The Princeton Review®

Cracking the

GRE®

PREMIUM

2018 Edition

The Staff of The Princeton Review

PrincetonReview.com

Penguin
Random
House

The Princeton Review®

The Princeton Review
555 W. 18th Street
New York, NY 10011
E-mail: editorialsupport@review.com

Published in the United States by Penguin Random House LLC, New York, and in Canada by Random House of Canada, a division of Penguin Random House Ltd., Toronto.

ISBN: 978-0-451-48765-0
eBook ISBN: 978-0-451-48766-7
ISSN: 1538-7210

Editor: Meave Shelton
Production Editors: Lee Elder and Melissa Duclos
Production Artist: Craig Patches

Printed in the United States of America on partially recycled paper.

10 9 8 7 6 5 4 3 2 1

2018 Edition

Editorial

Rob Franek, Editor-in-Chief
Casey Cornelius, VP Content Development
Mary Beth Garrick, Director of Production
Selena Coppock, Managing Editor
Meave Shelton, Senior Editor
Colleen Day, Editor
Sarah Litt, Editor
Aaron Riccio, Editor
Orion McBean, Editorial Assistant

Penguin Random House Publishing Team

Tom Russell, VP, Publisher
Alison Stoltzfus, Publishing Director
Jake Eldred, Associate Managing Editor
Ellen Reed, Production Manager
Suzanne Lee, Designer

Acknowledgments

The following people deserve thanks for their help with this book:

Many thanks to John Fulmer, National Content Director for the GRE, Kyle Fox, and Terry Serres for their hard work revising the 2018 edition.

The Princeton Review would also like to give a special thank-you to Jim Havens for his dedication and leadership in coordinating this project, as well as the following top-notch contributors: Chris Benson, Marty Cinke, Kevin Kelly, Sara Kuperstein, and Derek Smith.

Special thanks to Adam Robinson, who conceived of and perfected the Joe Bloggs approach to standardized tests, and many of the other successful techniques used by The Princeton Review.

Contents

Register Your

1 Go to **PrincetonReview.com/cracking**

2 You'll see a welcome page where you can register your book using the following ISBN: 9780451487650

3 After placing this free order, you'll either be asked to log in or to answer a few simple questions in order to set up a new Princeton Review account.

4 Finally, click on the "Student Tools" tab located at the top of the screen. It may take an hour or two for your registration to go through, but after that, you're good to go.

If you have noticed potential content errors, please email EditorialSupport@review.com with the full title of the book, its ISBN number (located above), and the page number of the error.

Experiencing technical issues? Please e-mail TPRStudentTech@review.com with the following information:

- your full name
- email address used to register the book
- full book title and ISBN
- your computer OS (Mac or PC) and Internet browser (Firefox, Safari, Chrome, etc.)
- description of technical issue

Book Online!

Once you've registered, you can...

- Take 4 full-length practice GRE exams

- Plan your review sessions with study guides based on your schedule—
4 weeks, 8 weeks, 12 weeks

- Watch tons of short videos in which Princeton Review teachers discuss GRE
question types and strategies, and work through practice problems step by step

- Read important advice about the GRE and graduate school

- Access crucial information about the graduate school application process,
including an application timeline

- Check to see if there have been any corrections or updates to this edition

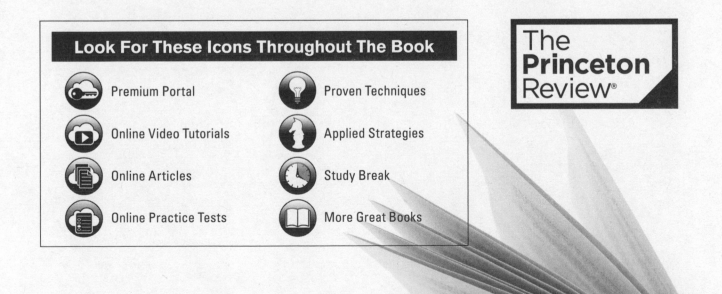

Look For These Icons Throughout The Book

🔑 Premium Portal

▶️ Online Video Tutorials

📄 Online Articles

📋 Online Practice Tests

💡 Proven Techniques

♟️ Applied Strategies

🕐 Study Break

📖 More Great Books

The Princeton Review®

Part I
Orientation

Chapter 1
Introduction

What is the GRE? Who makes the test? What's a good score? The answer to these questions and many others lie within this chapter. In the next few pages, we'll give you the lowdown on the things you need to know about the GRE.

CRACKING THE GRE

For a lot of people, taking a standardized test such as the GRE usually engenders a number of emotions—none of them positive. But here's the good news: The Princeton Review is going to make this whole ordeal a lot easier for you. We'll give you the information you will need to do well on the GRE, including our time-tested strategies and techniques.

A few years back, the GRE was rather significantly revised. This "new" version of the test supposedly allows graduate schools to get a better sense of an applicant's ability to work in a post-graduate setting—a goal that is unrealistic indeed, considering that the people who take the GRE are applying to programs as diverse as physics and anthropology.

However, it's safe to say that neither GRE—new or old—is a realistic measure of how well you'll do in grad school, or even how intelligent you are. In fact, the GRE provides a valid assessment of only one thing:

> The GRE assesses how well you take the GRE.

Got it? Even so, you still want to do well on the GRE, because you want grad schools to take you seriously when they consider your application. With this in mind, you should cultivate several very important skills when you're preparing for the test; each of them is attainable with the right guidance (which we'll give you), a strong work ethic (which you must provide), and a healthy dose of optimism. Who knows? Maybe after working through this book and learning how to crack the test, you'll actually look forward to taking the GRE.

So what exactly *is* this test you've heard so much about?

Strategies Galore
In this book you'll find The Princeton Review's trusted test-taking strategies to help you crack the GRE.

WHAT IS THE GRE?

The Graduate Record Examination (GRE) is a 3-hour, 45-minute exam that's used to rank applicants for graduate schools. The scored portion of the GRE consists of the following sections:

- One 30-minute Analysis of an Issue essay
- One 30-minute Analysis of an Argument essay
- Two 30-minute Verbal Reasoning sections
- Two 35-minute Quantitative Reasoning sections

The Verbal Reasoning sections test your skills on three different types of questions:

- Text Completion
- Sentence Equivalence
- Reading Comprehension

The Quantitative Reasoning sections measure your prowess in four areas:

- Arithmetic and Number Properties
- Algebra
- Geometry
- Data Analysis

Fun fact: It's possible your GRE score could come in handy if you are interested in law school. Check a school's admissions page for more info, as some schools are (or are considering) accepting GRE scores in lieu of LSAT scores. Your grad school options may have opened up even further!

WHY DO SCHOOLS REQUIRE IT?

Even though you will pay ETS $205 to take the GRE, it is important to note that you are not their primary customer. Their primary customers are the admissions offices at graduate programs across the United States. ETS provides admissions professionals with two important services. The first is a number, your GRE score. Everyone who takes the test gets a number. It is difficult for admissions committees to make a decision between a candidate with a 3.0 and a 3.2 GPA from drastically different schools and in two different majors. A GRE score, on the other hand, provides a quick and easy way for busy admissions offices to whittle a large applicant pool down to size.

Applicants could come from all over the world and will certainly have an enormous range in academic and professional experience. How does one compare a senior in college with a 32-year-old professional who has been out of college working in a different industry for the past 10 years? A GRE score is the only part of the application that allows for an apples-to-apples comparison among all applicants.

The second service that ETS provides is mailing lists. That's right; they will sell your name. You can opt out, but when you sit down to take the test, ETS will ask you a whole bunch of questions about your educational experience, family background, race, and gender, as well as other biographical data. All of this information goes into their database. In fact, ETS is one of the most important sources of potential applicants that many graduate programs have.

Another reason schools require the GRE is that it ensures that most graduate school applicants are qualified. It helps to weed out the people who might be considering grad school, but who can't get their act together enough to fill out applications. When you ask a program how important the GRE score is to the application, they may say, "it depends" or "not very" and that may be true as long as your score is in the top half. If your score is in the bottom half, however, it may mean that your application never gets seen.

So the GRE may have little relevance to any particular field of study you might be pursuing, but as long as it helps graduate programs uncover potential candidates, and as long as it is the only tool available to compare a diverse candidate pool, the GRE is here to stay.

WHO IS ETS?

Like most standardized tests in this country, the GRE is created and administered by Educational Testing Service (ETS), a private company located in New Jersey. ETS publishes the GRE under the sponsorship of the Graduate Record Examinations Board, which is an organization affiliated with the Association of Graduate Schools and the Council of Graduate Schools in the United States.

ETS is also the organization that brings you the SAT, the Test of English as a Foreign Language (TOEFL), the National Teacher Examination (NTE), and licensing and certification exams in dozens of fields, including hair styling, plumbing, and golf.

What to Take to the Test Center:
1. Your registration ticket
2. A photo ID and one other form of ID
3. A snack

TEST DAY

The GRE is administered at Prometric testing centers. This company specializes in administering tests on computer. They administer citizenship exams, professional health certifications, dental exams, accounting exams, and hundreds of other exams on computer. When you arrive at the center, they will check your ID, give you a clipboard with a form to fill out, and hand you a locker key. Despite the fact that they already have your information, you will be asked to fill out a long form on paper. This form includes an entire paragraph that you have to copy over—in cursive (they specify this)—that states that you are who you say you are and that you are taking the test for admissions purposes. This process will take you about 10 minutes, and you can complete it while you wait for them to call you into the testing room.

The locker is for all of your personal belongings, including books, bags, phones, bulky sweaters, and even watches. You are not allowed to take anything with you into the testing room.

When they call you into the testing room, they will first take a photo of you and, in some cases, fingerprint you before you go in. They will give you six sheets of scratch paper, stapled together to form a booklet, and two sharpened pencils with erasers. Then they lead you into the room where someone will start your test for you. The room itself will hold three or four rows of standard corporate cubicles, each with a monitor and keyboard. There will be other people in the room taking tests other than the GRE. Because people will be entering and exiting the room at different times, you will be provided with optional headphones.

Test Day Tips

- Dress in layers, so that you'll be comfortable regardless of whether the room is cool or warm.
- Don't bother to take a calculator; you're not allowed to use your own—just the one on the screen.
- Be sure to have breakfast, or lunch, depending on when your test is scheduled (but don't eat anything weird). Take it easy on the liquids and the caffeine.
- Do a few GRE practice problems beforehand to warm up your brain. Don't try to tackle difficult new questions, but go through a few questions that you've done before to help you review the problem-solving strategies for each section of the GRE. This will also help you put on your "game-face" and get you into test mode.
- Make sure to take photo identification to the test center. Acceptable forms of identification include your driver's license, photo-bearing employee ID cards, and valid passports.
- If you registered by mail, you must also take the authorization voucher sent to you by ETS.
- Stretch, drink some water, go to the bathroom, and do whatever you need to do in order to be prepared to sit for this four-hour test.

TEST STRUCTURE

While your test structure may vary, you should expect to see something like this when you sit down to take the exam:

The first section of the test collects all of your biographical information. If you fill this out, you will start getting mail from programs that have bought your name from ETS. In general, this is not a bad thing. If you don't want them to sell your name, or you don't want to spend the time answering their questions, you can click on a box that tells ETS not to share your information.

Once all of that is done, you will begin your first scored section, the essays. The two essays will be back to back. You have 30 minutes for each essay. Immediately after your second essay, you will get your first multiple-choice section. It may be math or verbal. You will have a 1-minute break between sections. Here is the structure of the test:

Section	Time	# of Questions
Biographical Information	+/– 10 minutes	–
Issue Essay	30 minutes	1
Argument Essay	30 minutes	1
Section 1	30 or 35 minutes	20
Section 2	30 or 35 minutes	20
Break	10 minutes	–
Section 3	30 or 35 minutes	20
Section 4	30 or 35 minutes	20
Section 5	30 or 35 minutes	20
Possible Research Section	Optional	Depends
Select Schools/Programs	5 minutes	Up to 4
Accept Scores	1 minute	–
Receive Scores	1 minute	–

More Online
For tons of information about the GRE, check out PrincetonReview.com/grad/gre-information

Here are some things to keep in mind:

- You will see five multiple-choice sections, but only four will count. The fifth is an "experimental" section. It can come at any time after the essays. At the end of the exam, you will know, based on the number of math or verbal sections, if the experimental section was math or verbal, but you will not know which section will not count toward your score.
- Math sections are 35 minutes. There are 20 math questions in each section. If your experimental section is math, your test will be five minutes longer than someone whose experimental section is verbal.
- Verbal sections are 30 minutes. There are 20 verbal questions in each section.
- For the computer-delivered test, the optional 10-minute break comes after the second multiple-choice section. For the paper-based test, the 10-minute break comes after the second Analytical Writing section.

A Note on the Paper-Based GRE
The computer-delivered GRE is the standard format for test takers. The paper-based GRE is far more rare and only offered up to three times a year. But if you want to learn more about the paper-and-pencil test, visit ETS.org.

- You may or may not get a research section. If you do, it will come last; it does not count toward your score, and it is optional.
- You must accept your scores and, if you choose, send your scores to selected programs prior to seeing your scores.
- If you choose not to accept your scores, neither you nor any program will ever see them.
- You may choose to send your scores to up to four graduate programs on the day of the test. This service is included in your testing fee.

The Experimental Section

ETS administers the experimental section to gather data on questions before they appear on real GREs. You will have no way of knowing in advance which multiple-choice section is experimental, so you need to do your best on all of them. Don't waste time worrying about which sections count and which section does not.

Research Section

At the end of the test, you may also have an unscored research section. At the beginning of this section, you will be told that it is an unscored research section, and that it will be used only to help develop and test questions for the GRE. You have the option to skip it if you want. You may be offered some sort of prize to induce you to take it, but by that point in the test you will probably be exhausted. If you're offered a research section, just go ahead and decline, get your scores, and go home.

The 10-Minute Break

You are given 1 minute between sections except for the second multiple-choice section, when you get a 10-minute break. Go to the bathroom, splash water on your face, wave your arms around. You want to re-oxygenate your brain. The goal, as much as it is possible, is to hit your brain's reset button. When you sit back down for the third multiple-choice section, you want to feel as if you are just sitting down at that computer for the first time that day. Your GRE test day is going to be a long and intense day, so be sure to take full advantage of break time.

Practice Like You Play
When tackling practice tests during your test preparation, be sure to mimic the real GRE and give yourself these timed breaks just like the real thing.

Accepting Your Scores

Before you see your scores, you will be given the opportunity to cancel them. There are very few reasons to do so. First, if you cancel your scores, you will never see them and you will have to go through the whole experience again, including paying an additional $205 to take the test again. Second, GRE scores are curved. Most people believe that they are doing worse while taking the test than they actually are. Third, you can make use of the GRE *ScoreSelect®* service.

ScoreSelect®

ScoreSelect® allows you to select which scores get sent to which schools. Options for sending scores depend on whether you are sending scores on the day of your test or after your test day. On test day, you have the following options for sending scores:

- **Most recent.** This option sends the results of the test you just took.
- **All.** This option sends all your scores from the last five years.

If you send your scores to schools after test day, you have even more options. After test day, your options are:

- **Most recent.** This option sends the scores from the test you took most recently.
- **All.** As above, this option sends all your GRE scores from the last five years.
- **Any.** Send just the scores you want to send. You can send one score or multiple scores. For example, if you have taken the GRE three times and your second score is your best, you can send just that score.

When you use *ScoreSelect®* after your test day, the score report that is sent to schools shows only the scores that you choose to send. The report does not indicate how many times you have taken the GRE nor does it indicate which that you have sent, for example, the second of three scores on record.

ScoreSelect® is another reason to think twice before cancelling your scores. Provided that you send your scores after your test date, your schools will never know that you didn't do as well as you would have liked or even that you took the test more than once if you don't want them to know.

Sending Additional Score Reports

On the day of your test, you can send your scores to up to four schools using the *ScoreSelect®* test day options. These score reports are included as part of the $205 fee that you pay to take the GRE. If you wish to send reports to additional schools, you'll need to request that these additional reports be sent after your test day. Each additional report costs $27. The fastest way to send additional score reports is to order them online using your My *GRE®* account that you create when you register to take the test.

WHAT DOES A GRE SCORE LOOK LIKE?

Every GRE score has two components: a scaled score and a percentile rank. GRE scores fall on a 130–170 point scale. However, your percentile rank is more important than your scaled score. Your percentile rank indicates how your GRE scores compare to those of other test takers. For example, a scaled score of 150 on the GRE translates to roughly the 43rd percentile, meaning that you scored better than 43 out of every 100 test takers—and worse than the other 57 percent of test takers. A score of 152 is about average, while scores of 163 and above are very competitive. Get the latest reported scores and percentiles at **PrincetonReview.com** and at **www.ets.org/gre**, the official ETS website for the GRE.

The essays are scored a little differently than the Verbal and Quantitative sections. All essays receive a scaled score of 0–6, in half-point increments. The corresponding percentiles are as follows:

Score	Analytical Writing Percentile
6.0	99
5.5	97
5.0	93
4.5	78
4.0	54
3.5	35
3.0	14
2.5	6
2.0	2
1.5	1
1.0	<1

In other words, a score of 5 on the essay portion of the GRE means you performed better than 93 percent of test takers.

How Much Does the GRE Matter?

Some programs consider the GRE very important, while others view it as more of a formality. Because the GRE is used for such a wide range of graduate studies, the relative weight it is given will vary from field to field and from school to school. A master's program in English literature will not evaluate the GRE the same way as a PhD program in physics, but it's hard to predict what the exact differences will be. A physics department may care more about the Math score than the Verbal score, but given that nearly all of its applicants will probably have high Math scores, a strong Verbal score might make you stand out and help you gain admission.

Do Your Research

GRE scores are used in a number of different ways. The first step in figuring out how to prepare for the GRE is figuring out how your scores will be used. The only way to do that is to contact the programs to which you plan to apply. Larger programs may have many of these questions already spelled out on their websites. Smaller programs, on the other hand, may not want to be pinned down to specific answers, and the answers may change from year to year. If you are applying to a smaller program, you will have to dig a bit deeper to get answers to some of these questions. Here are some things you should be asking.

1. **What scores do I need to be accepted?** The answer to this question is always "It depends." The GRE is not the only part of the application, and the quality of the applicant pool varies from year to year. Nevertheless, you need to have a target score so you can figure out how much work you need to put in between now and test day. If the school doesn't have or won't quote you a cutoff score, see if you can at least find out the average scores for last year's incoming class.

2. **Will you look at all parts of my score?** Some programs may care about your math score, but not your verbal score, and vice versa. Many programs don't use the essay scores at all. If a program doesn't care about your math or your essay score, then you know exactly where to put your prep time.

3. **Are scores used for anything else?** If your scores are to be used for placement or for scholarship, it would be good to know that now, while you still have time to prepare.

4. **How important are my scores?** In many ways, the importance of scores is a function of how competitive the program is. The scores may not matter much, but if it is a competitive program, every number will count.

5. **What do you do with multiple scores?** Depending upon your first scores, you may have to take the test a second time. It would be good to know, however, the importance of that first score. If a school is going to take the highest score, then you can relax a bit on test one, knowing that you can take it again if you need to.

If you plan your testing schedule well, you can send only your highest scores to the school using *ScoreSelect®*. Remember, however, that you must send your scores after your test day to use the *select any* option for *ScoreSelect®*.

In any case, remember that the GRE is only one part of an application to grad school. Admissions officers also consider many other factors, including

- undergraduate transcripts (that is, your GPA, relevant courses, and the quality of the school you attended)
- work experience
- any research or work you've done in that academic field
- subject GREs (for certain programs)
- essays (Personal Statements or other essays)
- recommendations
- interviews

The GRE can be a significant part of your graduate school application (which is why you bought this book), but it certainly isn't the only part.

Premium Portal
Head over to your Premium Portal for tons of pre-graduate school information and guidance.

SCHEDULING A TEST

You can schedule a test session for the GRE by calling 800-GRE-CALL or by registering online at **www.ets.org/gre**. Registering online is the easiest way to register. As part of the registration process, you'll create a MyGRE® account. The account will also allow you to see your scores online and make use of the GRE Diagnostic Service, which will give you some insight into your performance. You can also register through a local testing center (the list of centers is available online). After you get the list of local testing centers from ETS, you can call the one nearest you and set up an appointment. You can also call ETS at 609-771-7670 or e-mail them directly at their website to ask any general questions you have about the GRE.

Computer Testing Facts

- You can take the GRE almost any day—morning or afternoon, weekday or weekend. Appointments are scheduled on a first-come, first-served basis. You may take the test only once every 21 days. In addition, you cannot take the test more than five times in a continuous rolling 12-month period. Make sure to take your test early enough to book a second test date, if needed, before your applications are due.
- There's no real deadline for registering for the test (technically, you can register the day before). But there's a limited number of seats available on any given day and centers do fill up, sometimes weeks in advance. It's a good idea to register in advance, to give yourself at least a couple of weeks of lead time.

- The GRE is technically simple. Selecting an answer and moving to the next question involves three easy steps. All you need to do is point the mouse arrow at the answer and click, then click the "Next" button, and then click the "Answer Confirm" button to confirm your choice.

- Because the test is administered on a computer, it is impossible to write directly on the problems themselves (to underline text, cross out answer choices, and so on). Thus, all of your work must be done on scratch paper. Although the amount of scratch paper you may use is unlimited, requesting additional paper takes time. You should be efficient and organized in how you use it; learning to use your scratch paper effectively is one of the keys to scoring well on the GRE.

- When you've finished taking the test, you will be given the option to accept or cancel your scores. Of course, you have to make this decision before you learn what the scores are. If you choose to cancel your scores, they cannot be reinstated, and you will never learn what they were. No refunds are given for canceled scores, and your GRE report will reflect that you took the test on that day and canceled (though this shouldn't be held against you). If you choose to accept your scores, they cannot be canceled afterward. We suggest that unless you are absolutely certain you did poorly, you accept your score.

- You will receive your Verbal and Math scores the instant you finish the exam (provided that you choose not to cancel your score), but your Analytical Writing scores and "official" percentile scores for all three sections won't get to you until a few weeks later. If you registered for your test online, you'll be able to access your official scores through your My *GRE*® account.

- ETS offers the GRE® Diagnostic Service (**grediagnostic.ets.org**) as a free option for test takers to have a limited review of their tests. This service allows you to see the number of questions you missed and where they fell on the test, but you cannot review the actual questions. The diagnostic service also claims to let you know the difficulty of the questions you missed, but the scale used—a simple scale of 1 to 5—is not particularly useful.

Accommodated Testing

If you require accommodated testing, please see the Appendix at the end of this book. It contains information on the forms you'll need to fill out and procedures you'll need to follow to apply for accommodated testing. Be sure to start that application process well in advance of when you want to take your test, as it can take many weeks to complete.

HOW TO USE THIS BOOK

This book is chock full of our tried-and-true GRE test-taking techniques, some of which, at first, might seem to go against your gut instincts. In order to take full advantage of our methods, however, you'll have to trust them and use them consistently and faithfully.

Make sure to use the techniques on all of the practice problems you do and to thoroughly review the explanations for all of the questions—even the ones you get right. That way, the techniques will become second nature to you, and you'll have no problem using them on test day.

Practice for Technique

There is a finite amount of GRE material available in the world. Once you have used it all up, that's it. You don't get any more. Many people will work through the books, doing problems, looking for answers. When they get a problem right, they are happy. When they get a problem wrong, they are frustrated, and then they go on to the next problem. The problem with this approach is that you can churn through lots and lots of questions without ever actually getting better at taking the GRE. The techniques you use and the way you solve a problem are what matters. The results just tell you how you did. When you are practicing, always focus on your approach. When you get good at the techniques, your score will take care of itself. If you focus on just the results, you do nothing more than reinforce the way you are taking the test right now.

Additional Resources

In addition to the material in the book, we offer a number of other resources to aid you during your GRE preparation.

With your purchase of this book, you gain access to many helpful tools in your Premium Portal, which is the companion website that goes with this book. There you will find four full-length practice GRE exams, assorted videos in which Princeton Review teachers discuss GRE question types and strategies, plus tons of useful articles, essays, and information. Go to **PrincetonReview.com/cracking** to register. **PrincetonReview.com/gre** also contains a ton of useful information on graduate programs, financial aid, and everything else related to graduate school.

Real GREs

The practice problems in this book are designed to simulate the questions that appear on the real GRE. Part of your preparation, however, should involve working with real GRE problems. Working with real questions from past GRE exams is the best way to practice our techniques and prepare for the test. However, the only source of real GREs is the publisher of the test, ETS, which so far has refused to let anyone (including us) license actual questions from old tests.

Trust in the Techniques
What makes The Princeton Review's test prep so unique are our powerful test-taking strategies. Trust them and use them faithfully, and you won't be disappointed!

Extra Prep in Your Premium Portal
Follow the steps on the Register Your Book Online! page (page vi) to access the Premium Portal and find a bunch of great content designed to boost your test prep.

Therefore, we strongly recommend that you obtain *POWERPREP® II* software for the computer-based GRE revised General Test. You can download the *POWER-PREP® II* software directly from ETS's website. It contains two full-length adaptive revised General Tests. In addition, you can download the PDF *Practice Book for the Paper-based GRE® revised General Test*. While the format of the paper-based test is different from the computer-based test, the practice questions contained in the PDF are relevant and useful.

ETS also publishes *The Official Guide to the GRE® revised General Test*. This book can be found online or at most major book stores. Some of the practice questions in that book, however, are identical to the questions in the PDF, which is a free download.

Whatever you're using, always practice with scratch paper. As you prepare for the GRE, work through every question you do as if the question is being presented on a computer screen. This means not writing anything on the problems themselves. No crossing off answers, no circling, no underlining. Copy everything to scratch paper and do your work there. You shouldn't give yourself a crutch in your preparation that you won't have on the actual test.

About the Practice Tests in This Book

At the end of this book you'll find two full-length practice tests. Please note that these paper-and-pencil tests do not adapt to your performance like the real GRE. The actual GRE, as well as the online practice tests in your Student Tools, are computer-adaptive; that is, the number of questions you answer correctly on your first scored Math or Verbal section determines whether you'll get an easy, medium, or hard second section of that topic later in the test. A paper-and-pencil test, of course, is not adaptive by section. Scoring a paper-based test like the computer-adaptive GRE would require you to stop and score each section during the test in order to determine the difficulty level of your second section. But even this would not truly get you closer to the computer-adpative test experience, as you would be stopping to calculate scores—which, of course, is not something that happens during the real test. Much like the real exam, you won't know the difficulty level of the practice test questions. But you can still use the paper-and-pencil practice tests in this book as opportunities to practice with the question types and strategies, as well as work on your test-taking stamina.

MAKING A SCHEDULE

The GRE, like other standardized tests, is not a test for which you can cram. While you may have fond memories from your college days of spending the night before the midterm with a pot of coffee and a 500-page economics textbook, that strategy won't be as effective on the GRE. Why? Because, by and large, the GRE is a test of patterns, not of facts. This book does its best to reveal those patterns to you, but without sufficient time to practice and absorb the information in

Go Online!
Remember to check out your Student Tools to gain access to our computer-based practice tests for the GRE. Follow the steps on the Register Your Book Online! page, which can be found at the front of this book.

this book, your GRE score is not likely to improve. Thus, you should allow an adequate amount of time to fully prepare for the GRE.

You should allow yourself somewhere between 4 and 12 weeks to prepare for the GRE. Obviously we can't know exactly where you are in terms of your starting score, your target score, and the amount of time you can devote to studying, but in our experience, 4 weeks is about the minimum amount of time you'd want to spend, while 12 weeks is about the maximum. There are a number of reasons for these suggested preparation times. Attempting to prepare in fewer than 4 weeks typically does not allow sufficient time to master the techniques presented in this book. As you'll see, some of our approaches are counterintuitive and take some getting used to. Without adequate practice time, you may not have full confidence in the techniques. Additionally, vocabulary is part of the Verbal section of the GRE and it's difficult to substantially increase your vocabulary in a short period of time. Finally, as mentioned before, the GRE contains a number of patterns, and the more time you spend studying the test, the better you will be at recognizing these patterns.

On the other hand, spending an inordinate amount of time preparing for the GRE can have its downside as well. The first concern is a purely practical one: There is a finite amount of GRE practice material available. Budgeting six months of preparation time is unproductive because you'll run out of materials in less than half that time. Finally, spreading the material out over a long period of time may result in your forgetting some of the lessons from the beginning of your studies. It's better to work assiduously and consistently over a shorter time period than to dilute your efforts over a long time frame.

STAY UP TO DATE

We at The Princeton Review will continue to learn all about the GRE as it evolves. As you prepare for your GRE, make sure you periodically check both our website at **PrincetonReview.com** and the GRE website at **www.ets.org/gre** for the latest updates and information about the test.

WANT EVEN MORE PREP?

The Princeton Review offers an assortment of test preparation options: Classroom and online courses plus private and small group tutoring. We also have a bunch of other helpful GRE preparation books, including *Math Workout for the GRE, Verbal Workout for the GRE, 1,007 GRE Practice Questions,* and *Crash Course for the GRE.* When it comes to test preparation for the GRE, we've got you covered.

Now that we have that introduction out of the way, let's dive in and talk strategy.

Summary

○ The GRE is a 3-hour, 45-minute exam broken down into six sections and used by graduate schools to rank applicants.

○ The GRE tests your mathematical, verbal, and writing abilities.

○ The importance of your GRE score varies from program to program. Schools also consider your undergraduate record, your personal essays, and your relevant experience.

○ GRE tests can be scheduled online at **www.ets.org/gre**.

Chapter 2
General Strategy

This chapter contains some basic advice to get you into The Princeton Review mindset. You'll learn some core test-taking strategies to help you maximize your score. In addition, you'll see some of the different question formats you will probably encounter on test day.

CRACKING THE SYSTEM

Although ETS claims that the GRE measures "critical thinking, analytical writing, verbal reasoning, and quantitative reasoning skills that have been acquired over a long period of time," that isn't quite true. Again, what the GRE really measures is how well you take the GRE. The first step to bettering your GRE score is realizing that you can improve your score, in many cases substantially, by familiarizing yourself with the test and by practicing the techniques in this book.

I Thought the GRE Was Coach-Proof

ETS would have you believe that its tests are coach-proof, but that is simply untrue. In many ways, taking a standardized test is a skill and, as with any skill, you can become more proficient at it by both practicing and following the advice of a good teacher. Think of your GRE preparation as if you were practicing for a piano recital or a track meet; you wouldn't show up at the concert hall or track field without having put in hours of practice beforehand (at least we hope you wouldn't!). If you want to get a good score on the GRE, you'll have to put in the necessary preparation time.

Practice Your Way to Perfection
The GRE is not a test of intelligence. With practice, you can conquer the GRE.

Why Should I Listen to The Princeton Review?

Quite simply, because we monitor the GRE. Our teaching methods were developed through exhaustive analysis of all of the available GREs and careful research into the methods by which standardized tests are constructed. Our focus is on the basic concepts that will enable you to attack any problem, strip it down to its essential components, and solve it in as little time as possible.

Think Like the Test Writers

You might be surprised to learn that the GRE isn't written by distinguished professors, renowned scholars, or graduate school admissions officers. For the most part, it's written by ordinary ETS employees, sometimes with freelance help from local graduate students. You have no reason to be intimidated.

As you become more familiar with the test, you will also develop a sense of "the ETS mentality." This is a predictable kind of thinking that influences nearly every part of nearly every ETS exam. By learning to recognize the ETS mentality, you'll earn points even when you aren't sure why an answer is correct. You'll inevitably do better on the test by learning to think like the people who wrote it.

Cracking the System

"Cracking the system" is our phrase for getting inside the minds of the people who write these tests. This emphasis on earning points rather than pinpointing the correct answer may strike you as somewhat cynical, but it is crucial to doing well on the GRE. After all, the GRE leaves you no room to make explanations or justifications for your responses.

You'll do better on the GRE by putting aside your feelings about real education and surrendering yourself to the strange logic of the standardized test.

COMPUTER-ADAPTIVE TEST

As discussed briefly in Chapter 1, the GRE is a computer-adaptive test, or CAT for short. During the test, you will see two scored Math and Verbal sections, and the difficulty of the second scored section of either subject is determined by your performance on the first scored section. Depending on your performance in the first scored section of a subject, you will receive an easy, medium, or hard second section. Obviously enough, to achieve a high score on the GRE you need to get as many questions correct as you can, which means that the highest scores will result from performing well on the first scored section and the hardest of the second sections. However, the difficulty of an individual question plays no role in determining your score; that is, your score is calculated by your performance on the entirety of the scored sections, not just a handful of the hardest questions on a given section.

GENERAL STRATEGIES

1. Take the Easy Test First

Within a section, each question counts equally toward your score. There will inevitably be questions you are great at and questions you don't like. The beauty of the GRE is that there is no need to bow to Phoenician numerical hegemony; you can answer questions in any order you like. The question you can nail in 25 seconds is worth just as much as the question that will torture you for minutes on end. To maximize your score, leave the questions you don't like for last. If you are going to run out of time anywhere—and unless you are shooting for a 160 or higher, you should be running out of time—make sure that the questions that get chopped off are the ones you didn't want to answer anyway.

This strategy is called Take the Easy Test First. Skip early and skip often. Doing so will result in two passes through an individual section. On the first pass, cherry pick. Answer the questions you like. Get all of those easy points in the bank before time starts running short. You know that the hard questions—or the ones that you don't like—are going to take more time. Also, although you should never rush, everyone starts to feel the pressure of the clock as time starts running low. This is often when mistakes happen. Leave those difficult, time-consuming questions for the end of the test. If you run out of time or make some mistakes at that point, it won't matter because these are low percentage questions for you anyway.

2. Mark and Return

On your first pass through the questions, if you see a question you don't like, a question that looks hard, or a question that looks time consuming, you're going to walk on by and leave it for the end. Sometimes, however, a question that looks easy turns out to be more troublesome than you thought. The question may be trickier than it first appeared, or you may have simply misread it, and it seems hard only because you're working with the wrong information. From start to finish, the GRE is nearly a four-hour test. Over four hours your brain is going to get tired. When that happens, misreading a question is virtually inevitable. Once you read a problem wrong, however, it is almost impossible to un-read the problem and see it right. As long as you are still immersed in the problem, you could read it ten times in a row and you will read it the same wrong way each time.

Whether a question is harder than it first appeared, or made harder by the fact that you missed a key phrase or piece of information, the approach you've taken is not working. This is where the Mark button comes in.

Reset your brain by walking away from the problem, but Mark the question before you do. Do two or three other questions, and then return to the marked problem. When you walk away, your brain doesn't just forget the problem, it keeps on processing in the background. The distraction of the other questions helps your brain to consider the question from other angles. When you return to the problem, you may find that the part that gave you so much trouble the first time is now magically clear. If the problem continues to give you trouble, walk away again.

Staying with a problem when you're stuck burns time but yields no points. You might spend change numerals to two, three, five, or even six minutes on a problem but still be no closer to the answer. Spending five minutes to get one point will not get you enough points on a 30- or 35-minute section. In the five minutes you spend on a problem that you've misread, you could nail three or four easier questions. When you return to the question that gave you trouble, there is a good chance that you will spot your error, and the path to the correct answer will become clear. If it doesn't become clear, walk away again. Any time you encounter resistance on the test, do not keep pushing; bend like a reed and walk away. Use the Mark button to facilitate this key skill. Skip early and often so that you always have questions to distract your brain when you get stuck.

3. Use the Review Screen to Navigate

Within a single section you can mark an answered or unanswered question and return to it later. In fact you can skip any question you like and return to any question at any time you like. Navigating around a section is easy with the new Review Screen, which looks like this:

Question Number	Status	Marked
1	Not Answered	
2	Not Answered	✔
3	Not Answered	
4	Not Answered	
5	Not Answered	
6	Not Answered	
7	Answered	
8	Answered	
9	Answered	✔
10	Answered	✔
11	Answered	
12	Not Answered	

Simply click on a question and hit the button marked "Go To Question," and you will return directly to that question. This opens up a whole new realm of strategic opportunities for the savvy test taker.

4. There's No Penalty For Guessing

You should take the easy test first and you should spend most of your time on questions that you know how to answer, or are reasonably certain you can answer.

You will be able to answer some of the questions that you mark and move on from the second time around. A fresh set of eyes on a problem you've already seen is sometimes all it takes for a solution to present itself. But there may also be some questions that you do not know how to answer no matter how many times you look at them.

When you confront a question like this, try to eliminate any answer choice you can, but make sure to guess. There is no penalty for incorrect answers on the GRE. As a result, its better to guess than it is to leave a question blank. At least by guessing you stand a chance at getting lucky and guessing correctly.

Step 5

5. Use Process of Elimination

Because there are many more wrong answers on the GRE than there are credited answers, on some of the more difficult questions (those you do on your second pass) you'll actually be better served not by trying to find the *correct* answer, but instead by finding the wrong answers and using POE, Process of Elimination.

ETS Doesn't Care How You Get the Correct Answer

Remember when you were in high school, and even if you got a question wrong on a test, your teacher gave you partial credit? For example, maybe you used the right formula on a math question, but miscalculated and got the wrong result, so your teacher gave you some credit because you understood the concept.

Well, those days are over. There is no partial credit on the GRE. On the other hand, ETS doesn't know or care how you get the right answer. A lucky guess is worth just as many points as a question that you solve completely and correctly.

There is one thing for which we must thank ETS. They have actually given us the answers! For most problems, there are five answer choices, and one of them is correct. It is important to remember that the answer choices are part of the problem. Many of them will be clearly wrong and can, therefore, be eliminated. In fact, sometimes it is easier to identify the wrong answers and eliminate them than it is to find the right ones. This approach is called Process of Elimination, or POE.

POE will be crucial on the verbal side of the test. Vocabulary-based questions will include plenty of words you don't know. For such questions, you may not be able to identify the correct answer, but you will certainly be able to identify some wrong ones. Get rid of the wrong ones so that when you guess, you have a fifty-fifty shot and not a 20 percent chance. The same holds true for the reading comp questions, which will include plenty of answer choices that are clearly wrong.

On the math side of the test, ETS loves to sucker you into doing more math than is really necessary. You can often eliminate answer choices that are clearly too large or too small. Sometimes it is even more efficient to eliminate wrong answers than it is to do the math required to come up with the right one.

The Importance of Distractors

By using POE, you will be able to improve your score on the GRE by looking for wrong answers instead of right ones, on questions you find difficult. Why? Because, once you've eliminated the wrong ones, picking the right one can be a piece of cake.

Wrong answers on standardized multiple-choice tests are known in the testing industry as "distractors," or "trap answers." They are called distractors because their purpose is to distract test takers away from correct choices. Trap answers are specifically designed to appeal to test takers. Oftentimes, they're the answers that seem to scream out "pick me!" as you work through a question. However, these attractive answers are often incorrect.

Remembering this simple fact can be an enormous help to you as you sit down to take the test. By learning to recognize distractors, you will greatly improve your score.

Improve Your Odds Indirectly

Every time you're able to eliminate an incorrect choice on a GRE question, you improve your odds of finding the correct answer; the more incorrect choices you eliminate, the better your odds.

For this reason, some of our test-taking strategies are aimed at helping you arrive at ETS's answer indirectly. Doing this will make you much more successful at avoiding the traps laid in your path by the test writers. This is because most of the traps are designed to catch unwary test takers who try to approach the problems directly.

POE and Guessing

If you guessed blindly on a five-choice GRE problem, you would have a one-in-five chance of picking ETS's answer. Eliminate one incorrect choice, and your chances improve to one in four. Eliminate three, and you have a fifty-fifty chance of earning points by guessing. Get the picture?

6. Use Your Scratch Paper

ETS doesn't give you many useful tools on this test, so you have to make good use of the ones they do give you. You will get six sheets of scratch paper stapled into a booklet. You can get more by raising your hand during a section, but that takes time, so you will need an efficient system for using scratch paper.

Mistakes happen in your head, but good technique happens on scratch paper. When you do work in your head, you are really doing two things at once. The first is figuring out the answer at hand, and the second is keeping track of where you've been. Mistakes happen when you try to do two things in your head at once. It's better to park your thinking on your scratch paper. Get it out of your head and onto the page. Good things happen when you do.

On the math side, scratch paper is crucial. Not only is it important for performing complicated calculations, but when used properly, it can actually help to direct your thinking as you work through multi-step problems. In the math sections of this book, we will give you graphic set-ups for each math concept that you will encounter. Use them consistently, and they will become good habits that will pay big dividends in accuracy, even over a four-hour exam.

On the verbal side, scratch paper is every bit as essential. It will help you to track your progress, to focus on only one answer choice at a time, and to work through a series of answer choices efficiently. In the verbal section of this book, we will give you a process for using scratch paper efficiently and effectively.

Guess, but guess intelligently.

Remember
By crossing out a clearly incorrect choice, you permanently eliminate it from consideration.

Step 7

By training yourself to avoid careless errors, you will increase your score.

7. Double-Check

Get into the habit of double-checking all of your answers before you click on your answer choice—or answer choices. Make sure that you reread the directions and have done everything they asked you to—don't get the answer wrong just because you chose only one answer for a question that required you to choose two or more.

The only way to reliably avoid careless errors is to adopt habits that make them less likely to occur. Always check to see that you've transcribed information correctly to your scratch paper. Always read the problem at least twice and note any important parts that you might forget later. Always check your calculations. And always read the question one last time before selecting your answer.

Step 8

8. Let It Go

Every time you begin a new section, focus on that section and put the last section you completed behind you. Don't think about that pesky synonym from an earlier section while a geometry question is on your screen. You can't go back, and besides, your impression of how you did on a section is probably much worse than reality.

Step 9

9. Don't Make Any Last-Minute Lifestyle Changes

The week before the test is not the time for any major life changes. This is NOT the week to quit smoking, start smoking, quit drinking coffee, start drinking coffee, start a relationship, end a relationship, or quit a job. Business as usual, okay?

YOUR STARTING POINT

Before you dive in, you might wish to take one of the practice tests in this book or online to get a sense of where you are starting out from. It can be a good exercise to tackle a practice test before you know any strategies or have reviewed any content—while you have relatively fresh eyes to the test-taking experience. This will be a good initial impression and these first scores will show you what content areas need your focus. Of course, you'll review all necessary content for the GRE (won't you?), but this first test can serve as a helpful guide. Then as you learn strategies and review math and verbal content, you'll have a genuine sense of accomplishment.

Now let's get cracking!

Summary

o   You can increase your score on the GRE through practice and successful application of test-taking strategies.

o   The GRE uses a variety of question formats throughout the test.

o   Not all questions on the GRE are of equal difficulty. Your Personal Order of Difficulty should tell you which questions to spend time on and which to skip.

o   Accuracy is better than speed. Slow down and focus on accumulating as many points as possible. Forcing yourself to work faster results in careless errors and lower scores.

o   Process of Elimination is an extremely useful tool on the test. Use it to eliminate wrong answers and increase your odds of guessing correctly.

Part II
How to Crack the Verbal Section

Chapter 3
The Geography of the Verbal Section

The Verbal section of the GRE is designed to test your verbal reasoning abilities. This chapter will review the types of questions you will see, how to pace yourself, and the basic strategies that will best guide you through the Verbal section. Additionally, this chapter will cover the importance of vocabulary on the test, along with some useful tips on how to approach learning GRE vocabulary.

WHAT'S ON THE VERBAL SECTION

ETS claims that the Verbal section of the GRE accomplishes the following:

- places a greater emphasis on analytical skills and on understanding vocabulary in context rather than in isolation
- uses more text-based materials
- contains a broader range of reading selections
- tests skills that are more closely aligned with those used in graduate school
- expands the range of computer-enabled tasks

What does this mean for you?

- There won't be questions that involve analogies or antonyms on this test, as there were on the old version of the GRE.
- You'll see some wacky-looking question formats that you've probably never seen before.
- Though they say the new version of the test de-emphasizes vocabulary, there's no getting around the fact that the more vocabulary you know when you sit down to take the test, the better off you'll be. So vocabulary remains as important as it ever was. If you're especially eager to build your vocabulary, check out Chapter 8: Vocabulary for the GRE.

There are three types of questions on the Verbal section of the test:

- Text Completions
- Sentence Equivalence
- Reading Comprehension

Let's take a brief look at each question type.

Text Completions

Text Completion questions consist of short sections of text with one or more blanks; you are asked to choose the best word to place in each blank. You may see one blank in the text, in which case you will be offered five answer choices, or you may see two or three blanks, each of which will have three answer choices. No partial credit is given for getting some but not all blanks correct on a question, so be sure to read carefully.

Here is an example of a two-blank question:

> Fables often endure due to their (i) _____, often telling one simple narrative, based around one character. This is both by design, because direct statements are more easily remembered than florid ones, and by accident: As fables are passed from teller to teller, (ii) _____ details fall away, leaving only the essential story.

Blank (i)	Blank (ii)
bombast	· superfluous
objectivity	requisite
· simplicity	apocryphal

Sentence Equivalence

This is another vocabulary-oriented question type. Each question will consist of one sentence with six answer choices. Your job is to choose the two answer choices that logically complete the sentence. As with Text Completions, there is no partial credit, so you must select both correct answer choices to receive points.

Here's an example:

> He was a man of few words, _____ around all but his closest friends.

- ☐ laconic
- ☐ garrulous
- ☐ ascetic
- ☐ taciturn
- ☐ tempestuous
- ☐ ambiguous

Reading Comprehension

Reading comprehension accounts for about half of the Verbal questions you will see. Passages range from one to five paragraphs, and each passage can consist of one to five questions. No matter the length, the passages offer some type of argument that the author is trying defend, even if it's just the author's opinion. Therefore, some of the questions in this section will ask you to identify an author's point of view or the assumptions and premises upon which that point of view rests. Other Reading Comprehension questions will ask about details of specific information in the passage or provable from the passage, the structure or tone of the text, how a word is used in context, or the main idea. Fortunately, these questions rarely test you on your prior vocabulary knowledge. Furthermore, Reading Comprehension questions are like an open book test—everything you need is right there in the passage!

You will encounter three Reading Comprehension question formats:

Multiple Choice

Question 20 is based on this passage.

After examining the bodies of a dozen beached whales and finding evidence of bleeding around the animals' eyes and brains as well as lesions on their kidneys and livers, environmental groups fear that the Navy's use of sonar is causing serious harm to marine animals. A leading marine biologist reports that sonar induces whales to panic and surface too quickly, which causes nitrogen bubbles to form in their blood.

The argument above relies on which of the following assumptions?

○ Marine biologists have documented that other marine animals, including dolphins and sea turtles, have exhibited kidney and liver lesions.

○ No studies have been conducted on the possible detrimental effects of sonar on marine animals.

○ Whales in captivity panic only when exposed to man-made, rather than natural, sound waves.

○ The presence of nitrogen bubbles in the blood has been demonstrated to cause damage to various internal organs.

○ It is unlikely that the symptoms found in the beached whales could be caused by any known disease.

Select All That Apply

Questions 10 and 11 are based on this passage.

What was it about Oscar Wilde's only novel, *The Picture of Dorian Gray*, that caused it to create such an uproar when it was published in 1891? While critics attacked the quality of Wilde's formal elements, their denunciation merely masked the true concerns of many nineteenth-century critics. What these critics were actually railing against was the thematic content of Wilde's work, specifically his illustration of a lifestyle devoted to useless beauty. For many a nineteenth-century moralist, *The Picture of Dorian Gray* was nothing more than a primer for spiritual depravity. Wilde's ultimate sin was his leniency toward his protagonist, an unabashed hedonist. To the critics, allowing an evil character to escape his just desserts was an unforgivable sin. In their minds, Wilde's work was corrupting the genteel reading public by failing to show the proper consequences of immoral behavior.

Consider each of the choices separately and select all that apply.

The author of the passage would probably agree with which of the following statements?

☐ Most critics of Oscar Wilde's novel objected primarily to the lifestyle of its author.

☐ If *The Picture of Dorian Gray* were written in the twentieth century, the critical reaction would be less severe.

☐ Some critics of Wilde's *The Picture of Dorian Gray* believed that an author of a book had a moral responsibility to the book's audience.

Select a Sentence

Called by some the "island that time forgot," Madagascar is home to a vast array of unique, exotic creatures. One such animal is the aye-aye. First described by western science in 1782, it was initially categorized as a member of the order Rodentia. Further research then revealed that it was more closely related to the lemur, a member of the primate order. Since the aye-aye is so different from its fellow primates, however, it was given its own family: *Daubentoniidae*. The aye-aye has been listed as an endangered species and, as a result, the government of Madagascar has designated an island off the northeastern coast of Madagascar as a protected reserve for aye-ayes and other wildlife.

Select the sentence in the passage that most seriously weakens the author's claim that "this practice may result in the loss of a superb example of life's variety."

When you see a Select-a-Sentence question like the one above, you need to click on the sentence in the passage that you think answers the question.

HOW IS THE GRE VERBAL SECTION STRUCTURED?

The GRE has two scored multiple-choice verbal sections. Each will be 30 minutes long with 20 questions per section. The way you perform on one Verbal section will affect the difficulty of the next Verbal section you are given. Verbal sections tend to follow the same order. Roughly the first six questions will be Text Completion, the next five or six will be Reading Comprehension, followed by about four Sentence Equivalence questions, and then another four or five Reading Comprehension questions. In profile, the two verbal sections will look something like this:

A better performance on the first scored Verbal section will yield more difficult questions on the second one!

Question	1	2	3	4	5	6	7	8	9	10	11	12	13	14	15	16	17	18	19	20
Section 3	Text Completion						Reading Comprehension					Sentence Equivalence				Reading Comprehension				
Section 5	Text Completion						Reading Comprehension					Sentence Equivalence				Reading Comprehension				

BASIC STRATEGIES FOR THE GRE VERBAL SECTION

Here are some strategies that will help you on the Verbal section. We'll show you how to use them as we go through specific question types in the chapters ahead, but for now read through the strategies and get a sense of what they are before moving on.

Accuracy vs. Speed

Any timed test will cause at least some level of stress. While it is important to mark an answer to every question on the Verbal section, nobody has ever won a medal for getting the most questions wrong in the shortest amount of time. The key is to correctly answer the questions that you can get right. Be sure to apply each step of the techniques that we will cover in upcoming chapters. Don't let that clock force you to make silly mistakes!

Premium Portal
Check out our Premium Portal for helpful opinions and advice for GRE test takers.

Mark and Move On

While it is important to be careful and process-driven when you take the GRE, it is also important to allow yourself to see every question. After all, question 20 could be the easiest one on the test for you.

This is why the Mark button is important. If a question is not coming to you immediately, it is not necessarily something that you cannot answer. On the Reading Comprehension questions, for instance, you may struggle on a question that deals with the main idea of the passage. You may even have eliminated some answer choices. Don't give up yet! If you have invested time and work on a particular question, press the Mark button and move on. You may find that after answering the next question, perhaps on specific content from the passage, you have more insight and can return to the previously marked question to answer it with ease.

There is also use for the Mark button on Text Completions and Sentence Equivalences. Of course, some may have answer choices filled with vocabulary that you have never seen before. In that case, you may just want to guess and move on. On the other hand, you may be frustrated by a question that has answer choices with which you are familiar. Mark that question and move on. The time you could have spent staring at those answer choices could be better used on another one or two easier questions. Coming back to the earlier question with fresh eyes may help. If it doesn't, simply guess on that and other unanswered questions when there are two minutes remaining.

Bend—Don't Push

Mark and Move is a crucial technique. Sometimes you just get stuck in a mental rut, and continuing to stare at the same question is a waste of time. Mark it, move on, do a couple other questions, and come back. You'll be surprised how often you'll see something new just because you gave your brain a break!

Over the course of a nearly four-hour test, your brain *will* get tired. When that happens, you lose accuracy, make "silly" mistakes, and misread. Deal with this inevitable pressure by allowing yourself to move on whenever the words on the screen stop making sense. A fresh question can give you an opportunity to regain your focus.

Leave Nothing Blank

When you have two minutes left on a section, click the Review button and see which questions are unanswered. Click through each of those unanswered questions and pick something. You might be right, and there's no penalty for incorrect answers!

Process of Elimination (POE)

Determining correct answers on the Verbal sections of the GRE can be tricky. Answer choices on Reading Comprehension questions, for example, are constructed with "clever" wordings that make correct answers seem wrong and incorrect answers seem right.

So, reverse your approach. Instead of looking for the correct answer, eliminate the incorrect answer choices.

Using Process of Elimination (POE) will be the most effective way to avoid trap answer choices.

- Consider every answer choice, even if you think you know the answer.
- Eliminate any choice that contains something that you can point to and say, "Well, I know *that's* wrong."
- If a choice seems weird or confusing, or just doesn't make sense the first time you read it, leave it as an option.
- Cycle through the answer choices until you're down to one choice, and then pick it.

Your first impression of POE might be to think that it would take way too long, but don't knock it until you try it. Then try it again, and again. Most of the incorrect answer choices on the GRE Verbal sections can be quickly identified by spotting some minor detail that can't be supported. We'll discuss some of the ways to categorize these details in later chapters. For now, just realize that POE can actually be *faster* than trying to find the "right" answer. Before you pull out a stopwatch and time each method, realize that speed matters a lot less than accuracy.

> When you've eliminated four answer choices that you *know* are wrong, you know that you're left with the correct answer.

Need More Practice?
The Princeton Review's *Verbal Workout for the GRE, 6th Edition,* includes hundreds of drill questions for the Verbal and Analytical Writing sections.

Down to Two?

The most common situation you'll find yourself in is when you've eliminated all but two answer choices and you can't decide between them. Don't just pick one! Compare them and remind yourself what the answer to the question should look like. There's only one way to answer every question on the GRE, so if you can't see why one of the remaining choices is wrong, you are missing something. Find it. If you're really stuck, Mark and Move.

Stacking the Odds

Most likely, there will be some questions on the test that you *know* you won't be able to answer in time. POE can turn these questions into potential points. Before you just guess on a question, quickly consider if some of the answer choices are clearly wrong. If you can eliminate two choices on each of three different questions, you've got a good chance of getting a free point!

Consider the following question:

When studying human history, one must be aware that the _____ between historical periods are arbitrary; certainly none of the people alive at the time were aware of a shift from one era to another.

judgments
ideologies
innovations
demarcations
episodes

Here's How to Crack It

If you encountered this question on the GRE, you might not know what the best answer is (you'll learn how to approach questions like this in Chapter 4). However, you might see that some of the answer choices simply don't make sense. Choices (A), (B), and (C) don't seem to fit the sentence at all. By eliminating these wrong answers, you've suddenly given yourself a great chance of choosing the correct answer just by guessing, since only (D) and (E) are left. And if you realize that (E) doesn't make sense either, then you know the correct answer is (D), even if you're not sure what *demarcations* means.

POOD

Your Personal Order of Difficulty (POOD) should guide your approach to the Verbal section. Do you have a lot of success on Reading Comprehension and not much on vocabulary questions? Skip those six Text Completions for now and work your strengths. You do not want to be put in a situation in which you have to rush through the types of questions you would normally get correct simply because they show up later in the section.

With this in mind, think of the Verbal section as two tests—one easy and one difficult. Take the easy test first! Move briskly through the test, answering the questions that give you little trouble and skipping the questions that will bog you down. Do this all the way through question 20. Then go back and work those harder questions knowing that you will not have missed any easy points due to a lack of effective planning.

A Word on Vocabulary

While the GRE has scaled back on the sheer difficulty of vocabulary over the years, you still need to have a grasp on the words that are commonly used on the test if you want to see significant score improvements. In the coming chapters, we will go over strategies for answering Text Completion and Sentence Equivalence questions. However, there is no substitute for having a good understanding of the vocabulary that ETS tends to test. In Chapter 8, we offer the Key Terms List—a list of the most commonly used words tested on the GRE.

Effective ways to study vocabulary for the GRE may include the following:

- Prioritize words from the Key Terms List into three categories: Words I Know, Words I Sort of Know, and Words I Do Not Know. Spend most of your time studying the second group, followed by the final group.

- Read. You will absorb many of the words that will show up on the GRE by reading respected publications such as academic journals or some of the more highbrow newspapers and magazines.

- Keep a vocabulary list. When you come across new words on practice tests or practice problems, add them to your list. They have been used before on the GRE and they may very well be used again.

Stressed About Vocab?
Check out The Princeton Review's flashcards, *Essential GRE Vocabulary*, which includes 500 essential vocabulary words plus 50 customizable cards!

Summary

- The GRE Verbal section consists of two 30-minute sections, each containing 20 questions.

- The Verbal section is made up of Text Completions, Sentence Equivalences, and Reading Comprehension.

- Remember to utilize Process of Elimination (POE) to attack the wrong answers.

- Use your Personal Order of Difficulty (POOD) to ensure that you take the easy test first. Skip questions that seem difficult, and Mark and Move when questions get tough.

- Vocabulary is important. Prioritize the words from the Key Terms List into Words I Know, Words I Sort of Know, and Words I Do Not Know.

Chapter 4
Text Completions

If you took the SAT, you probably remember sentence completion questions. Well, they're back, retooled and renamed for the GRE. Text Completion questions test your ability to figure out which word or words best complete a given sentence or group of sentences. On the GRE, the sentence can have one, two, or even three blanks that you must fill. This chapter will show you The Princeton Review approach to Text Completions, a tried-and-true approach that will help you focus on exactly the parts of the sentences that you'll need to figure out the answer. Along the way we'll provide you with some valuable tips on using Process of Elimination to help you when you don't know all the vocabulary on a question.

PART 1: TEXT COMPLETION BASICS

WHAT'S A TEXT COMPLETION?

On each Verbal section of the GRE you can expect to see about six Text Completion questions, or approximately 30% of the total questions. Each question is made up of a passage consisting of one or more sentences—sometimes up to five! The passage has blanks in place of key words. There can be one, two, or three blanks. One-blank questions have five answer choices per blank, while two- and three-blank questions have three answer choices per blank. Your job is to select the combination of answer choices—one choice per blank—that best completes the text. The completed sentence(s) must make sense as a whole. In multiple-blank questions, credit is only given if all blanks are answered correctly.

Therefore, the correct choice for each blank depends on the meaning of the sentence as a whole. While at first glance, Text Completions may seem to focus on vocabulary, these questions are not just a glorified vocab quiz. Even more important is a critical understanding of context and the ability to recognize the internal logic of the passage. You cannot rely on word power alone.

But you *will* need a strategy for approaching Text Completion questions. This strategy is where we will begin our discussion of how to successfully navigate Text Completions.

THE BASIC APPROACH FOR TEXT COMPLETION QUESTIONS

Using the basic approach for Text Completion questions, you will examine the sentence or sentences in the passage, which will include clues and transition words that indicate the intended meaning of the sentence. Examining these clues and transitions, you will aim to come up with your own word for each blank to compare against the answer choices.

STEPS FOR TEXT COMPLETION QUESTIONS

Follow these steps for each blank in turn. For now, we'll only be working with one-blank questions. Later, we'll tell you how to handle questions with two and three blanks.

1. **Find the clues and transition words.** Ask yourself:
    *   *Who or what* is the blank describing?
    *   *What else* in the passage provides *insight* into that person or thing?
2. **Come up with your own word or phrase for the blank.** Write that word or phrase down on your scratch paper.
3. **Check each answer choice.**
    ✓ an answer that sort of matches your word
    ✗ an answer that does not at all match your word
    ? any word you don't know

Before tackling the nuts and bolts of these steps, let's try an example to get started:

_____○_____

Robert Ingersoll, although virtually unknown today, was _____ orator of the nineteenth century; people traveled hundreds of miles to hear his eloquent speeches.

a domineering
an eminent
an unobjectionable
a conventional
an execrable

Here's How to Crack It

1. **Find the clues and transition words.** First ask, "*Who* or *what* is the blank describing?" Before you try to fill the blank, you must consider what the blank is talking about! In this sentence, the blank describes the kind of *orator* that *Robert Ingersoll* was.

    Next ask, "*What else* in the passage provides *insight* into that person or thing?" Find information in the surrounding text that provides insight into the kind of orator that Ingersoll was. The sentence tells us that *people traveled hundreds of miles to hear his...speeches.* So he was obviously a good orator. The sentence also tells us that Ingersoll is *virtually unknown today.* The transition word *although* puts this insight into opposition to the word in the blank describing the kind of orator Ingersoll was. Now you know that he wasn't just a good orator but a well-known one.

2. **Come up with your own word or phrase for the blank.** Use the insights you've gained to come up with your own word for the blank. You don't have to come up with the perfect word, and it doesn't have to be a single word. It's better to be as literal as possible in order to capture your insights. Feel free to recycle language in the sentence when coming up with your own word. From Step 1, you know that Ingersoll was a well-known orator—recycled from the word *unknown*—and also a good one. To capture all that, you could just call him "famously good."

3. **Check each answer choice.** Only now that you've come up with your own word (or phrase in this case) compare that word or phrase to the answer choices. Compare each of the answer choices in turn to your own phrase, "famously good."

    Choice (A) is *domineering*, which means bossy, is not a match for "famously good." Eliminate (A). Choice (B), *eminent*, is a famous or respected person, so keep (B). The word *unobjectionable*, (C), means something that can't be objected to, so eliminate (C). Choice (D), *conventional*, is practically the opposite of "famously good", so eliminate it. Choice (E), *execrable*, might stump you, in which case you'd give it a question mark. *Execrable* means downright detestable. If you knew that, you'd eliminate the word. Either way, you'd go with the answer choice that you've assigned a checkmark, (B). Ingersoll was *an eminent* orator of the nineteenth century.

Congratulations on completing your first Text Completion question!

GET A CLUE!

Here's the good news about Text Completion questions: There is only ever one answer choice that is correct. We know that seems obvious enough, but it's worth mentioning. It gives you a touch of insight into the reality of the creation of Text Completion questions. Somewhere in the question, the information to determine the correct answer is present. There are no alternative interpretations or Mad-Lib style games for Text Completion questions. The information to justify the answer is always right in front of you.

The trick, as always, is to determine where and what that information is. Step 1 in approaching Text Completions is to find clues in the passage about the word for the blank. The *text* of the passage provides the *context* for the correct answer. Your mission is to determine the intended meaning of the passage, based on the information in the passage. That's why it's very important to do Step 1 first. *Do not move on to Step 2 or look at the answer choices until you've identified the clues in the sentence!*

The clue is the information in the sentence that provides insight into the word or phrase that goes in the blank. But before you can even look for clues, you want a concrete idea of what exactly is missing. That's why, when you start on each Text Completion question, you need to find the clue. And, you begin finding the clue by first asking yourself this question:

- *Who or what* is the blank describing?

Take a moment to make sure you understand what's being talked about by the blank. If it's not crystal-clear, then determine what part of speech the blank should be. An adjective will be easiest to work with, because then the blank merely describes the noun next to the blank. If it's a verb that's missing, the blank describes some action or process. If it's noun that's missing, the blank represents a person, thing, or idea—or often some aspect of another noun in the passage. Once you know what the blank is describing, ask yourself this question:

- *What else* in the passage provides *insight* into that person or thing?

The next order of business is to find the information in the passage that tells you something about the person or thing described by the blank. ETS *never* gives you a passage where the word that belongs in the blank is subject to opinion, debate, or poetic license. They always give you one or more pieces of information that offer insight into the topic of the blank. This information is the clue, and it's all there in the text.

To illustrate the importance of the clue, let's look at the following example:

> Sophocles, who wrote the play *Oedipus Rex*, was one of the most _____ playwrights of ancient Greece.

famous
bombastic
critical
prolific
eclectic

Who or what does the blank describe? It's an adjective describing the kind of playwright Sophocles was. What else in the sentence gives you insight into what kind of playwright Sophocles was? If you've come up empty-handed, that's because the sentence does not contain a clue. Based on what you may know about Sophocles, a few of the answer choices may work. To answer this question correctly, ETS would have to expect you to rely on outside knowledge about Sophocles. For fear of an army of angry lawyers knocking down their door, ETS will never produce a question that has a correct answer they cannot defend. The clue has to be there in the text. Let's try with another version of the same question:

Sophocles, who wrote the play *Oedipus Rex,* was one of the most _____ playwrights of ancient Greece, completing 123 plays in his lifetime—double that of any of his contemporaries.

famous
bombastic
critical
prolific
eclectic

Just as before, the blank should describe what kind of playwright Sophocles was. This time, however, you're given additional information: He completed *123 plays,* which was *double that of…his contemporaries.* Now you have something to work with in coming up with your own word. Sophocles wrote a lot of plays, so "productive" could be your word. You could even put down "adjective—wrote lots" on your scratch paper if you weren't able to come up with a single word that means "wrote lots." Remember that your job is to simply come up with a word or phrase that leads you to the correct answer. So, it's okay if your word is actually a phrase.

Now you're ready to take on the answer choices. The adjective *famous* is certainly tempting. Sophocles was unquestionably one of the most famous *playwrights of ancient Greece.* But this has no connection to the clue, which is all about the number of plays he wrote. This is a trap laid by ETS writers. ETS writers may not be able to use outside knowledge to create their correct answer choices, but they certainly can add in an incorrect answer choice relying on outside knowledge and hope the student does the rest. Assumptions and extrapolations are dangerous. One and only one of the answer choices matches the clue—(D), *prolific.* The other four words may indeed describe Sophocles and sound fine if inserted into the sentence. But only one answer choice will ever match the clue, and that's what counts.

A WORD ABOUT YOUR WORDS

Once you've found the clue in the passage, you've done most of the heavy lifting. Now it's time to come up with your own word to go in the blank. This is Step 2 of the basic approach.

This isn't about predicting the answer. You're just trying to come up with something that reflects the clues and will help you to identify the correct answer from among the choices. So don't waste time brainstorming the perfect GRE word to put in the blank. Think of your job as supplying the definition of what should go in the blank. To make your life easier, recycle! Just use a word or phrase recycled from the clues. What better way to capture the information you gleaned from the passage?

Practice: Finding the Clue

Underline the clue in each of the following sentences. Then, think of your own word for the blank and write it down. Answers can be found in Part V.

1 of 8

The _____ relationships in his life haunted Eugene O'Neill and are often reflected in the harrowing nature of many of his plays.

2 of 8

Mount Godwin-Austen, more commonly known as K2, is the second highest mountain in the world, with its _____ peaks reaching more than 28,000 feet high.

3 of 8

A wind-chill warning is issued when the temperature is projected to reach minus 25 degrees Fahrenheit or lower, the point at which the cold has _____ effects on living creatures.

4 of 8

Divers still stumble across unexploded shells, 70-year-old _____ from World War II, in the waters outside Tokyo.

5 of 8

Although some people use the terms interchangeably, mastodons and mammoths were quite _____ ; mammoths were hairy with long tusks, while mastodons had low-slung bodies and flatter skulls.

6 of 8

The mayor was definitely _____ ; he crafted his policies not with an eye toward their political consequences but instead toward their practical effects.

Be systematic! Ask yourself these questions. Who or what is the blank describing? What in the sentence gives insight into that?

The first-year law student was amazed at the
sheer _____ of the material he had to read
for his classes; he imagined that he would have to
read for hours and hours each day to finish it all.

Our word "ghoul" is _____ from the
Arabic word "Algol," the name for the Demon Star,
a star in the constellation Perseus.

NEXT, TRANSITIONS

Let's take another look at the mastodon/mammoth question from the preceding
Finding the Clue practice exercise:

Although some people use the terms
interchangeably, mastodons and mammoths were
quite _____ ; mammoths were hairy with
long tusks, while mastodons had low-slung bodies
and flatter skulls.

The first phrase of the sentence says that some people use the terms *mastodon* and
mammoth interchangeably. However, the clause after the semicolon describes each
animal, making it plain that they are very different in appearance. The clue to the
word that goes in the blank is the word *interchangeably*, but context indicates that
the word for the blank is the opposite of the clue. The reason you know this is
because the phrase containing the clue begins with the transition word *[a]lthough*.

Transition words tell the reader how a clue relates to the blank—whether the clue
has the same meaning as the blank or the opposite meaning. Consider the following two scenarios:

I won the lottery, *and*...
I won the lottery, *but*...

The first sentence is going to have a happy ending. The second one, not so much.
Changing a single word sets up dramatically different outcomes. The same scenarios could also have been written with different transition words placed at the
beginning:

Because I won the lottery, ...
Although I won the lottery, ...

Some transition words simply reinforce the clue. For these, you'd pick a word that agrees with the clue. Other transition words indicate that the word for the blank is the opposite of the clue. It's particularly important to take note of these contrast transitions.

Here are some of the most important transition words you'll encounter in Text Completion questions:

Same Meaning or Direction / Agreement		Opposite Meaning or Direction / Contrast	
accordingly	next	although	on the other hand
also	similarly	but	or
and	since	despite	previously
because	so	even though	rather than
consequently	therefore	however	still
for example	thus	in contrast	though
furthermore	too	instead	unfortunately
hence	; (semicolon)	nevertheless	whereas
in addition	: (colon)	nonetheless	while
moreover			yet

Two of the same-direction transition "words" are just punctuation marks. The semicolon is the equivalent of *and*, implying that the second clause follows logically from the first. The colon implies that the second clause is an explanation or illustration of the first. In either case, the clue for a blank in one part of the sentence will be found in the other part. Notice nuances in some of these transition words. Several of the same-direction words imply a cause-effect relationship: *accordingly*, *because*, *consequently*, *hence*, *so*, *therefore*, and *thus*. The word *previously* implies a change or contrast over time, and the word *unfortunately* implies a situation contrary to what was hoped for or expected.

Practice: Clues and Transitions

Underline the clues and circle the transition words in the following sentences; then come up with your own word for the blanks. Recycle the clues if possible. Answers can be found in Part V.

The star receiver is widely regarded as one of the top talents in the game, but his _____ performance as a rookie almost ended his career.

The prime minister received international _____ for her work; she brokered a diplomatic solution to a potential crisis.

While it is often assumed that drinking alcohol is detrimental to one's health, many studies have shown the _____ effects of having a glass or two of wine daily.

Despite the increasing technological connectivity of the modern world, many cultures still remain _____ from the global society.

Although many cultures view the toad as a symbol of ugliness and clumsiness, the Chinese revere the toad as a _____ symbol.

Stock analysts often use holiday sales to gauge future stock prices; thus, retail performance can be an important _____ of market trends.

It is somewhat ironic that while the population at large tends to have a negative view of the legal profession, individuals rarely display such _____ to their lawyers.

Methyl bromide is a pesticide that has devastating effects on insects; however, some believe it has the same _____ to humans.

PROCESS OF ELIMINATION STRATEGIES

After deciphering the clues in the passage and coming up with your own word for the blank, you arrive at the third and final step in Text Completion. In Step 3, you simply check each answer choice against the word you came up with. Use your scratch paper to mark any choice that's a match for your word with a ✓, any choice that's not a match with a ✗, and any word you don't know with a ?.

Ideally, your scratch paper will show one ✓, five ✗s, and no ?s. But life's not always that simple, and neither is the GRE. For those less-than-ideal situations, you'll need some POE skills and strategies to fall back on.

Here are some general points to keep in mind as you work through the answer choices.

- **Focus on the words you know.** Any answer choice that you know, you should be able to compare to your word and decisively mark with a ✓ or a ✗.
- **Never talk yourself into picking a word that you've eliminated.** Just because you know what it means does not mean the word is a better answer. If you are between choosing a word you've eliminated and choosing a word you don't know, pick the word you don't know.
- **Never eliminate a word you don't know.** If you have no good idea what an answer choice means, you can't rule it out as a match for your word.
- **Don't trust your ears.** If an answer choice matches your own word but doesn't sound quite right when inserted into the blank, it may still be correct. The question may be relying on a less common definition or usage of the word. Sometimes, too, the GRE will create a correct answer choice that's somewhat awkward while planting a trap answer that sounds better to the ear but has nothing to do with the clues.
- **Don't forget to Mark and Move.** There are certain situations where Mark and Move makes sense on Text Completion questions. You might be having difficulty finding the clues. You might be daunted by a multi-blank question. The definition of a familiar word may have momentarily slipped your mind. You might have gone through POE and have two answer choices with checkmarks. In such cases, step away from the question, answer a few other questions and return to the one you've skipped. It's the best way to reset your brain and get a fresh start on a difficult question.

Take a look at the following example:

Years of confinement in a sunless cell had left the prisoner wan and weakened, with a shockingly _____ appearance.

| sidereal |
| boisterous |
| etiolated |
| singular |
| circumscribed |

Here's How to Crack It

Begin by asking "Who or what is the blank describing?" The blank is describing *the prisoner's…appearance.* Now ask "What else in the passage provides insight into the prisoner's appearance? The sentence describes this as *wan and weakened.* Therefore, recycle the words "wan and weakened" as the word for the blank. Now evaluate the answer choices one at a time.

Upon evaluating the answer choices, many will find that they are a total nightmare. Resolutely work through the answer choices one by one, comparing them to "wan and weakened." Choice (A) is tough. If you don't know this word, you can't eliminate it, so mark with a question mark and leave it for now. You may know that (B), *boisterous,* means noisy and rowdy. If so, you can eliminate (B). The next choice, (C), is *etiolated*—another difficult word, so mark it with a question mark and move on. Choice (D) is *singular,* which we usually think of as the opposite of *plural.* It can also mean one-of-a-kind or unique. In either sense, it's not a match for "wan and weakened," so eliminate (D). The final choice, (E), is *circumscribed,* which means to restrict something, or draw around, so eliminate (E).

At this point, you have three eliminated choices and two with question marks, so pick one of the two unknowns. The bottom line is that by using careful POE you have increased your odds to one-in-two. By the way, the answer is (C), *etiolated,* which describes the pale appearance of plants grown with insufficient sunlight but by extension applies to anything feeble or sickly in appearance.

Positive and Negative Words

In some cases, your search for the clues will be less than conclusive. You might find the clues vague. You might be uncertain about the precise meaning of the word to go in the blank. Or, you may be faced with an intimidating lineup of answer choices. In situations such as these, try to simplify your POE. If you can determine whether the general sense of the word to go in the blank is positive or negative, you can separate the answer choices accordingly.

Look again at question 3 from the Finding the Clue practice exercise:

> A wind-chill warning is issued when the temperature is projected to reach minus 25 degrees Fahrenheit or lower, the point at which the cold has _____ effects on living creatures.

You might not be able to think of a good word to fit in the blank, but common sense (plus the clue that a *warning is issued*) tells you that *temperatures* of *minus 25 degrees…or lower* are bad for *living creatures*. So you can eliminate any answer choice that implies positive or beneficial—or even neutral!—effects on living creatures. This approach may not eliminate every answer choice (it may not eliminate any!), but every little bit helps. With a little thought, you might be able to take this positive/negative aspect of the passage a step further and eliminate any answer choice that doesn't reflect negative influences on *health* specifically.

It's important to remember that this strategy must not be your main approach to Text Completion questions. Your surest path to success remains the basic approach of finding clues and coming up with your own word to check the answer choices against. Positive/negative word associations can help you to leverage your vocabulary up to a point but should remain a tool of last resort.

THE FINAL WORD ON VOCABULARY

The strategies that we've been discussing emphasize critical assessment of the passage and smart POE. They're designed to make Text Completion questions as easy as possible and will get you far. Learning these strategies will also make you a better test-taker overall.

But there's no getting around it. At the end of the day, Text Completions are about knowing words and their definitions. These questions are about vocabulary. You'll see this most clearly (and painfully) on the questions where you successfully come up with a great word for the blank only to hit a slate of unfamiliar answer choices. Or the passage itself may be a minefield of verbiage, making it all but impossible to decipher the clues. The only solution for this predicament is to improve your vocabulary as much as possible, little by little, from now until test day.

Memorizing the Key Terms List of words in Chapter 8 is a good start. Try out the suggestions for Learning New Words at the beginning of that chapter (page 145). Deepen your vocabulary by exploring word roots as highlighted on page 73 of the Sentence Equivalence chapter. Bottom line: As you prepare for the GRE, keep learning new words every day, in whatever way works best for you. Make it fun!

PUTTING IT ALL TOGETHER

The following drill is your opportunity to apply all the skills and strategies you've learned so far. These are all one-blank Text Completion questions, each with five answer choices.

Remember how to go about it! Start by assessing the text to come up with your own word for the blank. Ignore the answer choices. Ask *who or what* the blank is describing—identifying the part of speech can clarify this. Then ask *what else* in the sentence gives insight into this person or thing. These are your clues, and you'll use transition words to determine whether the clues have the same or opposite meaning relative to the blank. Now, come up with a word or phrase for the blank. Use plain, descriptive, and literal language, recycling words from the clues if possible.

Compare each answer choice to your own word—eliminating words that don't match (✖), keeping the word that does (✓), and leaving any words you don't know (?). If it's not that straightforward, use your POE tools. Bear in mind that some words have figurative or uncommon usages that may sound awkward even if they are close to your own word and match the clues. If guessing, never choose a word you've eliminated over one you don't know.

Use the positive-and-negative approach to POE *only* if your understanding of the clues is vague or you're stumped by the majority of answer choices. If you wind up with two answer choices that work or find yourself paralyzed by a question for any other reason, use Mark and Move.

Good luck!

Text Completions Drill

Answers can be found in Part V.

Despite the smile that spread from ear to ear, her eyes relayed a certain _____ .

jubilance
sorrow
mischievousness
vision
liveliness

While grizzly bears have long, flat, and somewhat blunt claws, black bears have short, curved and_____ claws.

obtuse
abominable
barren
acute
fearful

One of social science's major themes is that of stability versus change; to what extent are individual personalities _____ or different over time?

transient
maladjusted
static
disturbed
discreet

The Erie Canal's completion caused _____ economic ripples; property values and industrial output along its route rose exponentially.

persistent
invaluable
incredulous
severe
prodigious

Voters have become so inured to the fickle nature of politicians that they responded to the levy of a new tax with _____ .

amazement
stolidity
exasperation
alarm
perplexity

It is desirable to expand the yield of a harvest only when _____ additions in time, exertion, and other variable factors of production are not also required.

predestined
commensurate
analogous
deliberate
indeterminate

PART 2: TEXT COMPLETION ADVANCED TOPICS

So far we have been dealing with one-sentence, one-blank Text Completions with five answer choices. But not all Text Completion questions are created equal. Some are designed to be more challenging, but ETS has a specific repertoire of techniques it uses to make hard Text Completion questions. While it's true you will never see the same question twice, ETS does repeatedly pull from the same bag of tricks to make questions harder. No matter how tricky a question looks, however, the ground rules remain the same: The text contains the clues that tell you what goes in the blank(s).

Let's take a quick look at how ETS mixes things up in advanced Text Completion questions:

- **More Blanks.** Some passages have questions with two or three blanks. In such questions, each blank has three answer choices, not five as in one-blank questions.
- **More Sentences.** Text Completion questions don't all have just a single sentence. Some are passages of up to five sentences. That means more to read and more to keep track of, but also more information about the blanks.
- **More Complicated Sentences.** ETS will make the structure of the sentence more difficult to read. They will make the language thicker and harder to follow.
- **Difficult Transitions.** Transitions—agreement or contrast between parts of a passage—may not always be marked by obvious words like *and*, *but*, *since*, and *although*. And some sentences contain multiple transitions.
- **Vocabulary.** The words in the answer choices may be more difficult. However, it's more typical for ETS to make harder Text Completion questions by including more challenging vocabulary in the passage itself.

STEPS FOR TWO- AND THREE- BLANK TEXT COMPLETIONS

For two- and three- blank text completion questions, there are only three answer choices per blank. With just three answer choices per blank, multiple-blank questions have a simpler POE per blank than one blank Text Completions. But that makes it even more important to analyze the text for clues about the word that goes in the blank. The strategies you've already learned in this chapter still apply, no matter how involved the question, but multiple blanks call for some slight modifications to the steps:

- **Start with the easiest blank.** This is not always the first blank. The easiest blank is the one with the most obvious clue. Read through the passage and determine the blank that has the most obvious clue and begin working there.

- **Answer each blank in turn.** Once you identify the blank with the strongest clue, work through the POE process for it first before moving on to another blank.
- **Reread the finished product.** Once you have selected answer choices for all the blanks, reread the entire passage with your choices. Make sure that it tells a consistent, logical story—the only possible story given the context of the passage.

Let's apply this modified approach to the following example:

Federal efforts to regulate standards on educational achievements have been met by (i) _____ from the states; local governments feel that government imposition represents an undue infringement on their (ii) _____ .

Blank (i)	Blank (ii)
receptivity	autonomy
intransigence	legislation
compromise	comportment

Here's How to Crack It

Without looking at any answer choices yet, scan the passage and determine which of the blanks has the more obvious clue. Because the second clause makes it clear that something bad is going on—*an undue infringement*, the first blank is easier to work with. The first blank is describing *the states'* reaction to *[f]ederal…standards on education achievements*. The sentence gives further insight into this by stating that *local governments* consider this *an…infringement*. The semicolon is a transition indicating agreement between the clauses. So, the word in the first blank describing the states' reaction will be something like "resistance." Now check the answer choices against "resistance." Choice (A) is the opposite of this, *receptivity*. Eliminate (A). If you don't know what *intransigence* means, then put a question mark next to (B). Choice (C), however, *compromise*, is not a match for "resistance." Even if you don't know what *intransigence* means, select (B) as it is the only non-eliminated answer. Now, work with the second blank.

The second blank describes something that *local governments* feel is negatively impacted by *government imposition*. The sentence provides insight into this by stating that *[f]ederal efforts to regulate standards on education achievements*, have not been well-received by *the states*. A word or phrase for the second blank, then, could be a descriptive phrase like "freedom from intervention by the federal government," which you might simplify to "the right to govern themselves." Now check the answer choices. Choice (D), *autonomy*, means independence or self-government.

This is a good match, so keep (D). Choice (E), *legislation*, is close but too neutral and broad given the clue. Eliminate (E). Choice (F), *comportment*, means demeanor or the way one carries oneself, so eliminate it.

The correct answer is *intransigence* and *autonomy*.

Let's try our hand at a three-blank question:

Many popular musicians have (i) _____ new digital technologies that allow them unprecedented control over their music. These musicians use computers to (ii) _____ and modify their songs, resulting in a level of musical precision often unattainable naturally. Of course, though, as is often the case with new technologies, some traditionalists (iii) _____ these developments.

Blank (i)	Blank (ii)	Blank (iii)
incorporated	energize	balk at
synthesized	delineate	revel in
alleviated	recast	retaliate at

Here's How to Crack It

The second blank has the strongest clue, so begin there. The second blank is a verb that describes what *musicians* do to their songs using *computers*. The sentence gives further insight into how musicians use computers to impact songs by stating that computers result in a *precision…unattainable naturally*. The transition word *and* indicates that the word for the blank should be similar to the word *modify,* which the passage uses to describe the contents of the blank. So, recycle this language and use a word such as "modify." Choice (D), *energize*, is not a match for "modify," so eliminate it. Choice (E), *delineate*, means to outline or to define, which is also not a match for "modify," so eliminate (E). Although both these words describe something that musicians could do to their songs, neither is as close a match for the word "modify" as (F), *recast*. Keep (F) and move on to the blank with the next strongest clue.

The blank with the next strongest clue is the first blank. The first blank should be a verb describing what *[m]any popular musicians* have done with *new digital technologies*. The passage gives further insight into what musicians have done with new technologies by stating technologies gives them *control over their music* and that *[t]hese musicians use computers*. Therefore, the word for the first blank should be something close to "use," so let's reuse that fairly neutral word. The word for

(A), *incorporated*, is a good fit, so keep (A). Choice (B), *synthesize*, is a trap answer. It may describe how musicians make their songs using digital technologies, but it doesn't describe what they do to these technologies. Eliminate (B). Choice (C), *alleviate*, means to make less severe, so also eliminate (C).

Now work with the third blank. The third blank is a verb describing the reaction of *traditionalists* to *these developments*. The passage provides further insight by stating that these are *new technologies* and the transition word *though* indicates that the reaction from *traditionalist* should be expected to be different than those of the musicians described earlier. Therefore, the traditionalists should have a negative reaction to new technologies, so a good phrase for the blank could simply be "don't like." Choice (G) is *balk at*, which matches "don't like," so keep (G). Choice (H), *revel in*, means celebrate, which is the opposite of "don't like," so eliminate (H). Choice (I) is *retaliate*, certainly negative but this extreme reaction is not suggested by the text, so eliminate (I).

The correct answer is *incorporated*, *recast*, and *balk at*.

RELATIONSHIP BETWEEN THE BLANKS

Sometimes, there is no clear clue for the blank. On occasion (maybe once per test), there is no clear clue because the blanks are related to each other. If you're struggling to find a clear clue for either blank, look for how the transition words connect the two blanks. If you find a transition word that connects the two blanks, come up with a pair of words that work for the blanks. Or, all you may be able to determine is that the two words go in the same or opposite directions.

Once you have a pair of words that work for the blanks, work through the choices for the first blank. When you find a word that works with your word, put a checkmark next to it and begin evaluating the words for the second blank. If you find a word in the answers that works for the second blank that also pairs well with the first blank, put a check next to it. Continue that process until you have gone through all of the potential answer choices for the first blank. If you end up with more than one pair of words that work for the blanks, re-evaluate the sentence and work those blanks again.

Oftentimes, students will be scared off of their game by questions like this with no clear clue. The good news is these types of questions are relatively rare. Just stick to the process and keep your cool. But because these questions only show up on average once per test, you can always make a guess and devote your time to more customary questions.

TRICKY TRANSITIONS

Transitions indicate that two parts of the sentence are the same or opposite, similar or different, agreeing or contrasting. Not every transition is flagged by the obvious transition words that we highlighted in the earlier section: *and, but, so, however, because, despite, since, although, instead,* etc. Let's take a look at examples of more elusive transitions:

> They were twins in _____ only: their personalities could not have been more _____.

The word *twins* indicates that similarity is expected. The word *only*, however, suggests that their similarity is limited to one aspect, because (note the transitional colon) another aspect, *their personalities*, was not twin-like. The word in the first blank should match "appearance"; the word in the second blank should match "different."

Here the similarity was implied by the word *twins*. Similarity or difference could be implied by a mere description of two things:

> Among dog breeds, the endearingly diminutive shihtzu has _____ close kinship to its lupine ancestors.

The word *close kinship* implies similarity between *the...shihtzu* and the wolf (*lupine ancestors*). However, the description of the shihtzu as *endearingly diminutive* contradicts our typical image of the wolf. Therefore, the word in the blank describing the *close kinship* between the two would be something like "(an) unexpectedly".

Suffice it to say there are many ways to set up agreement or contrast between two parts of a sentence. The GRE will often use time transitions to indicate some sort of change or difference. The GRE will also unfurl words such as *unexpected, surprising, ironic,* or *unfortunate*. These words imply opposition or contrast to what was expected or hoped for. Things really get complicated when a sentence contains more than one transition. Read the following example and its variations:

1. It's ironic that the striking nurses' chief grievance is _____ health care.
2. It's ironic that, while content with their salaries and vacation packages, the striking nurses' chief grievance is _____ health care.
3. It's ironic that, while pressing for better salaries and vacation packages, the striking nurses' chief grievance is _____ health care.
4. It's ironic that, while content with their salaries and vacation packages, the striking nurses' chief objective is _____ health care.

In the first sentence, the word *ironic* indicates opposition between two things in the sentence, *the striking nurses* and their *chief grievance* or complaint. This complaint has to do with the kind of *health care* they are receiving. Since nurses work in the health care field, it would be ironic for them to have "poor" or "inadequate" health care, so that should be their complaint. The second and third sentences are the same except for two very different transitional clauses: the clause in the second sentence implying that the nurses are happy with their *salaries and vacation packages*, the clause in the third sentence implying that they are not. Even though these transitional clauses have opposite meanings, they have no impact on the word in the blank. In all three sentences, the word in the blank is driven by the *ironic* opposition of *striking nurses* and their complaint of "inadequate" *health care*. In the fourth sentence, we replace the word *grievance* in sentence 2 with *objective*. While the irony of the nurses and their inadequate health care remains the same, changing *grievance* to *objective* means that the word in the blank must change from the kind of health care the nurses are complaining about ("inadequate") to the kind of health care they are aiming for ("better").

Including multiple transitions in a passage is a predictable trick that ETS uses to complicate Text Completion questions. So get used to recognizing and deciphering them! It's impossible to establish set rules for how these compound transitions add up. You must pay close attention to how they are related logically.

Text Completions Practice Set

Answers can be found in Part V.

With global interconnectedness on the rise, the conviction of the United States to remain neutral in World War I seemed ever more _____ .

presumptuous
futile
contemptuous
pragmatic
admirable

Upon visiting the Middle East in 1850, Gustave Flaubert was so _____ belly dancing that he wrote, in a letter to his mother, that the dancers alone made his trip worthwhile.

overwhelmed by
enamored of
taken aback by
beseeched by
flustered by

The human race is a very (i)_____ species, as the facade of calm that covers our anxiety and (ii)_____ is flimsy and effortlessly ruptured.

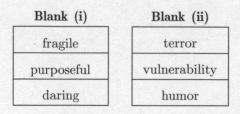

Blank (i)	Blank (ii)
fragile	terror
purposeful	vulnerability
daring	humor

The practice of purchasing books was primarily a (i)_____ of the well-to-do until the late 1800s, when the increased popularity of dime novels, the expansion in the number of bookstores, and the introduction of the paperback made books (ii)_____ the average man.

Blank (i)	Blank (ii)
conduit	dislikable to
prerogative	excitable to
plight	attainable by

Increasingly, the boundaries of congressional seats are drawn in order to protect incumbents, as legislators engineer the demographics of each district such that those already in office can coast to (i)_____ victory. Of course, there is always the possibility that the incumbent will face a challenge from within his or her own party. Nevertheless, once the primary is over, the general election is (ii)_____ .

Blank (i)	Blank (ii)
an ineluctable	seldom nugatory
an invidious	remarkably contentious
a plangent	merely denouement

While more (i)_____ professors continue to insist that video games will never be a proper object of study, the rising generation of more heterodox academics is inclined to view such talk as positively (ii)_____ .

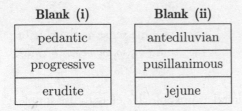

Blank (i)	Blank (ii)
pedantic	antediluvian
progressive	pusillanimous
erudite	jejune

Political predictions generally prove fairly accurate when the presumption that the future will be similar to the past is (i)_____ . In periods with substantial (ii)_____ in the political world, however, predictions can be (iii)_____ wrong.

Blank (i)	Blank (ii)	Blank (iii)
disproved	upswings	thoughtfully
stipulated	insurgencies	perilously
fulfilled	changes	carelessly

Water is one of the few molecules that is less (i)_____ as a solid than as a (ii)_____ ; if you need (iii)_____ , just look at the floating ice in your water glass.

Blank (i)	Blank (ii)	Blank (iii)
intriguing	vapor	an illustration
dense	plasma	an imbibement
aqueous	liquid	a discordance

As Molly was (i)_____ Spanish with her friends before their trip to Chile, she discovered that although she could comprehend her friends, she could not (ii)_____ her thoughts in the (iii)_____ language.

Blank (i)	Blank (ii)	Blank (iii)
mastering	acknowledge	inherent
disregarding	articulate	objective
practicing	disencumber	unfamiliar

People accustomed to thinking that the human lifespan (i)_____ the outer bounds of animal longevity tend to dismiss tales of musket balls being found in the shells of living turtles. Samantha Romney, however, argues that while such stories may be (ii)_____ , some turtles do indeed exhibit a phenomenon known as "negligible (iii)_____ ," showing no signs of aging even as they pass the two-century mark.

Blank (i)	Blank (ii)	Blank (iii)
belies	apocryphal	rejuvenation
demarcates	authentic	superannuation
antedates	heresy	senescence

Summary

○ In Text Completion questions, ignore the answer choices and come up with your own word for the blank(s), using the clues and transition words in the passage.

○ To find the clue, ask these questions: "*Who or what* is the blank describing" and "*What else* in the passage gives insight into that?"

○ Transition words tell you whether the word in the blank should have the same sense as the clue or the opposite sense. Transitions are often marked by obvious words like *and, but, so, however, because, despite, since, although, instead,* etc.

○ When coming up with your own word for the blank, be as literal as possible. It's okay to use simple words, a descriptive phrase, or language recycled from the clue.

○ After coming up with your own word for the blank, use POE to eliminate words that aren't matches for your word. Focus on the words you know. Never eliminate a word that you don't know.

○ If the clue is hard to decipher, you can simplify POE by determining if the word to go in the blank should be positive or negative. Then narrow down the answer choices by eliminating those that don't match.

○ If the sentence has two or three blanks, do the blanks one at a time. Pick the easiest blank to start with, ask the questions, find the clue, come up with a word, and use POE. Then repeat for the remaining blanks. When done, plug in all answer choices to double-check the meaning of the passage.

○ Harder questions may have less obvious transitions or more than one transition. Look out for anything that sets up a similarity or difference between two elements of the sentence—things, ideas, actions, etc. Pay attention to how transitions are related and the overall logic of the passage.

○ Use Mark and Move if you need a fresh start on a question. Answer a few other questions and then come back to the marked question.

○ Keep working on vocabulary every day! Learn prefixes, suffixes, and other word roots. Learn not just the main definition of a new word but the secondary and figurative meanings.

Chapter 5
Sentence
Equivalence

This chapter details a variation on the Text Completions you learned about in the prior chapter. Sentence Equivalence questions require you to find the best word to complete a sentence. For these questions, however, you'll have to pick the two answers that best complete the sentence; this means the two correct answers will be synonyms. Because both words create sentences that are equivalent—both have the same meaning— we refer to these types of questions as Sentence Equivalence questions. This chapter shows you how to apply the strategies you learned last chapter and use Process of Elimination to answer these questions.

WHAT'S A SENTENCE EQUIVALENCE?

Sentence Equivalence questions make up approximately 20% of the questions in any individual Verbal section. There are usually four Sentence Equivalence questions in each Verbal section. These questions are similar to Text Completion questions, as both require test-takers to select the answer choices that best complete the intended meaning of the given sentence. However, unlike Text Completion questions, Sentence Equivalence questions always have only one blank and six answer choices, and you will need to correctly select two answer choices to get credit for the question.

Sentence Equivalence questions look like this:

> Anthropologists contend that the ancient Mesopotamians switched from grain production to barley after excessive irrigation and salt accumulation made the soil _____ grains.

- ☐ indifferent to
- ☐ inhospitable to
- ☐ unsuitable for
- ☐ acrimonious to
- ☐ benignant to
- ☐ inured to

The goal of a Sentence Equivalence question is to choose the two answer choices that complete the sentence, fit the meaning of the sentence as a whole, and produce completed sentences that are alike in meaning.

A CAUTIONARY TALE ON SYNONYMS

A common mistake that test-takers make is expecting answer choices that produce completed sentences that are alike in meaning to be synonyms. The test-taker making this mistake believes when two synonyms are present in the answer choices, they must be the correct answer. The test writers know this is a commonly made assumption, so they use this information to trick test-takers into selecting the wrong answer choices. But this question type is called Sentence Equivalence, not Word Equivalence!

The first way they trick test-takers is by including a pair of synonyms in the answer choices that do not fit the meaning of the sentence as a whole. They are expecting a certain number of test-takers to scan the answer choices, find two answer choices that are synonyms, and select them as their answer. These test-takers will be sad to find that they have just been tricked by the test writers.

The second way the GRE writers trick test-takers is by ensuring that the two correct answer choices are not synonyms at all. The correct choices for Sentence Equivalence questions do not need to be exact synonyms, as long as both words correspond to the clues and the meaning of the sentence remains consistent with both words.

Sometimes, the test writers combine these two tricks and include as answer choices synonyms that are incorrect and correct answer choices that are not synonyms.

Let's look at an example:

> Unconventional political ideology is considered _____ existing main stream political ideology until the new ideas gather enough evidence and support to be adopted by or replace existing ideologies.
>
> ☐ in juxtaposition to
>
> ☐ inconsequential to
>
> ☐ deviant from
>
> ☐ a threat to
>
> ☐ in light of
>
> ☐ foreboding to

The correct answer is (B) and (C), even though *inconsequential to* and *deviant from* are not even near-synonyms. Don't worry too much yet about the best strategy to answer a question like this—we'll go over that later on. For now, let's just look at the correct and incorrect answer choices. In this example, each of the two correct answer choices is supported by a different clue in the sentence. *Inconsequential to* is supported by the fact that that the *unconventional political ideology* has yet to *gather enough support to...replace existing ideologies. Deviant from* is supported by the fact that the new ideology has yet to be *adopted by...existing ideologies.* In this context, however, both words give the same general meaning to the completed sentence. Notice also the two synonyms, *a threat to* and *foreboding to*, lying in wait for the unwary test-taker. These words may sound perfectly fine when plugged into the sentence, but they do not correspond to the clues in the sentence.

Of course, this doesn't mean that synonym pairs are always the wrong answer on Sentence Equivalence questions. In fact, the correct answers are often synonyms. But, answering a Sentence Equivalence question by picking any pair of synonyms is an unreliable strategy for conquering this portion of the GRE. At best, focusing on synonyms can be a last-resort approach for questions that you find difficult.

So, you ask, what is a good strategy?

Great question! We're glad you asked.

THE BASIC APPROACH FOR SENTENCE EQUIVALENCE QUESTIONS

The basic approach for Sentence Equivalence questions looks very similar to the basic approach for Text Completion questions. Much like Text Completion questions, Sentence Equivalence questions have clues and transition words built in, and you should come up with your own word or phrase for the blank before approaching the answer choices.

STEPS FOR SENTENCE EQUIVALENCE QUESTIONS

1. **Find the Clues and Transition words.**
2. **Come up with your own word or phrase for the blank.** Write that word or phrase down on your scratch paper.
3. **Check each answer choice and use your scratch paper.**
    - ✓ an answer that sort of matches your word
    - ✗ an answer that does not at all match your word
    - ? any word you don't know

CLUES AND TRANSITION WORDS

The first step in answering Sentence Equivalence questions is the same as that for Text Completions. You must find the clues and transition words in the sentence. *Do not move on to Step 2 or look at the answer choices until you've identified the clues and transition words in the sentence!* Consequently, as with Text Completion questions, much of your work for Sentence Equivalence questions happens by examining the sentence itself before considering the answer choices.

The clue is the words or phrases in the sentence that provide insight into the word or phrase that goes in the blank. When reading a Sentence Equivalence question and looking for the clue, ask yourself two questions:

- *Who or what* is the blank describing?
- *What else* in the sentence provides *insight* into that person or thing?

Transition words are words such as *and, but, so, however, because, despite, since, although, instead,* etc., that indicate how ideas in the sentence relate to each other. Thus, transition words convey important information about the intended meaning of a sentence. Some transition words, such as *but* and *however,* indicate that the portion of the sentence immediately following the transition word represents the opposite meaning to the other idea or action in the sentence. Here are some examples of sentences employing these sort of contrast transition words. The transition words are bolded.

I love coffee **but** I cannot tolerate the caffeine.
Although I love coffee, I cannot tolerate the caffeine.

Other transition words, such as *and, because,* and *since,* indicate that the portion of the sentence immediately following the transition word represents the same meaning as some other idea or action in the sentence. Here are some examples of sentences employing these sort of same direction transition words. The transition words are bolded.

I cannot tolerate caffeine, **so** I take my coffee decaffeinated.
Because I cannot tolerate caffeine, I take my coffee decaffeinated.

Try out the basic approach to Sentence Equivalence questions on the question we just saw:

Anthropologists contend that the ancient Mesopotamians switched from grain production to barley after excessive irrigation and salt accumulation made the soil _____ grains.

- ☐ indifferent to
- ☐ inhospitable to
- ☐ unsuitable for
- ☐ acrimonious to
- ☐ benignant to
- ☐ inured to

Here's How to Crack It

Begin working on this question by first looking for clues and transition words in the sentence. Ask yourself, *"Who or what is the blank describing?"* The blank describes what *the soil* was to *grains*—the relationship between the two. Now, ask yourself *"What else in the sentence provides insight into that person or thing?"*, or, in this case, what else in the sentence provides insight into the relationship of *the soil* to *grains*? The sentence states that *ancient Mesopotamians switched from grain production to barley* and that *excessive irrigation and salt accumulation* did something to *the soil*. These are the clues for the sentence.

Now that you've identified the clue, look for any transition words. In this sentence, the word *after* suggests that the switch from *grain production to barley* is the consequence of *irrigation and salt accumulation*'s impact on *the soil*. In other words, our two clues are in agreement and reflect the same meaning.

With all this in mind, now move on to Step 2. Come up with your own word or phrase for the blank that describes the effect on *the soil*'s relationship to *grains* brought about by *excessive irrigation and salt accumulation*—an effect that in turn would have caused *ancient Mesopotamians* to switch *from grain production to barley*. If ancient Mesopotamians had to switch from grain production to barley production, then excessive irrigation and salt accumulation must have made the soil bad for grains in some way. So, use the phrase "bad for" and move on to Step 3, checking the answer choices for any choice that indicates something "bad for."

Choice (A), *indifferent to*, does not mean something "bad for" so eliminate (A). Choice (B), *inhospitable to*, is a good match for "bad for" because if the soil was inhospitable to grain, it would explain why ancient Mesopotamians switched from grain production to barley production. Put a checkmark next to (B). Choice (C), *unsuitable for*, is also a good match for "bad for" as it would also explain why ancient Mesopotamians switched from grain production to barley production, so put another checkmark next to (C).

Don't stop evaluating the answer choices just because you found two that matched your word. Look at the remaining answer choices just in case another answer choice also matches. If that is the case, then you will need to reevaluate your interpretation of the sentence, or determine which words produce sentences that are closest in meaning. Choice (D), *acrimonious to,* may be a word you are unsure about, so put a question mark next to it. If you happen to know that *acrimonious* means angry or bitter, then you can eliminate this choice as not quite matching "bad for." Choice (E), *benignant to,* may also be a word you are unsure about, so put a question mark next to it as well. Choice (F), *inured to*, is not a good match for "bad" as inured means to grow accustomed to something, so eliminate (F).

You have two answer choices with checkmarks next to them, two choices with question marks next to them, and two choices that are eliminated. Select the two answer choices with checkmarks next to them, which is the correct answer.

———————————○———————————

Nice work.

Sentence Equivalence Drill

Work the following questions, using the same approach outlined in this chapter. Check your answers in Part V when you're done.

To any observer, ancient or _____ , the night sky appears as a hemisphere resting on the horizon.

- ☐ antiquated
- ☐ perceptive
- ☐ modern
- ☐ astute
- ☐ contemporary
- ☐ archaic

Researchers interested in the nature versus nurture debate use identical twins who were separated at birth to explore which personality characteristics are _____ and which arise through experience.

- ☐ intractable
- ☐ nascent
- ☐ erudite
- ☐ innate
- ☐ predilection
- ☐ inborn

The eccentric Canadian Prime Minister, Mackenzie King, often used séances to contact his dead pet dog for advice; despite this _____ behavior, the public had so much confidence in his ability as a leader that he was in power for 22 years.

- ☐ capricious
- ☐ lackluster
- ☐ poised
- ☐ unconventional
- ☐ repulsive
- ☐ decorous

The circulation of the blood makes human adaptability to the _____ conditions of life, such as fluctuating atmospheric pressure, level of physical activity, and diet, possible.

- ☐ inveterate
- ☐ dynamic
- ☐ timorous
- ☐ cowed
- ☐ turgid
- ☐ oscillating

Arriving in New Orleans days after Hurricane Zelda had passed and without an adequate number of vehicles of its own, the armed forces began to _____ any working form of transportation they could find, including a bus that had been chartered at great expense by a group of tourists.

- ☐ repatriate
- ☐ commandeer
- ☐ extradite
- ☐ interdict
- ☐ expurgate
- ☐ appropriate

LET'S TALK ABOUT VOCABULARY

The basic approach for Sentence Equivalence questions is going to be useful for each Sentence Equivalence question on the GRE. You're going to need to know how to proceed once you encounter a question. Knowing and believing in the basic approach is extremely valuable.

But, the basic approach can only get you so far. The truth is, for some Sentence Equivalence questions, if you do not know the meanings of the words in the answer choices, you'll likely end up guessing. There is only one, sure-fire defense against the possibility of guessing. That defense is having a robust vocabulary.

At the end of this section, we discuss in more detail vocabulary on the GRE. We have included the Key Terms List, which is a list of the words most commonly seen on the GRE. You should learn these words to stand the best chance of knowing many of the words you'll see on the GRE.

One of the best ways to help learn vocabulary, and to shed some light on unfamiliar words, is by understanding the roots of words.

Word Roots

Word roots are linguistic units that have distinct meanings. They're building blocks for words in modern English. Mastery of word roots can accelerate your vocabulary improvement. A knowledge of word roots can also sometimes help you infer enough about a mystery word to decide whether to keep or discard it as an answer choice. Here's a smattering of common word roots:

- *ben* or *bene*—good: *benefit, benefactor, benediction.*
- *mal* or *male*—bad: *malign, malfeasance, malediction.*
- *anthropo*—having to do with humankind: *anthropology, philanthropy, anthropocentric.*
- *cise* or *cide*—strike, cut, or kill: *incisive, circumcise, homicide.*
- *gen* or *gene*—origin, kind or type: *genesis, generate, genus, homogenous.*
- *morph* or *morpho*—form or shape: *morphology, amorphous, metamorphosis.*
- *vol* or *voli*—will or intention: *volunteer, voluntary, volition.*

Word roots are often combined. From the roots listed above you can now decipher several GRE-level words: *benevolence* (good intention), *malevolence* (bad intention), *anthropogenic* (caused by human activity), *anthropomorphic* (taking human form), *morphogenesis* (how something takes form), *genocide* (killing an entire group of people).

Prefixes and suffixes are especially common word roots. Just a handful of the prefixes you're sure to encounter: *ante* (before), *anti* (against), *circum* (around), *hyper* (over, above), *trans* (across). And here are some common suffixes: *able* (for adjectives indicating capability), *ism* (for nouns denoting a doctrine or belief), *less* (for adjectives indicating absence of something), *ly* (used to form adverbs from adjectives).

One good way to learn word roots is by noting the etymology (origin) of words that you look up in the dictionary. Look for word roots in your Key Terms List (in Chapter 8) and any other new words you learn.

But, learning the entirety of the Key Terms List or memorizing a couple of word roots, is in no way comprehensive. The GRE can test any word it wants, so unless you have a full working knowledge of the dictionary, its likely you'll come across some words on test day that you are unfamiliar with. That's okay.

In the following section we're going to outline for you some strategies for you to fall back on in case you are unsure how to proceed with a particular question, and you don't know what the words mean.

It's worth repeating here that the top strategy for all Sentence Equivalence questions is first to determine whether you know the words. Test-takers too often make the mistake of believing that the strategies suggested below are a cure-all (or, to use the GRE vocabulary, a nepenthe) for their Sentence Equivalence problems. We want to be very clear about this: there is no substitute for a killer vocabulary.

These strategies may not result in eliminating all the incorrect answer choices. But, if you can eliminate some, your chances of guessing correctly are certainly improved.

A PIECE OF ADVICE

When you come across a Sentence Equivalence question on test day, follow the basic approach. But, when you begin to evaluate the words in the answer choices the best thing you can do is be honest with yourself. If you don't know any of the words, then start thinking about some of the Process of Elimination strategies below. When confronted with a word they do not know, many test-takers will make the mistake of stubbornly staring at the word, convinced that if they continue to stare the word's meaning will appear. This behavior wastes valuable time that could be spent dealing with other questions and words that they do know.

So, on test day, if you don't know a word, just admit it and move on to process of elimination strategies. Or, if you don't know the meanings of most or all of the words in the answer choices, make a guess and move on to the next question.

PROCESS OF ELIMINATION STRATEGIES

Ideally, when you encounter a Sentence Equivalence question, you are able to discern the clues in the sentence clearly and come up with a spot-on word for the blank. Ideally, too, you will know the meaning of every answer choice.

Needless to say, this ideal scenario isn't the only situation you will come up against when working through the Sentence Equivalence questions in the verbal sections of the GRE. The precise nuance of the clues may elude you, making it hard to come up with a word for the blank. Or you may find yourself fuzzy, or even downright clueless, about the definition of some of the answer choices. Fret not. This happens to everyone!

Luckily, with two correct answer choices and four wrong ones, there are many opportunities for effective use of Process of Elimination. Let's look at a few of the POE strategies and considerations available to you.

Positive and Negative Words

One way to slice quickly through the lineup of answer choices is to decide whether the word in the blank should have a positive or negative connotation and then separate the answer choices into positive ones and negative ones. You don't need to know the exact dictionary definition of every answer choice if you can somewhat confidently identify it as positive or negative. However, note that with the exception of words such as "sizzle" words do NOT have meanings that relate to their sounds. So, don't fall for the trap of saying something like "Oh, that word sounds ugly so it must be a negative word." After all, pulchritude isn't a particularly nice sounding word but it means beauty. So, you can't separate words that you've never encountered before into positive or negative. But, you may remember that a word you've studied has a negative meaning even though you can't remember the precise meaning of that word.

Let's practice using this approach on the following question:

Despite the implications of their noble status, many aristocrats were virtually penniless and lived in a state of _____ .

- ☐ indigence
- ☐ opulence
- ☐ eminence
- ☐ penury
- ☐ depravity
- ☐ complacency

Can you identify any of the words as positive or negative?

Here's How to Crack It

The transition word that begins this sentence, *despite*, tells us that the *state* in which *many aristocrats…lived* is the opposite of *their noble status*. Because noble status is a positive idea, the word in the blank should be negative. This is reinforced by the additional clue that *many aristocrats were virtually penniless*. Evaluate the answer choices one at a time, eliminating positive words and holding onto negative words.

Choice (A), *indigence*, is an uncommon word. Instead of spending time trying to decipher whether it's positive or negative, just mark it with a question mark and move on. Choice (B) is another uncommon word, *opulence*, so give that one a question mark as well. Choice (C), *eminence*, is a positive word—think of someone described as *an eminent doctor* or as *an eminent author*. Therefore, eliminate (C) because the word in the blank has to be negative. Choice (D), *penury*, is another uncommon word, so mark it with a question mark. Choice (E), *depravity*, means moral corruption. This is certainly a negative word, but would you describe a penniless person as depraved? Not likely, so eliminate (E) as well. The final word, (F), is *complacency*, which means a feeling of self-satisfaction, so eliminate (F).

After all that, you have three answer choices remaining—(A) *indigence*, (B) *opulence*, and (D) *penury*. This is a much better situation than guessing from among all six. And if you happen to know that the word *opulence* is a positive word suggesting luxury, you've got the answer—it has to be (A) and (D).

———————————◯———————————

Let's move on to another strategy.

Synonym / No Synonym

One strategy is to look over the answer choices for synonym pairs and choose one of these pairs for the answer. However, the warning given earlier in the chapter still holds: It is sometimes the case that the correct answer choices will not be strict synonyms while synonym pairs can be found among the incorrect answer choices! Therefore, this strategy must be used with caution and considered a last resort. It's best reserved for times when you are pretty familiar with the words in the answer choices but having difficulty with the clue.

Consider this example:

———————————◯———————————

Because mercury has a variety of innocuous uses, including in thermometers and dental fillings, few people realize that it is one of the most _____ substances on the planet.

- ☐ acidic
- ☐ irritating
- ☐ mundane
- ☐ deleterious
- ☐ disagreeable
- ☐ pernicious

Here's How to Crack It

The clue here may be confusing, making it hard to come up with a word for the blank. So work with the answer choices to pair those that are synonyms and eliminate those with no synonyms. Evaluate the answer choices one at a time.

Start by eliminating (A), which has no synonyms among the other answer choices. Choice (B) is *irritating*. Scanning the other answer choices for a synonym, you'll find (E), *disagreeable*. If one of these is correct, the other is likely to be as well, so make them a pair. Choice (C) is *mundane*, which can mean either worldly or unexciting. This has no synonym among the other answer choices, so eliminate (C). Choice (D) is *deleterious*, a word similar in meaning to (F), *pernicious*, the only word remaining. Make these another pair.

This process eliminates two choices and leaves you with two pairs of synonyms. Guessing at this point will give you a 50/50 chance of getting the correct answer. If you've searched for the clue and come up empty-handed, those are not bad odds.

Here's how to choose between the answer choices. The blank should describe what kind of substance mercury is. The sentence gives the insight that *mercury has a variety of innocuous* or harmless *uses*. The transition word *because* suggests agreement between this clue and the blank. However, the sentence contains another transition in the phrase *few people*, which indicates that the word in the blank should actually be the opposite of *innocuous*. This insight makes the correct answer (D) and (F).

ADVANCED SENTENCE EQUIVALENCE QUESTIONS AND HOW TO CONQUER THEM

With Text Completion questions, we saw that GRE ups the difficulty by creating questions with multiple blanks. Some of these questions might even have two or more sentences! Neither of these complications occurs in Sentence Equivalence questions—they are always a single sentence containing a single blank. For Sentence Equivalence questions, the writers have some other tools to make questions difficult.

Difficult Transitions. When we introduced the topic of transitions, we focused on words such as *and, but, so, however, because, despite, since, although, instead,* etc. But not all transitions are marked by the obvious words that typically serve this function. Be on the lookout for less-than-obvious transitions. A transition can be any language indicating that two parts, ideas, or actions in the sentence are the same or opposite in sense. Let's consider these examples:

> Being a confirmed coffee snob, Boris reluctantly _____ the foul gas-station brew.
> Being a confirmed coffee snob, Boris surprised me by _____ the foul gas-station brew.

The clue in both sentences is that Boris is a coffee snob. In the first sentence, the adverb *reluctantly* implies that whatever he did with the gas-station brew was the opposite of his inclination. In the second sentence, the fact that Boris's actions were surprising again implies an action that is the opposite of the clue. In both cases, Boris has acted against his nature as a coffee snob. Therefore, the word in the blank should suggest that Boris was willing to drink the *foul gas-station brew*.

For another example, consider the use of *few people* in the mercury example used in the previous section, on page 76. There are many ways for a sentence to present things as the same or opposite, as agreeing or contrasting, as similar or different. Read carefully and critically!

Secondary Definitions. Sometimes the folks at ETS will make a question harder the old-fashioned way: with harder vocabulary.

There's no getting around it—your best defense against a lineup of scary answer choices is a formidable vocabulary. But it's not just about learning those polysyllabic, arcane, and unusual words. Many common words have less-common meanings or nuances that may be exploited on the test. The verb *apprehend*, for example, usually means to catch or arrest a wrongdoer. But it may also simply mean to perceive or to understand. While the verb *realize* commonly means to become fully aware of something, it can also mean to make something a reality. The adjective *fast* may describe something speedy or something fixed securely in place. And, as a verb, *flag* can mean to mark with a flag or to become droopy or tired. Moral of the story: When you learn a new word, take the time to learn the secondary and tertiary definitions as well.

Tips for Advanced Sentence Equivalence. Our tips for conquering the most difficult Sentence Equivalence questions fit within the three steps of the basic approach:

1. **Find the Clues and Transition words.**
   - Begin by asking "Who or what is the blank describing?" and "What else in the sentence gives insight into that person or thing?"
   - For Sentence Equivalence questions it may be difficult to identify the clue using the questions above. If that is the case, then start by determining the part of speech needed in the blank. This helps you to more concretely and efficiently answer the question, "Who or what is the blank describing?"
   - Transitions are not always clearly marked with words such as *and, but, so, however, because, despite, since, although, instead,* etc. Be alert to other ways that a sentence can make two parts the same or opposite, agreeing or contrasting.
2. **Come up with your own word or phrase for the blank.**
   - The more thoroughly you've done Step 1, the easier it will be to come up with a word for Step 2, and the better that word will predict the correct answer choices.
   - Do not be preoccupied with coming up with the perfect, most GRE-worthy word. Feel free to recycle from the clues in the sentence. Use a phrase instead of a single word. You do want a word or phrase that accurately reflects the clues. But your goal is not to have a scratch pad full of elegant words; it's to answer the questions quickly and correctly.
3. **Check each answer choice and use your scratch paper.**
   - Stick with the clues and the word you come up with. In reviewing the answer choices, if you have to choose between words you know that don't match and words you don't know, pick from the words you don't know! For example, if you have eliminated three answer choices and put question marks next to the other three, pick two from the ones that you've marked with question marks.
   - What makes a Sentence Equivalence question harder is often just the difficulty of the words in the answer choices. Your best defense is to build a strong vocabulary. Learn your word lists, and learn the range of meanings for each word.
   - The correct answer will not always be a pair of synonyms, and synonym pairs in the answer choices are not necessarily the correct answer. See the Cautionary Tale on Synonyms at the beginning of this chapter (page 66).

Let's put these advanced skills together in working through some more difficult questions.

Despite their outward negativity, many a cynic harbors an inner faith in the _____ of humankind.

☐ benevolence

☐ precocity

☐ parsimony

☐ ignobility

☐ antipathy

☐ probity

Here's How to Crack It

Find the clue for this Sentence Equivalence question by asking, "Who or what is the blank describing?" If the answer to that question is unclear, then determine the part of speech to more easily answer the question. In this case, the blank is a noun describing some aspect *of humankind* that *cynics* have *faith in*. Now ask, "What else in the sentence gives insight into that person or thing?" This clue comes from the introductory phrase, *[d]espite their outward negativity*. *Despite* is a transition word suggesting that *their outward negativity* is the opposite of their *inner faith in* some aspect *of humankind*. Therefore, the blank must refer to some positive aspect of humankind. Pick an appropriate word such as the "good" of humankind for the blank, or focus on positive words in the answer choices. Evaluate the answer choices individually.

Choice (A), *benevolence,* is a positive word so keep (A). Choice (B), *precocity,* is an uncommon word, so put a question mark next to this one. The same can be done for (C), *parsimony.* Choice (D) has the root word *noble* in it, which is certainly positive, but the prefix *ig* makes it a bad thing—think of the word *ignorant.* Eliminate this choice. Choice (E) has the prefix *anti-*, meaning against. This generally implies something negative, so eliminate (E). Choice (F), *probity,* is another tough word, so put a question mark next to it.

At this point, select (A), as it is the only choice with a checkmark next to it. Choices (B), (C), and (F) all have question marks, so if there is no way to further parse out what those words mean, pick one of them to go with (A) and move on. At the worst, you have a 1-in-3 choice of guessing correctly. Taking the POE a little further, you should also be able to eliminate (B). The word *precocity* is related to *precocious.* It also begins with the prefix *pre-*, meaning before—an idea that's neither positive nor negative. Choice (C), *parsimony,* means frugality, and (F), *probity,* means honesty and integrity. Thus, the correct answer is (A) and (F).

Let's try one more:

---○---

Formerly seen only on sailors and bikers, tattoos in the United States have become so _____ in urban culture as to lose any rebel cachet.

☐ prepossessing

☐ fascinating

☐ pedestrian

☐ peripheral

☐ marginal

☐ pervasive

Here's How to Crack It

Find the clue by asking first, "Who or what is the blank describing?" If the answer to that question is unclear, then determine the part of speech to more easily answer the question. In this case, the blank is an adjective describing what *tattoos have become…in urban culture.* Now ask, "What else in the sentence gives insight into that person or thing?" Clues here are that they were *[f]ormerly seen only on sailors and bikers* and that, as a consequence of what they've become, they have lost *any rebel cachet.* The word *formerly* is a transition word suggesting that tattoos—or specifically their cultural significance—have changed in some way. Therefore, the blank should suggest the opposite of being *seen only on sailors and bikers.* A good word might simply be "common," so use that for evaluating the answer choices. Evaluate the answer choices individually, looking for reasons to eliminate each.

Choice (A), *prepossessing*, might be unfamiliar. Trying to determine the meaning from its parts, you'd come up with something like "owning before." It's hard to see how this matches "common," so eliminate (A). Choice (B) is *fascinating.* While modern culture may be fascinated with tattoos, it doesn't match the word "common," so eliminate (B). Choice (C) is *pedestrian.* As an adjective, *pedestrian* can mean either walking on foot or ordinary. In the sense of ordinary, this is a good match for "common," so put a checkmark next to (C). Choice (D), *peripheral*, means at the edge of something—not a match for "common." Eliminate (D). Choice (E), *marginal*, means the same thing as *peripheral*, so eliminate it as well. The final choice is (F), *pervasive*, which describes something that is found everywhere. This could be another way of saying "common," so (F) earns a checkmark. The answer is (C) and (F).

Notice some pitfalls that we've avoided in this question. Two of the answer choices, *peripheral* and *marginal*, are synonyms but don't match "common." They'd be tempting if you missed the time transition implying that tattoos have changed from being something unusual. The words *prepossessing*, meaning impressive or pleasing, and *fascinating* are another decoy synonym pair. The correct answer choices, *pedestrian* and *pervasive*, aren't strict synonyms. Furthermore, recognizing *pedestrian* as a correct choice depends on knowing its secondary definition. These are all traps that might have tripped you up before, so you've learned a lot!

---○---

Sentence Equivalence Practice Set

Work the following questions, using all the techniques you've learned for Sentence Equivalence. Check your answers in Part V when you're done.

Possessed of an insatiable sweet tooth, Jim enjoyed all kinds of candy, but he had a special _____ for gumdrops, his absolute favorite.

- ☐ container
- ☐ affinity
- ☐ odium
- ☐ nature
- ☐ disregard
- ☐ predilection

Although the Wright brothers' first attempted flight in 1901 was a _____ and subsequent efforts similarly ended in failure, they persisted and ultimately made the first successful airplane flight in 1903.

- ☐ fiasco
- ☐ debacle
- ☐ hindrance
- ☐ feat
- ☐ triumph
- ☐ precedent

The fuel efficiency of most vehicles traveling at speeds greater than 50 miles per hour _____ as the vehicle's speed increases, due to the increased aerodynamic drag placed on the vehicle.

- ☐ equalizes
- ☐ adapts
- ☐ stabilizes
- ☐ diminishes
- ☐ increases
- ☐ wanes

Despite the vast amount of time Francis dedicated to learning six different languages, he was _____ communicator; his mastery of vocabulary and grammar failed to redress his inability to construct cogent prose.

- ☐ a florid
- ☐ an inept
- ☐ a prolific
- ☐ an astute
- ☐ a morose
- ☐ a maladroit

The twins' heredity and upbringing were identical in nearly every respect, yet one child remained unfailingly sanguine even in times of stress while her sister was prone to angry outbursts that indicated an exceptionally choleric _____ .

- ☐ genotype
- ☐ environment
- ☐ physiognomy
- ☐ incarnation
- ☐ temperament
- ☐ humor

Summary

- The approach for Sentence Equivalence questions is the same as for Text Completions. Ignore the answer choices, ask who or what the blank is describing, look for clues and transition words, fill in your own word for the blank, and check the answer choices against your word using POE. You must pick two answer choices.

- Identifying the part of speech that should go in the blank will help answer who or what the blank is describing.

- Pay close attention to transitions. Transitions indicate two parts of the sentence are the same or opposite in meaning. They are often marked by obvious words like *and, but, so, however, because, despite, since, although, instead,* etc. Other transitions are not as obvious but still important.

- If the clue is hard to decipher, you can simplify POE by determining if the word to go in the blank should be positive or negative. Then narrow down the answer choices by eliminating those that don't match.

- The two correct answer choices may not be strict synonyms.

- Sentence Equivalence questions can be made harder simply by having more difficult words in the answer choices. Keep working on vocabulary every day! Learn prefixes, suffixes, and other word roots.

Chapter 6
Reading
Comprehension

Reading Comprehension questions on the GRE can be quite deceptive. On the one hand, the answer to each question is somewhere in the passage. On the other hand, ETS is really good at crafting answers that seem right but are, in fact, wrong. This chapter will teach you the best way to approach the reading passages on the test and how to attack the questions. Furthermore, you'll learn how to use Process of Elimination to get rid of wrong answers and maximize your score.

WHAT YOU WILL SEE

On the GRE, you'll have about eight reading passages, varying in length from a mere 12 lines to more than 50 lines. After each passage, you'll be asked to answer a number of questions. Your task is to choose the best answer to each question based on what is stated or implied in the passage. Translation: The correct answer to every question is somewhere in the passage. In fact, think of Reading Comprehension questions as an open-book test. Your goal is simply to locate the answer within the passage.

Reading Comprehension and the Computer

Reading Comprehension questions are presented on a split screen. The passage is on the left side and stays there while you work on the questions; you may have to use the scroll bar to read the whole passage. The questions appear one at a time on the right side. It's very important to practice reading comprehension on the computer with The Princeton Review's online practice tests or ETS's free *POWERPREP® II* software (see Chapter 1), because you'll have to get used to not being able to circle or underline words, bracket text, write notes in the margin, and so on. But you can start practicing good habits right now. As you work through this chapter, and any time you practice reading comprehension on paper, don't allow yourself to write on the passage. Anything you write must be written on scratch paper. In your preparation for the GRE, never give yourself a crutch you won't actually have when you take the real test.

Let's get started.

READING AND THE GRE

Although it might seem that Reading Comprehension questions shouldn't be very hard, ETS makes these types of questions difficult by exploiting some common assumptions.

The reading skills you'll need to use for Reading Comprehension questions on the GRE are quite different from the ones you use in your everyday life. The biggest challenge will probably be the limited time you have to answer the questions.

For one thing, ETS (intentionally) chooses reading passages that are complicated and are concerned with unfamiliar and, in some cases, intimidating topics, hoping that you'll have a tough time absorbing the entirety of the passage in the short amount of time they give you. In many cases, that is exactly what happens: Test takers spend too much time trying to understand what they've read and not enough time working on the questions.

ETS also hopes that you will overanalyze the text. This level of critical thinking is wholly appropriate for most types of academic reading, but on the GRE it only leads to trouble. The way to crack the reading portion of the GRE is to read less into the passages, not more.

Although it may sound counterintuitive, in some ways the passage itself is the least important part of Reading Comprehension questions. This is for a simple reason—you don't get any points for reading the passage, and the only way to do well on the GRE is to amass as many points as possible.

Okay, now you're ready to take a look at our approach to Reading Comprehension questions.

READING COMPREHENSION: THE BASIC APPROACH

1. **Attack the Passage.** This step will vary slightly based on the length of the passage you're dealing with, but in each case, the goal is to read less, not more.
2. **Size Up the Questions.** Reading Comprehension questions on the GRE can ask you to do a variety of things. Make sure you know what the question's asking you to do.
3. **Find and Paraphrase the Answer.** This is the key. Always return to the passage to find your answer; never answer questions from memory!
4. **Use Process of Elimination.** You can use a number of helpful POE guidelines on Reading Comprehension questions. We'll go over these in detail in a moment.

Let's look at each step in some more detail.

ATTACK THE PASSAGE

Imagine you drop out of an airplane and land on a random college campus. You walk into a random building, pop into the first lecture hall you see, and stand in the back for ten minutes. When you come out, someone asks you a bunch of questions about what you've just heard. That is what reading comprehension is like on the GRE. You don't pick the topic; you don't start from the beginning; there is no title, no outline, and no table of contents. You are not in control.

The creators of the GRE are going to give you short and long passages filled with tons of information that you will never be tested on. They will try to suck you into these dense, badly written science or humanities passages in order to get you to waste time and to confuse you with useless information. Your job is to read as

Remember!
You don't have to read every single word of the passage in order to answer the questions.

little of the passage as you need to get started on the questions and then to let the questions tell you which facts to care about. To get started on the questions, you need to know only the main idea of the passage, the structure, and the tone.

Fortunately, you know most of this already. The truth is that all GRE passages are really about one of two things: a problem or a change. You may think a passage is about art history or geology or different kinds of rocks on Jupiter, but really, it's either about a problem or a change.

Furthermore, once you know whether it is about a problem or a change, you even know what the passage is likely to cover.

> Problem passages cover these questions:
>
> 1. What is the problem?
> 2. What caused the problem?
> 3. What are the effects of the problem?
> 4. Are there any solutions?
>
> Change passages cover these questions:
>
> 1. What was the old way?
> 2. What is the new way?
> 3. What caused the change?
> 4. What are the effects of the change?

Knowing how passages are organized will change the way you read. This information puts you back in control by allowing you to categorize the information you're given and to anticipate what is coming next. *Remember:* On the first reading, you just need the basics. Don't get sucked into details you don't need to know.

Once you know whether a passage is about a problem or a change, you just need enough information to answer the four standard problem or change questions. Feel free to skim the rest. If you are asked a question about something you skimmed over, you can always go back to find it.

There is one golden rule of reading comprehension: Always go back to the passage to find proof. If you cannot put your finger on a line that proves your answer choice, you should not pick it.

When you see reading comprehension passages, practice categorizing them as problem or change, and then practice anticipating what each paragraph is going to be about. Once you get good at this, you will find that *you* are in control, not them.

Try reading the following passage:

> Prior to 1735, there was no legal precedent for freedom of the press. The constitutional concept of freedom of the press traces its origins to 1735 and the libel trial of John Peter Zenger. Zenger, born in Germany, emigrated to America in 1710 and established *The New York Weekly Journal* in 1733. The *Journal* starkly opposed the policies of New York governor William Cosby and while Zenger did not write the majority of the critical pieces, he was arrested on libel charges in 1734. In the ensuing trial, widely followed by the populace, Zenger was defended by Andrew Hamilton, a Pennsylvania lawyer who was brought in after Cosby disbarred all the New York lawyers who offered to defend Zenger. Hamilton's brilliant defense of Zenger was predicated on the argument that since Zenger's criticisms involved verifiable facts, they could not possibly be considered libel. The judge agreed and acquitted the publisher, establishing the basic concept of freedom of the press that was to be enshrined in the United States Constitution some 57 years later.

Problem or change? _____

What was the old way? _____

What is the new way? _____

What caused the change?_____

What are the effects of the change? _____

Yes, the preceding passage is about freedom of the press, but it's really about a change. According to the old way, there was no freedom of the press, and reporters could be arrested. After the adoption of the new way, reporters writing verifiable facts could not be charged with libel. The cause of the change was the trial of John Peter Zenger, and the effect of the trial was the precedent of freedom that eventually became enshrined in the U.S. Constitution some 57 years later.

If you said that a lack of freedom of the press was a problem, don't worry. It was. The important thing is that you were the one in charge when you were reading, and you were the one asking the questions. Instead of passively letting information wash over you, hoping the important parts of the passage would stick, you became an active reader.

Now try again on a longer passage. Remember not to get bogged down by the details in the passage. Read for evidence of what the author thinks. Important statements in the passage contain the author's opinions, recommendations, and conclusions.

Stay focused on finding the main idea as you read.

What was it about Oscar Wilde's only novel, *The Picture of Dorian Gray*, that caused it to create such an uproar when it was published in 1891? While critics attacked the quality of Wilde's work, lambasting its plot as "incurably silly" and chiding the writer for using prose that was "clumsy" and "boring," these overt denunciations of the formal elements of Wilde's work merely masked the true concerns of many nineteenth-century critics. What these critics were actually railing against was the thematic content of Wilde's work, specifically his illustration of a lifestyle devoted to useless beauty. For many a nineteenth-century moralist, *The Picture of Dorian Gray* was nothing more than a primer for spiritual depravity. Wilde's ultimate sin was not his clunky plot or his sometimes cloying prose; it wasn't even his disregard for the time-honored tradition of English propriety. It was instead his leniency toward his protagonist. Wilde propagated the disdain of critics not simply because Dorian Gray was an unabashed hedonist, but because Wilde failed to punish his subject appropriately for his hedonism. To the critics, allowing an evil character to escape his just deserts was an unforgivable sin, and it was this transgression that resulted in such opprobrium for Wilde's work. In their mind, Wilde's work was corrupting the genteel reading public by failing to show the proper consequences of immoral behavior.

Problem or change? _____

What is the problem? _____

What caused it? _____

What are the effects? _____

Are there any solutions? _____

Here we have a longer passage about the critical response to Oscar Wilde's *The Picture of Dorian Gray.* You know that it is a problem in the very first sentence when you are told that the novel created "an uproar" and in the second sentence when you are told that critics "attacked" it. The cause of the problem doesn't come until the last third of the passage. The protagonist was a hedonist, but Wilde did not punish his character for his sins. The effect of this problem was the outrage from critics. No solution is offered. Everything else is just details. Transitions such as *Wilde's ultimate sin* and *It was instead* are good indicators that something important is being said.

Purpose

You will often see questions that ask about an author's purpose—that is, why the author bothered to write the passage, paragraph, or sentence at all. Purpose can be summed up with the acronym PRICE. The purpose of a paragraph, passage, or even an individual sentence is to Predict, Recommend, Inform, Correct, or Evaluate.

Most passages or paragraphs simply inform. Whenever an author begins to offer an opinion, however, he or she may be evaluating an argument, correcting a misperception, predicting an outcome, or even recommending a behavior.

With longer passages, it is helpful to go paragraph by paragraph and note the subject (the old way, the new way, the nature of the problem, and so on) and the purpose of each paragraph. Jot this information down on your scratch paper. Doing so will force you to actively assess each paragraph and will give you a map that you can use to find the answers for specific questions.

Here is a longer passage to try.

> Scientists researching the aging process are increasingly investigating the role of telomeres, portions of DNA on the ends of chromosomes found in every cell. The exact relationship between telomeres and aging is unknown. Unlike the rest of the chromosome, telomeres do not contain genes, the strands of DNA that code for particular enzymes and proteins. Telomeres primarily serve a protective role in cells, playing two key roles

Make sure that you scroll down as far as you can, to guarantee that you see the entire passage.

in maintaining healthy cells. First, telomeres prevent important genetic material from being lost during cell replication, functioning as a "cap" of sorts on the end of each chromosome. Second, telomeres serve as a biological marker that the chromosome is "complete"; without a telomere on the end of a chromosome, the body considers the chromosome defective and takes steps against it.

While the protective role of telomeres is fairly well understood, scientists are interested in another facet of telomeres. Telomeres contain between one to two thousand copies of a particular DNA sequence. Each time a cell divides, a minuscule bit of this DNA sequence is lopped off. When telomeres become too short, the cell becomes impaired, unable to divide, and prone to malfunction. Cells with critically short telomeres eventually die, leading many researchers to compare telomeres to biological clocks or fuses, counting down to the death of a cell.

This passage contains a lot of details. Don't get bogged down in them!

Although the role of telomeres in cellular aging and malfunction is well documented, new research is focused on searching for a link between cellular aging and aging and disease in humans. One study has found that subjects with shorter telomeres are more likely to develop cancers of the lungs and kidneys than those with longer telomeres. Furthermore, the study noted that the participants with the shortest telomeres were at a higher risk of developing heart disease and also appeared more prone to infectious diseases. Another study posited a link between telomere length and life span. In that study, patients with shorter telomeres died about 4 or 5 years earlier than those with telomeres of greater length.

Of course, many researchers are hesitant to conclude that shorter telomeres are a causative factor from this data, particularly because telomeres are susceptible to corruption from a number of factors besides cell division. For example, scientists have noted that telomeres are especially vulnerable to the byproducts of the body's oxidation process, by which oxygen is converted to energy. The byproducts of this process, called free radicals, can not only harm cells and DNA, but also artificially shorten telomeres.

Further research is necessary to better establish what link, if any, exists between telomeres and aging. One promising avenue to consider is whether lengthening damaged telomeres has the opposite effect on subjects, making them healthier and conferring greater longevity. And while some scientists optimistically believe that a full understanding of telomeres will eventually bestow dominion over the very aging process itself, such a scenario is both unlikely and not technologically feasible at this juncture.

Problem or change? _____

What was the problem? _____

What caused it? _____

What were the effects? _____

Is there any solution? _____

Need More Verbal Help?
Check out The Princeton Review's *Verbal Workout for the GRE* for more Text Completion, Sentence Equivalence, and Reading Comprehension practice.

The preceding passage is a long science passage with lots of technical information. In essence, however, it is about a problem. Scientists *think* that there is a link between telomeres and aging, but they don't *know*. The cause of the problem is that there is a link between the length of a telomere and the health of cells. The effect of this problem is lots of studies showing links between telomeres and different health problems. The solution, of course, is more research. The exact relationship is still unknown.

When you map the passage, paragraph by paragraph, you should come up with something like this:

Paragraph 1: What's a telomere? (Inform)
Paragraph 2: Shorter telomere = dead cell (Inform)
Paragraph 3: Effects of shorter telomeres (Inform)
Paragraph 4: Caution against conclusion (Inform)
Paragraph 5: Possible effects of finding link (Predict). Beating aging unlikely (Evaluate)

That is as much information as you need to answer Main Idea and Purpose questions, and as much as you need to get started on specific questions. If a question asks about the connection between telomeres and cell health, you know where to go. Until then, feel free to skim over the details.

SIZE UP THE QUESTIONS

Reading Comprehension questions vary in both format and what they require you to do. Let's take a look at the different types of questions you'll see on test day, and then go through strategies for tackling each type.

Question Formats

The Reading Comprehension questions on the GRE will appear in several different formats.

1. **Multiple Choice.** These are the standard, five-answer multiple-choice questions that ask you to choose a single answer.
2. **Select All That Apply.** These questions ask you to select more than one answer, similar to the way you answered Sentence Equivalence questions.
3. **Select in Passage.** These questions either refer you to a highlighted portion of the text or ask you to click on the portion of the text that contains a certain phrase or performs a certain function.

Question Tasks

While it might seem like there are tons of different reading comprehension tasks, there are really only two major types on the GRE.

1. **"Fetch" Questions.** Some questions simply require you to go to the passage and "fetch" some information. The information you are asked to fetch might be a fact from the reading, the meaning of a word, the author's tone, or the main idea of the passage.
2. **Reasoning Questions.** Other questions require a little more work than just returning to the passage and figuring out what the author says. Reasoning questions can ask you why an author used a particular word or sentence, what inferences you can draw from the passage, or who the author's intended audience may be. Reasoning questions may also ask critical reasoning-style "argument" questions about conclusions, premises, and assumptions.

Each of these question tasks may show up in any of the question formats above. Let's look at some of these questions in more detail.

Fetch Questions

Fetch, or retrieval, questions ask, in one form or another, "What does the passage say?" They are the most straightforward of reading questions, and simply require you to return to the passage and retrieve information. To answer a retrieval question, use the following steps:

The answer to a Reading Comprehension question has to be supported by the passage.

1. **Read the Question.** What kind of question are you dealing with?

2. **Make the Question Back into a Question.** Often the questions aren't questions at all; they're really incomplete sentences. To find an answer, you must first have a question. By putting the question into your own words, you interact qualitatively and actively with the question text. There is no possibility of your eyes glazing over or your brain going on autopilot (a real likelihood with a four-hour exam). To make the question into a question, simply start with a question word. Nine out of ten times *What* or *Why* will work, since most questions ask either *what* was said in the passage or *why* it was said.

3. **Find Proof.** This is the golden rule of reading comprehension. You will always be able to prove the correct answer with something in the passage. If you cannot put your finger on a specific word, phrase, or sentence that proves your answer choice, you can't pick it. To help find answers in the passage, use one or both of the following techniques:

   a. **Five Up/Five Down.** You can't trust ETS to put the correct answer exactly where they say it will be. If they highlight a portion of the passage, start reading five lines above and read until five lines below the highlighted passage. This way, you are always looking at things *in context*.

   b. **Lead Word.** A lead word is any word in the question that will be easy to skim for in the passage. Names, numbers, dates, large technical terms all make good lead words. Of course, once you find your lead word, read five lines up and five lines down (for a vocab-in-context question, you need to read only three lines up and three lines down).

4. **Link the Info in the Passage to the Question Task.** Once you find the relevant information in the passage take a moment to make sure that it addresses the question task. Is this all the author said? Are there other details that you need to consider?

5. **Use Process of Elimination.**

   a. **Avoid Extreme Statements.** No matter what the passage says, ETS can phrase a correct answer any way they like. They want correct answers that are difficult to argue with. That means *wishy-washy* language (often, many, usually). *Extreme* language (is, all, every, always) is too easy to prove wrong, so it almost always is incorrect.

   b. **Recycled Language.** ETS knows that most test-takers spend too long reading the passage. Then, they try to answer the questions by memory. So, ETS creates a lot of wrong answers by simply recycling memorable words and phrases back into the answer choices. These answers are very appealing because you'll remember reading something like that. But, the correct answer is usually a paraphrase of the information in the passage. Just remember that the more that an answer sounds like it is word for word from the passage, the less likely it is to be right. So be suspicious of answers that make you say "Wait! I remember reading that!"

c. **Half Right = All Wrong.** ETS likes to write answer choices that are half right; which also means they're half—and thus all—wrong. The first part of the answer choice will usually look good, but the second part will be incorrect. Make sure to read the entire choice carefully.

d. **Bad Comparisons.** Be suspicious of answers that contain comparison words such as *more...than, less...than, greater, faster, compared to,* etc. In most cases, the items in the answer choice are mentioned in the passage but they aren't compared in the passage. So, always be wary of answers that make comparisons. If you can't find the comparison in the passage, cross the answer off.

> Correct answers are paraphrases of information stated in the passage.

Let's try a fetch question with the short passage you saw before.

Prior to 1735, there was no legal precedent for freedom of the press. The constitutional concept of freedom of the press traces its origins to 1735 and the libel trial of John Peter Zenger. Zenger, born in Germany, emigrated to America in 1710 and established *The New York Weekly Journal* in 1733. The *Journal* starkly opposed the policies of New York governor William Cosby and while Zenger did not write the majority of the critical pieces, he was arrested on libel charges in 1734. In the ensuing trial, widely followed by the populace, Zenger was defended by Andrew Hamilton, a Pennsylvania lawyer who was brought in after Cosby disbarred all the New York lawyers who offered to defend Zenger. Hamilton's brilliant defense of Zenger was predicated on the argument that since Zenger's criticisms involved verifiable facts, they could not possibly be considered libel. The judge agreed and acquitted the publisher, establishing the basic concept of freedom of the press that was to be enshrined in the United States Constitution some 57 years later.

And here's the question:

The passage states that Zenger did all of the following EXCEPT

○ started his own newspaper

○ opposed the governor's administration

○ left his homeland to come to the United States

○ sought out Andrew Hamilton to defend him

○ based his criticisms on factual issues

Here's How to Crack It

Step 1:   **Read the Question.** Essentially, "What did Zenger do?" This is a fetch question.

Step 2:   **Make the Question Back into a Question.** What did Zenger do?

Step 3:   **Find Proof.** "Zenger" will make a nice lead word. Find the first instance of it in the passage and read from five lines above to five lines below.

Step 4:   **Link the Info in the Passage to the Question Task.** In the passage, we are told that Zenger "emigrated to America," "established *The New York Weekly Journal*," and "opposed the policies of New York governor William Cosby."

Step 5:   **Use Process of Elimination.** Use your scratch paper. Cross off (A), (B), and (C). Now we need more information, so go back to the passage and find more instances of the lead word *Zenger*. We are told that he "was defended by Andrew Hamilton" and that his "criticisms involved verifiable facts." Choice (D) says that Zenger "sought out Andrew Hamilton to defend him." One might assume that since Hamilton defended him, Zenger must have sought Hamilton out to do so. Be careful, and be literal. This is how they catch smart people. If you cannot prove your answer with something stated in the passage, you can't pick it. If the passage doesn't say Zenger sought out Hamilton, we can't assume it. Assumptions always get you into trouble on reading comp. If you're not convinced, don't get hung up; just give (D) the *maybe,* and move on. Choice (E) says that he "based his criticisms on factual issues." We have proof for this one, so cross it off. Choice (D) is the only one left. That must be our answer.

Always go back to the passage to verify your answer. Don't answer from memory.

Don't get hung up on an answer choice in the first pass, and be incredibly literal. If the passage doesn't say it, you can't pick it.

Let's try another fetch question. Try the next question, again based on the passage we've already studied:

Which of the following would most effectively replace the phrase predicated on as it is used in the passage?

○ derived from

○ extirpated on

○ conjectured on

○ covenanted on

○ relegated to

Here's How to Crack It

Treat this type of question just like a Text Completion problem. Go back to the passage and read the sentence that contains the highlighted phrase, imagining that the highlighted portion is missing: "Hamilton's brilliant defense of Zenger was _____ the argument that since Zenger's criticisms involved verifiable facts, they could not possibly be considered libel." Try to come up with your own word or phrase for the blank.

The clue is that the defense had something to do with the "argument that was…." A good phrase might be *based on* or *constructed on*. Now go to the answer choices and use POE. Does *derived from* mean based on? It's fairly close, so leave this choice. How about *extirpated*? Remember that if you're not sure of the meaning of this word, you can't eliminate it. Leave it for now. Choice (C) is not a match; *conjectured* means to guess or infer. A *covenant* is an agreement, so (D) doesn't make sense either. And *relegate* means to assign, so that's out too. If you're down to (A) and (B), go with the one you know works. Choice (A) definitely works, so that's our answer.

By the way, to *extirpate* means to tear up by the roots or destroy completely.

Remember to keep track of new vocabulary words as you work through this book!

Select-in-Passage Questions

Think of these as regular fetch questions, but the answer choices are in the passage rather than part of the question. Most of the time you will find these questions on short passages, but should they occur on a long passage, ETS will limit the scope of the question to a single paragraph. Follow the same steps as you would on a fetch question. Put the question into your own words. Anticipate the answer; then select it from the five or six sentences in the paragraph or passage.

Here's a practice Select-in-Passage question:

Prior to 1735, there was no legal precedent for freedom of the press. The constitutional concept of freedom of the press traces its origins to 1735 and the libel trial of John Peter Zenger. Zenger, born in Germany, emigrated to America in 1710 and established *The New York Weekly Journal* in 1733. The *Journal* starkly opposed the policies of New York governor William Cosby and while Zenger did not write the majority of the critical pieces, he was arrested on libel charges in 1734. In the ensuing trial, widely followed by the populace, Zenger was defended by Andrew Hamilton, a Pennsylvania lawyer who was brought in after Cosby disbarred all the New York lawyers who offered to defend Zenger. Hamilton's brilliant defense of Zenger was predicated on the argument that since Zenger's criticisms involved verifiable facts, they could not possibly be considered libel. The judge agreed and acquitted the publisher, establishing the basic concept of freedom of the press that was to be enshrined in the United States Constitution some 57 years later.

Select the sentence in which the author offers an opinion.

Here's How to Crack It

Select the sentence in which the author offers an opinion.

First, read the question and summarize it in your own words. The question is looking for an opinion, as opposed to a fact, and specifically, the author's opinion. Note that there are actually only seven sentences in this passage, so you have seven answer choices. One of them must contain an opinion. The other six, therefore, must be factual. This is a great case for POE. Write (A), (B), (C), (D), (E), (F), and (G) on your scratch paper so you have something to eliminate.

Sentences 1 and 2—All dates and facts. Cross off (A) and (B).

Sentence 3—More facts. Cross off (C).

Sentence 4—More facts. Cross off (D).

Sentence 5—More facts. Cross off (E).

Sentence 6—The author describes Hamilton's defense as "brilliant." This is an opinion, not a fact. This is a possible answer. Give it a check.

Sentence 7—More facts. Cross off (G). The correct answer is sentence 6.

Now that we've cracked the fetch questions, let's move onto the next major type: reasoning questions.

Reasoning Questions

Reasoning questions ask us to do a little more work to find the proof in the passage. The best answer is still based on the passage, but we need to do extra work to get it. Our steps for reasoning questions are pretty similar to those for fetch questions:

1. **Figure Out What the Question Wants**. Reasoning questions never ask for a simple fact from the passage. Instead, you'll need to figure out what type of information the question requires before you go back to the passage. For example, some reasoning questions may ask why an author brings up an example. Why do authors ever bring up examples? Well, to support a point that they either just made or are about to make. So, you need to find the point that the author uses the example to support.
2. **Return to the Passage**. You'll still need to return to the passage to find the answer. In general, reasoning questions will require you to read more of the passage than simple fetch questions because often you'll need to know the context for a particular piece of information.
3. **Answer in Your Own Words If Possible**. You'll be able to complete this step for some reasoning questions, but not for others. If you can't answer in your words, go right to the answers and use POE.

POE Guidelines for Reasoning Questions

On many reasoning questions you'll have to make aggressive use of POE. Much of the guidelines you used for fetch questions still apply. However, on reasoning questions, look out for answer choices that do the following:

1. **Go Beyond the Information Given**. Often, wrong answers on these questions will go beyond the scope of the passage. In most cases, the wrong answer simply makes a claim that is stronger than the claim in the passage. In other words, be on the look out for extreme language! Choose the answer that is closest to the information in the passage.

2. **Have the Wrong Tone**. Some reasoning questions, such as strengthen and weaken questions, can use extreme language while others, such as inference questions, generally should not. Make sure the tone of the answer choice is appropriate to the question task.

3. **Are Only Half Right**. Again, answers that are only half right are all wrong and you should eliminate them.

Here's a practice reasoning question and another familiar passage to work with:

What was it about Oscar Wilde's only novel, *The Picture of Dorian Gray*, that caused it to create such an uproar when it was published in 1891? While critics attacked the quality of Wilde's work, lambasting its plot as "incurably silly" and chiding the writer for using prose that was "clumsy" and "boring," these overt denunciations of the formal elements of Wilde's work merely masked the true concerns of many nineteenth-century critics. What these critics were actually railing against was the thematic content of Wilde's work, specifically his illustration of a lifestyle devoted to useless beauty. For many a nineteenth-century moralist, *The Picture of Dorian Gray* was nothing more than a primer for spiritual depravity. Wilde's ultimate sin was not his clunky plot or his sometimes cloying prose; it wasn't even his disregard for the time-honored tradition of English propriety. It was instead his leniency toward his protagonist. Wilde propagated the disdain of critics not simply because Dorian Gray was an unabashed hedonist, but because Wilde failed to punish his subject appropriately for his hedonism. To the critics, allowing an evil character to escape his just desserts was an unforgivable sin, and it was this transgression that resulted in such opprobrium for Wilde's work. In their mind, Wilde's work was corrupting the genteel reading public by failing to show the proper consequences of immoral behavior.

What sort of information do we need from the passage in order to answer this question?

The author of the passage would probably consider which one of the following situations most analogous to the response of the critics in the highlighted sentence?

A   ○ A college professor lowers a student's grade from an A to a B because the student is chronically late to class.

B   ○ An accountant refuses to help his clients cheat on their income tax returns.

C   ○ A politician attacks the character of his opponent even though it is his opponent's positions that the politician disagrees with.

D   ○ A district attorney indicts a person on a misdemeanor charge because he lacks the evidence to convict the person on a felony charge.

E   ○ A reporter files a story despite not having been able to verify all her sources.

Here's How to Crack It

This question wants us to figure out what the response of the critics is and then find a situation that is similar to it. First, return to the passage and read the highlighted sentence. Based on the sentence, it appears that the situation is that "the people attacked this thing for one reason, but there was really another reason they didn't like it."

Now you're ready to return to the answer choices and look for the best match. The situation in the first answer choice is not the same as what we've written; here the professor is penalizing a student for the student's poor performance in class. Eliminate it. Choice (B) doesn't match—the accountant is refusing to do something illegal. The third choice seems like a good match; the politician attacks his opponent for one reason (his character), but there was another reason (his policies) for his dislike of the candidate.

Let's check the remaining choices to make sure our answer is the best answer. In (D), the district attorney indicts on a lesser charge because of a lack of evidence for a more serious charge. This is somewhat similar, in that there is an overt element (the misdemeanor charge) and also a second factor which is not overt (the felony charge). However, the part of the answer choice that mentions the lack of evidence makes this choice worse than (C). It goes beyond the information presented in the passage because the original situation in the passage doesn't mention a lack of evidence on behalf of the critics. Finally, (E) is not a match at all. This situation involves a reporter who puts forth something that has not been verified, which isn't the same as criticizing something for one reason when there is another, deeper reason. Thus, (C) is our answer.

Ready for another reasoning question? It's based on the passage we just used.

---○---

Consider each of the choices separately and select all that apply.

The author of the passage would probably agree with which of the following statements?

A ☐ Most critics of Oscar Wilde's novel objected primarily to the lifestyle of its author.

B ☐ If *The Picture of Dorian Gray* were written in the twenty-first century, the critical reaction would be less severe.

C ☐ Some critics of Wilde's *The Picture of Dorian Gray* believed that an author of a book had a moral responsibility to the book's audience.

Here's How to Crack It

To answer this question, we have to figure out which answer choice the author might agree with. How the heck are we supposed to know what the author might think? Well, all we know about what the author thinks is what's found in the passage. In many ways, "author-agree" questions are very similar to inference questions. In both types of questions, the correct answer may not be explicitly stated in the passage, but there will be sufficient evidence in the passage to support the correct answer. The key here is to take each answer choice one by one and return to the passage to look for proof for it.

The first choice states that most critics objected to Wilde's lifestyle. Can you find any evidence of this in the passage? No. Nowhere does the passage mention his lifestyle. It says that the critics disagreed with the thematic content, but we can't assume that Wilde based his work on his own lifestyle (and of course, you can't use any outside knowledge you may have of Wilde's licentious life). Remember: You have to stay inside the scope of the passage—don't go beyond the information given. Thus, (A) is no good.

Now look at the second choice. Is there any evidence about how the author would feel if the book were released today? Nope. Of course, you may assume that the author would agree with this choice, but again, on the GRE that isn't good enough. We need direct evidence from the passage and there is none for this choice. So, goodbye to (B). Let's go to the third and final answer. Return to the passage and look for the part about the book's audience. The last two lines make it clear that some critics saw Wilde's book as corrupting the public and for this they attacked it. This would support (C), so (C) is the answer. Notice that in these multiple-choice, multiple-answer questions, there need not be two answers—sometimes there will just be one!

On Select All That Apply questions, don't feel compelled to choose more than one answer—sometimes only one choice will be correct!

---○---

FIND THE PARAPHRASE OF THE TEXT

Because the right answer to every Reading Comprehension question is literally right in front of you, ETS goes to great lengths to disguise the correct answer and to make the wrong answers more appealing. ETS does this by making the answer a clever paraphrase of the words in the text, one that basically states the same idea but usually avoids repeating words verbatim from the text. By paraphrasing, ETS is able to create right answers that "fly under the radar"; they don't stand out and they're easy to dismiss in favor of the trap answers.

Paraphrasing the information in the text is ETS's job. Your job is simpler. You just need to find the information in the passage that addresses the task of the question. Once you've found that information, you can compare each answer choice to your proof from the passage. If the answer choice is a good paraphrase of your proof from the passage, then that will very likely turn out to be the credited response.

As always, balance looking for the right answer with being suspicious of every answer. For most reading questions, there are more wrong answers than right answers. So, read each answer choice as though it is likely to be wrong.

USE PROCESS OF ELIMINATION

As you've surely noticed by now, the answer to a Reading Comprehension question is the one that is supported by evidence from the passage. Regardless of the question type or format, that rule is immutable. Here is a recap of other guidelines to use when you're using POE.

1. **Avoid Extreme Statements.** ETS prefers wishy-washy statements to extreme ones. When in doubt, pick the answer that has a weaker tone.
2. **Half Right = All Wrong.** ETS likes to write answer choices that are half right; which also means that they're half—and thus all—wrong. The first part of the answer choice will usually look good, but the second part will be incorrect. Make sure to read the entire choice carefully.
3. **Recycled Language.** Some wrong answer choices just take parts of the passage and garble them. These answers usually contain information that's taken directly from the passage rather than paraphrasing it. Eliminate them!
4. **Beyond the Information Given.** These answers go too far beyond what is written in the passage. If you can't point to a part of the passage that matches information in the answer choice, that choice is probably wrong.

Let's explore these guidelines in a little more detail.

ETS constructs correct answer choices that cannot be disputed. The more extreme a choice is, the less likely it is to be the answer.

Avoid Extreme Statements

Extreme statements are answer choices that make absolute claims. There are very few absolutes in the world, so you shouldn't expect ETS reading passages (which are all excerpted or based on actual academic papers) to contain extreme statements.

Certain words make choices extreme and, therefore, easy to dispute. Here are a few of these words.

Extreme answers are bad!

- must
- the first
- each
- every
- all
- the best
- only
- totally
- always
- no

You shouldn't automatically eliminate a choice that contains one of these words, but you should turn your attention to it immediately and attack it vigorously. If you can find even one exception, you can eliminate that choice.

Other words make choices moderate, more mushy, and therefore hard to dispute. Here are a few of these words.

Moderate answers are good!

- may
- can
- some
- many
- sometimes
- often

For example, consider the following two answer choices:

○ There is assuredly life on other planets or moons in the solar system.

○ Scientists believe that there may be life on other planets or moons in the solar system.

Without even looking at a passage, you should pick the second answer choice because it's more wishy-washy; the first choice is too strong for ETS's liking.

Half Right = All Wrong

Careful reading of the answer choices is essential on Reading Comprehension questions. Remember that your job is to find flaws in answer choices and eliminate them. Many people focus on what they like about an answer, rather than what's wrong with it. ETS loves to write answer choices that start out fine, but then say something wrong. Don't be taken in by the part of the answer you like. Use a critical eye when applying POE; don't look for reasons to keep disputed answer choices, look for reasons to eliminate them. One word can make an answer choice wrong if that word isn't supported by the passage.

If an answer choice is half wrong, it's all wrong. Focus on flaws and use Process of Elimination.

Look at the following example for the next three example questions:

> Within the atmosphere are small amounts of a number of important gases, popularly called "greenhouse gases," because they alter the flow of life- and heat-energy through the atmosphere, much as does the glass shell of a greenhouse. Their effect on incoming solar energy is minimal, but collectively they act as an insulating blanket around the planet. By absorbing and returning to the earth's surface much of its outgoing heat, these gases trap it within the lower atmosphere. A greenhouse effect is natural and essential to a livable climate on Earth.

The passage states which of the following about the effect of greenhouse gases on the environment?

○ Although their effect on incoming solar energy is minimal, the presence of artificial greenhouse gases is a danger to the planet.

○ The composite effect of the gases is necessary for maintaining a climate favorable to life on Earth.

In this case, the first answer starts out great—the passage does indeed state that the gases have a minimal effect on solar energy. But look at the rest of the passage. Does the passage ever talk about *artificial* greenhouse gases? Nope, so the first answer is half right, but all wrong. The second choice, however, is entirely supported by the passage. The second sentence states that *collectively they act*, while the final sentence says the greenhouse effect is *essential to a livable climate on Earth.*

Recycled Language

One of ETS's favorite tricks is to write answer choices that contain information from different parts of the passage than the one to which the question refers. If you aren't being careful, you'll think, "I remember something like that from the passage" and pick the wrong answer choice. This is one reason it's so important to use lead words and line references to guide you to the right part of the passage. Never answer a question from memory.

ETS also likes to conflate different parts of a passage to create an answer that uses a lot of words from the passage, but doesn't say a whole lot. For example, use the passage from the previous section to answer the following question.

The passage suggests which of the following about "greenhouse gases"?

○ They are a natural source of heat energy within the atmosphere.

○ They contribute to creating a habitable environment on Earth.

The first answer choice uses a lot of words from the passage, but says a whole lot of nothing. It garbles the information in the passage, which states that greenhouse gases *alter* heat energy. They are not a source of it. The second choice, which is the correct choice, is a nice paraphrase of the last sentence. It may not sound as "correct" as the other choice, but close examination shows it to be the better answer.

Beyond the Information Given

ETS takes its reading passages from textbooks, collections of essays, works of scholarship, and other sources of serious reading matter. However, be careful not to answer questions based on the fact that you did your undergraduate thesis on the topic, or that you once read a newspaper article about the topic at hand. The answers are in the passage; don't use outside knowledge.

Often, these answers will make common sense, but unfortunately you can't use that as a criterion on the GRE. Which of the following answer choices is beyond the information in the passage from before?

The author of the passage would probably agree with which of the following statements?

○ Without the presence of greenhouse gases, it is unlikely that the earth would be able to support life.

○ Air pollution may contribute to an increase in greenhouse gases, which will in turn lead to eventual warming of the earth.

Clearly, here the second choice is beyond the information given in the passage. It may be true and it makes common sense, but the passage never addresses it. Thus, it cannot be the correct answer on a GRE Reading Comprehension question.

Remember: All of the answers you need are on the screen.

UNDERSTANDING STRUCTURE IN READING AND WRITING

While the reading passages on the GRE may not represent some of the most engaging writing you've encountered, it is important to keep in mind the author's basic goal. Nonfiction writers want their writing to be understood; if you can't follow their arguments or their progression of ideas, they've failed in their jobs as writers. When you're reading or skimming a passage on the GRE, a good grasp of the structural elements in writing will aid your understanding.

First, pay attention to the structure of each paragraph. The most important information is probably going to be found at the beginning and end of the paragraph. While reading a passage, if your eyes start to glaze over, rest assured you're not the only one. Good authors know this and make sure to put key points where they are likely to stand out. So, focus on the beginning and end of each paragraph.

Second, look for transition words. Writers use these words as signposts to direct your reading. When you see same-direction transitions such as *for example, in addition, and*, or *furthermore*, you know the author is going to be supporting an earlier statement. If you already understand the point of the paragraph, feel free to skim through these lines. However, change-direction transitions like *although, but, yet*, and *however*, signify an important shift. Writers use words like this to direct the reader's attention to an important change or revelation in the progression of ideas.

Finally, the conclusion of the piece offers the author one last chance to get his or her point across. Always read the last paragraph. Does the piece wrap things up nicely or is there some doubt? Does the author suggest further avenues of inquiry? The way the passage ends can help you to understand the author's main point or primary purpose in writing the passage.

Paying attention to structural clues like the ones mentioned here can help you be a more effective reader. Following these principles in your own writing wouldn't hurt either.

Reading Comprehension Drill

Answers can be found in Part V.

Questions 1 through 4 are based on the following reading passage.

Called by some the "island that time forgot," Madagascar is home to a vast array of unique, exotic creatures. One such animal is the aye-aye. First described by western science in 1782, it was initially categorized as a member of the order Rodentia. Further research then revealed that it was more closely related to the lemur, a member of the primate order. Since the aye-aye is so different from its fellow primates, however, it was given its own family: *Daubentoniidae.* The aye-aye has been listed as an endangered species and, as a result, the government of Madagascar has designated an island off the northeastern coast of Madagascar as a protected reserve for aye-ayes and other wildlife.

Long before Western science became enthralled with this nocturnal denizen of Madagascar's jungles, the aye-aye had its own reputation with the local people. The aye-aye is perhaps best known for its large, round eyes and long, extremely thin middle finger. These adaptations are quite sensible, allowing the aye-aye to see well at night and retrieve grubs, which are one of its primary food sources, from deep within hollow branches. However, the aye-aye's striking appearance may end up causing its extinction. The people of Madagascar believe that the aye-aye is a type of spirit animal, and that its appearance is an omen of death. Whenever one is sighted, it is immediately killed. When combined with the loss of large swaths of jungle habitat, this practice may result in the loss of a superb example of life's variety.

Based on the information given in the passage, the intended audience would most likely be

○ visitors to a natural science museum

○ professors of evolutionary science

○ a third-grade science class

○ students of comparative religions

○ attendees at a world culture symposium

The author's attitude toward the aye-aye, as represented in the highlighted text, could best be described as

○ admiring

○ mystified

○ reverent

○ appalled

○ lachrymose

Select the sentence in the first paragraph that suggests the author's claim that "this practice may result in the loss of a superb example of life's variety" is unlikely to happen.

Consider each of the choices separately and select all that apply.

Which of the following statements can be logically inferred from the passage?

☐ Taxonomic classifications are not always absolute.

☐ The traditional religion of Madagascar involves augury.

☐ There are no longer enough resources on the main island to support the aye-aye population.

Questions 5 through 6 are based on the following reading passage.

A novel that is a bestseller is often, because of its popularity, not taken seriously as literature. Critics seem to presuppose that great literature must be somehow burdensome to the reader; it must be difficult for the uninitiated to understand. It is precisely this inverted snobbery that has hindered Isabel Allende's *The House of the Spirits* from gaining the critical attention it deserves.

Published in 1982, the novel draws deeply on the author's own family history. Allende is the first cousin once removed of former Chilean president Salvador Allende, who was murdered during a right-wing military coup in 1973. Yet rather than the to-be-expected socialist harangue, Allende subtly works her political message within the fabric of the compelling narrative she weaves. While Allende borrows a bit too freely from Gabriel García Márquez's work, she nevertheless has a powerful and original voice within the construct of magical realism.

The author of the passage would probably consider which of the following situations to be most analogous to the critics' viewpoint as it is described in the highlighted sentence?

○ Avant-garde movies with complicated storylines are deemed cinematically superior works to Hollywood blockbusters with straightforward narratives.

○ Scientific journals are thought of as providing coverage of natural events that is inferior to that provided by nature documentaries.

○ Poetry is considered superior literature to prose because it is shorter, and therefore the message it conveys is more easily understood.

○ Political diatribes are viewed as falling outside the accepted literary canon because they are too controversial.

○ A movie version of a popular novel is considered artistically superior to the original.

It can be inferred from the passage that

○ Allende's novel is a retelling of her family's political struggles

○ Allende's novel would have received more favorable reviews if critics had believed it to be great literature

○ Allende learned about magical realism from Gabriel García Márquez

○ Allende's novel could have been more compelling if she had included a stronger political message

○ readers might have expected Allende's work to be more political than it actually was

Questions 7 through 8 are based on the following reading passage.

Bronson Alcott is perhaps best known not for who he was, but for whom he knew. Indeed, Alcott's connections were impressive by any standards: He was a close confidante of such luminaries as Margaret Fuller, Ralph Waldo Emerson, and Henry David Thoreau. Yet, to remember the man solely by his associations is to miss his importance to nineteenth-century American philosophy as a whole and to the Transcendental Movement in particular. Admittedly, Alcott's gift was not as a writer. His philosophical treatises have rightly been criticized by many as being ponderous, esoteric, and lacking focus.

However, Alcott was an erudite orator, and it is in the text of his orations that one begins to appreciate him as a visionary. Most notably, Alcott advocated what were at the time polemical ideas on education. He believed that good teaching should be Socratic in nature and that a student's intellectual growth was concomitant with his or her spiritual growth.

It can be inferred from the passage that the author would agree with all of the following statements EXCEPT

- ○ Alcott should be remembered for his contributions to Transcendentalism
- ○ Alcott's ideas were ahead of those of many of his contemporaries
- ○ Alcott believed that learning should not neglect a student's spiritual education
- ○ Alcott's ideas about education were not always accepted by his compatriots
- ○ Alcott should not be regarded as a particularly gifted orator

It can be inferred that the author would agree with which of the following statements?

- ○ Transcendentalism was an esoteric field of inquiry promulgated by a select group of visionaries.
- ○ Alcott's prose style is not always easily understood.
- ○ A Socratic pedagogical style is difficult to align with spiritual teaching.
- ○ Alcott should be chiefly appreciated for the strengths of his association.
- ○ The text of Alcott's orations were widely accepted by his peers.

Questions 9 through 10 are based on the following reading passage.

    Echinosorex gymnura, known colloquially as the moonrat or gymnure, is one of the many fascinating creatures that inhabit the jungles of Southeast Asia. A close relative of the hedgehog, the moonrat likewise belongs to the order *Insectivora* and the family *Erinaceidae.* However, the family then splits into the sub-family *Hylomyinae,* which contains three separate genera and eight distinct species. The appearance and habitat of the moonrat are actually far more similar to those of various members of the order *Rodentia,* though its eating habits are more in line with its fellow insectivores. Ultimately, the taxonomic classification of this animal is useful only when considered along with other information regarding the animal's ecological niche.

Consider each of the choices separately and select all that apply.

Which of the following scenarios demonstrates the idea put forth by the author of this passage regarding animal classification?

☐ While studying a population of bears, scientists rely solely on the traditional taxonomic designations to identify likely hunting grounds.

☐ A team of medical researchers closely monitors the actions of the animals involved in a study and compares its findings with prevailing beliefs about those animals.

☐ A zookeeper designs a habitat for a new acquisition, disregards taxonomic classifications and instead focuses on observational data.

The author's tone could best be described as

○ exasperated

○ didactic

○ ambivalent

○ morose

○ laudatory

Summary

o   Before answering the questions, attack the passage. Read the passages looking for the main idea, structure, and tone. Remember that looking for problems or changes is the key to finding the main idea.

o   For short passages, read the entire passage. For medium passages, focus on the beginning and end. For longer passages, read the first few lines of each paragraph and the final lines of the entire passage.

o   Take a moment to understand the question task. Fetch questions ask you to retrieve information from the passage. Reasoning questions ask you to do something more than simply figure out what the author is saying.

o   Return to the passage to find the answer to the question. Don't answer from memory! Go back to the text and find the answer.

o   Try to come up with an answer in your own words before looking at the answer choices ETS provides. Remember to look for paraphrases of the text, not direct quotes.

o   Eliminate answers that contain extreme language, go beyond the information provided, garble the meaning of the text, or otherwise have information that you can't support from the text.

Chapter 7
Critical Reasoning

While ETS considers Critical Reasoning questions to fall within the category of Reading Comprehension questions, the questions are different enough to merit a separate discussion. Let's jump in!

CRITICAL REASONING

Critical Reasoning questions are composed of short reading passages, typically just one paragraph long, followed by a series of questions about the author's argument. You should expect to see anywhere from two to four Critical Reasoning questions within the two GRE Verbal sections.

Here's a sample Critical Reasoning passage and question:

> For more than fifty years, many evolutionary biologists posited that early fish such as *Eusthenopteron* developed limbs as a result of the need to drag themselves across short distances when their watery habitats dried up during periods of drought. However, new fossil evidence suggests that this hypothesis is incorrect. Fossilized remains of *Acanthostega*, a primitive fish, reveal that even though the animal had rudimentary limbs, it could not walk on land. *Acanthostega* lacked ankles, which means that its limbs couldn't support its weight; furthermore, its ribs were too short to prevent the organism's chest cavity from collapsing once the animal left water.

> Which of the following would most strengthen the author's argument?

> ○ The fossilized remains of the *Acanthostega* are the earliest known evidence of early fish.

> ○ The modern descendants of *Acanthostega* are not able to drag themselves across short distances on land.

> ○ Biologists have found that some aquatic species can successfully drag themselves across land even though these species do not possess ankles.

> ○ Any animal with a collapsed chest cavity is not able to survive long enough to travel even a short distance across land.

> ○ Some evolutionary biologists believe that the new fossils are not from *Acanthostega*.

The answer to this question, by the way, is (D). Not sure why? Keep reading.

What Exactly Is Critical Reasoning?

Critical reasoning is our term for a specific type of reading passage you'll encounter on the GRE. At first glance, Critical Reasoning passages resemble the short Reading Comprehension passages. However, what distinguishes critical reasoning from a regular reading comprehension passage is twofold:

1. The structure of the passage
2. The types of questions ETS will ask about it

We'll show you how to identify Critical Reasoning passages and the most effective way of tackling these questions as well.

BREAKING AN ARGUMENT DOWN

The key to doing well on Critical Reasoning questions is understanding how ETS authors construct an argument. All arguments contain two major parts—the conclusion, or the main point of the argument, and the premise—the facts that the author gives in support of his or her conclusion. Identifying these two parts is crucial to your success on these questions. Let's start our analysis of an author's argument in a Critical Reasoning passage by learning how to identify the conclusion.

Identifying the Conclusion

The conclusion is the most important part of the argument; quite simply, it is the reason the argument exists. The conclusion of an argument is generally a statement of opinion—it's the author's belief or prediction about a situation. Let's look at the sample Critical Reasoning passage again:

> For more than fifty years, many evolutionary biologists posited that early fish such as *Eusthenopteron* developed limbs as a result of the need to drag themselves across short distances when their watery habitats dried up during periods of drought. However, new fossil evidence suggests that this hypothesis is incorrect. Fossilized remains of *Acanthostega*, a primitive fish, reveal that even though the animal had rudimentary limbs, it could not walk on land. *Acanthostega* lacked ankles, which means that its limbs couldn't support its weight; furthermore, its ribs were too short to prevent the organism's chest cavity from collapsing once the animal left water.

You can identify the conclusion of the author's argument by asking yourself this question: What opinion does this author hold? Now underline the sentence that you think is the conclusion of the argument above.

The conclusion is the author's main point.

If you underlined "new fossil evidence suggests that this hypothesis is incorrect," you hit the nail on the head.

There are other ways of identifying conclusions in arguments. For example, often you can identify the conclusion by certain key words. Specifically, keep an eye out for the following:

therefore	*thus*	*consequently*	*and so*	*in conclusion*

You should also look for any words that indicate an opinion, such as the following:

suggest	*believe*	*hope*	*indicate*	*argue*	*follow*

Remember: The conclusion is often the author's opinion about what *might* happen.

In addition, a conclusion is often a belief about what should or might happen. Look for the following:

should	*would*	*must*	*will*

Practice: Identifying Conclusions

Underline the conclusions of the arguments in the following Critical Reasoning passages. Answers can be found in Part V.

1 of 5

Despite the support of the president, it is unlikely that the new defense bill will pass. A bipartisan group of 15 senators has announced that it does not support the legislation.

2 of 5

The earliest known grass fossils date from approximately 55 million years ago. Dinosaurs most likely disappeared from the earth around 60 million years ago. Based on this evidence, as well as fossilized remains of dinosaur teeth that indicate the creatures were more suited to eating ferns and palms, scientists have concluded that grass was not a significant part of the dinosaur diet.

3 of 5

Automaker X has lost over 2 billion dollars this year due to rising costs, declining automobile sales, and new governmental regulations. Because of the company's poor financial situation, it has asked its employees to pay more for health care and to accept a pay cut. However, the workers at automaker X are threatening to go on strike. If that happens, automaker X will have no choice but to file for bankruptcy.

4 of 5

The rise of obesity among citizens of country Y has been linked to a variety of health problems. In response to this situation, the country's largest health organization has called for food manufacturers to help combat the problem. Since the leading members of the nation's food industry have agreed to provide healthier alternatives, reduce sugar and fat content, and reduce advertisements for unhealthy foods, it is likely that country Y will experience a decrease in obesity-related health problems.

5 of 5

Recent advances in technology have led to a new wave of "smart" appliances, including refrigerators that note when food supplies are low and place an order at the grocery store, washing machines that automatically adjust the wash cycle and temperature based upon the clothes in the machine, and doorknobs that can identify the house owner and automatically open the door. A technology expert predicts that, due to these new innovations, machines will soon outnumber humans as the number-one users of the Internet.

Some Critical Reasoning questions ask you to find the conclusion of the argument. Here's an example:

Mutation breeding is a method of crop development that requires breeders to first find plants that randomly display the traits researchers are looking for, and then breed those plants with other plants displaying similar traits. In order to bring about the required mutations, researchers bombard plants with thermal neutrons, x-rays, and known carcinogenic chemicals in order to damage the plant's DNA. Today, almost all varieties of wheat grown commercially are products of mutation breeding. Ironically, when scientists discovered how to splice desirable genes directly into the plants, thus avoiding the use of harmful chemicals and radiation, critics derided the new process as potentially dangerous despite the lack of any supporting evidence, resulting in boycotts and bans on genetically modified foods.

The argument as a whole is structured to lead to which of the following conclusions?

○ Genetically modified food may have been unfairly stigmatized by its critics.

○ Mutation breeding produces safer food than does genetic modification.

○ Foods produced by genetic modification are healthier than foods produced by mutation breeding.

○ Researchers should stop using mutation breeding in order to modify foods.

○ Genetic modification of plants is more cost effective than mutation breeding of plants.

Here's How to Crack It

The conclusion, as you'll recall, is the author's opinion or belief. As you read the argument, look for indicators of the author's opinion. The first three sentences of the argument do not state opinions; the author is simply describing the method of mutation breeding. However, in the fourth sentence, the author uses the word *ironically*. This is an indicator of how the author feels. The author believes it is ironic that genetically modified foods are banned, despite *any supporting evidence* that they are dangerous, while foods created with mutation breeding, which use *harmful chemicals and radiation* account for *almost all varieties of wheat*.

Now we just need to find an answer choice that matches this opinion. Choice (A) looks pretty close, so let's hang on to it. Choice (B) is the opposite of what the author argues; the argument implies that genetic modification is safer. Choice (C) is close, but the argument doesn't really discuss which foods are "healthier," just that one type is banned and the other type isn't. Choice (D) also isn't discussed. The author thinks it's ironic that genetically modified foods are banned, but never states that mutation breeding should be stopped. Finally, (E) doesn't work because the argument doesn't express any opinion about cost effectiveness. Thus, (A) is correct.

Finding the Premise

After you identify the conclusion of an argument, your next task is to find the argument's premise. The premise (or premises—there can be more than one) is the evidence that the author gives in support of the conclusion.

You can find the premise of an argument in two ways. First, look for statements of fact. Critical Reasoning passages are usually based on statistics, surveys, polls, or reports and all of these things are premises—in fact, these are the most common types of premises. Second, you can use a strategy we call the "Why?" test. Once you've found the conclusion, ask yourself *why* you should accept it; the answer or answers to that question will be the premise(s). Let's look again at the passage from the beginning of the chapter:

> For more than fifty years, many evolutionary biologists posited that early fish such as *Eusthenopteron* developed limbs as a result of the need to drag themselves across short distances when their watery habitats dried up during periods of drought. However, new fossil evidence suggests that this hypothesis is incorrect. Fossilized remains of *Acanthostega*, a primitive fish, reveal that even though the animal had rudimentary limbs, it could not walk on land. *Acanthostega* lacked ankles, which means that its limbs couldn't support its weight; furthermore, its ribs were too short to prevent the organism's chest cavity from collapsing once the animal left water.

Why should you believe this conclusion?

What facts does the author give in support of the conclusion? In this argument, the author provides the following facts: (1) *Acanthostega* lacked ankles, and (2) the creature's ribs were too short to prevent its chest cavity from collapsing. These facts are the premises of the argument.

Is the statement a fact, something that you could verify or prove? Then it's a premise.

> *because*   *due to*   *since*   *based on*

Practice: Finding the Premise

For each of the following arguments, identify the premise or premises that support the conclusion. (Remember, you already found the conclusions in the exercise on page 117.) Answers can be found in Part V.

1 of 5

Despite the support of the president, it is unlikely that the new defense bill will pass. A bipartisan group of 15 senators has announced that it does not support the legislation.

Conclusion: _____

Why?

Premise: _____

2 of 5

The earliest known grass fossils date from approximately 55 million years ago. Dinosaurs most likely disappeared from the earth around 60 million years ago. Based on this evidence, as well as fossilized remains of dinosaur teeth that indicate the creatures were more suited to eating ferns and palms, scientists have concluded that grass was not a significant part of the dinosaur diet.

Conclusion: _____

Why?

Premise: _____

3 of 5

Automaker X has lost over 2 billion dollars this year due to rising costs, declining automobile sales, and new governmental regulations. Because of the company's poor financial situation, it has asked its employees to pay more for health care and to accept a pay cut. However, the workers at automaker X are threatening to go on strike. If that happens, automaker X will have no choice but to file for bankruptcy.

Conclusion: _____

Why?

Premise: _____

4 of 5

The rise of obesity among citizens of country Y has been linked to a variety of health problems. In response to this situation, the country's largest health organization has called for food manufacturers to help combat the problem. Since the leading members of the nation's food industry have agreed to provide healthier alternatives, reduce sugar and fat content, and reduce advertisements for unhealthy foods, it is likely that country Y will experience a decrease in obesity-related health problems.

Conclusion: _____

Why?

Premise: _____

5 of 5

Recent advances in technology have led to a new wave of "smart" appliances, including refrigerators that note when food supplies are low and place an order at the grocery store, washing machines that automatically adjust the wash cycle and temperature based upon the clothes in the machine, and doorknobs that can identify the house owner and automatically open the door. A technology expert predicts that, due to these new innovations, machines will soon outnumber humans as the number-one users of the Internet.

Conclusion: _____

Why?

Premise: _____

Okay. So you know how to identify the conclusion and premise(s) of an argument. Are you ready to try a Critical Reasoning question? Here's one way in which ETS will test your knowledge of the parts of an argument.

A common myth is that animals can sense an impending earthquake. And while most geophysicists dispute this assertion and claim that there is no way to predict an earthquake, a new hypothesis for predicting earthquakes is generating interest in the scientific community. This hypothesis is based on a well-known principle: **Subjecting rocks to extreme pressures causes the rocks to produce electrical currents**. Now, a leading physicist has proposed that this principle may help predict earthquakes. For example, an earthquake along the San Andreas Fault in California could produce hundreds of thousands of amperes (units of electrical current) that would disrupt the ionosphere surrounding the earth. **By monitoring the ionosphere for electrical fluctuations, scientists may be able to predict earthquakes.**

In the argument above, the two boldfaced statements play which of the following roles?

○ The first statement expresses the conclusion of the argument while the second statement provides support for that conclusion.

○ The first statement expresses the conclusion of the argument as a whole; the second statement provides a possible consequence of the conclusion.

○ The first statement presents support for the conclusion of the argument as a whole; the second statement states the conclusion of the argument.

○ The first statement expresses an intermediary conclusion of the argument while the second statement presents a possible objection to the intermediary conclusion.

○ The first statement provides support for a conclusion that the argument opposes; the second statement expresses the conclusion that the argument as a whole opposes.

Here's How to Crack It

The key to cracking this question is using the "Why?" test. Let's try using the "Why?" test on the two boldfaced statements and see which one works best. If we make the first statement the conclusion, we'd end up with something like this:

Conclusion: Subjecting rocks to extreme pressures causes the rocks to produce electrical currents.

Why?

Premise: By monitoring the ionosphere for electrical fluctuations, scientists may be able to predict earthquakes.

Does that make sense? Nope, so let's eliminate any answers that say that the first sentence is the argument's conclusion. That allows us to eliminate (A), (B), and (D). Now let's see what happens if we flip the statements around:

Conclusion: By monitoring the ionosphere for electrical fluctuations, scientists may be able to predict earthquakes.

Why?

Premise: Subjecting rocks to extreme pressures causes the rocks to produce electrical currents.

That makes much more sense. Choice (E) states that the argument opposes the conclusion, which it doesn't, so we can eliminate that choice. Choice (C) is the answer.

The "Why?" test helps to identify premises and conclusions.

Locating Assumptions

Although ETS frequently asks Critical Reasoning questions about the premise or the conclusion of an argument, there are a number of other question types that require you to work with one final part of an argument. The final part of an argument is the assumption. The assumption is never explicitly stated in the passage, which means that it can sometimes be tricky to find. Basically, the assumption is the missing link that connects the conclusion of an argument to its premise.

Let's look back at one of the arguments you've already worked on.

Conclusion: It is unlikely that the new defense bill will pass.

Why?

Premise: A bipartisan group of 15 senators has announced that it does not support the legislation.

In order for this argument to be convincing, the reader has to make an assumption that because 15 senators do not support the bill, the bill will probably not pass. If you don't assume that the opposition of 15 senators means that the bill is unlikely to pass, the argument fails. Thus, assumptions are necessary to a successful argument.

To find the assumption or assumptions in an argument, you need to look for a "gap" in the reasoning of the argument. You can often accomplish this by asking yourself the following question:

*Just because (**premise**) is true, does it really mean (**conclusion**) is true?*

For example, let's return to another of the arguments you've already tackled.

Conclusion: Country *Y* will experience a decrease in obesity-related health problems.

Why?

Premise: The leading members of the nation's food industry have agreed to provide healthier alternatives, reduce sugar and fat content, and reduce advertisements for unhealthy foods.

Now, let's ask ourselves the question: Just because it's true that the food industry has agreed to provide healthier alternatives, reduce sugar and fat content, and reduce advertisements for unhealthy foods, does it really mean that obesity-related health problems will decrease?

If you accept this argument, you must assume that the food industry's actions will lead to a decrease in obesity-related health problems. That's the missing link—or the assumption—required by the argument.

Practice: Locating Assumptions

For each of the following Critical Reasoning questions, identify the conclusion and the premise. Then note what assumption is required to make the argument work. Answers can be found in Part V.

1 of 4

City University recently announced the retirement of Professor Jones. Professor Jones is a leading biologist and widely published author and her presence was a major factor in many students' decisions to attend City University. The University predicts no decline in enrollment, however, because it plans to hire two highly credentialed biology professors to replace Professor Jones.

Conclusion: _____

Premise: _____

Assumption: _____

2 of 4

It is unjust to charge customers under the age of 25 more to rent a car than those over the age of 25. After all, most states allow people as young as 16 to have a driver's license and all states allow 18-year-olds the right to vote.

Conclusion: _____

Premise: _____

Assumption: _____

3 of 4

It is easy to demonstrate that extraterrestrial life exists by simply looking at our own solar system. In our solar system, there are eight planets and at least one of them obviously has life on it. Thus, roughly 12.5% of planets in the universe should have life on them.

Conclusion: _____

Premise: _____

Assumption: _____

4 of 4

State A is facing a serious budget shortfall for the upcoming year. Recent polls indicate that 58% of voters in Township B approve of a proposed 2-cent gasoline tax in order to make up the deficit. It is clear, therefore, that the leaders of State A should institute the gas tax.

Conclusion: _____

Premise: _____

Assumption: _____

CRITICAL REASONING QUESTION TYPES

Now that you've familiarized yourself with the basics of an argument, let's look at the types of argument questions you'll encounter on the GRE. Each of the following types of questions will require you to first identify the argument's premise and conclusion; after that, your task will vary depending on the type.

Reasoning Questions

Need More Verbal Help?

Check out *Verbal Workout for the GRE* for additional verbal review from The Princeton Review.

You can identify Reasoning questions because they will have the following question stems:

> In the argument given, the boldfaced statements play which of the following roles?

> Which of the following best describes the function of the boldfaced statements in the argument above?

> The argument above is structured to lead to which of the following conclusions?

For Reasoning questions, you must isolate the premise and conclusion, but you don't need to find the assumption.

Assumption Questions

Assumption questions are usually phrased in the following ways:

> The argument above assumes which of the following?

> The argument above relies on which of the following?

> The author's argument presupposes which of the following?

On Assumption questions, you need to first locate the premise and conclusion. After that, look for the gap as described in the "Locating Assumptions" section above.

Strengthen Questions

Strengthen questions will ask you to make the argument stronger. You'll be asked to do this by identifying answer choices that will support the assumption. Strengthen questions are often phrased as follows:

> Which one of the following, if true, would most strengthen the argument?

> Which of the following, if true, would most support the author's argument?

> Supporters of the argument would most likely cite which of following pieces of additional evidence?

To strengthen an argument, find the premise, the conclusion, and the assumption. The correct answer will be a premise that supports the assumption.

Weaken Questions

As we've learned, the assumption is what makes an argument work. It follows, then, that if you attack the assumption, you will weaken the argument. You can identify Weaken questions by looking for the following:

> Which one of the following, if true, would most weaken the argument?
>
> Which one of the following, if true, casts the most doubt on the argument above?
>
> Which one of the following, if true, would most undermine the author's argument?

On Weaken questions, once again you'll need to find the premise, conclusion, and assumption. The right answer will attack the assumption, breaking the link between the premise and the conclusion.

CRACKING CRITICAL REASONING QUESTIONS

Ready to tackle some Critical Reasoning questions? Let's go through steps you take when you run into one of these questions on the test.

The Basic Approach

When you identify a question as a Critical Reasoning question on the exam, go through the following steps:

1. **Read the Question Carefully.** Don't dive into the passage without being aware of exactly what you're dealing with—start by making sure that it really is critical reasoning and not a plain old reading comprehension passage.
2. **Analyze the Argument.** Identify the premise, conclusion, and assumption of the argument.
3. **Know What the Answer Needs to Do.** For each type of question, you can know what characteristic the right answer needs. For example, a Weaken question attacks the assumption of the argument.
4. **Use Process of Elimination.** Process of Elimination (POE) is a valuable tool. If you're not sure what the correct answer is, look for the wrong answers instead; eliminate them, and even if you still can't identify the correct answer, you have a much greater chance of guessing the correct answer.

Try going through these steps on the following question.

————————○————————

After examining the bodies of a dozen beached whales and finding evidence of bleeding around the animals' eyes and brains as well as lesions on their kidneys and livers, environmental groups fear that the Navy's use of sonar is causing serious harm to marine animals. A leading marine biologist reports that sonar induces whales to panic and surface too quickly, which causes nitrogen bubbles to form in their blood.

What type of question is this?

The argument above relies on which of the following assumptions?

○ Marine biologists have documented that other marine animals, including dolphins and sea turtles, have exhibited kidney and liver lesions.

○ No studies have been conducted on the possible detrimental effects of sonar on marine animals.

○ Whales in captivity panic only when exposed to man-made, rather than natural, sound waves.

○ The presence of nitrogen bubbles in the blood has been demonstrated to cause damage to various internal organs.

○ It is unlikely that the symptoms found in the beached whales could be caused by any known disease.

Here's How to Crack It

Let's apply the four-step basic approach:

1. **Read the Question Carefully.** This is an Assumption question—we know this because it asks you to determine what the argument relies on.
2. **Analyze the Argument.** Be sure to precisely identify the conclusion and premise. You should come up with the following:
   Conclusion: The Navy's use of sonar is causing serious harm to marine animals.
   Why?
   Premise: Surfacing too quickly causes nitrogen bubbles to form in the whale's blood.
   Next, we need to locate the assumption. Remember to use the question we introduced earlier—here it would be phrased as follows: "Just because the whales have nitrogen bubbles in their blood, does that really mean that sonar is causing them serious harm?"
3. **Know What the Answer Needs to Do.** Assumptions connect the premise to the conclusion. So, you want an answer that has something from both the premise and the conclusion in it.
4. **Use Process of Elimination.** Check out the gray box for some POE tips on Assumption questions.

Now, returning to the answer choices, let's see which one is best. Choice (A) is wrong; this choice doesn't connect the premise to the conclusion. Even though it states that other animals have exhibited similar symptoms, we need the answer choice to connect the symptoms—in whales—to the use of sonar. Choice (B) is wrong as well because it brings in information that isn't part of the original argument: It's irrelevant whether or not the Navy has conducted studies on the harmful effects of sonar. Choice (C) doesn't help much either; the argument is not concerned with the situations under which whales panic. Choice (D) looks pretty good. It connects the nitrogen bubbles found in the premise to the serious harm mentioned in the conclusion, so hold on to this choice. Remember that you always need to check all five answer choices; however, (E) is no good. Like (B), this choice brings in information that isn't relevant to the argument. The fact that the symptoms are unlikely to be caused by any known disease does not make the link between the sonar and the harm to the animals. Thus, (D) is the answer.

Eliminate answers that aren't relevant to the argument!

POE for Assumption Questions

When you're using POE on Assumption questions, always eliminate answer choices that do the following:

1. **Give New Information.** The assumption must link the premise and the conclusion. Any answer choices that discuss information that is not part of the original argument are wrong.
2. **Have the Wrong Tone.** The tone of the answer choice should match the tone of the argument. Arguments that have very strong conclusions require very strongly worded answer choices, and arguments that have milder tones require milder answer choices.
3. **Weaken the Argument.** The assumption is necessary to the argument. Eliminate any answer choice that would weaken or hurt the argument—unless of course you're dealing with a Weaken question!

Strengthen Questions

Here's another Critical Reasoning question:

Remember to identify the question type first.

Several companies have recently switched at least partially from memos written by hand on printer paper to memos written on a computer and sent electronically with no use of paper at all. Therefore, less printer paper will be used as a result of these changes than would have been used if these companies had continued to use handwritten memos.

Which of the following, if true, most strengthens the argument above?

○ Many of the companies that have switched to electronic memos have increased the number of memos sent.

○ More printer paper was used to create manuals for the use of electronic memos than was used to write handwritten memos.

○ Companies that used more printer paper were more likely to switch to electronic memos than companies that used less printer paper.

○ Some of the industries that have switched at least partially to electronic memos still primarily use printer paper for other operations.

○ The amount of printer paper needed to explain the electronic memos is less than the amount that would have been used for handwritten memos.

Here's How to Crack It

Let's again apply the four steps:

1. **Read the Question Carefully.** It's a Strengthen question; we know this because the word "strengthen" is actually used in the question!
2. **Analyze the Argument.** Find the premise, conclusion, and assumption. Here's what you should end up with:
   Conclusion: Less printer paper will be used as a result of electronic memos than would have been used with hand written memos. Why?

Premise: Several companies at least partially have switched from handwritten memos on printer paper to memos written on a computer and sent electronically.

Assumption: Companies use a lot of printer paper for handwritten memos; companies will stop using printer paper for memos; the amount of printer paper used for other operations won't increase.

3. **Know What the Answer Needs to Do.** To strengthen an argument, look for an answer that provides evidence that the assumption of the argument is valid.

4. **Use Process of Elimination.** Check out the gray box on this page for some POE guidelines on Strengthen questions.

Always check all five answer choices.

Choice (A) introduces the concept that the number of memos has increased in the companies that have switched to electronic memos. This does not strengthen an argument that less paper is being used, so eliminate (A). Choice (B) is a reversal of the passage, as this actually weakens the conclusion. If more printer paper was used to produce manuals than would have been used to write memos, then the amount of printer paper used overall would not decrease. Eliminate (B).

Choice (C) mentions that companies that used more printer paper were more likely to switch to electronic memos than those which used less printer paper. However, this does not address whether the electronic memos caused less printer paper to be used, as the companies using more printer paper prior to switching may not have been using that paper to make handwritten memos. Eliminate (C). Choice (D) indicates that companies that have switched to electronic memos still use printer paper for other operations. This does not strengthen the argument that less printer paper is being used, so eliminate (D). Choice (E) indicates that less printer paper is used to initiate the change than would have been used to write the memos, which would strengthen the claim that the total amount of printer paper used would decrease. The correct answer is (E).

POE for Strengthen Questions

When you're using POE on Strengthen questions, always eliminate answer choices that

1. **Are Only Half Good.** Some answers will be on the right track, but they won't strengthen the argument enough. Again, remember that you're looking for the *correct* answer, not an answer that might be good enough. You shouldn't have to make any assumptions about the answer choice in order for it to strengthen the argument.

2. **Weaken the Argument.** Typically, one of the answer choices will weaken the argument. Unless your task is to weaken the argument, you can easily eliminate it.

3. **Do Nothing.** Some answer choices do nothing to the argument; they neither strengthen nor weaken it. Get rid of these; they're decoys.

On Strengthen questions, note that answer choices that offer new information are okay, provided of course that they help strengthen the argument. Also note that answers that have strong tones are often correct for Strengthen questions.

Weaken Questions

Try one last Critical Reasoning question:

───────────────○───────────────

Psychologists have just completed an extensive study of recently divorced parents in order to determine which factors contributed most to the dissolution of the marriage. The researchers found that in a great majority of the cases of failed marriages, the couples ate, on average, fewer than 10 meals per week with each other. From this data, the psychologists have determined that a failure to spend time together during meal times is a major factor leading to divorce.

Which of the following, if true, would cast the most doubt on the researchers' hypothesis?

○ Many couples who have long and successful marriages eat together fewer than ten times per week.

Do you recognize what type of argument this is?

○ Most of the couples in the study who were unable to share meals with each other worked outside of the home.

○ People who lack a regular dining schedule tend to have more disorders and illnesses of the digestive system.

○ Couples in the study who reported that they ate together more than ten times per week also indicated that they tended to perceive their relationships with their spouses as healthy.

○ In many cases, people in unhappy marriages tend to express their displeasure by avoiding contact with their partners when possible.

Here's How to Crack It

This is a Weaken question. Once again, we'll break the argument down into its premise, conclusion, and assumption:

Conclusion: A failure to spend time together during meal times is a major factor leading to divorce.

Why?

Premise: In a great majority of the cases of failed marriages, the couples ate, on average, fewer than 10 meals per week with each other.

Assumption: A lack of time spent eating meals together causes marital problems; there is no other cause.

The assumptions are, first, that there is no other cause, and second, that the cause and effect are not reversed. Since we want to weaken this argument, we want to find an answer that attacks one of these assumptions.

Check out the gray box for POE guidelines on Weaken questions.

Looking through the answer choices, you can probably see right away that (A) is not the correct answer. The argument is not about what successful couples do; it is only concerned with divorced couples. Move on. Choice (B) doesn't really do anything to the argument; it's unclear how this information would affect the causal link assumed in the argument. The same goes for (C): All this choice indicates is that there may be other problems linked to eating—it doesn't address the connection between dining and marriage success.

Choice (D) seems like it might strengthen the argument. These couples are reporting a link between eating together more and perceiving their marriages as healthy. Eliminate this choice. Choice (E) is the answer. This answer choice shows that the researchers have reversed the cause and effect. It is not that a failure to dine together causes marital strife; rather, couples that are already unhappy express it by not eating together. This weakens the argument, and (E) is correct.

POE for Weaken Questions

The guidelines for Weaken questions are basically the same as those for Strengthen questions. Eliminate any answer choices that

1. **Are Half Good.** Make sure the answer attacks the assumption thoroughly.
2. **Strengthen the Argument.** Once again, one answer usually does the opposite of the question task—eliminate the odd man out.
3. **Do Nothing.** Some answer choices neither strengthen nor weaken the argument: Eliminate them.

As is the case with Strengthen questions, new information and extreme tones in Weaken questions need not be eliminated.

OTHER CRITICAL REASONING QUESTION TYPES

The GRE also contains Inference and Resolve/Explain questions, which require you to use different approaches from those you use for Weaken and Strengthen questions. Let's go through how to crack Inference and Resolve/Explain questions now.

> Inference and Resolve/Explain questions do not require you to find the premise and conclusion.

Inference Questions

An inference is a conclusion that's based on a set of given facts. You can identify Inference questions because they'll look a lot like the following:

> If the statements above are true, which of the following must also be true?
>
> Which of the following statements can be properly inferred from the information above?
>
> Based on the information above, which of the following can logically be concluded?

Here's an example:

⎯⎯⎯⎯⎯⎯⎯⎯⎯⎯◯⎯⎯⎯⎯⎯⎯⎯⎯⎯⎯

On Inference questions, you don't have to find the premise and conclusion.

The Mayville Fire Department always fills its employment vacancies "in-house"—when a firefighter retires or leaves the force, his or her position is filled by interviewing all qualified members of the Mayville Department who are interested in the position. Only if this process fails to produce a qualified candidate does the department begin interviewing potential employees from outside the department. This year, the Mayville Fire Department has hired three new firefighters from outside the department.

If the statements above are true, which of the following must also be true?

- ○ For the coming year, the Mayville Fire Department will be understaffed unless it hires three additional firefighters.

- ○ Firefighters hired from outside the Mayville Fire Department take longer to properly train for the job.

- ○ At the time of the vacancies in the Mayville Fire Department, either there were no qualified in-house candidates or no qualified in-house candidates were interested in the open positions.

- ○ The three firefighters who left the department had jobs for which no other members of the Mayville Fire Department were qualified to fill.

- ○ The three new firefighters are the first new employees hired by the Mayville Fire Department.

Here's How to Crack It

Inference questions are often associated with Critical Reasoning passages that are not structured like the clear-cut arguments we've seen thus far. Often these wacky arguments don't even have conclusions and premises; instead, they might simply resemble a set of facts.

Our strategy for approaching these types of questions, of course, begins with identifying them as Inference questions. However, for Step 2, don't attempt to identify a conclusion or premise; simply read the argument. If the argument is complex or hard to follow, don't spend too much time trying to untangle it. Most of the work on Inference questions should be done when you get to the answer choices.

For Inference questions, Step 3 is simple. You're just looking for an answer that is true based on the facts provided in the argument.

Check out the POE guidelines for Inference questions in the gray box on the next page.

Let's start with (A). This choice says that the department will be "understaffed." Is there any part of the argument that indicates that this is true? Nope, so eliminate this choice. Choice (B) states that firefighters from outside the department take longer to train, but the argument says nothing at all about training. Eliminate this choice. Choice (C) states that either there were no qualified candidates in house or there were no qualified candidates interested in the jobs. Returning to the argument, we see that the hiring policy is that a vacant "position is filled by interviewing all qualified members of the Mayville Department who are interested in the position."

Can you prove your answer choice? If not, eliminate it.

If this process fails, the department goes outside the department for candidates. Thus, since Mayville hired three new fire fighters from outside the department, (C) must be true.

Let's go through the remaining answers. Choice (D) is tempting, but on inference questions, we need to make sure that every part of the answer choice holds up to scrutiny. This answer states that no other members of the department were qualified to take the open positions. This could be true; however, based on the facts presented, it could also be true that there were qualified members who simply weren't interested in applying for the position. Thus, (D) isn't the best choice—it isn't better than (C). Finally, (E) goes beyond the information presented. There is no way of knowing whether these new firefighters were the first new employees. Choice (C) is still the best.

Resolve/Explain

Some Critical Reasoning questions will present you with a paradox—a set of facts that seem to contradict each other. On these questions, your task is to find the answer choice that best explains the contradiction. You can recognize these questions because they often contain the following phrases:

> Which of the following choices would best explain the situation presented above?

> Which of the following, if true, would best resolve the discrepancy above?

> Which of the following, if true, best reconciles the seeming paradox above?

Take a look at the following example:

Over the past ten years, the emergence of digital file sharing technology has threatened the traditional market for entire music albums. Internet users are now able to download single songs from their favorite artists, enabling them to acquire the songs they desire without having to purchase the entire album. Some music industry leaders contend that this practice causes untold financial losses, as the cost of individual songs is not enough to offset the money lost producing the songs that were not purchased from the rest of the album. However, consumer groups report that there has been an increase in the sales of entire music albums.

Which of the following, if true, would best explain the situation above?

○ Some consumers who have illegally downloaded songs from the Internet have been sued by major record companies.

○ Research indicates that persons who engage in file-sharing or song-downloading are usually only casual music fans.

○ The music industry is developing new technology to help prevent users from illegally downloading songs.

○ Music artists tend to release more material, on average, today than they did 10 years ago.

○ Entire music albums released now often include bonus features that are appealing to fans, such as interviews with the band and music videos, that are not available unless the entire album is purchased.

Here's How to Crack It

Like Inference questions, Resolve/Explain questions require a slightly different approach. Step 1 remains the same—read the question and identify the question type. Once you've identified the question as a resolve/explain question, read the critical-reasoning passage. However, instead of looking for a premise and conclusion, for Step 2 you're going to look for two facts that are in conflict. The basic pattern for a resolve/explain argument is as follows:

Fact I:
But
Fact II:

For the argument in the example, two facts are in conflict:

Fact I: Internet users are able to download individual songs instead of purchasing entire music albums.
But
Fact II: There has been an increase in entire music album sales.

For Resolve/Explain questions, the correct answer shows how both facts can be true at the same time. Proceed to Step 4, use POE, and as you read each answer choice, ask yourself the following question:

How can both Fact I and Fact II be true?

Check out the POE guidelines for Resolve/Explain questions in the gray box.

Let's use Process of Elimination on the answer choices in our example. The first answer choice doesn't resolve the conflict. It might explain why fewer users illegally download music, but it doesn't explain why entire music album sales have increased. Eliminate (A). Choice (B) does nothing to the paradox. The fact that the people who download music are casual fans doesn't really explain anything. Like (A), (C) is partly correct; however, it doesn't explain the increase in sales. Also, the answer choice states that the industry is "developing" technology; it doesn't state that the technology has been implemented yet. So this couldn't affect the current situation. Choice (D) doesn't help much either. You might assume that more material on the market means that sales could increase even with downloading, but that line of thought requires you to fill in too many missing pieces. The correct answer should do all the work. Look at (E). This choice states that entire music albums feature bonus material that is not available unless the entire album is purchased. This could explain both the fact that people are downloading individual songs and that entire music album sales are increasing. Since (E) is a more complete explanation, it's the correct answer.

WON'T ALL THIS TAKE TOO MUCH TIME?

While it may seem at first like you will need a lot of time to break down the arguments and apply the strategies, you'll get faster at doing this with practice. It's better to take your time and truly understand how the questions work than to rush through the problems, only to get them wrong.

Critical Reasoning Practice Set

In this practice set, follow the steps exactly as we have presented them. Answers can be found in Part V.

In 1989, corporate tax rates in some regions of the United States fell to their lowest level in 15 years, while the rates in other regions reached new highs. In 1974, similar conditions led to a large flight of companies from regions with unfavorable corporate tax policies to regions with favorable policies. There was, however, considerably less corporate flight in 1989.

Which of the following, if true about 1989, most plausibly accounts for the finding that there was less corporate flight in 1989 ?

○ The regions with the most favorable corporate tax policies had many of the same types of corporations as did those with unfavorable tax policies, but this was not true in 1974.

○ In contrast to 1974, office rental costs in the regions with the most favorable corporate tax policies were significantly higher than rental costs in other areas of the country.

○ In contrast to 1974, in 1989, the areas with the most favorable corporate tax policies reaped the most benefit from tax incentives, although the tax codes were particularly difficult to decipher.

○ Tax incentives offered by foreign countries were higher in 1989 than in 1974.

○ Individual tax incentives in the areas with favorable corporate tax policies were slightly lower than they were 15 years earlier in areas with favorable corporate tax policies.

Aramayo: Our federal government seems to function most efficiently when decision-making responsibilities are handled by only a few individuals. Therefore, our government should consolidate its leadership and move away from a decentralized representative democracy.

Tello: But moving our government in this direction could violate our constitutional mission to provide government of, for, and by the people.

Which of the following statements describes Tello's response to Aramayo?

○ Tello contradicts the reasoning used by Aramayo.

○ Tello uncovers an assumption used in Aramayo's reasoning.

○ Tello brings up a possible negative consequence of accepting Aramayo's argument.

○ Tello reveals the circular reasoning used by Aramayo.

○ Tello shows that Aramayo overgeneralizes a very special situation.

Business computer systems are designed to make workers more productive by automating a portion of the work that must be completed in a business process. As a result, the employee is free to perform more tasks that require human attention. Although productivity may be lost during a learning period, many businesses experience dramatic gains in productivity after installing a new computer system. While discussing the connection between productivity gains and computer systems, a well-respected business journal recently stated that the person who serves as the Chief Information Officer is the consummate business computer system.

By comparing a Chief Information Officer to business computer systems, the journal implicitly argues that

○ Chief Information Officers should always communicate the value of computer systems to their companies

○ the productivity of a company can be increased through the hiring of a Chief Information Officer

○ many companies have not improved their productivity with new computer systems

○ Chief Information Officers are more effective than are new computer systems

○ the impact of a Chief Information Officer on a company's productivity is difficult to measure

Whenever Joe does his laundry at the Main Street Laundromat, the loads turn out cleaner than they do when he does his laundry at the Elm Street Laundromat. Laundry done at the Main Street Laundromat is cleaner because the machines at the Main Street Laundromat use more water per load than do those at the Elm Street Laundromat.

Which of the following statements, if true, helps support the conclusion above?

○ The clothes washed at the Elm Street Laundromat were, overall, less clean than those washed at the Main Street Laundromat.

○ Joe uses the same detergent at both laundromats.

○ The machines at the Oak Street Laundromat use twice as much water as do those at the Main Street Laundromat.

○ Joe does three times as much laundry at the Main Street Laundromat as he does at the Elm Street Laundromat.

○ Joe tends to do his dirtier laundry at the Elm Street Laundromat.

According to the United States Postal Service bureau of information, the rate of complaints concerning late delivery was 30 times higher in 1991 than in 1964. Because the United States Postal Service changed neighborhood routes from a multiple-truck delivery system to a single-truck delivery system between 1964 and 1991, the enormous increase in complaints must be a result of this systematic change.

Which of the following, if true, weakens the conclusion drawn above?

○ In 1991, most late-mail complaints were reported to the appropriate United States Postal Service office, whereas in 1964 most were not.

○ Even in a multiple-truck delivery system, certain letters will arrive late.

○ According to the United States Postal Service bureau of information, most of the complaints concerning late delivery in 1991 were about registered mail.

○ The bulk amount of mail processed by the United States Postal Service was not much larger in 1991 than it was in 1964, before the systemic change occurred.

○ The change in neighborhood routes from a multiple-truck to a single-truck delivery system sometimes causes enormous increase in the price of stamps.

Summary

- Most Critical Reasoning questions require you to break down an argument. The conclusion is the main point of an argument. The premise is the fact cited in support of the conclusion.

- The assumption is used to link the premise and the conclusion with each other. Without an assumption, an argument breaks down.

- To crack a Critical Reasoning question, read the question first so you understand the task. Some questions require you to identify the conclusion and the premise of an argument. Others ask you to find the assumption or to strengthen or weaken the argument.

- After reading the question, break down the argument into its premise and conclusion and, if necessary, the assumption.

- Try to predict in your own words what the correct answer needs to do in order to answer the question.

Chapter 8
Vocabulary
for the GRE

Words, words, words. That's what you'll find in this chapter. The following pages contain the Key Terms List, a list of some of the most common words that appear on the GRE. There are also some handy tips on studying and learning new vocabulary words and exercises to test your progress. Be advised, though, that the words in the chapter ahead are just a starting point. As you prepare for your GRE, keep your eyes open for words you don't know and look them up!

VOCAB, VOCAB, VOCAB

As much as ETS would like to claim that the GRE doesn't rely much on vocabulary, the simple fact remains that many of the questions, answer choices, and reading passages contain some difficult vocabulary. You can't improve your score substantially without increasing your vocabulary. You might think that studying vocabulary is the most boring part of preparing for the GRE, but it's one of the most important, and it's also the one part of GRE preparation that's actually useful to you beyond the confines of the test itself. And the more words that you recognize (and know the meaning of) on the test, the easier it will be. So there's no avoiding the importance of vocabulary to your success on the GRE. Unfortunately, it is virtually impossible to fairly test someone's vocabulary on a standardized test. If you memorize 1,000 words and on test day none of those words appear, does that mean you have a bad vocabulary? Of course not—it just means that you've been victimized by the limitations of standardized testing.

This doesn't mean that you should take a defeatist attitude toward learning vocabulary! Even if you have only a few weeks before your test, you can still expand your vocabulary and increase your prospects of doing better on the GRE. One thing you have working in your favor is the fact that ETS loves to do the same things over and over. The words we've collected for you in this chapter are the words that appear most frequently on the GRE. So let's get started learning some new words!

Improving your vocabulary is one of the most important things you can do to improve your Verbal score.

Flashcards From Us
You can make your own flashcards or you can buy Essential GRE Vocabulary flashcards from us!

LEARN TO LOVE THE DICTIONARY

Get used to looking up words. ETS uses words that it believes the average college-educated adult should know. These words show up in newspaper and magazine articles, in books, and in textbooks. If you see a word you don't know while studying for the GRE or elsewhere, it's probably a good GRE word. Look it up and make a flash card. Dictionaries will give you the pronunciation, while digital apps can provide quick, handy look-ups for new words. Looking up words is a habit. You may have to force yourself to do it in the beginning, but it becomes more natural over time. Many of the techniques in this book will help you on the GRE but don't have much relevance in day-to-day life, but a great vocabulary and good vocabulary habits will add a tremendous amount of value to your graduate school career and beyond.

Learning New Words

How will you remember all the new words you should learn for the test? By developing a routine for learning new words. Here are some tips.

- To learn words that you find on your own, get into the habit of reading good books, magazines, and newspapers. Start paying attention to words you come across for which you don't know the definition. You might be tempted to just skip these, as usual, but train yourself to write them down and look them up.
- When you look up the word, say it out loud, being careful to pronounce it correctly. This will help you remember it.
- When you look up a word in the dictionary, don't assume that the first definition is the only one you need to know. The first definition may be an archaic one, or one that applies only in a particular context, so scan through all the definitions.
- Now that you've learned the dictionary's definition of a new word, restate it in your own words. You'll find it much easier to remember a word's meaning if you make it your own.
- Mnemonics—Use your imagination to create a mental image to fix the new word in your mind. For example, if you're trying to remember the word *voracious*, which means having an insatiable appetite for an activity or pursuit, picture an incredibly hungry boar, eating huge piles of food. The voracious boar will help you to recall the meaning of the word. The crazier the image, the better.
- Keep a vocabulary notebook, or make a file with a list of new vocabulary words and put it on your desktop. Simply having a notebook with you will remind you to be on the lookout for new words, and using it will help you to remember the ones you encounter. Writing something down also makes it easier to memorize. Jot down the word when you find it, note its pronunciation and definition (in your own words) when you look it up, and jot down your mnemonic or mental image. You might also copy the sentence in which you originally found the word, to remind yourself of how the word looks in context.
- Do the same thing with flash cards. Write the word on one side and the pronunciation, the meaning, and perhaps a mental image on the other. Stick five or six of your flash cards in your pocket every morning and use them whenever you can. Stuck on a delayed subway train? Look at your flashcards. Standing in a long line at the bank? Look at your flashcards. Sick of engaging in small talk with boring acquaintances? Look at your flashcards. (Only kidding about that last one.)
- Use your new word every chance you get. Make it part of your life. Insert it into your speech at every opportunity. Developing a powerful vocabulary requires lots of exercise.
- Learn word roots. Many words share similar origins. By learning these common roots, you'll be better able to work with words you've never seen before. A good dictionary should list the origin and roots of the words in it.

Learn new words little by little; don't try to learn a ton at once!

THE KEY TERMS LIST

You should start your vocabulary work by studying the Key Terms List, a list we've compiled of some of the most frequently tested words on the GRE. We put together this list by analyzing released GREs and keeping tabs on the test to make sure that these words are still popular with ETS. At the very least, answer choices that contain Key Terms make very good guesses on questions for which you don't know the answer. Each word on the Key Terms List is followed by the part of speech and a brief definition for the word. Some of the words on this list may have other definitions as well, but the definitions we have given are the ones most likely to appear on the GRE.

We've broken the Key Terms List down into four groups of about 75 words each. Don't try to learn all four groups of words at once—work with one list at a time. Write the words and their definitions down in a notebook or on flash cards. It is very important to write them down yourself, because this will help you remember them. Just glancing through the lists printed in this book won't be nearly as effective. Before doing the exercises for each group, spend some time studying and learning the words first. Then use the exercises as a way to test yourself. Answers for the matching exercises appear in Part V of this book.

Key Terms Group 1

abscond (verb)	to depart clandestinely; to steal off and hide
aberrant (adj.)	deviating from the norm (noun form: *aberration*)
alacrity (noun)	eager and enthusiastic willingness
anomaly (noun)	deviation from the normal order, form, or rule; abnormality (adj. form: *anomalous*)
approbation (noun)	an expression of approval or praise
arduous (adj.)	strenuous, taxing; requiring significant effort
assuage (verb)	to ease or lessen; to appease or pacify
audacious (adj.)	daring and fearless; recklessly bold (noun form: *audacity*)
austere (adj.)	without adornment; bare; severely simple; ascetic (noun form: *austerity*)
axiomatic (adj.)	taken as a given; possessing self-evident truth (noun form: *axiom*)
canonical (adj.)	following or in agreement with accepted, traditional standards (noun form: *canon*)
capricious (adj.)	inclined to change one's mind impulsively; erratic, unpredictable

censure (verb)	to criticize severely; to officially rebuke
chicanery (noun)	trickery or subterfuge
connoisseur (noun)	an informed and astute judge in matters of taste; expert
convoluted (adj.)	complex or complicated
disabuse (verb)	to undeceive; to set right
discordant (adj.)	conflicting; dissonant or harsh in sound
disparate (adj.)	fundamentally distinct or dissimilar
effrontery (noun)	extreme boldness; presumptuousness
eloquent (adj.)	well-spoken, expressive, articulate (noun form: *eloquence*)
enervate (verb)	to weaken; to reduce in vitality
ennui (noun)	dissatisfaction and restlessness resulting from boredom or apathy
equivocate (verb)	to use ambiguous language with a deceptive intent (adj. form: *equivocal*)
erudite (adj.)	very learned; scholarly (noun form: *erudition*)
exculpate (verb)	exonerate; to clear of blame
exigent (adj.)	urgent, pressing; requiring immediate action or attention
extemporaneous (adj.)	improvised; done without preparation
filibuster (noun)	intentional obstruction, esp. using prolonged speechmaking to delay legislative action
fulminate (verb)	to loudly attack or denounce
ingenuous (adj.)	artless; frank and candid; lacking in sophistication
inured (adj.)	accustomed to accepting something undesirable
irascible (adj.)	easily angered; prone to temperamental outbursts
laud (verb)	to praise highly (adj. form: *laudatory*)
lucid (adj.)	clear; easily understood
magnanimity (noun)	the quality of being generously noble in mind and heart, esp. in forgiving (adj. form: *magnanimous*)
martial (adj.)	associated with war and the armed forces
mundane (adj.)	of the world; typical of or concerned with the ordinary

nascent (adj.)	coming into being; in early developmental stages
nebulous (adj.)	vague; cloudy; lacking clearly defined form
neologism (noun)	a new word, expression, or usage; the creation or use of new words or senses
noxious (adj.)	harmful, injurious
obtuse (adj.)	lacking sharpness of intellect; not clear or precise in thought or expression
obviate (verb)	to anticipate and make unnecessary
onerous (adj.)	troubling; burdensome
paean (noun)	a song or hymn of praise and thanksgiving
parody (noun)	a humorous imitation intended for ridicule or comic effect, esp. in literature and art
perennial (adj.)	recurrent through the year or many years; happening repeatedly
perfidy (noun)	intentional breach of faith; treachery (adj. form: *perfidious*)
perfunctory (adj.)	cursory; done without care or interest
perspicacious (adj.)	acutely perceptive; having keen discernment (noun form: *perspicacity*)
prattle (verb)	to babble meaninglessly; to talk in an empty and idle manner
precipitate (adj.)	acting with excessive haste or impulse
precipitate (verb)	to cause or happen before anticipated or required
predilection (noun)	a disposition in favor of something; preference
prescience (noun)	foreknowledge of events; knowing of events prior to their occurring (adj. form: *prescient*)
prevaricate (verb)	to deliberately avoid the truth; to mislead
qualms (noun)	misgivings; reservations; causes for hesitancy
recant (verb)	to retract, esp. a previously held belief
refute (verb)	to disprove; to successfully argue against
relegate (verb)	to forcibly assign, esp. to a lower place or position
reticent (adj.)	quiet; reserved; reluctant to express thoughts and feelings
solicitous (adj.)	concerned and attentive; eager
sordid (adj.)	characterized by filth, grime, or squalor; foul

sporadic (adj.)	occurring only occasionally, or in scattered instances
squander (verb)	to waste by spending or using irresponsibly
static (adj.)	not moving, active, or in motion; at rest
stupefy (verb)	to stun, baffle, or amaze
stymie (verb)	to block; to thwart
synthesis (noun)	the combination of parts to make a whole (verb form: *synthesize*)
torque (noun)	a force that causes rotation
tortuous (adj.)	winding, twisting; excessively complicated
truculent (adj.)	fierce and cruel; eager to fight
veracity (noun)	truthfulness, honesty
virulent (adj.)	extremely harmful or poisonous; bitterly hostile or antagonistic
voracious (adj.)	having an insatiable appetite for an activity or pursuit; ravenous
waver (verb)	to move to and fro; to sway; to be unsettled in opinion

Group 1 Exercises

Match the following words to their definitions. Answers can be found in Part V.

1. improvised; without preparation
2. a newly coined word or expression
3. a song of joy and praise
4. to praise highly
5. truthfulness; honesty
6. artless; frank and candid
7. associated with war and the military
8. to retract a belief or statement
9. cursory; done without care or interest
10. troubling; burdensome
11. to criticize; to officially rebuke
12. winding; twisting; complicated
13. to block; to thwart
14. clear; easily understood

A. veracity
B. recant
C. extemporaneous
D. stymie
E. paean
F. lucid
G. laud
H. onerous
I. tortuous
J. neologism
K. martial
L. ingenuous
M. censure
N. perfunctory

Hold Up and Break
Did you just tackle Key Terms Group 1? Before you jump into Group 2, give yourself a break. Take a walk, get some air, eat a snack. Let the Group 1 words sink in before you dive into Group 2.

Key Terms Group 2

abate (verb)	to lessen in intensity or degree
accolade (noun)	an expression of praise
adulation (noun)	excessive praise; intense adoration
aesthetic (adj.)	dealing with, appreciative of, or responsive to art or the beautiful
ameliorate (verb)	to make better or more tolerable
ascetic (noun)	one who practices rigid self-denial, esp. as an act of religious devotion
avarice (noun)	greed, esp. for wealth (adj. form: *avaricious*)
axiom (noun)	a universally recognized principle (adj. form: *axiomatic*)
burgeon (verb)	to grow rapidly or flourish
bucolic (adj.)	rustic and pastoral; characteristic of rural areas and their inhabitants
cacophony (noun)	harsh, jarring, discordant sound; dissonance (adj. form: *cacophonous*)
canon (noun)	an established set of principles or code of laws, often religious in nature (adj. form: *canonical*)
castigation (noun)	severe criticism or punishment (verb form: *castigate*)
catalyst (noun)	a substance that accelerates the rate of a chemical reaction without itself changing; a person or thing that causes change
caustic (adj.)	burning or stinging; causing corrosion
chary (adj.)	wary; cautious; sparing
cogent (adj.)	appealing forcibly to the mind or reason; convincing
complaisance (noun)	the willingness to comply with the wishes of others (adj. form: *complaisant*)
contentious (adj.)	argumentative; quarrelsome; causing controversy or disagreement
contrite (adj.)	regretful; penitent; seeking forgiveness (noun form: *contrition*)
culpable (adj.)	deserving blame (noun form: *culpability*)
dearth (noun)	smallness of quantity or number; scarcity; a lack
demur (verb)	to question or oppose
didactic (adj.)	intended to teach or instruct
discretion (noun)	cautious reserve in speech; ability to make responsible decisions (adj. form: *discreet*)
disinterested (adj.)	free of bias or self-interest; impartial

dogmatic (adj.)	expressing a rigid opinion based on unproved or improvable principles (noun form: *dogma*)
ebullience (noun)	the quality of lively or enthusiastic expression of thoughts and feelings (adj. form: *ebullient*)
eclectic (adj.)	composed of elements drawn from various sources
elegy (noun)	a mournful poem, esp. one lamenting the dead (adj. form: *elegiac*)
emollient (adj.)/ (noun)	soothing, esp. to the skin; making less harsh; mollifying; an agent that softens or smoothes the skin
empirical (adj.)	based on observation or experiment
enigmatic (adj.)	mysterious; obscure; difficult to understand (noun form: *enigma*)
ephemeral (adj.)	brief; fleeting
esoteric (adj.)	intended for or understood by a small, specific group
eulogy (noun)	a speech honoring the dead (verb form: *eulogize*)
exonerate (verb)	to remove blame
facetious (adj.)	playful; humorous
fallacy (noun)	an invalid or incorrect notion; a mistaken belief (adj. form: *fallacious*)
furtive (adj.)	marked by stealth; covert; surreptitious
gregarious (adj.)	sociable; outgoing; enjoying the company of other people
harangue (verb)/ (noun)	to deliver a forceful or angry speech; ranting speech or writing.
heretical (adj.)	violating accepted dogma or convention (noun form: *heresy*)
hyperbole (noun)	an exaggerated statement, often used as a figure of speech (adj. form: *hyperbolic*)
impecunious (adj.)	lacking funds; without money
incipient (adj.)	beginning to come into being or to become apparent
inert (adj.)	unmoving; lethargic; sluggish
innocuous (adj.)	harmless; causing no damage
intransigent (adj.)	refusing to compromise (noun form: *intransigence*)
inveigle (verb)	to obtain by deception or flattery
morose (adj.)	sad; sullen; melancholy
odious (adj.)	evoking intense aversion or dislike
opaque (adj.)	impenetrable by light; not reflecting light
oscillation (noun)	the act or state of swinging back and forth with a steady, uninterrupted rhythm (verb form: *oscillate*)
penurious (adj.)	penny-pinching; excessively thrifty; ungenerous

pernicious (adj.)	extremely harmful in a way that is not easily seen or noticed
peruse (verb)	to examine with great care (noun form: *perusal*)
pious (adj.)	extremely reverent or devout; showing strong religious devotion (noun form: *piety*)
precursor (noun)	one that precedes and indicates or announces another
preen (verb)	to dress up; to primp; to groom oneself with elaborate care
prodigious (adj.)	abundant in size, force, or extent; extraordinary
prolific (adj.)	producing large volumes or amounts; productive
putrefy (verb)	to rot; to decay and give off a foul odor (adj. form: *putrid*)
quaff (verb)	to drink deeply
quiescence (noun)	stillness; motionlessness; quality of being at rest (adj. form: *quiescent*)
redoubtable (adj.)	awe-inspiring; worthy of honor
sanction (noun)/(verb)	authoritative permission or approval; a penalty intended to enforce compliance; to give permission or authority
satire (noun)	a literary work that ridicules or criticizes a human vice through humor or derision (adj. form: *satirical*)
squalid (adj.)	sordid; wretched and dirty as from neglect (noun form: *squalor*)
stoic (adj.)	indifferent to or unaffected by pleasure or pain; steadfast (noun form: *stoicism*)
supplant (verb)	to take the place of; to supersede
torpid (adj.)	lethargic; sluggish; dormant (noun form: *torpor*)
ubiquitous (adj.)	existing everywhere at the same time; constantly encountered; widespread
urbane (adj.)	sophisticated; refined; elegant (noun form: *urbanity*)
vilify (verb)	to defame; to characterize harshly
viscous (adj.)	thick; sticky (noun form: *viscosity*)

Group 2 Exercises

Match the following words to their definitions. Answers can be found in Part V.

1. brief; fleeting
2. a forceful or angry speech
3. arousing strong dislike or aversion
4. to free from blame or responsibility
5. arousing fear or awe; worthy of honor; formidable
6. unexpectedly harmful
7. to drink deeply
8. stinging; corrosive; sarcastic; biting
9. impressively great in size, force, or extent; enormous
10. greed; hunger for money
11. unmoving; lethargic
12. impartial; unbiased
13. lack; scarcity
14. to win over by deception, coaxing or flattery

A. pernicious
B. ephemeral
C. avarice
D. quaff
E. caustic

F. odious
G. dearth
H. inert
I. disinterested

J. exonerate
K. inveigle
L. prodigious
M. harangue
N. redoubtable

Key Terms Group 3

acumen (noun)	keen, accurate judgment or insight
adulterate (verb)	to reduce purity by combining with inferior ingredients
amalgamate (verb)	to combine several elements into a whole (noun form: *amalgamation*)
archaic (adj.)	outdated; associated with an earlier, perhaps more primitive, time
aver (verb)	to state as a fact; to declare or assert
bolster (verb)	to provide support or reinforcement
bombastic (adj.)	pompous; grandiloquent (noun form: *bombast*)
diatribe (noun)	a harsh denunciation
dissemble (verb)	to disguise or conceal; to mislead
eccentric (adj.)	departing from norms or conventions
endemic (adj.)	characteristic of or often found in a particular locality, region, or people
evanescent (adj.)	tending to disappear like vapor; vanishing
exacerbate (verb)	to make worse or more severe
fervent (adj.)	greatly emotional or zealous (noun form: *fervor*)
fortuitous (adj.)	happening by accident or chance

Break Time!
How did you do in Group 2? Take a moment to relax and let your mind rest before diving into Group 3. Remember to do this between each group of words so you don't overload your brain!

germane (adj.)	relevant to the subject at hand; appropriate in subject matter
grandiloquence (noun)	pompous speech or expression (adj. form: *grandiloquent*)
hackneyed (adj.)	rendered trite or commonplace by frequent usage
halcyon (adj.)	calm and peaceful
hedonism (noun)	devotion to pleasurable pursuits, esp. to the pleasures of the senses (a *hedonist* is someone who pursues pleasure)
hegemony (noun)	the consistent dominance of one state or group over others
iconoclast (noun)	one who attacks or undermines traditional conventions or institutions
idolatrous (adj.)	given to intense or excessive devotion to something (noun form: *idolatry*)
impassive (adj.)	revealing no emotion
imperturbable (adj.)	marked by extreme calm, impassivity, and steadiness
implacable (adj.)	not capable of being appeased or significantly changed
impunity (noun)	immunity from punishment or penalty
inchoate (adj.)	in an initial stage; not fully formed
infelicitous (adj.)	unfortunate; inappropriate
insipid (adj.)	lacking in qualities that interest, stimulate, or challenge
loquacious (adj.)	extremely talkative (noun form: *loquacity*)
luminous (adj.)	characterized by brightness and the emission of light
malevolent (adj.)	having or showing often vicious ill will, spite, or hatred (noun form: *malevolence*)
malleable (adj.)	capable of being shaped or formed; tractable; pliable
mendacity (noun)	the condition of being untruthful; dishonesty (adj. form: *mendacious*)
meticulous (adj.)	characterized by extreme care and precision; attentive to detail
misanthrope (noun)	one who hates all other humans (adj. form: *misanthropic*)
mitigate (verb)	to make or become less severe or intense; to moderate
obdurate (adj.)	unyielding; hardhearted; intractable
obsequious (adj.)	exhibiting a fawning attentiveness
occlude (verb)	to obstruct or block
opprobrium (noun)	disgrace; contempt; scorn
pedagogy (noun)	the profession or principles of teaching, or instructing

pedantic (adj.)	overly concerned with the trivial details of learning or education; show-offish about one's knowledge
penury (noun)	poverty; destitution
pervasive (adj.)	having the tendency to permeate or spread throughout
pine (verb)	to yearn intensely; to languish; to lose vigor
pirate (verb)	to illegally use or reproduce
pith (noun)	the essential or central part
pithy (adj.)	precise and brief
placate (verb)	to appease; to calm by making concessions
platitude (noun)	a superficial remark, esp. one offered as meaningful
plummet (verb)	to plunge or drop straight down
polemical (adj.)	controversial; argumentative
prodigal (adj.)	recklessly wasteful; extravagant; profuse; lavish
profuse (adj.)	given or coming forth abundantly; extravagant
proliferate (verb)	to grow or increase swiftly and abundantly
queries (noun)	questions; inquiries; doubts in the mind; reservations
querulous (adj.)	prone to complaining or grumbling; peevish
rancorous (adj.)	characterized by bitter, long-lasting resentment (noun form: *rancor*)
recalcitrant (adj.)	obstinately defiant of authority; difficult to manage
repudiate (verb)	to refuse to have anything to do with; to disown
rescind (verb)	to invalidate; to repeal; to retract
reverent (adj.)	marked by, feeling, or expressing a feeling of profound awe and respect (noun form: *reverence*)
rhetoric (noun)	the art or study of effective use of language for communication and persuasion
salubrious (adj.)	promoting health or well-being
solvent (adj.)	able to meet financial obligations; able to dissolve another substance
specious (adj.)	seeming true, but actually being fallacious; misleadingly attractive; plausible but false
spurious (adj.)	lacking authenticity or validity; false; counterfeit
subpoena (noun)	a court order requiring appearance and/or testimony
succinct (adj.)	brief; concise
superfluous (adj.)	exceeding what is sufficient or necessary
surfeit (verb)	an overabundant supply; excess; to feed or supply to excess (noun form: a *surfeit* of supplies)
tenacity (noun)	the quality of adherence or persistence to something valued; persistent determination (adj. form: *tenacious*)

tenuous (adj.)	having little substance or strength; flimsy; weak
tirade (noun)	a long and extremely critical speech; a harsh denunciation
transient (adj.)	fleeting; passing quickly; brief
zealous (adj.)	fervent; ardent; impassioned, devoted to a cause (a *zealot* is a zealous person)

Group 3 Exercises

Match the following words to their definitions. Answers can be found in Part V.

1. brief; concise; tersely cogent
2. prone to complaining; whining
3. fawning; ingratiating
4. marked by bitter, deep-seated resentment
5. controversial; argumentative
6. dominance of one state or group over others
7. uninteresting; tasteless; flat; dull
8. thin; flimsy; of little substance
9. excess; overindulgence
10. wasteful; recklessly extravagant
11. to appease; to pacify with concessions
12. to assert; to declare; to allege; to state as fact
13. pompous; grandiloquent
14. tending to vanish like vapor

A. hegemony
B. aver
C. insipid
D. pithy
E. placate
F. prodigal

G. querulous
H. surfeit
I. rancorous
J. bombastic
K. obsequious
L. evanescent

M. polemical
N. tenuous

Key Terms Group 4

acerbic (adj.)	having a sour or bitter taste or character; sharp; biting
aggrandize (verb)	to increase in intensity, power, influence, or prestige
alchemy (noun)	a medieval science aimed at the transmutation of metals, esp. base metals into gold (an *alchemist* is one who practices alchemy)
amenable (adj.)	agreeable; responsive to suggestion
anachronism (noun)	something or someone out of place in terms of historical or chronological context
astringent (adj.)	having a tightening effect on living tissue; harsh; severe; something with a tightening effect on tissue
contiguous (adj.)	sharing a border; touching; adjacent
convention (noun)	a generally agreed-upon practice or attitude
credulous (adj.)	tending to believe too readily; gullible (noun form: *credulity*)

What's Your Strategy?
Do you find flashcards helpful? Or do you prefer word lists? Or smartphone apps? Figure out the strategy that works best for you when it comes to learning vocabulary and stick to it!

cynicism (noun)	an attitude or quality of belief that all people are motivated by selfishness (adj. form: *cynical*)
decorum (noun)	polite or appropriate conduct or behavior (adj. form: *decorous*)
derision (noun)	scorn, ridicule, contemptuous treatment (adj. form: *derisive*; verb form: *deride*)
desiccate (verb)	to dry out or dehydrate; to make dry or dull
dilettante (noun)	one with an amateurish or superficial interest in the arts or a branch of knowledge
disparage (verb)	to slight or belittle
divulge (verb)	to disclose something secret
fawn (verb)	to flatter or praise excessively
flout (verb)	to show contempt for, as in a rule or convention
garrulous (adj.)	pointlessly talkative; talking too much
glib (adj.)	marked by ease or informality; nonchalant; lacking in depth; superficial
hubris (noun)	overbearing presumption or pride; arrogance
imminent (adj.)	about to happen; impending
immutable (adj.)	not capable of change
impetuous (adj.)	hastily or rashly energetic; impulsive and vehement
indifferent (adj.)	having no interest or concern; showing no bias or prejudice
inimical (adj.)	damaging; harmful; injurious
intractable (adj.)	not easily managed or directed; stubborn; obstinate
intrepid (adj.)	steadfast and courageous
laconic (adj.)	using few words; terse
maverick (noun)	an independent individual who does not go along with a group or party
mercurial (adj.)	characterized by rapid and unpredictable change in mood
mollify (verb)	to calm or soothe; to reduce in emotional intensity
neophyte (noun)	a recent convert; a beginner; novice
obfuscate (verb)	to deliberately obscure; to make confusing
obstinate (adj.)	stubborn; hard-headed; uncompromising
ostentatious (adj.)	characterized by or given to pretentious display; showy
pervade (verb)	to permeate throughout (adj. form: *pervasive*)
phlegmatic (adj.)	calm; sluggish; unemotional
plethora (noun)	an overabundance; a surplus
pragmatic (adj.)	practical rather than idealistic

presumptuous (adj.)	overstepping due bounds (as of propriety or courtesy); taking liberties
pristine (adj.)	pure; uncorrupted; clean
probity (noun)	adherence to highest principles; complete and confirmed integrity; uprightness
proclivity (noun)	a natural predisposition or inclination
profligate (adj.)	excessively wasteful; recklessly extravagant (noun form: *profligacy*)
propensity (noun)	a natural inclination or tendency; penchant
prosaic (adj.)	dull; lacking in spirit or imagination
pungent (adj.)	characterized by a strong, sharp smell or taste
quixotic (adj.)	foolishly impractical; marked by lofty romantic ideals
quotidian (adj.)	occurring or recurring daily; commonplace
rarefy (verb)	to make or become thin, less dense; to refine
recondite (adj.)	hidden; concealed; difficult to understand; obscure
refulgent (adj.)	radiant; shiny; brilliant
renege (verb)	to fail to honor a commitment; to go back on a promise
sedulous (adj.)	diligent; persistent; hard-working
shard (noun)	a piece of broken pottery or glass
soporific (adj.)	causing drowsiness; tending to induce sleep
sparse (adj.)	thin; not dense; arranged at widely spaced intervals
spendthrift (noun)	one who spends money wastefully
subtle (adj.)	not obvious; elusive; difficult to discern
tacit (adj.)	implied; not explicitly stated
terse (adj.)	brief and concise in wording
tout (verb)	to publicly praise or promote
trenchant (adj.)	sharply perceptive; keen; penetrating
unfeigned (adj.)	genuine; not false or hypocritical
untenable (adj.)	indefensible; not viable; uninhabitable
vacillate (verb)	to waver indecisively between one course of action or opinion and another
variegated (adj.)	multicolored; characterized by a variety of patches of different color
vexation (noun)	annoyance; irritation (verb form: *vex*)
vigilant (adj.)	alertly watchful (noun form: *vigilance*)
vituperate (verb)	to use harsh condemnatory language; to abuse or censure severely or abusively; to berate
volatile (adj.)	readily changing to a vapor; changeable; fickle; explosive (noun form: *volatility*)

Group 4 Exercises

Match the following words to their definitions. Answers can be found in Part V.

1. acid or biting; bitter in taste or tone
2. sleep-inducing; causing drowsiness
3. a surplus; an overabundance
4. one with superficial interest in a subject
5. arrogance; overbearing pride
6. sharing a border; touching; adjacent
7. talking too much; rambling
8. something out of place in history or chronology
9. difficult to understand; obscure; hidden
10. dull; unimaginative; ordinary
11. unemotional; calm
12. stubborn; obstinate; difficult to manage or govern
13. condemn with harsh, abusive words; berate
14. foolishly impractical; marked by lofty ideals

A. anachronism
B. contiguous
C. dilettante
D. intractable
E. prosaic
F. quixotic
G. recondite
H. vituperate

I. acerbic
J. garrulous
K. hubris
L. soporific

M. phlegmatic

N. plethora

BEYOND THE KEY TERMS LIST

So you've finished the Key Terms List and you're now the master of many more words than you were before. What to do next? Why, go *beyond the Key Terms List* of course! The Key Terms List was just the beginning. To maximize your score on the GRE you must be relentless in increasing your vocabulary. Don't let up. Keep learning words until the day you sit down for the exam. The following lists of extra words don't have exercises, so just keep working with your notebook or flash cards and get your friends to quiz you. You are a vocabulary machine!

Beyond the Key Terms Group 1

The following list contains some of those simple-sounding words with less common secondary meanings that ETS likes to test on the GRE.

alloy (verb)	to commingle; to debase by mixing with something inferior; *unalloyed* means pure
appropriate (verb)	to take for one's own use; to confiscate
arrest, arresting (verb)/(adj.)	to suspend; to engage; holding one's attention: as in arrested adolescence, an arresting portrait
august (adj.)	majestic, venerable
bent (noun)	leaning, inclination, proclivity, tendency

broach (verb)	to bring up; to announce; to begin to talk about
brook (verb)	to tolerate; to endure; to countenance
cardinal (adj.)	major, as in cardinal sin
chauvinist (noun)	a blindly devoted patriot
color (verb)	to change as if by dyeing, i.e., to distort, gloss, or affect (usually the first)
consequential (adj.)	pompous, self-important (primary definitions are: logically following; important)
damp (verb)	to diminish the intensity or check the vibration of a sound
die (noun)	a tool used for shaping, as in a tool-and-die shop
essay (verb)	to test or try; to attempt; to experiment
exact (verb)	to demand; to call for; to require; to take
fell (verb)	to cause to fall by striking
fell (adj.)	inhumanly cruel
flag (verb)	to sag or droop; to become spiritless; to decline
flip (adj.)	sarcastic, impertinent, as in flippant: a flip remark
ford (verb)	to wade across the shallow part of a river or stream
grouse (verb)	to complain or grumble
guy (noun)	a rope, cord, or cable attached to something as a brace or guide; to steady or reinforce using a guy: Think *guide*. (verb form: *guyed, guying*)
intimate (verb)	to imply, suggest, or insinuate
list (verb)	to tilt or lean to one side
lumber (verb)	to move heavily and clumsily
meet (adj.)	fitting, proper
milk (verb)	to exploit; to squeeze every last ounce of
mince (verb)	to pronounce or speak affectedly; to euphemize, to speak too carefully. Also, to take tiny steps; to tiptoe
nice (adj.)	exacting, fastidious, extremely precise
occult (adj.)	hidden, concealed, beyond comprehension
pedestrian (adj.)	commonplace, trite, unremarkable, quotidian
pied (adj.)	multicolored, usually in blotches
pine (verb)	to lose vigor (as through grief); to yearn
plastic (adj.)	moldable, pliable, not rigid
pluck (noun)	courage, spunk, fortitude
prize (verb)	to pry, to press or force with a lever; something taken by force, spoils
rail (verb)	to complain about bitterly

rent (verb)	torn (past tense of *rend*); an opening or tear caused by such
quail (verb)	to lose courage; to turn frightened
qualify (verb)	to limit
sap (verb)	to enervate or weaken the vitality of
sap (noun)	a fool or nitwit
scurvy (adj.)	contemptible, despicable
singular (adj.)	exceptional, unusual, odd
stand (noun)	a group of trees
steep (verb)	to saturate or completely soak, as in to let a tea bag steep
strut (noun)	the supporting structural cross-part of a wing
table (verb)	to remove (as a parliamentary motion) from consideration
tender (verb)	to proffer or offer
waffle (verb)	to equivocate; to change one's position
wag (noun)	wit, joker

Beyond the Key Terms Group 2

abjure (verb)	to renounce or reject solemnly; to recant; to avoid
adumbrate (verb)	to foreshadow vaguely or intimate; to suggest or outline sketchily; to obscure or overshadow
anathema (noun)	a solemn or ecclesiastical (religious) curse; accursed or thoroughly loathed person or thing
anodyne (adj.)/(noun)	soothing; something that assuages or allays pain or comforts
apogee (noun)	farthest or highest point; culmination; zenith
apostate (noun)	one who abandons long-held religious or political convictions
apotheosis (noun)	deification; glorification to godliness; an exalted example; a model of excellence or perfection
asperity (noun)	severity, rigor; roughness, harshness; acrimony, irritability
asseverate (verb)	to aver, allege, or assert
assiduous (adj.)	diligent, hard-working, sedulous
augury (noun)	omen, portent
bellicose (adj.)	belligerent, pugnacious, warlike

calumniate (verb)	to slander, to make a false accusation; *calumny* means slander, aspersion
captious (adj.)	disposed to point out trivial faults; calculated to confuse or entrap in argument
cavil (verb)	to find fault without good reason
celerity (noun)	speed, alacrity; think *accelerate*
chimera (noun)	an illusion; originally, an imaginary fire-breathing she-monster
contumacious (adj.)	insubordinate, rebellious; *contumely* means insult, scorn, aspersion
debacle (noun)	rout, fiasco, complete failure
denouement (noun)	an outcome or solution; the unraveling of a plot
descry (verb)	to catch sight of
desuetude (noun)	disuse
desultory (adj.)	random; aimless; marked by a lack of plan or purpose
diaphanous (adj.)	transparent, gauzy
diffident (adj.)	reserved, shy, unassuming; lacking in self-confidence
dirge (noun)	a song of grief or lamentation
encomium (noun)	glowing and enthusiastic praise; panegyric, tribute, eulogy
eschew (verb)	to shun or avoid
excoriate (verb)	to censure scathingly, to upbraid
execrate (verb)	to denounce, to feel loathing for, to curse, to declare to be evil
exegesis (noun)	critical examination, explication
expiate (verb)	to atone or make amends for
extirpate (verb)	to destroy, to exterminate, to cut out, to exscind
fatuous (adj.)	silly, inanely foolish
fractious (adj.)	quarrelsome, rebellious, unruly, refractory, irritable
gainsay (verb)	to deny, to dispute, to contradict, to oppose
heterodox (adj.)	unorthodox, heretical, iconoclastic
imbroglio (noun)	difficult or embarrassing situation
indefatigable (adj.)	not easily exhaustible; tireless, dogged
ineluctable (adj.)	certain, inevitable
inimitable (adj.)	one of a kind, peerless

insouciant (adj.)	unconcerned, carefree, heedless
inveterate (adj.)	deep rooted, ingrained, habitual
jejune (adj.)	vapid, uninteresting, nugatory; childish, immature, puerile
lubricious (adj.)	lewd, wanton, greasy, slippery
mendicant (noun)	a beggar, supplicant
meretricious (adj.)	cheap, gaudy, tawdry, flashy, showy; attracting by false show
minatory (adj.)	menacing, threatening (reminds you of the Minotaur, a threatening creature indeed)
nadir (noun)	low point, perigee
nonplussed (adj.)	baffled, bewildered, at a loss for what to do or think
obstreperous (adj.)	noisily and stubbornly defiant, aggressively boisterous
ossified (adj.)	tending to become more rigid, conventional, sterile, and reactionary with age; literally, turned into bone
palliate (verb)	to make something seem less serious, to gloss over, to make less severe or intense
panegyric (noun)	formal praise, eulogy, encomium; *panegyrical* means expressing elaborate praise
parsimonious (adj.)	cheap, miserly
pellucid (adj.)	transparent, easy to understand, limpid
peroration (noun)	the concluding part of a speech; flowery, rhetorical speech
plangent (adj.)	pounding, thundering, resounding
prolix (adj.)	long-winded, verbose; *prolixity* means verbosity
propitiate (verb)	to appease; to conciliate; *propitious* means auspicious, favorable
puerile (adj.)	childish, immature, jejune, nugatory
puissance (noun)	power, strength; *puissant* means powerful, strong
pusillanimous (adj.)	cowardly, craven
remonstrate (verb)	to protest, to object
sagacious (adj.)	having sound judgment; perceptive, wise; like a sage
salacious (adj.)	lustful, lascivious, bawdy
salutary (adj.)	remedial, wholesome, causing improvement
sanguine (adj.)	cheerful, confident, optimistic
saturnine (adj.)	gloomy, dark, sullen, morose

sententious (adj.)	aphoristic or moralistic; epigrammatic; tending to moralize excessively
stentorian (adj.)	extremely loud and powerful
stygian (adj.)	gloomy, dark
sycophant (noun)	toady, servile, self-seeking flatterer; parasite
tendentious (adj.)	biased; showing marked tendencies
timorous (adj.)	timid, fearful, diffident
tyro (noun)	novice, greenhorn, rank amateur
vitiate (verb)	to corrupt, to debase, to spoil, to make ineffective
voluble (adj.)	fluent, verbal, having easy use of spoken language

Part III
How to Crack the Math Section

Chapter 9
The Geography of
the Math Section

This chapter contains an overview of the content and structure you'll see on the Math section of the GRE. It provides valuable information on pacing strategies and the various question formats you'll encounter on the GRE. It also goes over how to use basic test-taking techniques such as Process of Elimination and Ballparking as they relate to math questions. After finishing this chapter, you'll have a good idea of what the Math section of the GRE looks like and some basic approaches to help you navigate it.

WHAT'S IN THE MATH SECTION

The GRE Math section primarily tests math concepts you learned in seventh through tenth grades, including arithmetic, algebra, and geometry. ETS alleges that the Math section tests the reasoning skills that you'll use in graduate school, but what the Math section primarily tests is your comfort level with some basic math topics and your ability to take a test with strange-looking questions under timed conditions.

The Math section of the exam consists of two 35-minute sections, each of which will consist of 20 questions. The first 7 or 8 questions of each section will be *quantitative comparisons* (quant comp, for short). The remainder will consist of multiple-choice or numeric-entry questions.

Junior High School?

The Math section of the GRE mostly tests how much you remember from the math courses you took in seventh, eighth, ninth, and tenth grades. But here's some good news: GRE math is easier than SAT math. Why? Because many people study little or no math in college. If the GRE tested college-level math, everyone but math majors would bomb the test.

If you're willing to do a little work, this is good news for you. By brushing up on the modest amount of math you need to know for the test, you can significantly increase your GRE Math score. All you have to do is shake off the dust.

Predictable Questions

The beauty of a standardized test is that it is, well, standardized. Standardized means predictable. We know exactly what ETS is going to test and how they're going to test it. The math side of the test consists of a series of utterly predictable questions, to which we have designed a series of highly scripted responses. ETS wants you to see each problem as a new challenge to solve. What you will find, however, is that there are only about 20 math concepts that are being tested. All of the questions you will see are just different ways of asking about these different concepts. Most of these concepts you already know. Once you recognize what's being tested, even the trickiest questions become familiar and easy to solve.

It's Really a Reading Test

Head to your Premium Portal to watch top-notch Princeton Review instructors talk about the GRE Math section and walk you through sample problems.

In constructing the Math section, ETS is limited to the math that nearly everyone has studied: arithmetic, basic algebra, basic geometry, and elementary statistics. There's no calculus (or even precalculus), no trigonometry, and no major-league algebra or geometry. Because of these limitations, ETS has to resort to traps in order to create hard problems. Even the most commonly missed GRE math problems are typically based on relatively simple principles. What makes the problems difficult is that these simple principles are disguised.

Many test takers have no problem doing the actual calculations involved in the math questions on the GRE; in fact, you'll even be allowed to use a calculator (more on that soon). However, on this test your ability to carefully read the problems and figure out how to set them up is more important than your ability to make calculations.

As you work through this section, don't worry about how quickly you're doing the problems. Instead, take the time to really understand what the questions are asking; pay close attention to the wording of the problems. Most math errors are the result of careless mistakes caused by not reading the problem carefully enough!

Read and Copy Carefully

You can do all the calculations right and still get a question wrong. How? What if you solve for x but the question asked for the value of $x + 4$? Ugh. Always reread the question before you choose an answer. Take your time and don't be careless. The problem will stay on the screen as long as you want it to, so reread the question and double-check your work before answering it.

Or how about this? The radius of the circle is 5, but when you copied the picture onto your scratch paper, you accidentally made it 6. Ugh! If you make a mistake copying down information from the screen, you'll get the question wrong no matter how perfect your calculations are. You have to be extra careful when copying down information.

THE CALCULATOR

As we mentioned before, on the GRE you'll be given an on-screen calculator. The calculator program on the GRE is a rudimentary one that gives you the five basic operations: addition, subtraction, multiplication, division, and square root, plus a decimal function and a positive/negative feature. It follows the order of operations, or PEMDAS (more on this topic in Chapter 10). The calculator also has the ability to transfer the answer you've calculated directly into the answer box for certain questions. The on-screen calculator can be a huge advantage—if it's used correctly!

As you might have realized by this point, ETS is not exactly looking out for your best interests. Giving you a calculator might seem like an altruistic act, but rest assured that ETS knows that there are certain ways in which calculator use can be exploited. Keep in mind the following:

1. **Calculators Can't Think**. Calculators are good for one thing and one thing only: calculation. You still have to figure out how to set up the problem correctly. If you're not sure what to calculate, then a calculator isn't helpful. For example, if you do a percent calculation on your calculator and then hit "Transfer Display," you will have to remember to move the decimal point accordingly, depending on whether the question asks for a percent or a decimal.

2. **The Calculator Can Be a Liability**. ETS will give you questions that you can solve with a calculator, but the calculator can actually be a liability. You will be tempted to use it. For example, students who are uncomfortable adding, subtracting, multiplying, or dividing fractions may be tempted to convert all fractions to decimals using the calculator. Don't do it. You are better off mastering fractions than avoiding them.

Working with exponents and square roots is another way in which the calculator will be tempting but may yield really big and awkward numbers or long decimals. You are much better off learning the rules of manipulating exponents and square roots. Most of these problems will be faster and cleaner to solve with rules than with a calculator. The questions may also use numbers that are too big for the calculator. Time spent trying to get an answer out of a calculator for problems involving really big numbers will be time wasted. Find another way around.

3. **A Calculator Won't Make You Faster.** Having a calculator should make you more accurate, but not necessarily faster. You still need to take time to read each problem carefully and set it up. Don't expect to blast through problems just because you have a calculator.

4. **The Calculator Is No Excuse for Not Using Scratch Paper.** Scratch paper is where good technique happens. Working problems by hand on scratch paper will help to avoid careless errors or skipped steps. Just because you can do multiple functions in a row on your calculator does not mean that you should be solving problems on your calculator. Use the calculator to do simple calculations that would otherwise take you time to solve. Make sure you are still writing steps out on your scratch paper, labeling results, and using set-ups. Accuracy is more important than speed!

Of course, you should not fear the calculator; by all means, use it and be grateful for it. Having a calculator should help you eliminate all those careless math mistakes.

GEOGRAPHY OF A MATH SECTION

Each of the two Math sections contains 20 questions. Test takers are allowed 35 minutes per section. The first 7 or 8 questions of each Math section are quantitative comparisons, while the remainder are a mixed bag of problem solving, all that apply, numeric entry, and charts and graphs. Each section covers a mixture of algebra, arithmetic, quantitative reasoning, geometry, and real-world math.

QUESTION FORMATS

Much like the Verbal section, the Math portion of the GRE contains a variety of different question formats. Let's go through each type of question and discuss how to crack it.

Standard Multiple Choice

These questions are the basic five-answer multiple-choice questions. These are great candidates for POE (Process of Elimination) strategies we will discuss later in this chapter.

Multiple Choice, Multiple Answer

These questions appear similar to the standard multiple-choice questions; however, on these you will have the opportunity to pick more than one answer. There can be anywhere from three to eight answer choices. Here's an example of what these will look like:

If $\frac{1}{12} < x < \frac{1}{6}$, then which of the following could be the value of x ?

Indicate all such values.

A □ $\frac{2}{9}$

B □ $\frac{1}{5}$

C □ $\frac{2}{15}$

D □ $\frac{1}{10}$

E □ $\frac{2}{25}$

Your approach on these questions won't be radically different from the approach you use on standard multiple-choice questions. But obviously, you'll have to consider all of the answers—make sure you read each question carefully and remember that more than one answer can be correct. For example, for this question, you'd click on (C) and (D). You must select *every* correct choice to get credit for the problem.

Quantitative Comparison Questions

Quantitative comparison questions, hereafter affectionately known as "quant comp" questions, ask you to compare Quantity A to Quantity B. These questions have four answer choices instead of five, and all quant comp answer choices are the same. Here they are:

- ○ Quantity A is greater.
- ○ Quantity B is greater.
- ○ The two quantities are equal.
- ○ The relationship cannot be determined from the information given.

Your job is to compare the two quantities and choose one of these answers.

Quant comp problems test the same basic arithmetic, algebra, and geometry concepts as do the other GRE math problems. So, to solve these problems, you'll apply the same techniques you use on the other GRE math questions. But quant comps also have a few special rules you need to remember.

There Is No "(E)"

Because there are only four choices on quant comp questions, after you use POE to eliminate all of the answer choices you can, your odds of guessing correctly are even better. Think about it this way: Eliminating even one answer on a quant comp question will give you a one-in-three chance of guessing correctly.

If a Quant Comp Question Contains Only Numbers, the Answer Can't Be (D)

Any quant comp problem that contains only numbers and no variables must have a single solution. Therefore, on these problems, you can eliminate (D) immediately because the larger quantity can be determined. For example, if you're asked to compare $\frac{3}{2}$ and $\frac{3}{4}$, you can determine which fraction is larger, so the answer cannot be (D).

Compare, Don't Calculate

Do only as much work as you need to.

You don't always have to calculate the exact value of each quantity before you compare them. After all, your mission is simply to compare the two quantities. It's often helpful to treat the two quantities as though they were two sides of an equation. Anything you can do to both sides of an equation, you can also do to both quantities. You can add the same number to both sides, you can multiply both sides by the same positive number, and you can simplify a single side by multiplying it by one.

If you can simplify the terms of a quant comp, you should always do so.

Here's a quick example:

---------------○---------------

Quantity A	Quantity B
$\dfrac{1}{16} + \dfrac{1}{7} + \dfrac{1}{4}$	$\dfrac{1}{4} + \dfrac{1}{16} + \dfrac{1}{6}$

○ Quantity A is greater.

○ Quantity B is greater.

○ The two quantities are equal.

○ The relationship cannot be determined from the information given.

Here's How to Crack It

Don't do any calculating! Remember: Do only as much work as you need to in order to answer the question! The first thing you should do is eliminate (D). After all, there are only numbers here. After that, get rid of numbers that are common to both columns (think of this as simplifying). Both columns contain a $\dfrac{1}{16}$ and a $\dfrac{1}{4}$, so because we're talking about addition, they can't make a difference to the outcome. With them gone, you're merely comparing the $\dfrac{1}{7}$ in column A to the $\dfrac{1}{6}$ in column B. Now we can eliminate (C) as well—after all, there is no way that $\dfrac{1}{7}$ is equal to $\dfrac{1}{6}$. So, we're down to two choices, (A) and (B). If you don't remember how to compare fractions, don't worry—it's covered in Chapter 10 (Math Fundamentals). The answer to this question is (B).

---------------○---------------

Okay, let's talk about another wacky question type you'll see in the Math section.

Numeric Entry

Some questions on the GRE won't even have answer choices, and you'll have to generate your own answer. Here's an example:

Each month, Renaldo earns a commission of 10.5% of his total sales for the month, plus a salary of $2,500. If Renaldo earns $3,025 in a certain month, what were his total sales?

Click on the answer box and type in a number. Backspace to erase.

Here's How to Crack It

On this type of question, POE is not going to help you! That means if you're not sure how to do one of these questions, you should immediately move on. Leave it blank and come back to it in your second pass through the test.

If Renaldo earned $3,025, then his earnings from the commission on his sales are $3,025 – $2,500 = $525. So, $525 is 10.5% of his sales. Set up an equation to find the total sales: $525 = \frac{10.5}{100}x$, where x is the amount of the sales. Solving this equation, $x = 5,000$. (We'll review how to set up and solve equations like this in later chapters.)

To answer this question, you'd enter 5000 into the box. Alternately, you could transfer your work directly from the on-screen calculator to the text box.

MAXIMIZE YOUR SCORE

As you're probably aware by now, doing well on the Math section will involve more than just knowing some math. It will also require the use of some good strategies. Let's go through some good strategies now. Make sure you read this section carefully; it will be important for you to keep these techniques in mind as you work through the content chapters that follow this one!

The Two Roles of Techniques

The techniques are there to ensure that the questions that you should get right, you do get right. A couple of careless errors on easy questions will kill your score. The techniques are not just tools; they are proven standard approaches that save time and effort and guarantee points. Use these techniques on every question. Turn them into habits that you use every time.

Take the Easy Test First

The GRE offers the opportunity to mark a question and return to it. Since all questions count equally toward your score, why not do the easy ones first? Getting questions right is far more important than getting to every question, so start with the low hanging fruit. There is no law that says you have to take the test in the order in which it is given. If you see a question you don't like, keep moving. Play to your strengths and get all of the questions that you're good at in the bank, before you start spending time on the hard ones. It makes no sense to spend valuable minutes wrestling with hard questions while there are still easy ones on the table. It makes even less sense if you end up having to rush some easy ones (making mistakes in the process), as a result. Free yourself from numerical hegemony! Take the easy test first!

Bend, Don't Push

Eighty percent of the errors on the math side of the test are really reading errors. The GRE is nearly a four-hour-long test, so at some point during this time your brain will get tired. When this happens you will read, see, or understand questions incorrectly. Once you see a problem wrong, it is nearly impossible to see it correctly. When this happens, even simple problems can become extremely frustrating. If you solve a problem and your answer is not one of the choices, this is what has happened. When you would swear that a problem can't be solved, this is what has happened. When you have absolutely no idea how to solve a problem, this is what has happened. If you find yourself with half a page full of calculations and are no closer to the answer, this is what has happened. When you find yourself in this scenario, you can continue to push on that problem all day and you won't get any closer.

There is a good chance that you are already familiar with this frustration. The first step is to learn to recognize it when it is happening. Here are some keys to recognizing when you are off track.

You know you are off track when...

- You have spent more than three minutes on a single problem.
- Your hand is not moving.
- You don't know what to do next.
- Your answer is not one of the choices.
- You're spending lots of time with the calculator and working with some ugly numbers.

Once you recognize that you are off track, stop and take a deep breath. Then move on to the next question. Continuing to push on a problem, at this point, is a waste of your time. You could easily spend three or four precious minutes on this problem and be no closer to the answer. Spend those three or four minutes on other questions. That time should be yielding you points, not frustration.

After you have done two or three other questions, return to the one that was giving you trouble. Most likely, the reason it was giving you trouble is that you missed something or misread something the first time around. If the problem is still difficult, walk away again.

This is called Bend, Don't Push. The minute you encounter any resistance on the test, walk away. Bend. There are plenty of other easier points for you to get with that time. Then return to the problem a few questions later. It's okay to take two or three runs at a tough problem. If you run out of time before returning to the question, so be it. Your time is better spent on easier problems anyway, since all problems count the same.

Forcing yourself to walk away can be difficult, especially when you have already invested time in a question. You will have to train yourself to recognize resistance when it occurs, to walk away, and then to remember to come back. Employ this technique anytime you are practicing for the GRE. It will take some time to master. Be patient and give it a chance to work. With this technique, there are no questions that are out of your reach on the GRE.

POE: Ballparking and Trap Answers

Use Process of Elimination whenever you can on questions that are in standard multiple-choice format. Always read the answer choices before you start to solve a math problem because often they will help guide you—you might even be able to eliminate a couple of answer choices before you begin to calculate the answer.

Two effective POE tools are Ballparking and Trap Answers.

You Know More Than You Think

Say you were asked to find 30 percent of 50. Wait—don't do any math yet. Let's say that you glance at the answer choices and you see these:

- ○ 5
- ○ 15
- ○ 30
- ○ 80
- ○ 150

Think about it. Whatever 30 percent of 50 is, it must be less than 50, right? So any answer choice that's greater than 50 can't be right. That means you should eliminate both (D) and (E) before you even do any calculations! Thirty percent is less than half, so we can get rid of anything greater than 25, which means that (C) is gone too. What is 10 percent of 50? Eliminate (A). You're done. The only answer left is (B). This process is known as Ballparking. Remember that the answers are part of the question. There are more than four times the number of wrong answers on the GRE as there are right ones. If it were easy to find the right ones, you wouldn't need this book. It is almost always easier to identify and eliminate the wrong answers than it is to calculate the right one. Just make sure that you are using your scratch paper to eliminate answer choices instead of keeping track in your head.

Ballparking helps you eliminate answer choices and increases your odds of zeroing in on the correct answer. The key is to eliminate any answer choice that is "out of the ballpark."

Let's look at another problem:

A 100-foot rope is cut so that the shorter piece is $\frac{2}{3}$ the length of the longer piece. What is the length of the shorter piece in feet?

- ○ 75
- ○ $66\frac{2}{3}$
- ○ 50
- ○ 40
- ○ $33\frac{1}{3}$

Need More Math Review?

Check out *Math Workout for the GRE* for even more math practice.

Here's How to Crack It

Now, before we dive into the calculations, let's use a little common sense. The rope is 100 feet long. If we cut the rope in half, each part would be 50 feet. However, we didn't cut the rope in half; we cut it so that there's a longer part and a shorter part. What has to be true of the shorter piece then? It has to be less than 50 feet. If it weren't, it wouldn't be shorter than the other piece. So looking at our answers, we can eliminate (A), (B), and (C) without doing any real math. That's Ballparking. By the way, the answer is (D).

Trap Answers

ETS likes to include "trap answers" in the answer choices to their math problems. Trap answers are answer choices that appear correct upon first glance. Often these answers will look so tempting that you'll choose them without actually bothering to complete the necessary calculations. Watch out for this! If a problem seems way too easy, be careful and double-check your work.

Look at the this problem:

The price of a jacket is reduced by 10%. During a special sale, the price is discounted by another 10%. The special sale price is what percent less than the original price of the jacket?

- ○ 15%
- ○ 19%
- ○ 20%
- ○ 21%
- ○ 25%

Here's How to Crack It

The answer might seem like it should be 20 percent. But wait a minute: Does it seem likely that the GRE is going to give you a problem that you can solve just by adding 10 + 10? Probably not. Choice (C) is a trap answer.

To solve this problem, imagine that the original price of the jacket is $100. After a 10 percent discount the new price is $90. But now when we take another 10 percent discount, we're taking it from $90, not $100. 10 percent of 90 is 9, so we take off another $9 from the price and our final price is $81. That represents a 19 percent total discount because we started with a $100 jacket. The correct answer is (B).

HOW TO STUDY

Make sure you learn the content of each of the following chapters before you go on to the next one. Don't try to cram everything in all at once. It's much better to do a small amount of studying each day over a longer period; you will master both the math concepts and the techniques if you focus on the material a little bit at a time. Just as we have been telling you in earlier chapters, let the content sink in by taking short study breaks between study sessions and giving yourself plenty of time to prepare for the GRE. Slow and steady wins the race!

Practice, Practice, Practice

Practice may not make perfect, but it sure will help. Use everyday math calculations as practice opportunities. Balance your checkbook without a calculator! Make sure your check has been added correctly at a restaurant, and figure out the exact percentage you want to leave for a tip. The more you practice simple adding, subtracting, multiplying, and dividing on a day-to-day basis, the more your arithmetic skills will improve for the GRE.

After you work through this book, be sure to practice doing questions on our online tests and on real GREs. There are always sample questions at **www.ets.org/ gre**, and practice will rapidly sharpen your test-taking skills.

Finally, unless you trust our techniques, you may be reluctant to use them fully and automatically on the real GRE. The best way to develop that trust is to practice before you get to the real test.

Your Premium Portal contains tons of informational videos, practice tests, helpful articles, and more to help with your GRE preparation. Head over there and take advantage of this fantastic resource!

Summary

- The GRE contains two 35-minute Math sections. Each section has 20 questions.

- The GRE tests math concepts up to about the tenth-grade level of difficulty.

- You will be allowed to use a calculator on the GRE. The calculator is part of the on-screen display.

- The Math section employs a number of different question formats, including multiple choice, numeric entry, and quantitative comparison questions.

- Use the Two-Pass system on the Math section. Find the easier questions and do them first. Use your remaining time to work some of the more difficult questions.

- When you get stuck on a problem, walk away. Do a few other problems to distract your brain, and then return to the question that was giving you problems.

- Ballpark or estimate the answers to math questions and eliminate answers that don't make sense.

- Watch out for trap answers. If an answer seems too easy or obvious, it's probably a trap.

- Always do your work on your scratch paper, not in your head. Even when you are Ballparking, make sure that you are eliminating answer choices on your scratch paper. If your hand isn't moving, you're stuck and you need to walk away, or you're doing work in your head, which leads to errors.

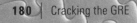

Chapter 10
Math Fundamentals

Numbers and equations form the basis of all the math questions on the GRE. Simply put, the more comfortable you are working with numbers and equations, the easier the math portion of the exam will be. This chapter gives you a review of all the basic mathematical concepts including properties of numbers, factors and multiples, fractions and decimals, math vocabulary, and some basic rules of math.

GET FAMILIAR

To do well on the GRE Math section, you'll have to be comfortable working with numbers. The concepts tested on the GRE are not exceptionally difficult, but if you are even the least bit skittish about numbers you'll have a harder time working the problems.

This chapter will familiarize you with all the basics you need to know about numbers and how to work with them. If you're an arithmophobe or haven't used math in a while, take it slowly and make sure you're comfortable with this chapter before moving onto the succeeding ones.

GRE MATH VOCABULARY

Quick—what's an integer? Is 0 even or odd? How many even prime numbers are there?

Before we go through our techniques for specific types of math problems, we'll acquaint ourselves with some basic vocabulary and properties of numbers. The GRE loves to test your knowledge of integers, fractions, decimals, and all those other concepts you probably learned years ago. Make sure you're comfortable with the topics in this chapter before moving on. Even if you feel fairly at ease with number concepts, you should still work through this chapter. ETS is very good at coming up with questions that require you to know ideas forwards and backwards.

The math terms we will review in this section are very simple, but that doesn't mean they're not important. Every GRE math question uses simple terms, rules, and definitions. You absolutely need to know this math "vocabulary." Don't worry; we will cover only the math terms that you *must* know for the GRE.

Digits

Digit refers to the numbers that make up other numbers. There are 10 digits: 0, 1, 2, 3, 4, 5, 6, 7, 8, 9, and every number is made up of one or more digits. For example, the number 10,897 has five digits: 1, 0, 8, 9, and 7. Each of the digits in a number has its own name, which is designated by a place value. In the number 10,897

- 7 is the ones or units digit.
- 9 is the tens digit.
- 8 is the hundreds digit.
- 0 is the thousands digit.
- 1 is the ten-thousands digit.

Numbers

A **number** is made up of either a digit or a collection of digits. There are, of course, an infinite number of numbers. Basically, any combination of digits you can imagine is a number, which includes 0, negative numbers, fractions and decimals, and even weird numbers such as $\sqrt{2}$.

GRE problems like to try to trip you up on the difference between a number and an integer.

Integers

The **integers** are the numbers that have no fractional or decimal part, such as –6, –5, –4, –3, –2, –1, 0, 1, 2, 3, 4, 5, 6, and so on.

Notice that fractions, such as $\frac{1}{2}$, are not integers.

Remember that the number zero is an integer! The values of positive integers increase as they move away from 0 (6 is greater than 5); the values of negative integers decrease as they move away from zero (–6 is less than –5).

Remember: Fractions are NOT integers.

PROPERTIES OF NUMBERS AND INTEGERS

Now that you've learned the proper names for various types of numbers, let's look at properties of numbers and integers.

Positive or Negative

Numbers can be positive or negative. Negative numbers are less than zero, while positive numbers are greater than zero. Zero itself is neither positive nor negative—all other numbers are either positive or negative.

Even or Odd

Only integers possess the property of being even or odd. Fractions, decimals, and other non-integers cannot be described as even or odd. Integers that are even are those that are divisible by 2; odd integers are those integers that are not divisible by 2. Put another way, even integers have a remainder of 0 when divided by 2 while odd integers have a remainder of 1 when divided by 2.

- Here are some even integers: –4, –2, 0, 2, 4, 6, 8, 10.
- Here are some odd integers: –3, –1, 1, 3, 5, 7, 9, 11.

Zero

Zero is a special little number. It is an integer, but it is neither positive nor negative. However, try to remember these facts about zero:

- 0 is even.
- 0 plus any other number is equal to that other number.
- 0 multiplied by any other number is equal to 0.
- You cannot divide by 0.

Zero has a number of special properties that are tested frequently on the GRE. Technically, zero is a multiple of every number, but this fact is rarely tested on the GRE.

Keep in Mind

- Fractions are neither even nor odd.
- Any integer is even if its units digit is even; any integer is odd if its units digit is odd.
- The results of adding and multiplying odd and even integers are as follows:
  - even + even = even
  - odd + odd = even
  - even + odd = odd
  - even × even = even
  - odd × odd = odd
  - even × odd = even

Be careful: Don't confuse odd and even with positive and negative!

If you have trouble remembering some of these rules for odd and even, don't worry. As long as you remember that there are rules, you can always figure them out by plugging in numbers. Let's say you forget what happens when an odd number is multiplied by an odd number. Just pick two odd numbers, say 3 and 5, and multiply them. $3 \times 5 = 15$. Now you know: odd × odd = odd.

Consecutive Integers

Consecutive integers are integers listed in order of value without any integers missing in between them. Here are some examples:

- 0, 1, 2, 3, 4, 5
- −6, −5, −4, −3, −2, −1, 0
- −3, −2, −1, 0, 1, 2, 3

By the way, fractions and decimals cannot be consecutive, only integers can be consecutive. However, you can have different types of consecutive integers. For example consecutive even integers could be 2, 4, 6, 8, 10. Consecutive multiples of four could be 4, 8, 12, 16.

Absolute Value

The **absolute value** of a number is equal to its distance from 0 on the number line, which means that the absolute value of any number is always positive, whether the number itself is positive or negative. The symbol for absolute value is a set of double lines: | |. Thus $|-5| = 5$, and $|5| = 5$ because both −5 and 5 are a distance of 5 from 0 on the number line.

FACTORS, MULTIPLES, AND DIVISIBILITY

Now let's look at some ways that integers are related to each other.

Factors

A **factor** of a particular integer is a number that will divide evenly into the integer in question. For example, 1, 2, 3, 4, 6, and 12 are all factors of 12 because each number divides evenly into 12. In order to find all the factors of a particular integer, write down the factors systematically in pairs of integers that, when multiplied together, make 12, starting with 1 and the integer itself:

- 1 and 12
- 2 and 6
- 3 and 4

If you always start with 1 and the integer itself and work your way up, you'll make sure you get them all.

Multiples

The **multiples** of an integer are all the integers for which the original integer is a factor. For example, the multiples of 8 are all the integers of which 8 is a factor: 8, 16, 24, 32, 40, and so on. Note that there are an infinite number of multiples for any given number. Also, zero is a multiple of every number, although this concept is rarely tested on the GRE.

There are only a few factors of any number; there are many multiples of any number.

Prime Numbers

A **prime number** is an integer that only has two factors: itself and one. Thus, 37 is prime because the only integers that divide evenly into it are 1 and 37, while 10 is not prime because its factors are 1, 2, 5, and 10.

Here is a list of all the prime numbers that are less than 30: 2, 3, 5, 7, 11, 13, 17, 19, 23, 29.

Here are some other facts about primes that are important to remember:

- 0 is not a prime number.
- 1 is not a prime number.
- 2 is the only even prime number.
- Prime numbers are positive integers. There's no such thing as a negative prime number or a prime fraction.

1 is not prime!

Divisibility

An integer is always divisible by its factors. If you're not sure if one integer is divisible by another, a surefire way to find out is to use the calculator. However, there are also certain rules you can use to determine whether one integer is a factor of another.

- An integer is divisible by 2 if its units digit is divisible by 2. For example, we know just by glancing at it that 598,447,896 is divisible by 2, because the units digit, 6, is divisible by 2.
- An integer is divisible by 3 if the sum of its digits is divisible by 3. For example, we know that 2,145 is divisible by 3 because 2 + 1 + 4 + 5 = 12, and 12 is divisible by 3.
- An integer is divisible by 4 if its last two digits form a number that's divisible by 4. For example, 712 is divisible by 4 because 12 is divisible by 4.
- An integer is divisible by 5 if its units digit is either 0 or 5. For example, 23,645 is divisible by 5 because its units digit is 5.
- An integer is divisible by 6 if it's divisible by both 2 and 3. For example, 4,290 is divisible by 6 because it is divisible by 2 (it's even) and by 3 (4 + 2 + 9 = 15, which is divisible by 3).
- An integer is divisible by 8 if its last three digits form a number that's divisible by 8. For example, 11,640 is divisible by 8 because 640 is divisible by 8.
- An integer is divisible by 9 if the sum of its digits is divisible by 9. For example, 1,881 is divisible by 9 because 1 + 8 + 8 + 1 = 18, which is divisible by 9.
- An integer is divisible by 10 if its units digit is 0. For example, 1,590 is divisible by 10 because its units digit is 0.

Remainders

If one integer is not divisible by another—meaning that the second integer is not a factor of the first number—you'll have an integer left over when you divide. This left-over integer is called a **remainder**; you probably remember working with remainders in grade school.

If a question asks about a remainder, don't use the calculator. Use long division.

For example, when 4 is divided by 2, there's nothing left over so there's no remainder. In other words, 4 is divisible by 2. You could also say that the remainder is 0.

On the other hand, 5 divided by 2 is 2, with 1 left over; 1 is the remainder. Thirteen divided by 8 is 1, with 5 left over as the remainder.

Note that remainders are always less than the number that you are dividing by. For example, the remainder when 13 is divided by 7 is 6. What happens if you divide 14, the next integer, by 7? The remainder is 0.

Here's one more thing to know about remainders. What's the remainder when 5 is divided by 6? The remainder is 5 because 5 can be divided by 6 zero times and the amount that remains is 5. When the positive integer you are dividing by is greater than the integer being divided, the remainder will always be the number being divided.

MORE MATH VOCABULARY

In a way, the Math section is almost as much of a vocabulary test as the Verbal section. Below, you'll find some more standard terms that you should commit to memory before you do any practice problems.

Term	Meaning
sum	the result of addition
difference	the result of subtraction
product	the result of multiplication
quotient	the result of division
divisor	the number you divide by
numerator	the top number in a fraction
denominator	the bottom number in a fraction
consecutive	in order from least to greatest
terms	the numbers and expressions used in an equation

BASIC OPERATIONS WITH NUMBERS

Now that you've learned about numbers and their properties, you're ready to begin working with them. As we mentioned above, there are four basic operations you can perform on a number: addition, subtraction, multiplication, and division.

Order of Operations

When you work with numbers you can't just perform the four operations in any way you please. Instead, there are some very specific rules to follow, which are commonly referred to as the **order of operations.**

It is absolutely necessary that you perform these operations in exactly the right order. In many cases, the correct order will be apparent from the way the problem is written. In cases in which the correct order is not apparent, you need to remember the following mnemonic.

> Please Excuse My Dear Aunt Sally, or **PEMDAS.**

What does PEMDAS stand for?

$$P \mid E \mid \underset{\rightarrow}{MD} \mid \underset{\rightarrow}{AS}$$

P stands for "parentheses." Solve anything in parentheses first.

E stands for "exponents." Solve exponents next. (We'll review exponents soon.)

M stands for "multiplication" and **D** stands for "division." The arrow indicates that you do all the multiplication and division together in the same step, going from left to right.

A stands for "addition" and **S** stands for "subtraction." Again, the arrow indicates that you do all the addition and subtraction together in one step, from left to right.

Let's look at an example:

---○---

$$12 + 4(2 + 1)^2 \div 6 - 7 =$$

Here's How to Crack It

Start by doing all the math inside the parentheses. 2 + 1 = 3. Now the problem looks like this:

$$12 + 4(3)^2 \div 6 - 7 =$$

Next we have to apply the exponent. $3^2 = 9$. Now this is what we have:

$$12 + 4(9) \div 6 - 7 =$$

Now we do multiplication and division from left to right. 4 × 9 = 36, and 36 ÷ 6 = 6, which gives us

$$12 + 6 - 7 =$$

Finally, we do the addition and subtraction from left to right. 12 + 6 = 18, and 18 − 7 = 11. Therefore,

$$12 + 4(2 + 1)^2 \div 6 - 7 = 11$$

---○---

Multiplication and Division

When multiplying or dividing, keep the following rules in mind:

- positive × positive = positive   2 × 2 = 4
- negative × negative = positive   −2 × −2 = 4
- positive × negative = negative   2 × −2 = −4
- positive ÷ positive = positive   8 ÷ 2 = 4
- negative ÷ negative = positive   −8 ÷ −2 = 4
- positive ÷ negative = negative   8 ÷ −2 = −4

Before taking the GRE, you should have your times tables memorized from 1 through 15. It will be a tremendous advantage if you can quickly and confidently recall that 7 × 12 = 84, for example.

It seems like a small thing, but memorizing your times tables will really help you on test day.

FRACTIONS, DECIMALS, AND PERCENTAGES

One of the ways ETS tests your fundamental math abilities is through Fractions, Decimals, and Percents. So let's expand our conversation on math fundamentals to include these concepts.

Fractions

A **fraction** expresses the number of parts out of a whole. In the fraction $\frac{2}{3}$, for instance, the top part, or **numerator**, tells us that we have 2 parts, while the bottom part of the fraction, the **denominator**, indicates that the whole, or total, consists of 3 parts. We use fractions whenever we're dealing with a quantity that's between two whole numbers.

Notice that the fraction bar is simply another way of expressing division. Thus, the fraction $\frac{2}{3}$ is just expressing the idea of "2 divided by 3."

Fractions are important on the GRE. Make sure you're comfortable with them.

Reducing and Expanding Fractions

Fractions express a relationship between numbers, not actual amounts. For example, saying that you did $\frac{1}{2}$ of your homework expresses the same idea whether you had 10 pages of homework to do and you've done 5 pages, or you had 50 pages to do and you've done 25 pages. This concept is important because on the GRE you'll frequently have to reduce or expand fractions.

To reduce a fraction, express the numerator and denominator as the products of their factors. Then cross out, or "cancel," factors that are common to both the numerator and denominator. Here's an example:

$$\frac{16}{20} = \frac{2 \times 2 \times 2 \times 2}{2 \times 2 \times 5} = \frac{\cancel{2} \times \cancel{2} \times 2 \times 2}{\cancel{2} \times \cancel{2} \times 5} = \frac{2 \times 2}{5} = \frac{4}{5}$$

You can achieve the same result by dividing the numerator and denominator by the factors that are common to both. In the example you just saw, you might realize that 4 is a factor of both the numerator and the denominator. That is, both the numerator and the denominator can be divided evenly (without a remainder) by 4. Doing this yields the much more manageable fraction $\frac{4}{5}$.

When you confront GRE math problems that involve fractions with great numbers, always reduce them before doing anything else.

Look at each of the following fractions:

$$\frac{1}{4} \qquad \frac{2}{8} \qquad \frac{6}{24} \qquad \frac{18}{72} \qquad \frac{90}{360} \qquad \frac{236}{944}$$

What do you notice about each of these fractions? They all express the same information! Each of these fractions expresses the relationship of "1 part out of 4 total parts."

Adding and Subtracting Fractions

Adding and subtracting fractions that have a common denominator is easy—you just add the numerators and put the sum over the common denominator. Here's an example:

$$\frac{1}{10} + \frac{2}{10} + \frac{4}{10} =$$

$$\frac{1+2+4}{10} = \frac{7}{10}$$

In order to add or subtract fractions that have different denominators, you need to start by finding a common denominator. You may remember your teachers from grade school imploring you to find the "lowest common denominator." Actually, any common denominator will do, so find whichever one you find most comfortable working with.

> **Why Bother?**
> You may be wondering why, if the GRE allows the use of a calculator, you should bother learning how to add or subtract fractions or to reduce them or even know any of the topics covered in the next few pages. While it's true that you can use a calculator for these tasks, for many problems it's actually slower to do the math with the calculator than without. Scoring well on the GRE Math section requires a fairly strong grasp of the basic relationships among numbers, fractions, percents, and so on, so it's in your best interest to really understand these concepts rather than to rely on your calculator to get you through the question. In fact, if you put in the work now, you'll be surprised at how easy some of the problems become, especially when you don't have to refer constantly to the calculator to perform basic operations.

$$\frac{7}{8} - \frac{5}{12} = \frac{21}{24} - \frac{10}{24} = \frac{11}{24}$$

Here, we expanded the fraction $\frac{7}{8}$ into the equivalent fraction $\frac{21}{24}$ by multiplying both the numerator and denominator by 3. Similarly, we converted $\frac{5}{12}$ to $\frac{10}{24}$ by multiplying both denominator and numerator by 2. This left us with two fractions that had the same denominator, which meant that we could simply subtract their numerators.

When adding and subtracting fractions, you can also use a technique we call the Bowtie. The Bowtie method accomplishes exactly what we just did in one fell swoop. To use the Bowtie, first multiply the denominators of each fraction. This gives you a common denominator. Then multiply the denominator of each fraction by the numerator of the other fraction. Take these numbers and add or subtract them—depending on what the question asks you to do—to get the numerator of the answer. Then reduce if necessary.

The Bowtie method is a convenient shortcut to use when you're adding and subtracting fractions.

$$\frac{2}{3} + \frac{3}{4} =$$

$$\frac{2}{3} \times \frac{3}{4} = \frac{8}{12} + \frac{9}{12} = \frac{17}{12}$$

and

$$\frac{2}{3} - \frac{3}{4} =$$

$$\frac{2}{3} \times \frac{3}{4} = \frac{8}{12} - \frac{9}{12} = -\frac{1}{12}$$

Multiplying Fractions

Multiplying fractions is relatively straightforward when compared to addition or subtraction. To successfully multiply fractions, multiply the first numerator by the second numerator and the first denominator by the second denominator. Here's an example:

$$\frac{4}{5} \times \frac{10}{12} = \frac{40}{60} = \frac{2}{3}$$

When multiplying fractions, you can make your life easier by reducing before you multiply. Do this once again by dividing out common factors.

$$\frac{4}{5} \times \frac{10}{12} = \frac{4}{5} \times \frac{5}{6} = \frac{20}{30} = \frac{2}{3}$$

Also remember that when you're multiplying fractions, you can even reduce diagonally; as long as you're working with a numerator and a denominator of opposite fractions, they don't have to be in the same fraction. So you end up with:

$$\frac{4}{5} \times \frac{5}{6} = \frac{2}{1} \times \frac{1}{3} = \frac{2}{3}$$

Of course, you get the same answer no matter what method you use, so attack fractions in whatever fashion you find easiest.

Multiplying fractions is a snap: Just multiply straight across, numerator times numerator and denominator times denominator.

Dividing Fractions

Dividing fractions is just like multiplying fractions, with one crucial difference: Before you multiply, you have to to find the reciprocal of the second fraction. To do this, all you need to do is flip the fraction upside down! Put the denominator on top of the numerator and then multiply just like before. In some cases, you can also reduce before you multiply. Here's an example:

$$\frac{2}{3} \div \frac{4}{5} = \frac{2}{3} \times \frac{5}{4} = \frac{1}{3} \times \frac{5}{2} = \frac{5}{6}$$

ETS tests problems that involve fractions which have numerators or denominators that are themselves fractions. These problems might look intimidating, but if you're careful, you won't have any trouble with them. All you have to do is remember what we said about a fraction being shorthand for division. Always rewrite the expression horizontally. Here's an example:

$$\frac{7}{\frac{1}{4}} = 7 \div \frac{1}{4} = \frac{7}{1} \times \frac{4}{1} = \frac{28}{1} = 28$$

Comparing Fractions

Sometimes ETS will test your ability to compare two fractions to decide which is greatest. These are typically found on quant comp questions. There are a couple of ways to accomplish this. One is to find equivalent fractions that have a common denominator. If the fraction is fairly simple this is a good strategy, but oftentimes the common denominator may be hard to find or work with.

If the denominator is hard to find or work with, you can use a variant of the Bowtie technique. In this variant, you don't have to multiply the denominators together; instead, just multiply the denominators and the numerators. The fraction with the greater product in its numerator is the greater fraction. Let's say we had to compare the following fractions:

$$\frac{3}{7} \qquad \frac{7}{12}$$

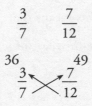

Multiplying the first denominator by the second numerator yields 49. This means the numerator of the second fraction $\left(\dfrac{7}{12}\right)$ is 49. Multiplying the second denominator by the first numerator gives you 36, which means the first fraction has a numerator of 36. Since 49 is greater than 36, $\dfrac{7}{12}$ is greater than $\dfrac{3}{7}$.

Comparing More Than Two Fractions

You may also be asked to compare more than two fractions. On these types of problems, don't waste time trying to find a common denominator for all of them. Simply use the Bowtie to compare two of the fractions at a time.

Here's an example:

Which of the following statements is true?

$\bigcirc\ \dfrac{3}{8} < \dfrac{2}{9} < \dfrac{4}{11}$

$\bigcirc\ \dfrac{2}{5} < \dfrac{3}{7} < \dfrac{4}{13}$

$\bigcirc\ \dfrac{4}{13} < \dfrac{2}{5} < \dfrac{3}{7}$

$\bigcirc\ \dfrac{3}{7} < \dfrac{3}{8} < \dfrac{2}{5}$

$\bigcirc\ \dfrac{2}{9} < \dfrac{3}{7} < \dfrac{3}{8}$

Here's How to Crack It

As you can see, it would be a nightmare to try to find common denominators for all these fractions, so instead we'll use the Bowtie method. Simply multiply the denominators and numerators of a pair of fractions and note the results. For example, to check answer choice (A), we first multiply 8 and 2, which gives us a numerator of 16 for the fraction $\dfrac{2}{9}$. But multiplying 9 and 3 gives us a numerator of 27 for the first fraction. This means that $\dfrac{3}{8}$ is greater than $\dfrac{2}{9}$, and we can eliminate choice (A), because the first part of it is wrong. Here's how the rest of the choices shape up:

○ $\dfrac{2}{5} < \dfrac{3}{7} < \dfrac{4}{13}$ Compare $\dfrac{3}{7}$ and $\dfrac{4}{13}$; $\dfrac{3}{7}$ is greater. Eliminate (B).

○ $\dfrac{4}{13} < \dfrac{2}{5} < \dfrac{3}{7}$ These fractions are in order.

○ $\dfrac{3}{7} < \dfrac{3}{8} < \dfrac{2}{5}$ $\dfrac{3}{7}$ is greater than $\dfrac{3}{8}$. Eliminate (D).

○ $\dfrac{2}{9} < \dfrac{3}{7} < \dfrac{3}{8}$ $\dfrac{3}{7}$ is greater than $\dfrac{3}{8}$. Eliminate (E).

The answer is (C).

Converting Mixed Numbers into Fractions

A **mixed number** is a number that is represented as an integer and a fraction, such as $2\dfrac{2}{3}$. In most cases on the GRE, you should get rid of mixed fractions by converting them to improper fractions. How do you do this? By multiplying the denominator of the fraction by the integer, then adding that result to the numerator, and then putting the whole thing over the denominator. In other words, for the fraction above we would get $\dfrac{3 \times 2 + 2}{3}$ or $\dfrac{8}{3}$.

The result, $\dfrac{8}{3}$, is equivalent to $2\dfrac{2}{3}$. The only difference is that $\dfrac{8}{3}$ is easier to work with in math problems. Also, answer choices are usually not given in the form of mixed numbers.

Improper fractions have a numerator that is greater than the denominator. When you convert mixed numbers, you'll get an improper fraction as the result.

Decimals

Decimals are just fractions in disguise. Basically, decimals and fractions are two different ways of expressing the same thing. Every decimal can be written as a fraction, and every fraction can be written as a decimal. For example, the decimal 0.35 can be written as the fraction $\dfrac{35}{100}$: These two numbers, 0.35 and $\dfrac{35}{100}$, have the same value.

To turn a fraction into its decimal equivalent, all you have to do is divide the numerator by the denominator. Here, for example, is how you would find the decimal equivalent of $\dfrac{3}{4}$:

$$\dfrac{3}{4} = 3 \div 4 = 4\overline{)3.00}^{\,0.75}$$

Try this problem:

$$\frac{1}{3} + \frac{2}{5} = x$$

$$y = 3$$

Quantity A   **Quantity B**

$$\frac{y}{x}$$ 4

○ Quantity A is greater.

○ Quantity B is greater.

○ The two quantities are equal.

○ The relationship cannot be determined
   from the information given.

Here's How to Crack It

Begin this quant comp question by solving for *x*. The common denominator is easy to find, as it is 15, so adjust the fractions to have the denominator of 15.

$$\frac{1}{3} + \frac{2}{5} = \frac{5}{15} + \frac{6}{15} = \frac{11}{15}$$

The problem gives the value of *y* so now solve for Quantity A. Quantity A is $\left(\frac{3}{\frac{11}{15}}\right)$ which equals $3 \times \frac{15}{11} = \frac{45}{11}$. Now compare this to Quantity B. Dividing 45 by 11 yields a result slightly greater than 4, which means that Quantity A is greater than Quantity B and the correct answer is (A).

Comparing Decimals

Which is greater: 0.00099 or 0.001? ETS loves this sort of problem. You'll never go wrong, though, if you follow these easy steps.

- Line up the numbers by their decimal points.
- Fill in the missing zeros.

Here's how to answer the question we just asked. First, line up the two numbers by their decimal points.

$$0.00099$$
$$0.001$$

Now fill in the missing zeros.

$$0.00099$$
$$0.00100$$

Can you tell which number is greater? Of course you can. 0.00100 is greater than 0.00099, because 100 is greater than 99.

Digits and Decimals

Sometimes ETS will ask you questions about digits that fall after the decimal point as well. Suppose you have the number 0.584.

- 0 is the units digit.
- 5 is the tenths digit.
- 8 is the hundredths digit.
- 4 is the thousandths digit.

Another way to convert a fraction into a percentage is to divide the numerator by the denominator and multiply the result by 100. So, $\frac{3}{5} = 3 \div 5 = 0.6 \times 100 = 60\%$.

Percentages

A **percentage** is just a special type of fraction, one that always has 100 as the denominator. Percent literally means "per 100" or "out of 100" or "divided by 100." If your best friend finds a dollar and gives you 50¢, your friend has given you 50¢ out of 100, or $\frac{50}{100}$ of a dollar, or 50 percent of the dollar. To convert fractions to percentages, just expand the fraction so it has a denominator of 100:

$$\frac{3}{5} = \frac{60}{100} = 60\%$$

For the GRE, you should memorize the following percentage-decimal-fraction equivalents. Use these friendly fractions and percentages to eliminate answer choices.

$0.01 = \frac{1}{100} = 1\%$ $0.333... = \frac{1}{3} = 33\frac{1}{3}\%$ $0.666... = \frac{2}{3} = 66\frac{2}{3}\%$

$0.1 = \frac{1}{10} = 10\%$ $0.4 = \frac{2}{5} = 40\%$ $0.75 = \frac{3}{4} = 75\%$

$0.8 = \frac{4}{5} = 80\%$

$0.2 = \frac{1}{5} = 20\%$ $0.5 = \frac{1}{2} = 50\%$ $1.0 = \frac{1}{1} = 100\%$

$0.25 = \frac{1}{4} = 25\%$ $0.6 = \frac{3}{5} = 60\%$ $2.0 = \frac{2}{1} = 200\%$

Converting Decimals to Percentages

In order to convert decimals to percentages, just move the decimal point two places to the right. For example, 0.8 turns into 80 percent, 0.25 into 25 percent, 0.5 into 50 percent, and 1 into 100 percent.

Translation

One of the best ways to handle percentages in word problems is to know how to translate them into an equation that you can manipulate. Use the following table to help you translate percentage word problems into equations you can work with.

These translations apply to any word problem, not just percent problems.

Word	Equivalent Symbol
percent	$\overline{100}$
is	=
of, times, product	×
what (or any unknown value)	any variable *(x, k, b)*

Here's an example:

○
---

56 is what percent of 80 ?

- ○ 66%
- ○ 70%
- ○ 75%
- ○ 80%
- ○ 142%

Here's How to Crack It

To solve this problem, let's translate the question and then solve for the variable. So, "56 is what percent of 80," in math speak, is equal to

$$56 = \frac{x}{100}(80)$$

$$56 = \frac{80x}{100}$$

Don't forget to reduce the fraction: $56 = \frac{4}{5}x$.

Now multiply both sides of the equation by the reciprocal, $\frac{5}{4}$.

$$\frac{5}{4}(56) = x$$

$$\frac{56 \times 5}{4} = x$$

$$\frac{280}{4} = x = 70$$

The correct answer is (B), 70%.

---○---

Let's try a quant comp example.

---○---

5 is r percent of 25

s is 25 percent of 60

Quantity A   **Quantity B**

r s

○ Quantity A is greater.

○ Quantity B is greater.

○ The two quantities are equal.

○ The relationship cannot be determined from the information given.

Here's How to Crack It
First translate the first statement.

$$5 = \frac{r}{100}(25)$$

$$5 = \frac{25r}{100}$$

$$5 = \frac{r}{4}$$

$$(4)(5) = \left(\frac{r}{4}\right)(4)$$

$$20 = r$$

That takes care of Quantity A. Now translate the second statement.

$$s = \frac{25}{100}(60)$$

$$s = \frac{1}{4}(60)$$

$$s = 15$$

So Quantity A is greater than Quantity B. The answer is (A).

Percentage Increase/Decrease

Rather than asking for percents, ETS typically will test your knowledge by asking for percent change. Percent change is the percentage by which something has increased or decreased. To find percent change, use the following formula.

$$\text{Percent Change} = \frac{\text{Difference}}{\text{Original}} \times 100$$

When presented with a percent change problem, you will typically be given two numbers. The "difference" is the result when the lesser number is subtracted from the greater number. The "original" is whichever number you started with. If the question asks you to find a **percent increase**, then the original number is the **lesser number**. If the question asks you to find a **percent decrease**, then the original number is the **greater number**.

On the GRE, a percent change will not be stated as a negative number. Instead, the problem will ask for a percent decrease. So, if something declined by 50%, the problem will ask for a percent decrease and the answer will be stated as 50%. Note that when you use the percent change formula, you always subtract the lesser number from the greater number to find the difference. Doing so ensures that you get a positive result.

On percent increase problems, the original is always the smaller number. On percent decrease problems, the original is the larger number.

Here's an example.

During a certain three-month period, Vandelay Industries reported a $3,500 profit. If, over the next three-month period, Vandelay Industries reported $6,000 profit for those months, by approximately what percent did Vandelay Industries' profit increase?

○ 25%

○ 32%

○ 42%

○ 55%

○ 70%

Here's How to Crack It

Let's use the percent change formula we just learned. The first step is to find the difference between the two numbers. The initial profit was $3,500 and the final profit is $6,000. The difference between these two numbers is 6,000 − 3,500 = 2,500. Next, we need to divide this number by the original, or starting, value.

One way to help you figure out what value to use as the original value is to check to see whether you're dealing with a percent increase or a percent decrease question. Remember that on a percent increase question, you should always use the lesser of the two numbers as the denominator and on a percent decrease question you need to use the greater of the two numbers as the denominator. Because the question asks to find the percent increase, the number we want to use for our denominator is 3,500. The percent increase fraction looks like this: $\frac{2,500}{3,500}$. This can be reduced to $\frac{25}{35}$ by dividing by 100, and reduced even further by dividing by 5. The reduced fraction is $\frac{5}{7}$, which is approximately 70% (remember that the fraction bar means divide, so if you divide 5 by 7, you'll get 0.71). Thus, (E) is the correct answer.

Here's another question.

Model	Original Price	Sale Price
A	$12,000	$9,500
B	$16,000	$13,000
C	$10,000	$7,500
D	$17,500	$13,000
E	$20,000	$15,500
F	$22,000	$16,000

The table above shows the original price and the sale price for six different models of cars. For which car models is the percent decrease at least 25% ?

Indicate <u>all</u> such models.

☐ A

☐ B

☐ C

☐ D

☐ E

☐ F

Here's How to Crack It

The task of this question is to identify a 25% or greater percent decrease between the two prices for the different car models. Use the percent change formula for all of the models to solve this question. Start with model A. Using the calculator, subtract 9,500 from 12,000 to get 2,500. This is the difference. Divide it by the original, 12,000, to get about 0.2, which when multiplied by 100 is 20%. Since 20% is less than 25%, eliminate (A). Try the next one. 16,000 − 13,000 = 3,000. Divide 3,000 by 16,000. The result is less than 25%, so eliminate (B). Repeat this process for each of the answer choices. Choices (C), (D), and (F) are the correct answers.

A FEW LAWS

These two basic laws are not necessary for success on the GRE, so if you have trouble with them, don't worry too much. However, ETS likes to use these laws to make certain math problems more difficult. If you're comfortable with these two laws, you'll be able to simplify problems using them, so it's definitely worth it to use them.

Associative Laws

There are two associative laws—one for addition and one for multiplication. For the sake of simplicity, we've lumped them together.

Here's what you need to know:

> When you are adding or multiplying a series of numbers, you can regroup the numbers in any way you'd like.

Here are some examples:

$$4 + (5 + 8) = (4 + 5) + 8 = (4 + 8) + 5$$
$$(a + b) + (c + d) = a + (b + c + d)$$
$$4 \times (5 \times 8) = (4 \times 5) \times 8 = (4 \times 8) \times 5$$
$$(ab)(cd) = a(bcd)$$

Distributive Law

This is often tested on the GRE. Here's what it looks like:

$$a(b + c) = ab + ac$$
$$a(b - c) = ab - ac$$

Here's an example:

———————◯———————

$$12(66) + 12(24) = \text{?}$$

Here's How to Crack It

This is in the same form as *ab* + *ac*. Using the distributive law, this must equal 12(66 + 24), or 12(90) = 1,080.

———————◯———————

Math Fundamentals Drill

Test your new skills and check your answers in Part V.

If a prime number, p, is squared and the result is added to the next prime number greater than p, which of the following integers could be the resulting sum?

Indicate all such integers.

A ☐ 3

B ☐ 4

C ☐ 7

D ☐ 14

E ☐ 58

F ☐ 60

G ☐ 65

H ☐ 69

A bookstore will only order books that come in complete cases. Each case has 150 books and costs $1,757.

Quantity A	Quantity B
The number of books that can be ordered for $10,550	The number of books that can be ordered for $12,290

○ Quantity A is greater.

○ Quantity B is greater.

○ The two quantities are equal.

○ The relationship cannot be determined from the information given.

If the product of two distinct integers is 91, then which of the following could be the sum of the two integers?

Indicate all such sums.

A ☐ −92

B ☐ −91

C ☐ 7

D ☐ 13

E ☐ 20

Which of the following is the digit for the sum of all of the distinct prime integers less than 20 ?

○ 4

○ 5

○ 6

○ 7

○ 8

During a sale, a store decreases the prices on all of its scarves by 25 to 50 percent. If all of the scarves in the store were originally priced at $20, which of the following prices could be the sale price of a scarf?

Indicate all such prices.

A ☐ $8

B ☐ $10

C ☐ $12

D ☐ $14

E ☐ $16

$$-2, 3, -5, -2, 3, -5, -2, 3, -5,...$$

In the sequence above, the first 3 terms repeat without end. What is the product of the 81st term through the 85th term?

Quantity A	**Quantity B**
$4\left(\dfrac{1}{2}x + 2y\right)$	$2x + 8y$

○ Quantity A is greater.

○ Quantity B is greater.

○ The two quantities are equal.

○ The relationship cannot be determined from the information given.

Quantity A	**Quantity B**
The greatest number of consecutive nonnegative integers which have a sum less than 22	6

○ Quantity A is greater.

○ Quantity B is greater.

○ The two quantities are equal.

○ The relationship cannot be determined from the information given.

If x is the remainder when a multiple of 4 is divided by 6, and y is the remainder when a multiple of 2 is divided by 3, what is the greatest possible value of $x + y$?

○ 2

○ 3

○ 5

○ 6

○ 9

$$12 - \left(\frac{6}{3} - 4 \times 3\right) - 8 \times 3 =$$

○ −46

○ −30

○ −18

○ −6

○ −2

Summary

- Familiarity with the basic math concepts on the GRE is essential to achieving a great score.

- Digits are the numbers that make up other numbers, which are collections of digits, and those other numbers are determined by the place value of the digits.

- Integers are numbers with no fractional part (such as –6, –1, 1, 10, etc.) and can be positive or negative, and even or odd.

- Zero is an integer that is neither positive nor negative.

- Consecutive integers are integers listed in some sort of order.

- The absolute value of a number is that number's distance away from zero on a number line.

- A factor of a particular integer is an integer that divides evenly into that integer.

- A multiple of a number is a number that has the original number as a factor.

- Prime numbers only have two factors: 1 and the number itself.

- Divisibility is the ability for one number to be divided into another number with a result that is an integer. If a number divided by another number and the result is not an integer, the amount that is leftover is called the remainder.

- Always follow the order of operations when working a math problem.

- Fractions, decimals, and percents are all ways of expressing parts of integers and can be manipulated and compared.

- The associative and distributive laws are useful ways to group and regroup numbers.

Chapter 11
Algebra (And When to Use It)

The basics for math on the GRE are often used in the context of algebra. While comfort with algebraic operations is a good skill to have, plugging in numbers in lieu of doing the algebra is often a much faster way of getting the correct answer. This chapter provides an introduction to the strategies we call Plugging In and Plugging In The Answers, as well as explains how to deal with exponents and square roots, and how to manipulate equations, inequalities, quadratic equations, and simultaneous equations.

Why Plug In?

Plugging In is a powerful tool that can greatly enhance your math score, but you may be wondering why you should Plug In when algebra works just fine. Here's why:

Plugging In converts algebra problems into arithmetic problems. No matter how good you are at algebra, you're better at arithmetic. Why? Because you use arithmetic every day, every time you go to a store, balance your checkbook, or tip a waiter. Chances are you rarely use algebra in your day-to-day activities.

Plugging In is oftentimes more accurate than algebra. When you plug in real numbers, you make the problems concrete rather than abstract. Once you're working with real numbers, it's easier to notice when and where you've messed up a calculation. It's much harder to see where you went wrong (or to even know you've done something wrong) when you're staring at a bunch of x's and y's.

The GRE allows the use of a calculator. A calculator can do arithmetic but it can't do algebra, so Plugging In allows you to take advantage of the calculator function.

ETS expects its students to attack the problems algebraically and many of the tricks and the traps built into the problem are designed to catch students who use algebra. By Plugging In, you'll avoid these pitfalls.

As you can see, there are a number of excellent reasons for Plugging In. Mastering this technique can have a significant impact on your score.

PLUGGING IN

Many of the hardest questions you might encounter on the GRE involve algebra. Algebra questions are generally difficult for two reasons. First, they are often complicated, multistep problems. Second, ETS studies the types of mistakes that people make when they solve questions using algebra. They generate wrong answers for the questions based on these common algebraic errors. So, if you aren't careful, you can make an algebraic mistake and still find your answer among the choices.

If you are one of the many students who take the GRE and struggle with Algebra, you're in luck. Plugging In is a strategy that will turn even the hardest, messiest GRE algebra problem into an arithmetic problem.

Let's look at an example of how Plugging In can make a seemingly messy algebra problem much easier to work with.

Dale gives Miranda x bottles of water. He gives Marcella two fewer bottles of water than he gives to Miranda and he gives Mary three more bottles of water than he gives to Marcella. How many bottles of water did Dale give to Miranda, Marcella and Mary, in terms of x ?

- ○ $3x - 1$
- ○ $3x$
- ○ $3x + 1$
- ○ $3x + 2$
- ○ $x - 2$

Here's How to Crack It

This problem can definitely be solved using algebra. However, the use of Plugging In makes this problem much easier to solve. The problem has one variable in it, x, so start plugging in by picking a number for x. An easy number to use would be 10, so use your scratch paper and write down $x = 10$. Now read the problem again and follow the directions, only this time do the arithmetic instead of the algebra on the scratch paper. So, Miranda gets 10 bottles of water. The problem then states that Marcella gets two fewer bottles of water than Miranda, so Marcella gets 8 bottles. Next, Mary gets three more bottles than Marcella, so Mary gets 11 bottles. That's a total of 10 + 8 + 11 = 29 bottles of water. The problem asks how many bottles of water Dale gave to Miranda, Marcella, and Mary, so the answer to the question is 29 bottles of water. This is the target answer, which should always be circled on the scratch paper so you don't forget it. Now plug in 10 for the variable x in all the answer choices and see which answer choice equals 29. Be sure to check all five answer choices.

(A) $3(10) - 1 = 29$ Looks good!
(B) $3(10) = 30$ Nope
(C) $3(10) + 1 = 31$ Nope
(D) $3(10) + 2 = 32$ Nope
(E) $10 - 2 = 8$ Nope

The correct answer to this question is (A), and if you successfully completed the algebra you would have gotten the same answer. Pretty easy compared to the algebra, huh?

As you can see, Plugging In turned this algebra problem into an arithmetic problem. The best news is that you can solve any problem with variables by using Plugging In.

Here are the steps:

Step 1:   **Recognize the opportunity.** See variables in the problem and answer choices? Get ready to Plug In. The minute you see variables in a question or answer choices, you should start thinking about opportunities to Plug In.

Step 2:   **Set up the scratch paper.** Plugging In is designed to make your life easier. Why make it harder again by trying to solve problems in your head? You are not saving any notable amount of time by trying to work out all the math without writing it down, so use the scratch paper. Even if it seems like an easy question of translating a word problem into an algebraic equation, remember that there are trap answer choices. Whenever you recognize the opportunity to Plug In, set up the scratch paper by writing answer choices (A) through (E) down before you start to solve.

Plugging In
This technique can be achieved by following these five simple steps. Plugging in numbers in place of variables can make algebra problems much easier to solve.

Step 3: **Plug In.** If the question asks for "x apples," come up with a number for x. The goal here is to make your life easier, so plugging in numbers such as 2, 3, 5, 10, 100 are all good strategies. However, for the first attempt at Plugging In on any given problem, avoid the numbers 1 or 0. These numbers can oftentimes create a situation where more than one answer choice produces the target answer. If you plug in a number and the math starts getting difficult (for example, you start getting fractions or negative numbers), don't be afraid to just change the number you plug in.

Step 4: **Solve for the Target.** The Target is the value the problem asks you to solve for. Remember to always circle the Target so you don't forget what it is you are solving for.

Step 5: **Check all of the answer choices.** Anywhere you see a variable, plug in the number you have written down for that variable and do the arithmetic. The correct answer is the one that matches the Target. If more than one answer matches the Target, just plug in a different number for the variables and test the answer choice you were unable to eliminate with the original number.

Can I Just Plug In Anything?

Plug in numbers that make the calculations EASY.

You can plug in any numbers you like, as long as they're consistent with any restrictions stated in the problem, but it's more effective if you use easy numbers. What makes a number easy? That depends on the problem, but in most cases, lesser numbers are easier to work with than greater numbers. Usually, it's best to start with a lesser number, such as 2 for example. Avoid the numbers 0 and 1; both 0 and 1 have special properties, which you'll hear more about later. You want to avoid these numbers because they will often make more than one answer choice match the target. For example, if we plug in 0 for a variable such as x, then the answers 2x, 3x, and 5x would all equal 0. Also, try to avoid plugging in any numbers that are repeats of numbers that show up a lot in the question or answer choices. If you can avoid plugging in 0, 1, or repeat numbers, you can oftentimes avoid situations that may make you have to Plug In again.

Good Numbers Make Life Easier

Plug in real numbers for variables to turn algebra into arithmetic!

However, numbers of lesser value aren't always the best choices for Plugging In. What makes a number good to work with depends on the context of the problem, so be on the lookout for clues to help choose the numbers you are going to use to Plug In. For instance, in a problem involved percentages the numbers 10 and 100 are good numbers to use. In a problem that involves minutes or seconds any multiple or factor of 60, such as 30 or 120 are often good choices.

Let's use the Plugging In steps from above to work through the following problem.

———————◯———————

Mara has six more than twice as many apples as Robert and half as many apples as Sheila. If Robert has x apples, then, in terms of x, how many apples do Mara, Robert, and Sheila have combined?

◯ $2x + 6$

◯ $2x + 9$

◯ $3x + 12$

◯ $4x + 9$

◯ $7x + 18$

On the GRE, Plugging In is often more accurate, and easier, than doing the algebra.

Here's How to Crack It

Step 1:   **Recognize the opportunity.** Look at the question. There is the variable x in the question stem and the answer choices. This is a clear indication to start thinking about Plugging In.

Step 2:   **Set up the scratch paper.** Keep yourself organized by listing out answer choices (A) through (E) on the scratch paper. Leave some space to work the problem.

Step 3:   **Plug In.** Plug in a good number. The problem states that Robert has x apples, and doesn't indicate that the number of apples needs to be anything specific, so choose an easy number such as $x = 4$.

Step 4:   **Solve for the Target.** Now use $x = 4$ to read the problem again and solve for the target. The problem states that "Mara has six more than twice as many apples as Robert." If Robert has 4 apples, then Mara must have 14. Next, the problem states that Mara has "half as many apples as Sheila." That means that Sheila must have 28 apples. The question asks for the number of apples that Robert, Sheila, and Mara have combined so add $4 + 14 + 28 = 46$ apples. This is the target number, so circle it.

Step 5: **Check all of the answer choices.** Plug in $x = 4$ for all of the variables in the answer choices and use the scratch paper to solve them, eliminating any answer choice that does not equal 46.

(A) $2(4) + 6 = 14$—This is not 46, so eliminate it.

(B) $2(4) + 9 = 17$—Eliminate this too.

(C) $3(4) + 12 = 24$—Also not 46, so eliminate this.

(D) $4(4) + 9 = 25$—This is still not 46, so eliminate this as well.

(E) $7(4) + 18 = 46$—Bingo! This is the correct answer.

Always be on the lookout for variables and if you see them, get ready to Plug In!

On the GRE, plug in for variables in the question and answer choices. Remember to plug in numbers that will be easy to work with based on the problem, as some numbers can end up causing more trouble than they are worth.

When Plugging In, follow these rules:

1. Avoid plugging in 0 or 1. These numbers, while easy to work with, have special properties.
2. Avoid plugging in numbers that are already in the problem; this often leads to more than one answer matching your target.
3. Avoid plugging in the same number for multiple variables. For example, if a problem has x, y, and z in it, pick three different numbers to plug in for the three variables.
4. Avoid plugging in conversion numbers. For example, don't use 60 for a problem involving hours, minutes, or seconds.

Finally, Plugging In is a powerful tool, but you **must remember to always check all five answer choices when you Plug In.** In certain cases, two answer choices can yield the same target. This doesn't necessarily mean you did anything wrong; you just hit some bad luck. When this happens, just plug in different numbers, solve for a new target, and recheck the answer choices that worked the first time.

PLUGGING IN THE ANSWERS (PITA)

Some questions may not have variables in them but will try to tempt you into using algebra to solve them. We call these Plugging In the Answers questions, or PITA for short. These are almost always difficult problems but once you recognize the opportunity to PITA, these questions turn into simple arithmetic questions. In fact, the hardest part of these problems is often identifying them as opportunities for PITA. The beauty of these questions is that they take advantage of one of the inherent limitations of a multiple-choice test: the answers are given to you. ETS has actually given you the answers, and only one of them is correct. The essence of this technique is to systematically Plug In the Answers to see which answer choice works given the information in the problem.

Let's look at an example of a Plugging In the Answers question.

Strategy!
At the left is a tried-and-true Princeton Review strategy, PITA (which has nothing to do with the delicious type of bread).

An office supply store sells binder clips that cost 14 cents each and binder clips that cost 16 cents each. If a customer purchases 85 binder clips from this store at a total cost of $13.10, how many 14-cent binder clips does the customer purchase?

- ○ 16
- ○ 25
- ○ 30
- ○ 35
- ○ 65

Are you tempted to try to set up an algebraic equation? Are there no quickly identifiable variables? Are the answer choices real numbers? Try Plugging In the Answers!

Here's How to Crack It

ETS would like you to solve this problem using algebra, and there is a good chance that you started to think about the variables you could use to set up some equations to solve this problem. That urge to do algebra is actually the first sign that you can solve this problem using Plugging In the Answers. Other signs that you can Plug In the Answers to solve this problem are that the question asks for a specific amount and that the numbers in the answer choices reflect that specific amount. With all these signs, it's definitely time to Plug In the Answers!

Start by setting up your scratch paper. To do so, just list the five answer choices in a column, with the actual numbers included. Since the problem is asking for the number of 14-cent binder clips purchased, these answer choices have to represent the number of 14-cent binder clips purchased. Label this column 14¢.

The answer choices will always be listed in either ascending or descending numerical order, so when you Plug In the Answers, start with (C). By determining whether or not (C) works, you can eliminate the other answer choices that are either greater or less than (C), based on the result of this answer choice.

This effectively cuts the amount of work you need to do in half. So, start with the idea that the customer purchased 30 binder clips that cost 14 cents each. What can you figure out with this information? You'd know that the total spent on these binder clips is 30 × $0.14 = $4.20. So, make a column with the heading "amount spent" and write $4.20 next to (C). Now, look for the next thing you'd know from this problem. If the customer purchased a total of 85 binder clips and 30 of them cost 14 cents each, that means that the customer purchased 55 16-cent binder clips. Make another column with the heading "16¢" and write 55 in the row for (C). Next, make another column for the amount spent on 16-cent binder clips, label it "amount spent," and write 55 × $0.16 = $8.80 under this column in the row for (C). The next piece of information in the problem is that the customer spends a total of $13.10 on the binder clips. This information allows you to determine if (C) is correct. All Plugging In the Answers questions contain a condition like this that lets you decide if the answer is correct. In this case, $4.20 + $8.80 = $13.00, which is less than $13.10, so eliminate (C). Since the total was not great enough, you can determine that to increase the total, the customer must have purchased more 16-cent binder clips. Since (D) and (E) would increase the number of 14-cent binder clips purchased, they cannot be correct. Eliminate (D) and (E) as well.

Now, do the same steps starting with (B). If the customer purchased 25 of the 14-cent binder clips, they cost $3.50. The customer also purchased 60 of the 16-cent binder clips at a cost of $9.60. The total amount spent is $3.50 + $9.60 = $13.10. Since this matches the amount spent in the problem, (B) is correct.

Here's what your scratch paper should look like after this problem:

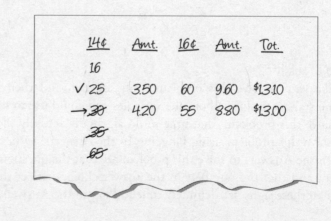

When you want to Plug In the Answers, here are the steps that you should follow.

Step 1: **Recognize the opportunity.** There are three ways to do this. The first indications are the phrases "how much…," "how many…," or "what is the value of…." When you see one of these phrases in a question, its a good indicator that you may be able to Plug In the Answers. The second tip-off is specific numbers in the answer choices in ascending or descending order. The last tip-off is your own inclination. If you find yourself tempted to write your own algebraic formulas and to invent your own variables to solve the problem, it's a good sign that you can Plug In the Answer choices.

Step 2: **Set up the scratch paper.** The minute you recognize the opportunity, list the numbers in the answer choices in a column on the scratch paper.

Step 3: **Label the first column.** The question asks you to find a specific number of something so the answer choices must be options for that number. At the top of the column above the answer choices, write down what the numbers represent.

Step 4: **Start with (C).** Choice (C) will always be the number in the middle. This the most efficient place to start because it will allow you to eliminate as many as three answer choices if it is wrong.

Step 5: **Create your spreadsheet.** Use (C) to work through the problem. It is always easier to understand the problem using a specific number. Work through the problem one step at a time, and every time you have to do something with the number, make a new column. Each column is a step in solving the problem that you may need to use again with a different answer choice, so don't leave anything out.

Step 6: **Repeat with the other answer choices.** On single-answer multiple-choice questions, only one answer choice can work. If (C) is correct, you are finished with the problem. If it is not correct, you may be able to determine if the value of the number is too great or too small. If it is too great, you can eliminate it and every answer choice that it is greater than. The same thing can be done if the value of the resulting answer is lesser than the value indicated by the problem. At this point, you have basically created your own little spreadsheet that is specfically designed to calculate the correct answer. Check the remaining answer choices by using the spreadsheet. As soon as you find an answer choice that works, you're finished.

On PITA questions, you don't need to check all five answer choices because only one of them can be correct. Once you have found an answer that works with the problem, select it and move on to the next problem. PITA is a great tool but it requires a high level of organization, so make sure to keep track of everything that you do on the scratch paper.

PLUGGING IN ON QUANTITATIVE COMPARISON QUESTIONS

Quantitative comparison questions often test your knowledge of the properties of fractions, zero, one, negatives, and other weird numbers.

Quantitative comparison, or quant comp, questions with variables can be extremely tricky because the obvious answer is often wrong, whereas finding the correct answer may involve a scenario that is not commonly thought of. On the other hand, there is a simple set-up and approach that you can use to help find the correct answers. As always, whenever you see variables, replace them with real numbers. On quant comp questions, however, it is crucial that you Plug In more than once and specifically that you plug in different kinds of numbers that may not occur to you to think of initially. A good way to help you think of this is to always keep the nature of the answer choices in mind. Picking (A) means that you believe that the quantity in column A will *always* be greater than Quantity B—*no matter what number you plug in.* Choice (B) means that the quantity in column B will *always* be greater than Quantity A—*no matter what number you plug in,* and so forth. To prove that one of these statements is true you have to plug in every possible number that could change the outcome. Don't worry. We have a simple process to help figure out what to plug in and how to track your progress as you do.

Here are the steps:

Step 1:   **Recognize the opportunity.** The first seven or eight questions of any Math section will be quant comp. When a quant comp question appears and you see variables, you know that you can Plug In.

Step 2:   **Set up the scratch paper.** The minute you see quant comp and variables set up the scratch paper. The recommended set up should look something like the diagram below. Place Quantity A and B on either side. Quant comp questions only have four potential answer choices, so write (A), (B), (C), and (D) down as well, so you can eliminate answers as you go. Finally, leave space to write down the numbers that you plug in for the variables in between the Quantities, so you can stay organized.

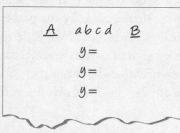

Step 3: **Plug In and eliminate.** Start with an easy number, just like outlined in the earlier Plugging In section, but make sure that you also follow any conditions in the problem. With the number you plugged in for the variable, solve for Quantity A and Quantity B and write the solutions down. If Quantity A is greater than Quantity B, eliminate (B) and (C). If Quantity B is greater than Quantity A, eliminate (A) and (C). If both quantities are the same, eliminate (A) and (B).

Step 4: **Plug In again using FROZEN numbers.** On quant comp questions with variables, you always need to Plug In more than once and the second time you do it, you need to use FROZEN numbers. FROZEN is an acronym that will be explained in the next section, as well the entire concept behind why to Plug In more than once, so keep reading!

Always Plug In More Than Once on Quant Comp Questions

Quant comp questions only have four options for answer choices but one of those options, (D), can be selected if the relationship between Quantity A and Quantity B cannot be determined based on the information given. After you Plug In the first time, you need to Plug In again but this time you need to try and choose a number that will produce a different outcome for the question. While the first time you Plug In you can usually reliably eliminate two of answer choices (A), (B), or (C), you Plug In again to try and make sure that you can eliminate (D). Choice (D) can be eliminated only when you have a high level of confidence that no matter what number you plug in, the answer will always remain the same. If even one of the numbers you choose creates a different answer, (D) should be selected.

So, to eliminate (D) you need to choose a different number. But what makes a number different and what makes for a good number to choose that might create a different outcome for the problem? When you Plug In for the second (or sometimes third or fourth) time in a quant comp question, you should pick a FROZEN number. FROZEN is an acronym that highlights different types of numbers and it stands for:

Fractions
Repeats
One
Zero
Extremes
Negatives

On quant comp questions, plug in easy numbers such as 2 or 5, and eliminate two choices. Then plug in FROZEN numbers (Fractions, Repeats, One, Zero, Extremes, Negatives) to try to disprove your first answer. If different numbers give you different answers, you've proved that the answer is (D).

Fractions are numbers such as $\frac{1}{2}$ or $\frac{1}{4}$ that are great to use if the problem contains exponents or roots, as fractions respond to these two stimuli in a different way from whole numbers. Repeats are numbers that are found in the question stem, can be used in both Quantities, or numbers that are implied by the question stem (such as using the number 60 if the question is about seconds, minutes, or hours). One and zero are special numbers because they can result in two quantities being equal to each other, and each has a unique effect on other numbers. Extreme numbers are numbers such as 10 or 100 that should be used to see if the relationship between the quantities changes for numbers that are greater than the one that was initially chosen. Negative numbers, such as –2 or –3, are numbers that create different outcomes when plugged in for variables, as they can make Quantities negative or positive, which can alter the outcome.

FROZEN numbers can also be combined to create different numbers, such as –100, $-\frac{1}{2}$, or –1. Often ETS will create a quant comp question that has a correct answer that depends on using these types of numbers. They do that because they know that most people will not think of these numbers, which is why it is important to Plug In more than once and, when you do, use FROZEN numbers.

Let's look at an example problem:

Quantity A	**Quantity B**
$2x^3$	$4x^2$

○ Quantity A is greater.

○ Quantity B is greater.

○ The two quantities are equal.

○ The relationship cannot be determined from the information given.

Here's How to Crack It

Step 1: **Recognize the opportunity.** This is a quant comp question and there are variables in the quantities, so this is a Plug In problem.

Step 2: **Set up the scratch paper.** Get yourself organized and ready to answer the problem by setting up the scratch paper.

Step 3: **Plug In.** Let's start with an easy number such as 2. Plug in 2 for x. When $x = 2$, the quantity in column A is $2 \times 2^3 = 16$, and the quantity in column B is $4 \times 2^2 = 16$ as well. Since both quantities are equal in this case, neither Quantity A nor Quantity B is always greater than the other, so eliminate choices (A) and (B).

Step 4: **Plug In again using FROZEN numbers.** Now look at the problem and try to decide on a FROZEN number for x that may create a different answer. Try One. If $x = 1$, then Quantity A is $2 \times 1^3 = 2$ and Quantity B is $4 \times 1^2 = 4$. Quantity B is now greater than Quantity A, which means that (C) is incorrect. Eliminate (C) and select (D), which is the correct answer.

If you chose to follow the recommended setup for the scratch paper, it should look like this:

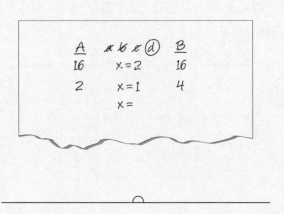

You might also have noticed that choosing different FROZEN numbers, such as Fractions or Zero, would also yield a different result that would have allowed you to eliminate (C). This is not uncommon as ETS is hoping you forget to use these FROZEN numbers when Plugging In. Make sure you use these numbers aggressively on quant comp problems because they can radically affect the relationship between the two Quantities.

PLUGGING IN ON FRACTION AND PERCENT PROBLEMS

Plugging In on fraction and percent problems is a great way to make these problems much easier.

Now that you've become familiar with fractions and percents, we'll show you a great method for solving many of these problems. When you come to regular multiple-choice questions, or multiple-choice, multiple-answer questions, that involve fractions or percents, you can simply plug in a number and work through the problem using that number. This approach works even when the problem doesn't have variables in it. Why? Because, as you know, fractions and percents express only a relationship between numbers—the actual numbers don't matter. For example, look at the following problem:

A recent survey of registered voters in City X found that $\frac{1}{3}$ of the respondents support the mayor's property tax plan. Of those who did not support the mayor's plan, $\frac{1}{8}$ indicated they would not vote to reelect the mayor if the plan were implemented. Of all the respondents, what fraction indicated that they would not vote for the mayor if the plan were enacted?

What important information is missing from the problem?

- ○ $\frac{1}{16}$
- ○ $\frac{1}{12}$
- ○ $\frac{1}{6}$
- ○ $\frac{1}{3}$
- ○ $\frac{2}{3}$

Here's How to Crack It

Even though there are no variables in this problem, we can still Plug In. On fraction and percent problems, ETS will often leave out one key piece of information: the total. Plugging In for that missing value will make your life much easier. What crucial information did ETS leave out of this problem? The total number of respondents. So let's plug in a value for it. Let's say that there were 24 respondents to the survey. 24 is a good number to use because we'll have to work with $\frac{1}{3}$ and $\frac{1}{8}$, so we want a number that's divisible by both those fractions. Working through the problem with our number, we see that $\frac{1}{3}$ of the respondents support the plan. $\frac{1}{3}$ of 24 is 8, so that means 16 people do not support the plan. Next, the problem says that $\frac{1}{8}$ of those who do not support the plan will not vote for the mayor. $\frac{1}{8}$ of 16 is 2, so 2 people won't vote for the mayor. Now we just have to answer the question: Of all respondents, what fraction will not vote for the mayor? Well, there were 24 total respondents and we figured out that 2 aren't voting. So that's $\frac{2}{24}$, or $\frac{1}{12}$. Choice (B) is the one we want.

ALGEBRA: OPERATIONS WITH VARIABLES

While Plugging In is a great strategy to make algebra problems easy on the GRE by turning them into arithmetic, in many cases being comfortable manipulating variables in an equation is necessary to answering a question. Plugging In will help you solve for a variable in a question but sometimes the question only requires you to manipulate an equation to get the correct answer.

Dealing with Variables

The previous chapter familiarized you with number concepts and the previous section showed you how to turn algebra into arithmetic by using Plugging In. However, its time to learn the basics of dealing with variables and manipulating equations to help make problems easier to work with and give you the best opportunity to optimize your score.

Manipulating Equations

When working with equations, you can do pretty much anything you want to them as long as you follow the golden rule:

> Whatever you do on one side of the equals sign you must also do on the other side.

Don't assume you'll always need to solve for the variable on the GRE; sometimes you'll simply have to manipulate the equation to get the answer.

Solving for One Variable

Let's begin the discussion of manipulating equations with one variable by solving for one variable. When presented with an equation with one variable, start by isolating the variable on one side of the equation and the numbers on the other side. You can do this by adding, subtracting, multiplying, or dividing both sides of the equation by the same number. Just remember that anything you do to one side of an equation, you must do to the other side. Let's look at a simple example:

$$3x - 4 = 5$$

Here's How to Crack It

When presented with a problem like this, your goal is to isolate the variable on one side of the equation with all the real numbers, or constants, on the other. In the example above, begin manipulating this question by adding 4 to both sides of the equation. In general, you can eliminate negative numbers by adding them to both sides of the equation, just as you can eliminate positives by subtracting them from both sides of the equation.

$$
\begin{aligned}
3x - 4 &= 5 \\
+\,4 &= +\,4 \\
\hline
3x &= 9
\end{aligned}
$$

The variable is not quite isolated yet, as it is still being multiplied by 3. In the same way that you manipulated the equation earlier by moving the 4 to the other side of the equation, you must move the 3. Since the 3 is being multiplied to the variable, move it by doing the opposite operation, in this case division. This allows you to solve for x and finish the problem.

$$\frac{3x}{3} = \frac{9}{3}$$

$$x = 3$$

Let's try another one:

---○---

$$5x - 13 = 12 - 20x$$

Here's How to Crack It

Again, we want to get all the x values on the same side of the equation. This time, however, there is more than one instance of x so begin the question by combining the x values.

$$
\begin{array}{r}
5x - 13 = 12 - 20x \\
+\ 20x \qquad\qquad +\ 20x \\
\hline
25x - 13 = 12
\end{array}
$$

Now that the values of x are combined, isolate the x by moving the negative 13 to the other side of the question.

$$
\begin{array}{r}
25x - 13 = 12 \\
+\ 13 + 13 \\
\hline
25x = 25
\end{array}
$$

Solve for x by finishing the isolation by moving the 25 that it is being multiplied by.

$$
\begin{array}{c}
25x = 25 \\
\dfrac{25x}{25} = \dfrac{25}{25} \\
x = 1
\end{array}
$$

---○---

As the problems get more involved, make sure to keep yourself organized by utilizing the scratch paper given to you.

Let's try one more that is slightly more complicated.

$$5x + \frac{3}{2} = 7x$$

Here's How to Crack It

The first thing you probably notice here is the fraction. Whenever you see an equation like this that contains a fraction, begin by "clearing" the fraction. To clear the fraction, multiply all the terms in the equation by the denominator of the fraction. In this case, multiply all the terms by 2.

$$10x + 3 = 14x$$

Notice how all the terms have by multiplied by 2! This is very important, so don't forget to do it! Now, manipulate the equation to collect all the x's on the same side of the equation.

$$
\begin{array}{r}
10x + 3 = 14x \\
-10x \qquad -10x \\
\hline
3 = 4x
\end{array}
$$

Now finish isolating the x by moving the 4.

$$3 = 4x$$
$$\frac{3}{4} = \frac{4x}{4}$$
$$\frac{3}{4} = x$$

You must always do the same thing to both sides of an equation.

WORKING WITH TWO VARIABLES

Many times, however, an equation on the GRE will involve two variables. An example of an equation with two variables looks like this:

$$3x + 10y = 64$$

Here's How to Crack It

The important thing to note about this situation is that we cannot solve this equation. Why, you ask? The problem is that since there are two variables, there are many possible solutions to this equation, all of which are equally valid. For example, plugging in the values $x = 8$ and $y = 4$ would satisfy the equation. But the equation would also be satisfied if you plugged in the values $x = 10$ and $y = 3.4$. Therefore, the GRE cannot test an equation with two variables without either providing a definitive way to solve for one of the variables, or providing a second equation. By giving two equations, you are able to find definitive values for the variables. So a more likely problem would look something like this:

$$3x + 10y = 64$$
$$6x - 10y = 8$$

Now there are 2 variables and 2 equations, which means we can solve for the variables. When two equations are given, look to combine them by adding or subtracting the entire equations. We do this so that we can cancel out one of the variables, leaving us with a simple equation with one variable. In this case, it's easier to add the two equations together, which will eliminate the y variable as seen below.

$$
\begin{array}{rl}
3x + 10y &= 64 \\
+\,6x - 10y &= 8 \\
\hline
9x &= 72
\end{array}
$$

Add these two equations to get $9x = 72$. This is a simple equation, just like the ones discussed in the previous section, which we can solve to find $x = 8$. Once we've done that, we can solve for the other variable by inserting the value of x into one of the original equations. For example, if we substitute $x = 8$ into the first equation, we get $3(8) + 10y = 64$, we can solve to find that $y = 4$.

You can't solve an equation with two variables unless you have a second equation.

The GRE will rarely give you two equations that line up as nicely as the above example does, though. You are more likely to find two equations with two variables and, while the variables match, the numbers associated with the variables are not equal. In this case, you will need to manipulate one equation so the numbers associated with a variable are equal. Doing this will allow the elimination of a variable when the two equations are added or subtracted. Try the next problem as an example.

---○---

$$4x + 7y = 41$$
$$- \quad 2x + 3y = 19$$

Here's How to Crack It

Notice here that the numbers associated with the variables are not equal, which means that you cannot eliminate a variable. Adding the two equations yields $6x + 10y = 60$. That doesn't help; it's a single equation with two variables, which is impossible to solve. Subtracting the equations leaves $2x + 4y = 22$, which is also a single equation with two variables. To solve this system of equations, we need to make the coefficient for one of the variables in the first equation equal to the coefficient for that same variable in the second equation. In this case, try multiplying the second equation by 2.

$$2(2x + 3y) = 2(19)$$

This gives us the following:

$$4x + 6y = 38$$

Now we can subtract this equation from the first equation. Doing this operation yields $y = 3$. Now we can substitute $y = 3$ into either one of the original equations to find that $x = 5$.

---○---

Simultaneous Equations

Thus far, we have learned how to manipulate equations with one variable and two equations with two variables in order to solve for the variables. However, it is not uncommon for ETS to give you two equations and ask you to use them to find the value of a given expression. Much like manipulating two equations with two variables, all you need to do is add or subtract the two equations! The only difference is this time you won't end up solving for an individual variable.

Here's an example:

If $5x + 4y = 6$ and $4x + 3y = 5$, then what does $x + y$ equal?

Here's How to Crack It

Remember that the problem is asking you to solve for $x + y$. This may appear like you need to solve for the variables individually, but try to add or subtract the equations first to see what they yield. First, try adding the two equations together.

$$\begin{array}{r} 5x + 4y = 6 \\ + \ 4x + 3y = 5 \\ \hline 9x + 7y = 11 \end{array}$$

Since the problem wants the value of $x + y$ and this gives us the value of $9x + 7y$ this is not useful. So try subtracting the two equations.

$$\begin{array}{r} 5x + 4y = 6 \\ -(4x + 3y = 5) \\ \hline x + \ y = 1 \end{array}$$

Bingo. The value of the expression $(x + y)$ is exactly what we're looking for. You could have tried to solve for each variable individually and solved the problem that way, but since the question is asking for the value of an expression, it was easier to manipulate the equations like this. So remember, on the GRE you may see two equations written horizontally. Now you know that you don't need complicated math to solve them! Just rewrite the two equations, putting one on top of the other, and simply add or subtract them.

INEQUALITIES

The difference between an equation and an inequality is that in an equation one side always equals the other and in an inequality one side does *not* equal the other. Equations contain equal signs, while inequalities contain one of the following symbols:

$\neq$	is not equal to
$>$	is greater than
$<$	is less than
$\geq$	is greater than or equal to
$\leq$	is less than or equal to

The good news is that inequalities are manipulated in the same way that you manipulated any of the equations in the previous sections of this chapter. However, there is one critical difference. When you multiply or divide both sides of an inequality by a negative number, the direction of the inequality symbol must change. So, if the inequality $x > y$ is multiplied by -1, the resulting inequality is $-x < -y$.

To see this rule in action, take a look at the following inequality:

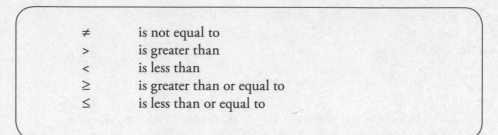

$$12 - 6x > 0$$

Here's How to Crack It

There are two ways to solve this inequality. You could manipulate this inequality without ever multiplying or dividing by a negative number by just adding $6x$ to both sides and then dividing both sides of the inequality by the positive 6. In this case, the sign would not change, as seen below.

$$
\begin{array}{r}
12 - 6x > 0 \\
\underline{+\,6x > +\,6x} \\
12 > 6x
\end{array}
$$

$$\frac{12}{6} > \frac{6x}{6}$$

$$2 > x$$

The other way to solve this inequality is to subtract 12 from both sides first. This will create a situation where you need to divide both sides of the equation by −6, as shown below.

$$12 - 6x > 0$$
$$\underline{-12 \qquad > -12}$$
$$-6x > -12$$
$$\frac{-6x}{-6} < \frac{-12}{-6}$$
$$x < 2$$

Notice that the sign flipped because you divided both sides by a negative number, but the answer for both methods of solving this inequality is the same thing. The first answer says that the number 2 is greater than x, and the second says that x is less than the number 2!

Inequalities show up on the GRE in a variety of ways. For instance, ETS may give you a range for two variables and then ask you to combine them in some way. This type of problem looks like the following question:

If $0 \leq x \leq 10$ and $-10 \leq y \leq -1$, then what is the range for $x - y$?

Here's How to Crack It

First, determine what the question is asking you to do. The question is asking you to solve for the range for the expressions $x - y$. To determine this you need to consider all possible combinations of $x - y$. Since the inequalities are ranges themselves, find the greatest and least possible values of $x - y$ by calculating the largest x minus the largest y, the largest x minus the least y, the least x minus the largest y, and the least x minus the least y. The greatest value of x is 10 and the least value of x is 0. The greatest value of y is −1 and the least value is −10. Calculate these values and keep yourself organized by writing this all down on the scratch paper.

Flip the sign! When you multiply or divide both sides of an inequality by a negative number, the greater than/less than sign points the opposite way.

The calculations look as follows:

$$10 - (-1) = 11$$
$$10 - (-10) = 20$$
$$0 - (-1) = 1$$
$$0 - (-10) = 10$$

Since the least possible value of $x - y$ is $0 - (-1) = 1$ and the greatest possible value of $x - y$ is $10 - (-10) = 20$, the range is $1 \le x - y \le 20$.

○

QUADRATIC EQUATIONS

Quadratic equations are special types of equations that involve four terms. Here is an example of a quadratic:

$$(x + 4)(x - 7)$$

In order to work with quadratics on the GRE, you must be familiar with two concepts: FOIL and factoring.

FOIL

When you see a quadractic, you need to multiply every term in the first set of parentheses by every term in the second set of parentheses. Use the acronym FOIL to remember this method. FOIL stands for *first, outer, inner, last*. For example, if you see $(x + 4)$ $(x + 3)$, you would multiply the first terms $(x \times x)$, the outer terms $(x \times 3)$, the inner terms $(4 \times x)$, and the last terms (4×3), as follows:

$$(x \times x) + (x \times 3) + (4 \times x) + (4 \times 3) =$$
$$x^2 + 3x + 4x + 12 =$$
$$x^2 + 7x + 12$$

We know to use plus signs inside the parentheses because both the 7 and the 12 are positive. Now we have to think of two numbers that, when added together, give us 7, and when multiplied together, give us 12.

Quadratic Equations

There are three quadratic equations that frequently appear on the GRE. Knowing these equations both in their factored and unfactored forms, can drastically improve your time on these questions. Here they are:

1. Factored form: $x^2 - y^2$ (the difference between two squares)
    Unfactored form: $(x + y)(x - y)$

2. Factored form: $(x + y)^2$
    Unfactored form: $x^2 + 2xy + y^2$

3. Factored form: $(x - y)^2$
    Unfactored form: $x^2 - 2xy + y^2$

Find these numbers by listing the factor pairs of 12. Those pairs are 1 and 12, 2 and 6, and 3 and 4. The only pair that equals 7 when they are added together is 4 and 3, so insert those into the equation.

$$(x + 4)(x + 3) = 0$$

To find the solutions, set each factor equal to 0 and solve. So, $x + 4 = 0$ and $x + 3 = 0$. So x can either be -4 or -3.

Let's look at a question that uses quadratics that you may see on the GRE.

Quantity A	Quantity B
$(4 + \sqrt{6})(4 - \sqrt{6})$	10

○ Quantity A is greater.

○ Quantity B is greater.

○ The two quantities are equal.

○ The relationship cannot be determined from the information given.

Here's How to Crack It

First, eliminate (D) because there are only numbers in this question, so the answer can be determined. Now, Quantity A looks like a job for FOIL! Multiply the first terms, and you get 16. Multiply the outer terms and you get $-4\sqrt{6}$. Multiply the inner terms to get $4\sqrt{6}$. Multiply the last terms to get -6. So, Quantity A is now $16 - 4\sqrt{6} + 4\sqrt{6} - 6$. The two inner terms cancel each other out and all the remains is $16 - 6$, or 10. Since Quantity B is also equal to 10, the two answer choices are equal and the correct answer is (C). You might also notice that Quantity A is one of the common quadratics: $(x + y)(x - y) = x^2 - y^2$. Therefore, $(4 + \sqrt{6})(4 - \sqrt{6}) = 4^2 - (\sqrt{6})^2 = 16 - 6 = 10$.

Factoring

The process of factoring "undoes" the FOIL process. Factoring is commonly tested on the GRE so you should be very familiar with the process. Think of factoring as taking a quadratic in the opposite direction of FOIL. Here is a quadratic in its unfactored, or expanded, form:

$$x^2 - 10x + 24$$

We are going to factor this quadratic using the following steps:

1. Separate the x^2 into $(x \quad)(x \quad)$.
2. Find the factors of the third term that, in this case the number 24, when added or subtracted, yield the second term, the number 10. Note here that we are not concerned with the variable x.
3. Figure out the signs (+/–) for the terms. The signs have to yield the middle number when added and the last term when multiplied.

If we apply these steps to the quadratic given earlier, we begin the problem by splitting x^2 into

$$(x \quad)(x \quad)$$

Next, write down the factors of the third term, 24. The factors are 1 and 24, 2 and 12, 3 and 8, and 4 and 6. Of these pairs of factors, which contains two numbers that we can add or subtract to get the second term, 10? 4 and 6 is the only pair that works, so put those into the parentheses.

$$(x \quad 4)(x \quad 6)$$

The final step is to figure out the signs. We need to end up with a negative 10 and a positive 24. If we add –6 and –4, we'll get –10. Similarly, if we multiply –6 and –4, we'll end up with 24. So the factored form of the quadratic is

$$(x - 4)(x - 6)$$

Solving Quadratic Equations

ETS likes to use quadratic equations because they have an interesting quirk; when you solve a quadratic equation, you usually get two possible answers as opposed to one. For this reason, quadratic equations are perfect ways for ETS to try to trick you.

Here's an example:

Quadratic equations usually have two solutions.

$$x^2 + 2x - 15 = 0$$

Quantity A   **Quantity B**

2   x

○ Quantity A is greater.

○ Quantity B is greater.

○ The two quantities are equal.

○ The relationship cannot be determined from the information given.

Here's How to Crack It

In order to solve a quadratic equation, the equation must be set equal to zero. Normally, this will already be the case on the GRE, as it is in this example. But if you encounter a quadratic equation that isn't set equal to zero, you must first manipulate the equation so that it is. Next you must factor the equation; otherwise you cannot solve it. So let's factor the quadratic equation in this example. We need to figure out the factors of 15 that we can add or subtract to give us 2. The only possible factors are 3 and 5. In order to get a negative 15 and a positive 2, we need to use 5 and –3. So that leaves us

$$(x - 3)(x + 5) = 0$$

Next, we're going to solve each of the two factors within parentheses separately:

$$x - 3 = 0 \text{ and } x + 5 = 0$$

Thus, $x = 3$ and $x = -5$. If $x = 3$, then Quantity B is greater, but if $x = -5$ then Quantity A is greater. This means that the correct answer is (D).

Let's try another one:

⌀

If $x^2 + 8x + 16 = 0$, then what is the value of x ?

```
┌──────────────┐
│              │
│              │
└──────────────┘
```

Click on the answer box and type in a number.
Backspace to erase.

Here's How to Crack It

Let's factor the equation. Start with $(x\quad)(x\quad)$. Next, find the factors of 16 that add or subtract to 8. The factors of 16 are 1 and 16, 2 and 8, and 4 and 4. Of these pairs, only 4 and 4 have a sum of 8. Since we have a positive 8 and a positive 16, the signs for both numbers must be positive. Thus, we end up with $(x + 4)(x + 4)$ = 0. Now, we need to solve the equation. If $x + 4 = 0$, then $x = -4$. This is the number we'd enter into the text box on the GRE.

⌀

Let's look at one more example.

⌀

If x and y are positive integers, and if
$x^2 + 2xy + y^2 = 25$, then what is the value of
$(x + y)^3$?

○ 5

○ 15

○ 50

○ 75

○ 125

Here's How to Crack It

While this problem may look like a lot of work, if you have committed the common quadratic equations from earlier in this section to memory the answer is easier to come by. The equation in this question is reflective of the common quadratic: $x^2 + 2xy + y^2 = (x + y)^2$. The question tells us that $x^2 + 2xy + y^2$ is equal to 25, which means that $(x + y)^2$ is also equal to 25. Think of $x + y$ as one unit that, when squared, is equal to 25. Since this question specifies that x and y are positive integers, what positive integer squared equals 25? The number 5 does, so $x + y = 5$. The question is asking for $(x + y)^3$. In other words, what's 5 cubed, or $5 \times 5 \times 5$? The answer is (E), 125.

⌀

EXPONENTS AND SQUARE ROOTS

Finally, the last section of this chapter is going to deal with exponents and square roots. Questions with exponents and square roots are common on the GRE and solving these questions often requires manipulating the exponents or roots. Here's the information you need to know in order to work with them.

What Are Exponents?

Exponents are a sort of mathematical shorthand for repeated multiplication. Instead of writing $(2)(2)(2)(2)$, you can use an exponent and write 2^4. The little 4 is the **power** and the 2 is called the **base**. The power tells you how many times to multiply the base by itself. Knowing this terminology will be helpful in following the discussion in this section.

The Five Rules of Working with Exponents

For the GRE there are five major rules that apply when you work with exponents. The more comfortable you are with these rules, the more likely you will be to approach an exponent question with confidence and get the answer correct!

The first three rules deal with the combination and manipulation of exponents. Those three rules are represented by the acronym **MADSPM** , which stands for:

> **M**ultiply
> **A**dd
>
> **D**ivide
> **S**ubtract
>
> **P**ower
> **M**ultiply

These three rules will be explained in more detail shortly, but for now just remember:

- when you see exponents with equal bases which are being **multiplied**, you **add** the powers;
- when equal bases are **divided** you **subtract** the exponents; and
- when an exponent is raised to a **power**, you **multiply** the powers.

The fourth rule is the definition of a **negative exponent**. The fifth and final rule is the definition of a **zero exponent**.

The Multiply-Add Rule of Exponents

When two exponents with equal bases are multiplied, you must add the exponents. Consider the following example:

$$3^2 \times 3^3$$

As defined earlier, a power just tells you how many times to multiply a base by itself. So another way to write this expression is:

$$3^2 \times 3^3 = (3 \times 3)(3 \times 3 \times 3) = 3^5$$

As you can see, the number of bases, which in this case is the integer 3, that are actually being multiplied together is five, as there are two 3's that are represented by 3^2 and three 3's that are represented by 3^3.

Now solve this question more quickly by using the multiply-add rule.

$$3^2 \times 3^3 = 3^{2+3} = 3^5$$

The Divide-Subtract Rule of Exponents

When two exponents with equal bases are divided, you must subtract the exponents. Consider the following example and expand the exponents to make it clear.

$$\frac{5^3}{5^2} = \frac{5 \times 5 \times 5}{5 \times 5} = \frac{5}{1} = 5$$

Now, instead of expanding the exponents just apply the divide-subtract rule for the same problem.

$$\frac{5^3}{5^2} = 5^{3-2} = 5^1 = 5$$

The Power-Multiply Rule of Exponents

When an expression with an exponent is raised to another power, multiply the powers together. Consider the following example and expand the exponents to make it clear.

$$(6^2)^3 = (6^2)\,(6^2)\,(6^2) = (6 \times 6)\,(6 \times 6)\,(6 \times 6) = 6^6$$

Now, apply the power-multiply rule to solve the same problem.

$$(6^2)^3 = 6^{2 \times 3} = 6^6$$

For all of these rules, the bases must be the same. So, for example, you could not divide-subtract the expression $\dfrac{3^3}{2^2}$ because the bases are not the same.

Negative Exponents

A negative exponent is another way ETS uses exponents on the GRE. Consider the following example.

$$\frac{8^3}{8^5} = 8^{3-5} = 8^{-2} = \frac{1}{8^2} = \frac{1}{64}$$

So when you have a negative exponent, all that needs to be done is to put the entire expression in a fraction, with 1 in the numerator and the exponent in the denominator, and change the negative exponent to a positive. A term raised to a negative power is the reciprocal of that term raised to the positive power.

Zero Exponents

Sometimes ETS will give you an exponent question that, after you have successfully manipulated it, results in a base number raised to a power of 0. Any nonzero number raised to a power of 0 is equal to 1. Consider the following example.

$$4^3 \times 4^{-3} = 4^{3-3} = 4^0 = 1$$

Exponent Tips Beyond the Five Rules

Sometimes you will have an exponent problem for which none of the five rules discussed apply. If you reach this point there are two tips to keep you moving forward.

Tip 1: Rewrite Terms Using Common Bases

ETS will always write questions that work out nicely, so if none of the bases in an exponent question seem to match up, see if you can find a way to rewrite the bases so that they match, and you will be able to use one of the five rules.

Tip 2: Look for a Way to Factor the Expression

Factoring the expression is often a way to reveal something about the exponent expression that you may not have noticed before. If you get stuck with an exponent question try to factor the expression and see if there is a way to use one of the five rules.

It will be uncommon for ETS to just test one or two of these concepts on a GRE problem. Most times, two or more of these concepts will be combined to create a problem. Let's look at a couple of examples.

If $y \neq 0$, which of the following is equivalent to $\dfrac{y^9}{y\left(y^2\right)^3}$?

○ y

○ y^2

○ y^3

○ y^4

○ y^5

Here's How to Crack It

Begin by simplifying the denominator of the fraction. Use the power-multiply rule to combine $(y^2)^3$ into y^6. Since a number, or in this case a variable, by itself is the same thing as having that number or variable raised to a power of 1, use the add-multiply rule to combine $y(y^6)$ into y^7. Now use the divide-subtract rule to solve the problem; the correct answer is (B).

Let's look at another problem.

Quantity A	Quantity B
$15^{15} - 15^{14}$	$15^{14}(14) - 1$

○ Quantity A is greater.

○ Quantity B is greater.

○ The two quantities are equal.

○ The relationship cannot be determined from the information given.

Here's How to Crack It

The question wants you to compare the two quantities but since none of the rules for exponents apply here, see if there is something else you can do to this problem. The expression in Quantity A can be factored so begin there. Quantity A is now $15^{15} - 15^{14} = 15^{14}(15 - 1)$, which is the same thing as $15^{14}(14)$. Notice how this is the same as Quantity B, except Quantity B is 1 less than $15^{14}(14)$. Therefore, Quantity A is greater and the correct answer is (A).

Take a look at one more exponent problem.

If $x \neq 0$ and $64^3 = 8^x$ then what is the value of x^2 ?

- ○ 5
- ○ 6
- ○ 25
- ○ 36
- ○ 64

Here's How to Crack It

Solve this question by determining the value for x. To solve for x in this equation, start by rewriting the exponent expressions using a common base. Since 64 can be written as 8^2, the equation can be rewritten as $(8^2)^3 = 8^x$. Since the bases are the same, for the equation to be equal the powers have to be the same as well. $(8^2)^3$ can be rewritten as 8^6 because of the power-multiply rule, so if $8^6 = 8^x$ then $x = 6$. Now plug that number into the value for x^2. This is now 6^2 which equals 36, so the correct answer is (D).

The Peculiar Behavior of Exponents

- Raising a number greater than 1 to a power greater than 1 results in a greater number. For example, $2^2 = 4$.

- Raising a fraction that's between 0 and 1 to a power greater than 1

  results in a lesser number. For example, $\left(\frac{1}{2}\right)^2 = \frac{1}{4}$.

- A negative number raised to an even power results in a positive number. For example, $(-2)^2 = 4$, because $(-2)(-2) = 4$.

- A negative number raised to an odd power results in a negative number. For example, $(-2)^3 = -8$, because $(-2)(-2)(-2) = -8$.

- A number raised to the first power ALWAYS results in the number itself. For example, $1,000^1 = 1,000$.

What Is a Square Root?

The radical sign $\sqrt{}$ indicates the **square root** of a number. For example, $\sqrt{4}$ means that some number times itself is equal to 4. In this case, since $2^2 = 4$ it can be determined that $\sqrt{4} = 2$. Think of square roots as the opposite of exponents. If you want to eliminate a square root in an equation, all you need to do is raise that square root to a power of 2. Just remember to do that for all of the elements in the equation!

Square roots can only exist on the GRE with nonnegative numbers. If the problem states that $x^2 = 16$, then $x = \pm 4$ as both a positive and a negative 4, when multiplied by itself, yields 16. However, when you find the square root of any number, the result will always be positive.

Rules for Square Roots

There are rules that dictate what you can and cannot do with square roots, just like there are rules about exponents.

You can multiply and divide any square roots, but you can add or subtract roots only when the number under the radical sign is the same.

Adding and Subtracting Square Roots

You can only add or subtract square roots if the values under the radical sign are equal. So, for example, the expression $2\sqrt{5} + 4\sqrt{5}$ can be simplified to $6\sqrt{5}$ because the value under the radical sign is equal. Conversely, the expression $3 + 2\sqrt{5}$ cannot be reduced any further because the values of the roots are not the same.

> Rules for Adding and Subtracting Square Roots
>
> $$a\sqrt{r} + b\sqrt{r} = (a+b)\sqrt{r}$$
> $$a\sqrt{r} - b\sqrt{r} = (a-b)\sqrt{r}$$

Multiplying and Dividing Square Roots

Any square roots can be multiplied or divided. There aren't any restrictions on this so keep an eye out for opportunities to combine roots by multiplying or dividing that could make a root easier to work with. For example, $\sqrt{3} \times \sqrt{12} = \sqrt{36} = 6$. Roots can be divided as well; for example, $\sqrt{\dfrac{12}{3}} = \dfrac{\sqrt{12}}{\sqrt{3}} = \sqrt{4} = 2$.

> Rules for Multiplying and Dividing Square Roots
>
> $$a\sqrt{r} \times b\sqrt{s} = (a \times b)\sqrt{rs}$$
>
> $$\sqrt{\frac{a}{b}} = \frac{\sqrt{a}}{\sqrt{b}}$$

Simplifying Square Roots

Often times when you multiply square roots on the GRE, you will not get numbers under the radical sign that work out perfectly. When this happens, you will need to simplify the square root. You simplify a square root by looking for ways to factor the number under the root that results in a least one perfect square. A perfect square is an integer that when the square root of that integer is taken, the result is another integer. For example, 4 is a perfect square because $\sqrt{4} = 2$. Similarly, 9 and 25 are perfect squares because $\sqrt{9} = 3$ and $\sqrt{25} = 5$, respectively. Look at the following expression and try to simplify it.

$$\sqrt{2} \times \sqrt{10}$$

You can combine this expression to result in $\sqrt{20}$. However, this is not in the most simplified form. Look for ways to factor 20 in which one of the pairs of numbers is a perfect square. The factors of 20 are 1 and 20, 2 and 10, and 4 and 5. Since 4 is a perfect square, this can now be simplified even further.

$$\sqrt{2} \times \sqrt{10} = \sqrt{20} = \sqrt{4 \times 5} = \sqrt{4} \times \sqrt{5} = 2\sqrt{5}$$

Now let's take a look at some examples of how ETS might test roots on the GRE.

What is the value of the expression $3\sqrt{80} - 2\sqrt{5}$?

- ○ $4\sqrt{5}$
- ○ $5\sqrt{3}$
- ○ $10\sqrt{5}$
- ○ $12\sqrt{3}$
- ○ $20\sqrt{5}$

Here's How to Crack It

The problem is subtracting roots. Since roots cannot be subtracted unless the numbers under the radical sign are equal, look for a way to simplify the roots. Since 5 cannot be simplified any further, work with 80. The factors of 80 are 1 and 80, 2 and 40, 4 and 20, 5 and 16, and 8 and 10. Two of these pairs of factors contain a perfect square, but one contains a perfect square and a prime number. This is a good thing. This means that it could be reduced no further, so choose 5 and 16 and simplify to read $3\sqrt{80} = 3\sqrt{5 \times 16} = (3 \times 4)\sqrt{5} = 12\sqrt{5}$. Now that the bases are equal, subtract the expression to find that $12\sqrt{5} - 2\sqrt{5} = 10\sqrt{5}$, which is (C). The same answer would have been found if the numbers 4 and 20 had been chosen as the factors of 80, but there would have been another round of simplifying the root, as 20 would have needed to be reduced to 4 and 5 as factors.

Here's another problem.

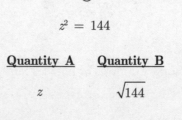

$$z^2 = 144$$

Quantity A	**Quantity B**
z	$\sqrt{144}$

- ○ Quantity A is greater.
- ○ Quantity B is greater.
- ○ The two quantities are equal.
- ○ The relationship cannot be determined from the information given.

Here's How to Crack It

The trap answer here is (C). Remember that if $z^2 = 144$, then the value of z is either 12 or –12. However, when a value is under a radical sign—that is, when you're looking for the square root—it can only be positive. Therefore, Quantity A could be 12 or –12 and Quantity B can only be 12. Since there is no way to ensure that one is always greater than the other, the correct answer is (D).

———————◯———————

Try one more problem:

———————◯———————

What is the value of $\dfrac{\sqrt{75}}{\sqrt{27}}$?

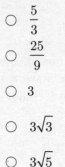

◯ $\dfrac{5}{3}$

◯ $\dfrac{25}{9}$

◯ 3

◯ $3\sqrt{3}$

◯ $3\sqrt{5}$

To Simplify Roots:
1. Rewrite the number as the product of two factors, one of which is a perfect square.
2. Use the multiplication rule for roots.

Here's How to Crack It

First, simplify each of these roots. $\sqrt{75}$ has a factor that is a perfect square—25, so it can be rewritten as $\sqrt{25 \times 3}$ and simplified to $5\sqrt{3}$. $\sqrt{27}$ has the perfect square 9 as a factor, so it can be written as $\sqrt{9 \times 3}$ and then simplified to $3\sqrt{3}$. This means that $\dfrac{\sqrt{75}}{\sqrt{27}}$ is equal to $\dfrac{5\sqrt{3}}{3\sqrt{3}}$; the $\sqrt{3}$ in the numerator and denominator cancel, leaving $\dfrac{5}{3}$. The correct answer is (A).

———————◯———————

Algebra (And When to Use It) Drill

Now it's time to try out what you have learned on some practice questions. Try the following problems and then check your answers in Part V.

The original selling price of an item at a store is 40 percent more than the cost of the item to the retailer. If the retailer reduces the price of the item by 15 percent of the original selling price, then the difference between the reduced price and the cost of the item to the retailer is what percent of the cost of the item to the retailer?

Percent

Click on each box and type in a number.
Backspace to erase.

$$x^2 + 8x = -7$$

Quantity A	**Quantity B**
x	0

○ Quantity A is greater.

○ Quantity B is greater.

○ The two quantities are equal.

○ The relationship cannot be determined from the information given.

If $3^3 \times 9^{12} = 3^x$, what is the value of x ?

Click on the answer box and type in a number.
Backspace to erase.

If $A = 2x - (y - 2c)$ and $B = (2x - y) - 2c$, then $A - B =$

○ $-2y$

○ $-4c$

○ 0

○ $2y$

○ $4c$

A merchant sells three different sizes of canned tomatoes. A large can costs the same as 5 medium cans or 7 small cans. If a customer purchases an equal number of small and large cans of tomatoes for the same amount of money needed to buy 200 medium cans, how many small cans does she purchase?

○ 35

○ 45

○ 72

○ 199

○ 208

If $6k - 5l = 27$ and $3l - 2k = -13$ and $5k - 5l = j$, what is the value of j ?

Click on the answer box and type in a number.
Backspace to erase.

If a is multiplied by 3 and the result is 4 less than 6 times b, what is the value of $a - 2b$?

○ -12

○ $-\dfrac{4}{3}$

○ $-\dfrac{3}{4}$

○ $\dfrac{4}{3}$

○ 12

Quantity A	Quantity B
$\dfrac{2^{-4}}{4^{-2}}$	$\dfrac{\sqrt{64}}{-2^3}$

○ Quantity A is greater.

○ Quantity B is greater.

○ The two quantities are equal.

○ The relationship cannot be determined from the information given.

$$11x + 14y = 30 \text{ and } 3x + 4y = 12$$

Quantity A	Quantity B
$x + y$	$(x + y)^{-2}$

○ Quantity A is greater.

○ Quantity B is greater.

○ The two quantities are equal.

○ The relationship cannot be determined from the information given.

If $x = 3a$ and $y = 9b$, then all of the following are equal to $2(x + y)$ EXCEPT

○ $3(2a + 6b)$

○ $6(a + 3b)$

○ $24(\dfrac{1}{4}a + \dfrac{3}{4}b)$

○ $\dfrac{1}{3}(18a + 54b)$

○ $12(\dfrac{1}{2}a + \dfrac{3}{4}b)$

Summary

- Plugging In converts algebra problems to arithmetic problems. Plug In by replacing variables in the question with real numbers or by working backwards from the answer choices provided.

- Use easy numbers first when Plugging In for variables. If the need arises to Plug In again, use the FROZEN numbers to help eliminate tricky answer choices on math problems.

- The golden rule of equations: Whatever you do to one side of the equation, you must do to the other. This applies to all equations, whether they are equal or not.

- In order to solve an equation with two variables, you need two equations. Stack them up and add or subtract to cancel out one of the variables.

- Inequalities are manipulated the same way that other equations are, with one notable difference: Always remember to flip the sign when you multiply or divide by a negative number.

- Use the FOIL process to expand quadratics. To solve a quadratic equation, set it equal to zero, and factor.

- An exponent is shorthand for repeated multiplication. When in doubt on exponent problems, look to find common bases or ways to factor the expressions.

- Think of a square root as the opposite of an exponent. Square roots are always positive.

Chapter 12
Real World Math

Real world math is our title for the grab bag of math topics that will be heavily tested on the GRE. This chapter details a number of important math concepts, many of which you've probably used at one point or another in your daily adventures, even if you didn't recognize them. After completing this chapter, you'll have brushed up on important topics such as ratios, proportions, and averages. You'll also learn some important Princeton Review methods for organizing your work and efficiently and accurately answering questions on these topics.

EVERYDAY MATH

A few years ago when ETS reconfigured the GRE, they wanted the Math section to test more of what they call "real life" scenarios that a typical graduate student might see. You can therefore expect the math questions on the GRE to heavily test topics such as proportions, averages, and ratios—mathematical concepts that are theoretically part of your everyday life. Regardless of whether that's true of your daily life or not, you'll have to master these concepts in order to do well on the GRE Math section.

RATIOS AND PROPORTIONS

If you're comfortable working with fractions and percentages, you'll be comfortable working with ratios and proportions, because ratios and proportions are simply special types of fractions. Don't let them make you nervous. Let's look at ratios first and then we'll deal with proportions.

What Is a Ratio?

A ratio is just another type of fraction.

Recall that a fraction expresses the relationship of a part to the whole. A **ratio** expresses a different relationship: part to part. Imagine yourself at a party with 8 women and 10 men in attendance. Remembering that a fraction expresses a part-to-whole relationship, what fraction of the partygoers are female? $\frac{8}{18}$, or 8 women out of a total of 18 people at the party. But what's the ratio, which expresses a part to part relationship, of women to men? $\frac{8}{10}$, or as ratios are more commonly expressed, 8 : 10. You can reduce this ratio to 4 : 5, just like you would a fraction.

On the GRE, you may see ratios expressed in several different ways:

$$x : y$$
the ratio of x to y
$$x \text{ is to } y$$

In each case, the ratio is telling us the relationship between parts of a whole.

Every Fraction Can Be a Ratio, and Vice Versa

Every ratio can be expressed as a fraction. A ratio of 1 : 2 means that the total of all the parts is either 3 or a multiple of 3. So, the ratio 1 : 2 can be expressed as the fraction $\frac{1}{2}$, or the *parts* of the ratio can be expressed as fractions *of the whole* as $\frac{1}{3}$ and $\frac{2}{3}$. Likewise, the fraction $\frac{1}{3}$ expresses the ratio 1 : 3. So if a question says "the ratio of *x* to 2*y* is $\frac{1}{3}$," then that would be expressed as $\frac{x}{2y} = \frac{1}{3}$.

Treat a Ratio Like a Fraction

Anything you can do to a fraction you can also do to a ratio. You can cross-multiply, find common denominators, reduce, and so on.

Find the Total

The key to dealing with ratio questions is to find the whole, or the total. Remember: A ratio tells us only about the parts, not the total. In order to find the total, add the numbers in the ratio. A ratio of 2 : 1 means that there are three total parts. A ratio of 2 : 5 means that we're talking about a total of 7 parts. And a ratio of 2 : 5 : 7 means there are 14 total parts. Once you have a total you can start to do some fun things with ratios.

For example, let's say you have a handful of pennies and nickels. If you have 30 total coins and the pennies and nickels are in a 2 : 1 ratio, how many pennies do you have? The total for our ratio is 3, meaning that out of every 3 coins, there are 2 pennies and 1 nickel. So if there are 30 total coins, there must be 20 pennies and 10 nickels. Notice that $\frac{20}{10}$ is the same as $\frac{2}{1}$, is the same as 2 : 1!

Like a fraction, a ratio expresses a relationship between numbers.

When you are working with ratios, there's an easy way not only to keep track of the numbers in the problem but also to quickly figure out the values in the problem. It's called the Ratio Box. Let's try the same question, but with some different numbers; if you have 24 coins in your pocket and the ratio of pennies to nickels is 2 : 1, how many pennies and nickels are there? The Ratio Box for this question is below, with all of the information we're given already filled in.

The minute you see the word "ratio," draw a Ratio Box on your scratch paper.

	Pennies	Nickels	Total
ratio	2	1	**3**
multiply by			
actual numbers			**24**

Remember that ratios are relationships between numbers, not actual numbers, so the real total is 24; that is, you have 24 actual coins in your pocket. The ratio total (the number you get when you add the number of parts in the ratio) is 3.

The middle row of the table is for the multiplier. How do you get from 3 to 24? You multiply by 8. Remember when we talked about finding equivalent fractions? All we did was multiply the numerator and denominator by the same value. That's exactly what we're going to do with ratios. This is what the Ratio Box looks like now:

The multiplier is the key concept in working with ratios. Just remember that whatever you multiply one part by, you must multiply *every* part by.

	Pennies	Nickels	Total
ratio	2	1	**3**
multiply by	8	8	**8**
actual numbers			**24**

Now let's finish filling in the box by multiplying everything else.

	Pennies	Nickels	Total
ratio	2	1	**3**
multiply by	8	8	**8**
actual numbers	16	8	**24**

Therefore, of the 24 coins 16 are pennies and 8 are nickels.

Let's try a GRE example.

Need More Math Review?

Check out *Math Workout for the GRE.* If you're in a hurry, pick up *Crash Course for the GRE.*

Flour, eggs, yeast, and salt are mixed by weight in the ratio of 11 : 9 : 3 : 2, respectively. How many pounds of yeast are there in 20 pounds of the mixture?

○ $1\frac{3}{5}$

○ $1\frac{4}{5}$

○ 2

○ $2\frac{2}{5}$

○ $8\frac{4}{5}$

Here's How to Crack It

The minute you see the word *ratio*, draw a Ratio Box on your scratch paper and fill in what you know.

	Flour	Eggs	Yeast	Salt	Total
ratio	11	9	3	2	
multiply by					
actual numbers					20

First, add all of the numbers in the ratio to get the ratio total.

	Flour	Eggs	Yeast	Salt	Total
ratio	11	9	3	2	25
multiply by					
actual numbers					20

Now, what do we multiply 25 by to get 20?

$$25x = 20$$

$$\frac{25x}{25} = \frac{20}{25}$$

$$x = \frac{20}{25}$$

$$x = \frac{4}{5}$$

So $\frac{4}{5}$ is our "multiply by" number. Let's fill it in.

	Flour	Eggs	Yeast	Salt	Total
ratio	11	9	3	2	25
multiply by	$\frac{4}{5}$	$\frac{4}{5}$	$\frac{4}{5}$	$\frac{4}{5}$	$\frac{4}{5}$
actual numbers					20

The question asks for the amount of yeast, so we don't have to worry about the other ingredients. Just look at the yeast column. All we have to do is multiply 3 by $\frac{4}{5}$ and we have our answer: $3 \times \frac{4}{5} = \frac{12}{5} = 2\frac{2}{5}$, which is (D).

———○———

What Is a Proportion?

So you know that a fraction is a relationship between part and whole, and that a ratio is a relationship between part and part. A **proportion** is an equivalent relationship between two fractions or ratios. Thus, $\frac{1}{2}$ and $\frac{4}{8}$ are proportionate because they are equivalent fractions. But $\frac{1}{2}$ and $\frac{2}{3}$ are not in proportion because they are not equal ratios.

The GRE often contains problems in which you are given two proportional, or equal, ratios from which one piece of information is missing. These questions take a relationship or ratio, and project it onto a larger or smaller scale. Proportion problems are recognizable because they always give you three values and ask for a fourth value. Here's an example:

———○———

If the cost of a one-hour telephone call is $7.20, what would be the cost in dollars of a 10-minute telephone call at the same rate?

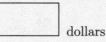 dollars

Click on the answer box and type in a number.
Backspace to erase.

The key to proportions is setting them up correctly.

Here's How to Crack It

It's very important to set up proportion problems correctly. That means placing your information on your scratch paper. Be especially careful to label *everything*. It takes only an extra two or three seconds, but doing this will help you catch lots of errors.

For this question, let's express the ratios as dollars over minutes, because we're being asked to find the cost of a 10-minute call. That means that we have to convert 1 hour to 60 minutes (otherwise it wouldn't be a proportion).

$$\frac{\$}{\min} = \frac{\$7.20}{60} = \frac{x}{10}$$

Now cross-multiply.

$$60x = (7.20)(10)$$
$$60x = 72$$
$$\frac{60x}{60} = \frac{72}{60}$$
$$x = \frac{6}{5}$$

Now we can enter 1.20 into the box.

<table>
<tr><td>

Relationship Review

You may have noticed a trend in the preceding pages. Each of the major topics covered—fractions, percents, ratios, and proportions—described a particular relationship between numbers. Let's review:

- A fraction expresses the relationship between a part and the whole.
- A percent is a special type of fraction, one that expresses the relationship of part to whole as a fraction with the number 100 in the denominator.
- A ratio expresses the relationship between part and part. Adding the parts of a ratio gives you the whole.
- A proportion expresses the relationship between equal fractions, percents, or ratios.
- Each of these relationships shares all the characteristics of a fraction. You can reduce them, expand them, multiply them, and divide them using the exact same rules you used for working with fractions.

</td></tr>
</table>

AVERAGES

The **average** (arithmetic mean) of a list of numbers is the sum, or total value, of all the numbers in the list divided by the number of numbers in the list. The average of the list 1, 2, 3, 4, 5 is equal to the total of the numbers (1 + 2 + 3 + 4 + 5, or 15) divided by the number of numbers in the list (which is 5). Dividing 15 by 5 gives us 3, so 3 is the average of the list.

ETS always refers to an average as an "average (arithmetic mean)." This confusing parenthetical remark is meant to keep you from being confused by other more obscure kinds of averages, such as geometric and harmonic means. You'll be less confused if you simply ignore the parenthetical remark and know that average means total of the elements divided by the number of elements.

GRE average problems always give you two of the three numbers needed.

Think Total

Don't try to solve average problems all at once. Do them piece by piece. The key formula to keep in mind when doing problems that involve averages is

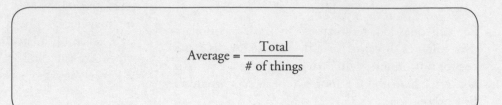

$$\text{Average} = \frac{\text{Total}}{\text{\# of things}}$$

The minute you see the word *average*, draw an Average Pie on your scratch paper.

Drawing an Average Pie will help you organize your information.

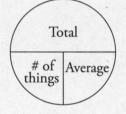

Here's how the Average Pie works. The *total* is the sum of the numbers being averaged. The *number of things* is the number of different elements that you are averaging. And the *average* is, naturally, the average.

Say you wanted to find the average of 4, 7, and 13. You would add those numbers to get the total and divide that total by three.

$$4 + 7 + 13 = 24$$
$$\frac{24}{3} = 8$$

Which two pieces of the pie do you have?

Mathematically, the Average Pie works like this:

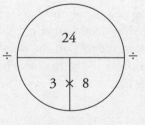

The horizontal bar is a division bar. If you divide the *total* by the *number of things*, you get the *average*. If you divide the total by the *average*, you get the *number of things*. If you have the *number of things* and the *average*, you can simply multiply them together to find the *total*. This is one of the most important things you need to be able to do to solve GRE average problems.

Using the Average Pie has several benefits. First, it's an easy way to organize information. Furthermore, the Average Pie makes it clear that if you have two of the three pieces, you can always find the third. This makes it easier to figure out how to approach the problem. If you fill in the number of things, for example, and the question wants to know the average, the Average Pie shows you that the key to unlocking that problem is finding the total.

Try this one.

---○---

The average (arithmetic mean) of seven numbers is 9 and the average of three of these numbers is 5. What is the average of the other four numbers?

○   4

○   5

○   7

○   10

○   12

Draw a new Average Pie each time you encounter the word *average* in a question.

Here's How to Crack It

Let's take the first sentence. You have the word *average*, so draw an Average Pie and fill in what you know. We have seven numbers with an average of 9, so plug those values into the Average Pie and multiply to find the total.

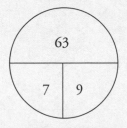

Now we also know that three of the numbers have an average of 5, so draw another Average Pie, plug those values into their places, and multiply to find the total of those three numbers.

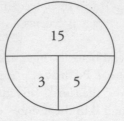

The question is asking for the average of the four remaining numbers. Draw one more Average Pie and plug in 4 for the number of things.

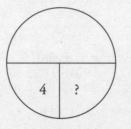

In order to solve for the average, we need to know the total of those four numbers. How do we find this? From our first Average Pie we know that the total of all seven numbers is 63. The second Average Pie tells us that the total of three of those numbers was 15. Thus, the total of the remaining four has to be 63 − 15, which is 48. Plug 48 into the last Average Pie, and divide by 4 to get the average of the four numbers.

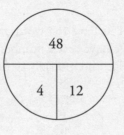

The average is 12, which is (E).

Let's try one more.

The average (arithmetic mean) of a set of 6 numbers is 28. If a certain number, y, is removed from the set, the average of the remaining numbers in the set is 24.

Quantity A	**Quantity B**
y	48

○ Quantity A is greater.

○ Quantity B is greater.

○ The two quantities are equal.

○ The relationship cannot be determined from the information given.

Here's How to Crack It

All right, let's attack this one. The problem says that the average of a set of six numbers is 28, so let's immediately draw an Average Pie and calculate the total.

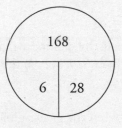

If a certain number, y, is removed from the set, there are now five numbers left. We already know that the new average is 24, so draw another Average Pie.

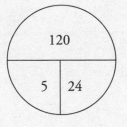

The difference between the totals must be equal to y. $168 - 120 = 48$. Thus, the two quantities are equal, and the answer is (C).

Up and Down

Averages are very predictable. You should make sure you automatically know what happens to them in certain situations. For example, suppose you take three tests and earn an average score of 90. Now you take a fourth test. What do you know?

If your average goes up as a result of the fourth score, then you know that your fourth score was higher than 90. If your average stays the same as a result of the fourth score, then you know that your fourth score was exactly 90. If your average goes down as a result of the fourth score, then you know that your fourth score was less than 90.

MEDIAN, MODE, AND RANGE

Don't confuse median and mode!

The **median** is the middle value in a list of numbers; above and below the median lie an equal number of values. For example, in the list of numbers (1, 2, 3, 4, 5, 6, 7) the median is 4, because it's the middle number (and there are an odd number of numbers in the list). If the list contained an even number of integers such as (1, 2, 3, 4, 5, 6) the median is the average of 3 and 4, or 3.5. When looking for the median, sometimes you have to put the numbers in order yourself. What is the median of the list of numbers (13, 5, 6, 3, 19, 14, 8)? First, put the numbers in order from least to greatest, (3, 5, 6, 8, 13, 14, 19). Then take the middle number. The median is 8. Just think *median* = *middle* and always make sure the numbers are in order.

When you see the word *median* in a question, put the numbers in the problem in order.

The **mode** is the number in a list of numbers that occurs most frequently. For example, in the list (2, 3, 4, 5, 3, 8, 6, 9, 3, 9, 3) the mode is 3, because 3 shows up the most. Just think *mode* = *most*.

The **range** is the difference between the greatest and the least numbers in a list of numbers. So, in the list of numbers (2, 6, 13, 3, 15, 4, 9), the range is 15 (the greatest number in the list) − 2 (the least number in the list), or 13.

Here's an example:

Set $F = \{4, 2, 7, 11, 8, 9\}$

What do we need to do to the numbers in this set?

Quantity A	**Quantity B**
The range of Set F	The median of Set F

○ Quantity A is greater.

○ Quantity B is greater.

○ The two quantities are equal.

○ The relationship cannot be determined from the information given.

Here's How to Crack It

Let's put the numbers in order first, so it'll be easier to see what we have: $\{2, 4, 7, 8, 9, 11\}$. First, let's look at Quantity A: The range is the greatest number, or 11, minus the least number, or 2. That's 9. Now let's look at Quantity B: The minute you see the word *median*, be sure to put the numbers in order. The median is the middle number of the set, but because there are two middle numbers, 7 and 8, we have to find the average. Or do we? Isn't the average of 7 and 8 clearly going to be smaller than the number in Quantity A, which is 9? Yes, in quant comp questions, we compare, not calculate. The answer is (A).

STANDARD DEVIATION

Standard deviation is one of those phrases that math people like to throw around to scare non-math people, but it's really not that scary. The GRE might ask you questions about standard deviation, but you'll never have to actually calculate it; instead, you'll just need a basic understanding of what standard deviation is. In order to understand standard deviation, we must first look at something all standardized testers should be familiar with, the bell curve.

You'll never have to calculate the standard deviation on the GRE.

Your Friend the Bell Curve

The first thing to know about a bell curve is that the number in the middle is the mean.

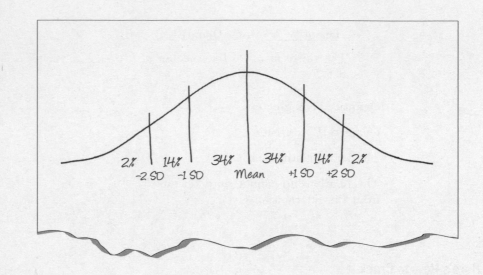

Imagine that 100 students take a test and the results follow a normal distribution. When you see the phrase *normal distribution*, draw a bell curve. Let's say that the average score on this test is an 80. Put 80 in the middle of the curve. You also know that 2% of the students got a 96 or higher. Put a 96 above the right 2% line on the curve.

Standard deviation measures how much a score differs from the norm (the average) in even increments. The curve tells us that a score earned by only 2% of the students is two standard deviations from the norm. If the norm is 80 and 96 is two standard deviations away, then one standard deviation on this test is 8 points. Why? Remember that standard deviations are even increments. If the average is 80 and the score two standard deviations from the norm is 96, then the difference is 16. So, one standard deviation is half of that difference, or 8. The score at one standard deviation greater than the norm is, therefore, 88. Two standard deviations above the norm is 96, while two standard deviations below the norm is 64. One standard deviation below the norm is 72. Fill these in on your bell curve.

Now you know quite a bit about the distribution of scores on this test: 68% of the students received a score between 72 and 88, and 98% percent scored above a 64. That's all there is to know about standard deviations. The percentages don't change, so memorize those. When you see the phrase, just draw a bell curve and fill in what you know. Here's what the curve looks like for this test:

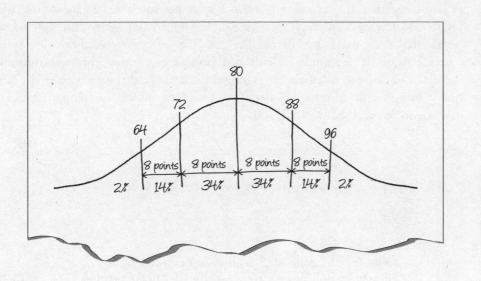

Here's an example of how ETS might test standard deviation:

Quantity A

The standard deviation of a list of data consisting of 10 integers ranging from –20 to –5

Quantity B

The standard deviation of a list of data consisting of 10 integers ranging from 5 to 20

○ Quantity A is greater.

○ Quantity B is greater.

○ The two quantities are equal.

○ The relationship cannot be determined from the information given.

Here's How to Crack It

ETS is hoping you'll make a couple of wrong turns on this problem. The first trap they set is that one list of numbers contains negative integers while the other doesn't—but this doesn't mean that one list has a negative standard deviation. Standard deviation is defined as the distance a point is from the mean, so it can never be negative. The second trap is that ETS hopes you'll waste a lot of time trying to calculate standard deviation based on the information given. But you know better than to try to do that. Remember that ETS won't ask you to calculate standard deviation; it's a complex calculation. Plus, as you know, you need to know the mean in order to calculate the standard deviation and there's no way we can find it based on the information here. Thus, we have no way of comparing these two quantities, and the answer is (D).

───────────○───────────

Now let's try a question that will make use of the bell curve.

───────────○───────────

The fourth grade at School X is made up of 300 students who have a total weight of 21,600 pounds. If the weight of these fourth-graders has a normal distribution and the standard deviation equals 12 pounds, approximately what percentage of the fourth-graders weigh more than 84 pounds?

○ 12%

○ 16%

○ 36%

○ 48%

○ 60%

Here's How to Crack It

This one's a little tougher than the earlier standard deviation questions. The first step is to determine the average weight of the students, which is $\dfrac{21,600}{300} = 72$ pounds. If the standard deviation is 12 pounds, then 84 pounds places us exactly one standard deviation above the mean, or at the $50 + 34 = 84$th percentile (remember the bell curve?). Because 16 percent of all students weigh more than 84 pounds, the answer is (B).

───────────○───────────

RATE

Rate problems are similar to average problems. A rate problem might ask for an average speed, distance, or the length of a trip, or how long a trip (or a job) takes. To solve rate problems, use the Rate Pie.

A rate problem is really just an average problem.

```
        _____
      /  Distance   \
     /      or        \
  ÷ |    Amount       | ÷
     _____|_____/
      \ Time × Rate /
       \_____|_____/
```

The Rate Pie works exactly the same way as the Average Pie. If you divide the *distance* or *amount* by the *rate,* you get the *time.* If you divide the *distance* or *amount* by the *time,* you get the *rate.* If you multiply the *rate* by the *time,* you get the *distance* or *amount.*

Let's take a look.

It takes Carla three hours to drive to her brother's house at an average speed of 50 miles per hour. If she takes the same route home, but her average speed is 60 miles per hour, what is the time, in hours, that it takes her to drive home?

○ 2 hours

○ 2 hours and 14 minutes

○ 2 hours and 30 minutes

○ 2 hours and 45 minutes

○ 3 hours

Here's How to Crack It

The trip to her brother's house takes three hours, and the rate is 50 miles per hour. Plug those numbers into a Rate Pie and multiply to find the distance.

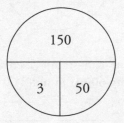

So the distance is 150 miles. On her trip home, Carla travels at a rate of 60 miles per hour. Draw another Rate Pie and plug in 150 and 60. Then all you have to do is divide 150 by 60 to find the time.

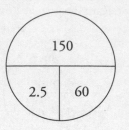

So it takes Carla two and a half hours to get home. That's (C).

Try another one.

A machine can stamp 20 envelopes in 4 minutes. How many of these machines, working simultaneously, are needed to stamp 60 envelopes per minute?

○ 5
○ 10
○ 12
○ 20
○ 24

Here's How to Crack It

First we have to find the rate per minute of one machine. Plug 20 and 4 into a Rate Pie and divide to find the rate.

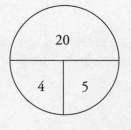

The rate is 5. If one machine can stamp 5 envelopes per minute, how many machines do you need to stamp 60 per minute? 60 ÷ 5 = 12, or (C).

CHARTS

Every GRE Math section has a few questions that are based on a chart or graph (or on a group of charts or graphs). But don't worry; the most important thing that chart questions test is your ability to remember the difference between real-life charts and ETS charts.

In real life, charts are often provided in order to display information in a way that's easier to understand. Conversely, ETS constructs charts to hide information you need to know and to make that information harder to understand.

Chart questions frequently test percents, percent change, ratios, proportions, and averages.

Chart Questions

There are usually two or three questions per chart or per set of charts. Like the Reading Comprehension questions, chart questions appear on split screens. Be sure to click on the scroll bar and scroll down as far as you can; there may be additional charts underneath the top one, and you want to make sure you've seen all of them.

Chart problems just recycle the basic arithmetic concepts we've already covered: fractions, percentages, and so on. This means you can use the techniques we've discussed for each type of question, but there are two additional techniques that are especially important to use when doing chart questions.

On charts, look for the information ETS is trying to hide.

Don't Start with the Questions: Start with the Charts

Take a minute to note the following key bits of information from any chart you see.

- **Information in titles:** Make sure you know what each chart is telling you.
- **Asterisks, footnotes, parentheses, and small print:** Often there will be crucial information hidden away at the bottom of the chart. Don't miss it!
- **Funny units:** Pay special attention when a title says "in thousands" or "in millions." You can usually ignore the units as you do the calculations, but you have to use them to get the right answer.

Using Your Smarts on Charts
Pay attention to small details like footnotes, parentheses, tiny print, and even odd units. These usually provide key insights that will enrich your understanding of the chart.

Don't try to work
with huge values.
Ballpark instead!

Approximate, Estimate, and Ballpark

Like some of our other techniques, you have to train yourself to estimate when working with charts and graphs questions. You should estimate, not calculate exactly, in the following situations:

- whenever you see the word *approximately* in a question
- whenever the answer choices are far apart in value
- whenever you start to answer a question and you justifiably say to yourself, "This is going to take a lot of calculation!"

Review those "friendly" percentages and their fractions from earlier in the chapter. Try estimating this question:

What is approximately 9.6 percent of 21.4 ?

Here's How to Crack It

Use 10 percent as a friendlier percentage and 20 as a friendlier number. One-tenth of 20 is 2 (it says "approximately"—who are you to argue?). That's all you need to do to answer most chart questions.

Chart Problems

Make sure you've read everything on the chart carefully before you try the first question.

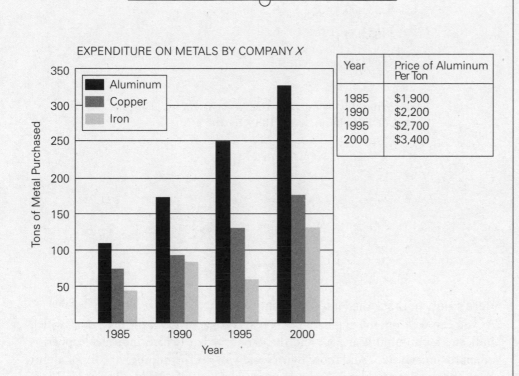

EXPENDITURE ON METALS BY COMPANY *X*

Year	Price of Aluminum Per Ton
1985	$1,900
1990	$2,200
1995	$2,700
2000	$3,400

Approximately how many tons of aluminum and copper combined were purchased in 1995 ?

- ○ 125
- ○ 255
- ○ 325
- ○ 375
- ○ 515

How much did Company *X* spend on aluminum in 1990 ?

- ○ $675,000
- ○ $385,000
- ○ $333,000
- ○ $165,000
- ○ $139,000

Approximately what was the percent increase in the price of aluminum from 1985 to 1995 ?

- ○   8%
- ○ 16%
- ○ 23%
- ○ 30%
- ○ 42%

Here's How to Crack the First Question

As you can see from the graph on the previous page, in 1995, the black bar (which indicates aluminum) is at 250, and the dark gray bar (which indicates copper) is at approximately 125. Add those figures and you get the number of tons of aluminum and copper combined that were purchased in 1995: 250 + 125 = 375. That's (D). Notice that the question says "approximately." Also notice that the numbers in the answer choices are pretty far apart.

Here's How to Crack the Second Question

We need to use the chart and the graph to answer this question, because we need to find the number of tons of aluminum purchased in 1990 and multiply it by the price per ton of aluminum in 1990 in order to figure out how much was spent on aluminum in 1990. The bar graph tells us that 175 tons of aluminum was purchased in 1990, and the little chart tells us that aluminum was $2,200 per ton in 1990. 175 × $2,200 = $385,000. That's (B).

Here's How to Crack the Third Question
Remember that percent increase formula from earlier in this chapter?

$$\text{Percent change} = \frac{\text{Difference}}{\text{Original}} \times 100$$

We'll need to use the little chart for this one. In 1985, the price of aluminum was $1,900 per ton. In 1995, the price of aluminum was $2,700 per ton. Now let's use the formula. $2,700 - 1,900 = 800$, so that's the difference. This is a percent increase problem, so the original number is the smaller one. Thus, the original is 1,900, and our formula looks like this: Percent change $= \frac{800}{1,900} \times 100$. By canceling the 0's in the fraction you get $\frac{8}{19} \times 100$, and multiplying gives you $\frac{800}{19}$. At this point you could divide 800 by 19 to get the exact answer, but because they're looking for an approximation, let's round 19 to 20. What's $800 \div 20$? That's 40, and (E) is the only one that's close.

Real World Math Drill

Now it's time to try out what you have learned on some practice questions. Try the following problems and then check your answers in Part V.

Sadie sells half the paintings in her collection, gives one-third of her paintings to friends, and keeps the remaining paintings for herself. What fraction of her collection does Sadie keep?

Click on each box and type in a number.
Backspace to erase.

$$5x - 2y = 2y - 3x$$

Quantity A	**Quantity B**
x	y

○ Quantity A is greater.

○ Quantity B is greater.

○ The two quantities are equal.

○ The relationship cannot be determined from the information given.

Questions 3 through 5 refer to the following graph.

PERCENT OF POPULATION IN NEW ENGLAND
BY STATE IN YEAR *X* AND YEAR *Y*

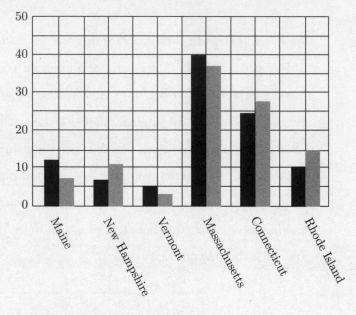

■ Year *X*: Total New England population= 15 million
▨ Year *Y*: Total New England population= 25 million

If the six New England states are ranked by population in Year *X* and Year *Y*, how many states would have a different ranking from Year *X* to Year *Y* ?

○ None

○ One

○ Two

○ Three

○ Four

In Year X, the population of Massachusetts was approximately what percent of the population of Vermont?

○ 50%

○ 120%

○ 300%

○ 800%

○ 1,200%

By approximately how much did the population of Rhode Island increase from Year X to Year Y ?

○ 750,000

○ 1,250,000

○ 1,500,000

○ 2,250,000

○ 3,375,000

A water jug with a capacity of 20 gallons is 20 percent full. At the end of every third day, water is added to the jug. If the amount of water added is equal to 50 percent of the water in the jug at the beginning of that day, how many days does it take for the jug to be at least 85% full?

○ 4

○ 6

○ 12

○ 15

○ 20

Towns A, B, C, and D are all in the same voting district. Towns A and B have 3,000 people each who support referendum R and the referendum has an average (arithmetic mean) of 3,500 supporters in towns B and D and an average of 5,000 supporters in Towns A and C.

Quantity A	**Quantity B**
The average number of supporters of Referendum R in Towns C and D	The average number of supporters of Referendum R in Towns B and C

○ Quantity A is greater.

○ Quantity B is greater.

○ The two quantities are equal.

○ The relationship cannot be determined from the information given.

A company paid $500,000 in merit raises to employees whose performances were rated A, B, or C. Each employee rated A received twice the amount of the raise that was paid to each employee rated C; and each employee rated B received one-and-a-half times the amount of the raise that was paid to each employee rated C. If 50 workers were rated A, 100 were rated B, and 150 were rated C, how much was the raise paid to each employee rated A ?

○ $370

○ $625

○ $740

○ $1,250

○ $2,500

Questions 9 through 11 refer to the following graphs.

NUMBER OF STUDENTS IN GRADES
9 THROUGH 12 FOR SCHOOL DISTRICT
X IN 1995 AND 2013

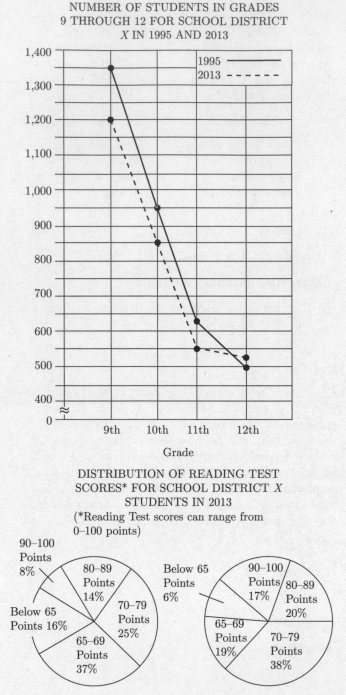

DISTRIBUTION OF READING TEST
SCORES* FOR SCHOOL DISTRICT X
STUDENTS IN 2013
(*Reading Test scores can range from
0–100 points)

9th Grade Students

10th–12th Grade Students

In 2013, the median reading test score for ninth-grade students was in which score range?

○ Below 65 points

○ 65–69 points

○ 70–79 points

○ 80–89 points

○ 90–100 points

10 of 12

If the number of students in grades 9 through 12 comprised 35 percent of the number of students in School District X in 1995, then approximately how many students were in School District X in 1995 ?

○ 9,700

○ 8,700

○ 3,400

○ 3,000

○ 1,200

11 of 12

Assume that all students in School District X took the reading test each year. In 2013, approximately how many more ninth-grade students had reading test scores in the 70–79 point range than in the 80–89 point range?

○ 470

○ 300

○ 240

○ 170

○ 130

One ounce of Solution X contains only ingredients a and b in a ratio of 2 : 3. One ounce of Solution Y contains only ingredients a and b in a ratio of 1 : 2. If Solution Z is created by mixing solutions X and Y in a ratio of 3 : 11, then 630 ounces of Solution Z contains how many ounces of a ?

○   68

○   73

○   89

○   219

○   236

Summary

- A ratio expresses a part to part relationship. The key to ratio problems is finding the total. Use the ratio box to organize ratio questions.

- A proportion expresses the relationship between equal fractions, percents, or ratios. A proportion problem always provides you with three pieces of information and asks you for a fourth.

- Use the Average Pie to organize and crack average problems.

- The median is the middle number in a set of values. The mode is the value that appears most frequently in a set. The range of a set is the difference between the largest and smallest values in the set.

- You will never have to calculate standard deviation on the GRE.

- Standard deviation problems are really average and percent problems. Make sure you know the percentages associated with the bell curve: 34%, 14%, 2%.

- Use the Rate Pie for rate questions.

- On chart questions, make sure you take a moment to understand what information the chart is providing. Estimate answers to chart questions whenever possible.

Chapter 13
Geometry

Chances are you probably haven't used the Pythagorean theorem recently or had to find the area of a circle in quite a while. However, you'll be expected to know geometry concepts such as these on the GRE. This chapter reviews all the important rules and formulas you'll need to crack the geometry problems on the GRE. It also provides examples of how such concepts will be tested on the GRE Math section.

Expect to see a handful
of basic geometry
problems on each of
your Math sections.

WHY GEOMETRY?

Good question. If you're going to graduate school for political science or linguistics or history or practically anything that doesn't involve math, you might be wondering why the heck you have to know the area of a circle or the Pythagorean theorem for this exam. While we may not be able to give you a satisfactory answer to that question, we can help you do well on the geometry questions on the GRE.

WHAT YOU NEED TO KNOW

The good news is that you don't need to know much about actual geometry to do well on the GRE; we've boiled down geometry to the handful of bits and pieces that ETS actually tests.

Before we begin, consider yourself warned: Since you'll be taking your test on a computer screen, you'll have to be sure to transcribe all the figures onto your scrap paper accurately. All it takes is one mistaken angle or line and you're sure to get the problem wrong. So make ample use of your scratch paper and always double-check your figures. Start practicing now, by using scratch paper with this book.

Another important thing to know is that you cannot necessarily trust the diagrams ETS gives you. Sometimes they are very deceptive and are intended to confuse you. Always go by what you read, not what you see.

DEGREES, LINES, AND ANGLES

For the GRE, you will need to know that

1. A line is a 180-degree angle. In other words, a line is a perfectly flat angle.
2. When two lines intersect, four angles are formed; the sum of these angles is 360 degrees.
3. When two lines are perpendicular to each other, their intersection forms four 90-degree angles. Here is the symbol ETS uses to indicate perpendicular lines: ⊥ .

4.   Ninety-degree angles are also called *right angles*. A right angle on the GRE is identified by a little box at the intersection of the angle's arms.

90°

5.   The three angles inside a triangle add up to 180 degrees.
6.   The four angles inside any four-sided figure add up to 360 degrees.
7.   A circle contains 360 degrees.
8.   Any line that extends from the center of a circle to the edge of the circle is called a *radius* (plural is *radii*).

Vertical Angles

Vertical angles are the angles that are across from each other when two lines intersect. Vertical angles are always equal. In the drawing below, angle x is equal to angle y (they are vertical angles) and angle a is equal to angle b (they are also vertical angles).

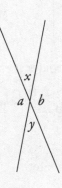

On the GRE, the measure of only one of the vertical angles is typically shown. But usually you'll need to use the other angle to solve the problem.

Parallel Lines

Parallel lines are lines that never intersect. When a pair of parallel lines is intersected by a third, two types of angles are formed: big angles and small angles. Any big angle is equal to any big angle, and any small angle is equal to any small angle. The sum of any big angle and any small angle will always equal 180.

When ETS tells you that two lines are parallel, this is what is being tested. The symbol for parallel lines and the word *parallel* are both clues that tell you what to look for in the problem. The minute you see either of them, immediately identify your big and small angles; they will probably come into play.

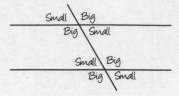

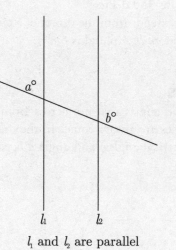

l_1 and l_2 are parallel

Quantity A	**Quantity B**
$a + b$	180

○ Quantity A is greater.

○ Quantity B is greater.

○ The two quantities are equal.

○ The relationship cannot be determined from the information given.

Here's How to Crack It

Notice that you're told that these lines are parallel. Here's one very important point: You need to be told that. You can't assume that they are parallel just because they look like they are.

Okay, so as you just learned, only two angles are formed when two parallel lines are intersected by a third line: a big angle (greater than 90 degrees) and a small one (smaller than 90 degrees). More importantly, you learned that all the big angles are equal, and all the small angles are equal. Therefore, the angle directly across l_1 from angle a is the same as angle b. These now form a straight line, so $a + b = 180$, and the correct answer is (C).

TRIANGLES

Triangles are perhaps ETS's favorite geometrical shape. Triangles have many properties, which make them great candidates for standardized test questions. Make sure you familiarize yourself with the following triangle facts.

Triangles are frequently tested on the GRE.

The Rule of 180°

Every triangle contains three angles that add up to 180 degrees. You must know this fact cold for the exam. This rule applies to every triangle, no matter what it looks like. Here are some examples:

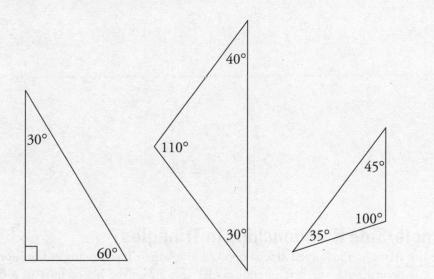

Equilateral Triangles

An **equilateral triangle** is a triangle in which all three sides are equal in length. Because all of the sides are equal in these triangles, all of the angles are equal. Each angle is 60 degrees because 180 divided by 3 is 60.

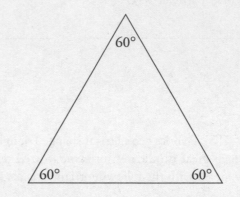

Isosceles Triangles

An **isosceles triangle** is a triangle in which two of the three sides are equal in length. This means that two of the angles are also equal.

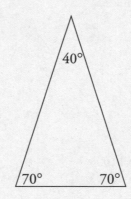

Angle/Side Relationships in Triangles

In any triangle, the longest side is opposite the largest interior angle; the shortest side is opposite the smallest interior angle. That's why the hypotenuse of a right triangle is its longest side—there couldn't be another angle in the triangle bigger than 90 degrees. Furthermore, equal sides are opposite equal angles.

Perimeter of a Triangle

The perimeter of a triangle is simply a measure of the distance around it. All you have to do to find the perimeter of a triangle is add up the lengths of the sides.

The Third Side Rule

Why is it impossible for the following triangle to exist?

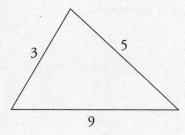

This triangle could not exist because the length of any one side of a triangle is limited by the lengths of the other two sides. This can be summarized by the **third side rule**:

> The length of any one side of a triangle must be less than the sum of the other two sides and greater than the difference between the other two sides.

This rule is not tested frequently on the GRE, but when it is, it's usually the key to solving the problem. Here's what the rule means in application: Take the lengths of any two sides of a triangle. Add them together, then subtract one from the other. The length of the third side must lie between those two numbers.

Take the sides 3 and 5 from the triangle above. What's the longest the third side could measure? Just add and subtract. It could not be as long as 8 (5 + 3) and it could not be as short as 2 (5 − 3).

Therefore, the third side must lie between 2 and 8. It's important to remember that the third side cannot be equal to either 2 or 8. It must be greater than 2 and less than 8.

Try the following question:

A triangle has sides 4, 7, and x. Which of the following could be the perimeter of the triangle?

Indicate <u>all</u> such perimeters.

☐ 13

☐ 16

☐ 17

☐ 20

☐ 22

Here's How to Crack It

Remember the third side rule of triangles here, which is how to find possible lengths of the third side of a triangle when given the two other sides. The third side rule dictates that the length of the third side of a triangle must be greater than the difference, but less than the sum, of the length of the two known sides. In this particular problem, the two known sides are 4 and 7. The difference between 4 and 7 is 3, and the sum of 4 and 7 is 11, so the third side of the triangle must be greater than 3 and less than 11. This can be represented by the expression $3 < x < 11$. Use these values to create a range for the possible perimeter of the triangle. If the third side of the triangle is 3, and the other two sides are 4 and 7, the perimeter is $3 + 4 + 7 = 14$. If the third side of the triangle is 11, and the other two sides are 4 and 7, then the perimeter is $11 + 4 + 7 = 22$. Because the third side of the triangle is *greater* than 3 and *less* than 11, the perimeter of the triangle must be *greater* than 14 and *less* than 22. This can be represented by the expression $14 < perimeter < 22$. The only answer choices that fall in that range are (B), (C), and (D), which are the correct answers.

Area of a Triangle

The area of any triangle is equal to its height (or altitude) multiplied by its base, divided by 2, so

$$A = \frac{1}{2}bh$$

The height of a triangle is defined as the length of a perpendicular line drawn from the point of the triangle to its base.

Any time you see the word *area* or any other word that indicates that a formula is to be used, write the formula on your scratch paper and park the information you're given directly underneath.

The height of a triangle must be perpendicular to the base.

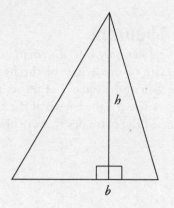

This area formula works on any triangle.

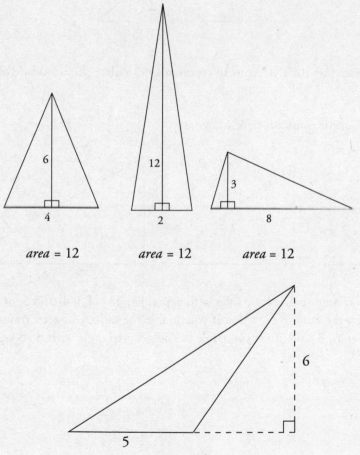

area = 12   *area* = 12   *area* = 12

area = 15

ETS will sometimes try to intimidate you by using multiples of the common Pythagorean triples. For example, you might see a 10-24-26 triangle. That's just a 5-12-13 in disguise.

The Pythagorean Theorem

The Pythagorean theorem applies only to right triangles. This theorem states that in a right triangle, the square of the length of the hypotenuse (the longest side, remember?) is equal to the sum of the squares of the lengths of the two other sides. In other words, $c^2 = a^2 + b^2$, where c is the length of the hypotenuse and a and b are the lengths of the other sides. (The two sides that are not the hypotenuse are called the legs.)

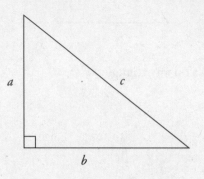

You can always use the Pythagorean theorem to calculate the third side of a right triangle.

Here are the most common right triangles:

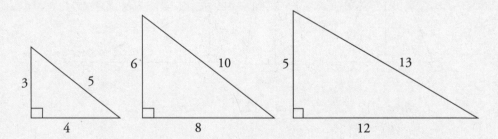

Note that a triangle could have sides with actual lengths of 3, 4, and 5, or 3 : 4 : 5 could just be the ratio of the sides. If you double the ratio, you get a triangle with sides equal to 6, 8, and 10. If you triple it, you get a triangle with sides equal to 9, 12, and 15.

Let's try an example.

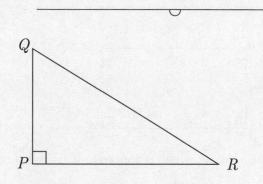

In the figure above, if the distance from point P to point Q is 6 miles and the distance from point Q to point R is 10 miles, what is the distance from point P to point R ?

○ 4

○ 5

○ 6

○ 7

○ 8

Here's How to Crack It

Once you've sensitized yourself to the standard right triangles, this problem couldn't be easier. When you see a right triangle, be suspicious. One leg is 6. The hypotenuse is 10. The triangle has a ratio of 3 : 4 : 5. Therefore, the third side (the other leg) must be 8.

The Pythagorean theorem will sometimes help you solve problems that involve squares or rectangles. For example, every rectangle or square can be divided into two right triangles. This means that if you know the length and width of any rectangle or square, you also know the length of the diagonal—it's the shared hypotenuse of the hidden right triangles.

Here's an example:

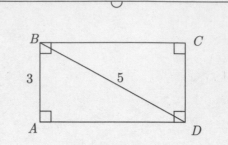

In the rectangle above, what is the area of triangle *ABD* ?

Click on the answer box and type in a number.
Backspace to erase.

Here's How to Crack It

We were told that this is a rectangle (remember that you can never assume!), which means that triangle *ABD* is a right triangle. Not only that, but it's a 3 : 4 : 5 right triangle (with a side of 3 and a hypotenuse of 5, it must be), with side *AD* = 4. So, the area of triangle *ABD* is $\frac{1}{2}$ the base (3) times the height (4). That's $\frac{1}{2}$ of 12, or 6. Enter that value into the box.

Right Isosceles Triangles

If you take a square and cut it in half along its diagonal, you will create a right isosceles triangle. The two sides of the square stay the same. The 90-degree angle will stay the same, and the other two angles that were 90 degrees each get cut in half and are now 45 degrees. The ratio of sides in a right isosceles triangle is $x : x : x\sqrt{2}$. This is significant for two reasons. First, if you see a problem with a right triangle and there is a $\sqrt{2}$ anywhere in the problem, you know what to look for. Second, you always know the length of the diagonal of a square because it is one side times the square root of two.

You always know the length of the diagonal of a square because it is one side of the square times $\sqrt{2}$.

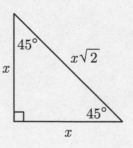

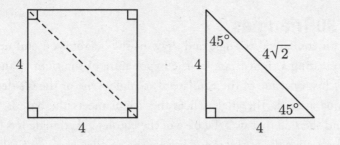

Let's try an example involving a special right triangle.

———————————○———————————

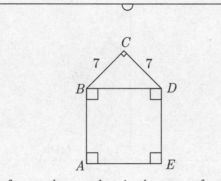

In the figure above, what is the area of square *ABDE* ?

○ $28\sqrt{2}$

○ 49

○ $49\sqrt{2}$

○ 98

○ $98\sqrt{2}$

Here's How to Crack It

In order to figure out the area of square *ABDE*, we need to know the length of one of its sides. We can get the length of *BD* by using the isosceles right triangle attached to it. *BD* is the hypotenuse, which means its length is $7\sqrt{2}$. To get the area of the square we have to square the length of the side we know, or $\left(7\sqrt{2}\right)\left(7\sqrt{2}\right) =$ (49)(2) = 98. That's (D).

———————————○———————————

You can always calculate the area of an equilateral triangle because you know that the height is one half of one side times $\sqrt{3}$.

30 : 60 : 90 Triangles

If you take an equilateral triangle and draw in the height, you end up cutting it in half and creating a right triangle. The hypotenuse of the right triangle has not changed; it's just one side of the equilateral triangle. One of the 60-degree angles stays the same as well. The angle where the height meets the base is 90 degrees, naturally, and the side that was the base of the equilateral triangle has been cut in half. The smallest angle, at the top, opposite the smallest side, is 30 degrees. The ratio of sides on a 30 : 60 : 90 triangle is $x : x\sqrt{3} : 2x$. Here's what it looks like:

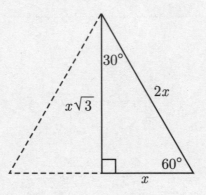

This is significant for two reasons. The first is that if you see a problem with a right triangle and one side is double the other or there is a $\sqrt{3}$ anywhere in the problem, you know what to look for. The second is that you always know the area of an equilateral triangle because you always know the height. The height is one half of one side times the square root of 3.

Here's one more:

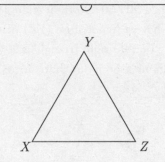

Triangle XYZ in the figure above is an equilateral triangle. If the perimeter of the triangle is 12, what is its area?

○ $2\sqrt{3}$

○ $4\sqrt{3}$

○ 8

○ 12

○ $8\sqrt{3}$

If you see $\sqrt{2}$ or $\sqrt{3}$ in the answer choices of the problem, it's a tip-off that the problem is testing special right triangles.

Here's How to Crack It

Here we have an equilateral triangle with a perimeter of 12, which means that each side has a length of 4 and each angle is 60 degrees. Remember that in order to find the area of a triangle, we use the triangle area formula: $A = \frac{1}{2}\,bh$, but first we need to know the base and the height of the triangle. The base is 4, which now gives us $A = \frac{1}{2}\,4h$, and now the only thing we need is the height. Remember: The height always has to be perpendicular to the base. Draw a vertical line that splits the equilateral triangle in half. The top angle is also split in half, so now we have this:

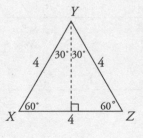

What we've done is create two 30 : 60 : 90 right triangles, and we're going to use one of these right triangles to find the height. Let's use the one on the right. We know that the hypotenuse in a 30 : 60 : 90 right triangle is always twice the length of the short side. Here we have a hypotenuse (*YZ*) of 4, so our short side has to be 2. The long side of a 30 : 60 : 90 right triangle is always equal to the short side multiplied by the square root of 3. So if our short side is 2, then our long side must be $2\sqrt{3}$. That's the height.

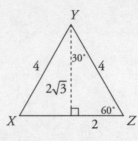

Finally, we return to our area formula. Now we have $A = \dfrac{1}{2} \times 4 \times 2\sqrt{3}$. Multiply it out and you get $A = 4\sqrt{3}$. The answer is (B).

FOUR-SIDED FIGURES

The four angles inside any figure that has four sides add up to 360 degrees. That includes rectangles, squares, and parallelograms. Parallelograms are four-sided figures made out of two sets of parallel lines whose area can be found with the formula $A = bh$, where *h* is the height of a line drawn perpendicular to the base.

Perimeter of a Rectangle

The perimeter of a rectangle is just the sum of the lengths of its four sides.

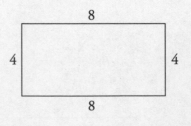

perimeter = 4 + 8 + 4 + 8

Area of a Rectangle

The area of a rectangle is equal to its length times its width. For example, the area of the rectangle above is 32 (or 8 × 4).

Squares

A square has four equal sides. The perimeter of a square is, therefore, four times the length of any side. The area of a square is equal to the length of any side times itself, or in other words, the length of any side, squared. The diagonal of a square splits it into two 45 : 45 : 90, or isosceles, right triangles.

CIRCLES

Circles are a popular test topic for ETS. There are a few properties that the GRE likes to test over and over again and problems with circles also always seem to use that funny little symbol π. Here's all you need to know about circles.

> **The World of Pi**
>
> You may remember being taught that the value of pi (π) is 3.14, or even 3.14159. On the GRE, π = 3ish is a close enough approximation. You don't need to be any more precise than that when doing GRE problems.
>
> What you might not recall about pi is that pi (π) is the ratio between the circumference of a circle and its diameter. When we say that π is a little bigger than 3, we're saying that every circle is about three times as far around as it is across.

Chord, Radius, and Diameter

A **chord** is a line that connects two points on the circumference of a circle. The **radius** of a circle is any line that extends from the center of the circle to a point on the circumference of the circle. The **diameter** of a circle is a line that connects two points on the circumference of the circle and that goes through the center of the circle. Therefore, the diameter of a circle is twice as long as its radius. Notice as well that the diameter of a circle is also the longest chord and that a radius is not a chord.

The radius is always the key to circle problems.

Circumference of a Circle

The **circumference** of a circle is like the perimeter of a triangle: It's the distance around the outside. The formula for finding the circumference of a circle is 2 times π times the radius, or π times the diameter.

Circumference is just a fancy way of saying perimeter.

> circumference = $2\pi r$ or πd

If the diameter of a circle is 4, then its circumference is 4π, or roughly 12+. If the diameter of a circle is 10, then its circumference is 10π, or a little more than 30.

An **arc** is a section of the outside, or circumference, of a circle. An angle formed by two radii is called a **central angle** (it comes out to the edge from the center of the circle). There are 360 degrees in a circle, so if there is an arc formed by, say, a 60-degree central angle, and 60 is $\frac{1}{6}$ of 360, then the arc formed by this 60-degree central angle will be $\frac{1}{6}$ of the circumference of the circle.

Area of a Circle

The area of a circle is equal to π times the square of its radius.

When working with π, leave it as π in your calculations. Also, leave $\sqrt{3}$ as $\sqrt{3}$. The answer will have them that way.

$$\text{area} = \pi r^2$$

Let's try an example of a circle question.

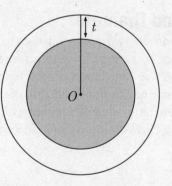

In the wheel above, with center O, the area of the entire wheel is 169π. If the area of the shaded hubcap is 144π, then $t =$

Click on the answer box and type in a number.
Backspace to erase.

Here's How to Crack It

We have to figure out what t is, and it's going to be the length of the radius of the entire wheel minus the length of the radius of the hubcap. If the area of the entire wheel is 169π, the radius is $\sqrt{169}$, or 13. If the area of the hubcap is 144π, the radius is $\sqrt{144}$, or 12. $13 - 12 = 1$. Enter this value into the box.

───────────────○───────────────

Let's try another one.

───────────────○───────────────

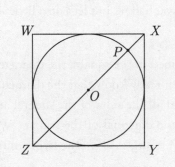

In the figure above, a circle with the center O is inscribed in square $WXYZ$. If the circle has radius 3, then $PZ =$

- ○ 6
- ○ $3\sqrt{2}$
- ○ $6 + \sqrt{2}$
- ○ $3 + \sqrt{3}$
- ○ $3\sqrt{2} + 3$

Ballparking answers will help you eliminate choices.

Here's How to Crack It

Inscribed means that the edges of the shapes are touching. The radius of the circle is 3, which means that PO is 3. If Z were at the other end of the diameter from P, this problem would be easy and the answer would be 6, right? But Z is beyond the edge of the circle, which means that PZ is a little more than 6. Let's stop there for a minute and glance at the answer choices. We can eliminate anything that's "out of the ballpark"—in other words, any answer choice that's less than 6, equal to 6 itself, or a lot more than 6. Remember when we told you to memorize a few of those square roots?

Let's use them:

(A) Exactly 6? Nope.

(B) That's 1.4 × 3, which is 4.2. Too small.

(C) That's 6 + 1.4, or 7.4. Not bad. Let's leave that one in.

(D) That's 3 + 1.7, or 4.7. Too small.

(E) That's (3 × 1.4) + 3, which is 4.2 + 3, or 7.2. Not bad. Let's leave that one in too.

So we eliminated three choices with Ballparking. We're left with (C) and (E). You could take a guess here if you had to, but let's do a little more geometry to find the correct answer.

Because this circle is inscribed in the square, the diameter of the circle is the same as a side of the square. We already know that the diameter of the circle is 6, so that means that ZY, and indeed all the sides of the square, are also 6. Now, if ZY is 6, and XY is 6, what's XZ, the diagonal of the square? Well, XZ is also the hypotenuse of the isosceles right triangle XYZ. The hypotenuse of a right triangle with two sides of 6 is $6\sqrt{2}$. That's approximately 6 × 1.4, or 8.4.

The question is asking for PZ, which is a little less than XZ. It's somewhere between 6 and 8.4. The pieces that aren't part of the diameter of the circle are equal to 8.4 – 6, or 2.4. Divide that in half to get 1.2, which is the distance from the edge of the circle to Z. That means that PZ is 6 + 1.2, or 7.2. Check your remaining answers: Choice (C) is 7.4, and (E) is 7.2. Bingo! The answer is (E).

THE COORDINATE SYSTEM

On a coordinate system, the horizontal line is called the **x-axis** and the vertical line is called the **y-axis**. The four areas formed by the intersection of these axes are called **quadrants**. The point where the axes intersect is called the **origin**. This is what it looks like:

Coordinate geometry questions often test basic shapes such as triangles and squares.

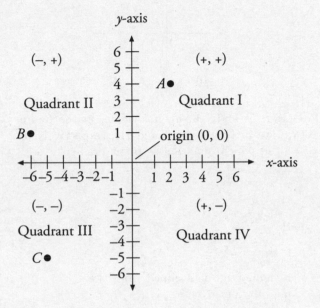

To express any point in the coordinate system, you first give the horizontal value, then the vertical value, or (*x*, *y*). In the diagram above, point *A* can be described by the coordinates (2, 4). That is, the point is two spaces to the right of the origin and four spaces above the origin. Point *B* can be described by the coordinates (–6, 1). That is, it is six spaces to the left and one space above the origin. What are the coordinates of point *C*? Right, it's (–5, –5).

Here's a GRE example:

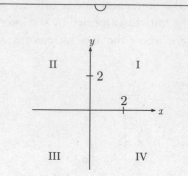

Points $(x, 5)$ and $(-6, y)$, not shown in the figure above, are in Quadrants I and III, respectively. If $xy \neq 0$, in which quadrant is point (x, y) ?

○ IV

○ III

○ II

○ I

○ It cannot be determined from the information given.

Here's How to Crack It

If point $(x, 5)$ is in Quadrant I, that means x is positive. If point y is in Quadrant III, then y is negative. The quadrant that would contain coordinate points with a positive x and a negative y is Quadrant IV. That's (A).

Slope

Trickier questions involving the coordinate system might give you the equation for a line on the grid, which will involve something called the slope of the line. The equation of a line is

$$y = mx + b$$

In this equation x and y are both points on the line, b stands for the y-intercept, or the point at which the line crosses the y-axis, and m is the slope of the line.

Slope is defined as the vertical change divided by the horizontal change, often called "the rise over the run" or the "change in y over the change in x."

$$\text{Slope} = \frac{\text{rise}}{\text{run}} = \frac{(y_2 - y_1)}{(x_2 - x_1)}$$

Sometimes on the GRE, m is written instead as a, as in $y = ax + b$. You'll see all this in action in a moment.

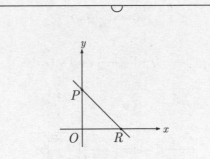

The line $y = -\dfrac{8}{7}x + 1$ is graphed on the rectangular

coordinate axes.

Quantity A	**Quantity B**
OR	*OP*

○ Quantity A is greater.

○ Quantity B is greater.

○ The two quantities are equal.

○ The relationship cannot be determined from the information given.

Here's How to Crack It

The y-intercept, or b, in this case is 1. That means the line crosses the y-axis at 1. So the coordinates of point P are $(0, 1)$. Now we have to figure out what the coordinates of point R are. We know the y-coordinate is 0, so let's stick that into the equation (the slope and the y-intercept are constant; they don't change).

$$y = mx + b$$

$$0 = -\frac{8}{7}x + 1$$

Now let's solve for x.

$$0 = -\frac{8}{7}x + 1$$

$$0 - 1 = -\frac{8}{7}x + 1 - 1$$

$$-1 = -\frac{8}{7}x$$

$$\left(-\frac{7}{8}\right)(-1) = \left(-\frac{7}{8}\right)\left(-\frac{8}{7}\right)x$$

$$\frac{7}{8} = x$$

So the coordinates of point R are $(\frac{7}{8}, 0)$. That means OR, in Quantity A, is equal to $\frac{7}{8}$, and OP, in Quantity B, is equal to 1. The answer is (B).

Another approach to this question would be to focus on the meaning of slope. Because the slope is $-\frac{8}{7}$, that means the vertical change is 8 and the horizontal change is 7. In other words, you count up 8 and over 7. Clearly the rise is more than the run; thus OP is more than OR.

Incidentally, if you're curious about the difference between a positive and negative slope, any line that rises from left to right has a positive slope. Any line that falls from left to right has a negative slope. (A horizontal line has a slope of 0, and a vertical line is said to have "no slope.")

VOLUME

You can find the volume of a three-dimensional figure by multiplying the area of a two-dimensional figure by its height (or depth). For example, to find the volume of a rectangular solid, you would take the area of a rectangle and multiply it by the depth. The formula is *lwh* (length × width × height). To find the volume of a circular cylinder, take the area of a circle and multiply by the height. The formula is πr^2 times the height (or $\pi r^2 h$).

DIAGONALS IN THREE DIMENSIONS

There's a special formula that you can use if you are ever asked to find the length of a diagonal (the longest distance between any two corners) inside a three-dimensional rectangular box. It is $a^2 + b^2 + c^2 = d^2$, where a, b, and c are the dimensions of the figure (kind of looks like the Pythagorean theorem, huh?).

Take a look:

What is the length of the longest distance between any two corners in a rectangular box with dimensions 3 inches by 4 inches by 5 inches?

○ 5

○ 12

○ $5\sqrt{2}$

○ $12\sqrt{2}$

○ 50

Here's How to Crack It

Let's use our formula, $a^2 + b^2 + c^2 = d^2$. The dimensions of the box are 3, 4, and 5.

$$3^2 + 4^2 + 5^2 = d^2$$
$$9 + 16 + 25 = d^2$$
$$50 = d^2$$
$$\sqrt{50} = d$$
$$\sqrt{25 \times 2} = d$$
$$\sqrt{25} \times \sqrt{2} = d$$
$$5\sqrt{2} = d$$

That's (C).

Questions that ask about diagonals are really about the Pythagorean theorem.

Don't confuse surface area with volume.

SURFACE AREA

The surface area of a rectangular box is equal to the sum of the areas of all of its sides. In other words, if you had a box whose dimensions were $2 \times 3 \times 4$, there would be two sides that are 2 by 3 (this surface would have an area of 6), two sides that are 3 by 4 (area of 12), and two sides that are 2 by 4 (area of 8). So, the total surface area would be $6 + 6 + 12 + 12 + 8 + 8$, which is 52.

Key Formulas and Rules

Here is a review of the key rules and formulas to know for the GRE Math section.

Lines and angles

- All straight lines have 180 degrees.
- A right angle measures 90 degrees.
- Vertical angles are equal.
- Parallel lines cut by a third line have two kinds of angles: big angles and small angles. All of the big angles are equal and all of the small angles are equal. The sum of a big angle and a small angle is 180 degrees.

Triangles

- All triangles have 180 degrees.
- The angles and sides of a triangle are in proportion—the largest angle is opposite the largest side and the smallest side is opposite the smallest angle.
- The Pythagorean theorem is $c^2 = a^2 + b^2$ where c is the length of the hypotenuse.
- The area formula for a triangle is

    $A = \dfrac{bh}{2}$.

Quadrilaterals

- All quadrilaterals have 360 degrees.
- The area formula for a squares and rectangles is bh.

Circles

- All circles have 360 degrees.
- The radius is the distance from the center of the circle to any point on the edge.
- The area of a circle is πr^2.
- The circumference of a circle is $2\pi r$.

PLUGGING IN ON GEOMETRY PROBLEMS

Remember: Whenever you have a question that has answer choices, like a regular multiple-choice question or a multiple-choice, multiple-answer question that has variables in the answer choices, Plug In. On geometry problems, you can plug in values for angles or lengths as long as the values you plug in don't contradict either the wording of the problem or the laws of geometry (you can't have the interior angles of a triangle add up to anything but 180, for instance).

Here's an example:

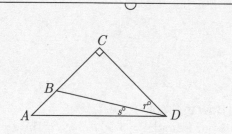

In the drawing above, if $AC = CD$, then $r =$

- ○ $45 - s$
- ○ $90 - s$
- ○ s
- ○ $45 + s$
- ○ $60 + s$

Here's How to Crack It

See the variables in the answer choices? Let's Plug In. First of all, we're told that *AC* and *CD* are equal, which means that *ACD* is an isosceles right triangle. So angles *A* and *D* both have to be 45 degrees. Now it's Plugging In time. The smaller angles, *r* and *s*, must add up to 45 degrees, so let's make *r* = 40 degrees and *s* = 5 degrees. The question asks for the value of *r*, which is 40, so that's our target answer. Now eliminate answer choices by plugging in 5 for *s*.

       (A) 45 − 5 = 40. Bingo! Check the other choices to be sure.

       (B) 90 − 5 = 85. Nope.

       (C) 5. Nope.

       (D) 45 + 5 = 50. Eliminate it.

       (E) 60 + 5 = 65. No way.

By the way, we knew that the correct answer couldn't be greater than 45 degrees, because that's the measure of the entire angle *D*, so you could have eliminated (D) and (E) right away.

DRAW IT YOURSELF

When ETS doesn't include a drawing with a geometry problem, it usually means that the drawing, if supplied, would make ETS's answer obvious. In cases like this, you should just draw it yourself. Here's an example:

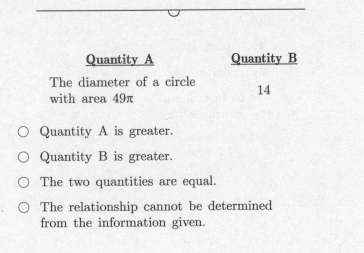

Quantity A	Quantity B
The diameter of a circle with area 49π	14

  ○ Quantity A is greater.

  ○ Quantity B is greater.

  ○ The two quantities are equal.

  ○ The relationship cannot be determined from the information given.

Don't forget to Plug In on geometry questions. Just pick numbers according to the rules of geometry.

Here's How to Crack It

Visualize the figure. If the area is 49π, what's the radius? Right: 7. And if the radius is 7, what's the diameter? Right: 14. The answer is (C).

Redraw

On tricky quant comp questions, you may need to draw the figure once, eliminate two answer choices, and then draw it another way to try to disprove your first answer and to see if the answer is (D). Here's an example of a problem that might require you to do this:

For quant comp geometry questions, draw, eliminate, and REDRAW; it's like Plugging In twice.

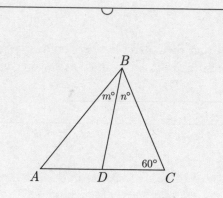

D is the midpoint of AC.

Quantity A	Quantity B
m	n

○ Quantity A is greater.

○ Quantity B is greater.

○ The two quantities are equal.

○ The relationship cannot be determined from the information given.

Here's How to Crack It

Are you sure that the triangle looks exactly like this? Nope. We know only what we are told—that the lengths of *AD* and *DC* are equal; from this figure, it looks like angles *m* and *n* are also equal. Because this means that it's possible for them to be, we can eliminate (A) and (B). But let's redraw the figure to try to disprove our first answer.

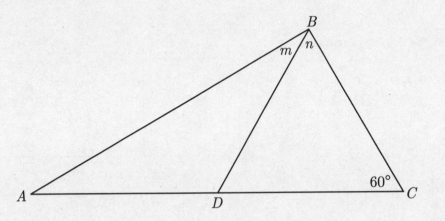

Try drawing the triangle as stretched out as possible. Notice that *n* is now clearly greater than *m,* so you can eliminate (C), and the answer is (D).

Geometry Drill

Think you have mastered these concepts? Try your hand at the following problems and check your work after you have finished. You can find the answers in Part V.

Which of the following could be the degree measures of two angles in a right triangle?

Indicate <u>all</u> such angles.

- ☐ 20° and 70°
- ☐ 30° and 60°
- ☐ 45° and 45°
- ☐ 55° and 55°
- ☐ 75° and 75°

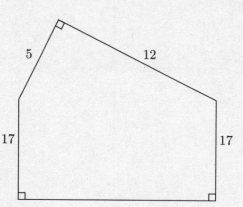

What is the perimeter of the figure above?

- ○ 51
- ○ 64
- ○ 68
- ○ 77
- ○ 91

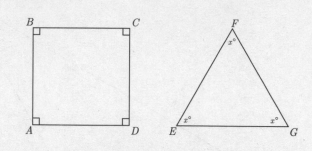

$$AB = BC = EG$$

$$FG = 8$$

Quantity A	Quantity B
The area of square $ABCD$	32

- ○ Quantity A is greater.
- ○ Quantity B is greater.
- ○ The two quantities are equal.
- ○ The relationship cannot be determined from the information given.

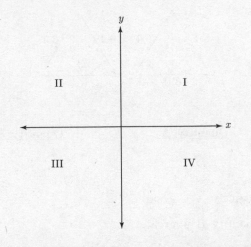

(*a*, 6) is a point (not shown) in Quadrant I.

(–6, *b*) is a point (not shown) in Quadrant II.

Quantity A	**Quantity B**
a	*b*

○ Quantity A is greater.

○ Quantity B is greater.

○ The two quantities are equal.

○ The relationship cannot be determined from the information given.

5 of 15

A piece of twine with length of *t* is cut into two pieces. The length of the longer piece is 2 yards greater than 3 times the length of the shorter piece. Which of the following is the length, in yards, of the longer piece?

○ $\dfrac{t+3}{3}$

○ $\dfrac{3t+2}{3}$

○ $\dfrac{t-2}{4}$

○ $\dfrac{3t+4}{4}$

○ $\dfrac{3t+2}{4}$

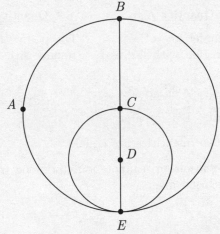

The circle with center *D* is drawn inside the circle with center *C*, as shown in the figure above. If $CD = 3$, what is the area of semicircle *EAB* ?

○ $\dfrac{9}{2}\pi$

○ 9π

○ 12π

○ 18π

○ 36π

7 of 15

For the final exam in a scuba diving certification course, Karl navigates from one point in a lake to another. Karl begins the test *x* meters directly beneath the boat and swims straight down toward the bottom of the lake for 8 meters. He then turns to his right and swims in a straight line parallel to the surface of the lake and swims 24 meters, at which point he swims directly from his location, in a straight line, back to the boat. If the distance that Karl swims back to the boat is 26 meters, what is the value of *x* ?

 meters

Click on the answer box and type in a number. Backspace to erase.

Quantity A	**Quantity B**
The circumference of a circular region with radius r	The perimeter of a square with side r

○ Quantity A is greater.

○ Quantity B is greater.

○ The two quantities are equal.

○ The relationship cannot be determined from the information given.

Triangle ABC is contained within a circle with center C. Points A and B lie on the circle. If the area of circle C is 25π, and the measure of angle ACB is $60°$, which of the following are possible lengths for side AB of triangle ABC?

Indicate all such lengths.

☐ 3

☐ 4

☐ 5

☐ 6

☐ 7

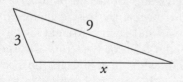

Quantity A	**Quantity B**
x	5.9

○ Quantity A is greater.

○ Quantity B is greater.

○ The two quantities are equal.

○ The relationship cannot be determined from the information given.

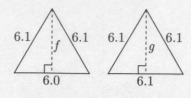

Quantity A	**Quantity B**
f	g

○ Quantity A is greater.

○ Quantity B is greater.

○ The two quantities are equal.

○ The relationship cannot be determined from the information given.

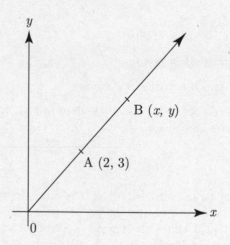

Given points $A(2, 3)$ and $B(x, y)$ in the rectangular coordinate system above, if $y = 4.2$, then $x =$

○ 2.6

○ 2.8

○ 2.9

○ 3.0

○ 3.2

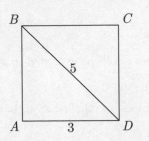

In rectangle *ABCD* above, which of the following is the area of the triangle *ABD* ?

○   6

○   7.5

○   10

○   12

○   15

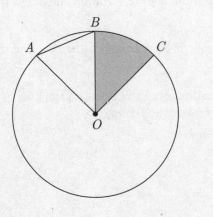

The circle above has a center *O*.
$$\angle AOB = \angle BOC$$

Quantity A

The area of
triangle *AOB*

Quantity B

The area of the
shaded region

○ Quantity A is greater.

○ Quantity B is greater.

○ The two quantities are equal.

○ The relationship cannot be determined from the
information given.

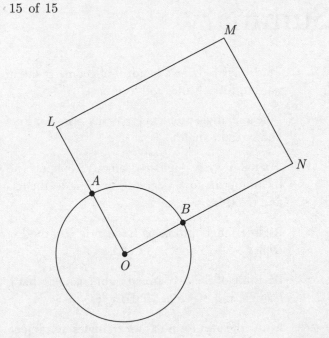

The circumference of the circle with center *O* shown
above is 15π. *LMNO* is a parallelogram and
$\angle OLM = 108°$. What is the length of minor arc *AB* ?

○   15π

○   9π

○   3π

○   2π

○   π

Summary

- There may only be a handful of geometry questions on the GRE, but you'll be expected to know a fair number of rules and formulas.

- Line and angle problems typically test your knowledge of vertical angles, parallel lines, right angles, and straight angles.

- Triangles are a popular geometry topic on the GRE. Make sure you know your triangle basics, including the total degrees of a triangle, the relationship between the angles and sides of a triangle, and the third side rule.

- Right triangle problems frequently test the Pythagorean theorem and the common Pythagorean triples 3 : 4 : 5 and 5 : 12 : 13.

- Be aware of the two special right triangles that ETS likes to torture test takers with: the 45 : 45 : 90 triangle and 30 : 60 : 90 triangle.

- Know the area formulas for triangles, rectangles, squares, and circles.

- Problems involving the xy-coordinate plane frequently test common geometry concepts such as the area of a triangle or a square. Other plane geometry questions will test you on slope and the equation of a line.

- Slope is defined as "rise over run." Find it by finding the change in y-coordinates (the rise) and the change in x-coordinates (the run).

- The equation of a line is $y = mx + b$, where x and y are the coordinates of any point on the line, m is the slope and b is the y-intercept, the point at which the line crosses the y-axis.

- Don't forget to Plug In on geometry problems!

Chapter 14
Math Et Cetera

There are a few more math topics that may appear on the GRE that don't fit nicely into the preceding chapters. This chapter looks at some of these leftover topics, including probability, permutations and combinations, and factorials. The topics in this chapter are not essential to your GRE Math score, because these areas are not tested as frequently as the topics detailed earlier. However, if you feel confident with the previous math topics, and you're looking to maximize your GRE Math score, this chapter will show you all you need to know to tackle these more obscure GRE problems.

OTHER MATH TOPICS

These topics show up rarely on the GRE, but if you're going for a very high score, they are useful to know.

The bulk of the GRE Math section tests your knowledge of fundamentals, basic algebra, and geometry. However, there are a few other topics that may appear. These "et cetera" concepts usually show up only once or twice per test (although at higher scoring levels they may appear more frequently) and often cause anxiety among test takers. Many test takers worry excessively about probability problems, for example, even though knowledge of more familiar topics such as fractions and percents will be far more important in determining your GRE math score. So tackle these problems only after you've mastered the rest. If you find these concepts more difficult, don't worry—they won't make or break your GRE score.

PROBABILITY

If you flip a coin, what's the probability that it will land heads up? The probability is equal to one out of two, or $\frac{1}{2}$. What is the probability that it won't land heads up? Again, one out of two, or $\frac{1}{2}$. If you flip a coin nine times, what's the probability that the coin will land on heads on the tenth flip? Still 1 out of 2, or $\frac{1}{2}$. Previous flips do not affect the outcome of the current coin flip.

You can think of probability as just another type of fraction. **Probabilities** express a special relationship, namely the chance of a certain outcome occurring. In a probability fraction, the denominator is the total number of possible outcomes that may occur, while the numerator is the number of outcomes that would satisfy the criteria. For example, if you have 10 shirts and 3 of them are black, the probability of selecting a black shirt from your closet without looking is $\frac{3}{10}$.

Think of probability in terms of fractions:

- If it is impossible for something to happen—if no outcomes satisfy the criteria—then the numerator of the probability fraction is 0 and the probability is equal to 0.
- If something is certain to happen—if all possible outcomes satisfy the criteria—then the numerator and denominator of the fraction are equal and the probability is equal to 1.
- If it is possible for something to occur, but it will not definitely occur, then the probability of it occurring is between 0 and 1.

Since probability is expressed as a fraction, it can also be expressed as a decimal or a percentage. A probability of one-half is equivalent to a probability of 0.5 or 50%.

$$\text{probablity} = \frac{\text{number of possible outcomes that satisfy the condition}}{\text{number of total possible outcomes}}$$

Let's see how it works.

At a meeting of 375 members of a neighborhood association, $\frac{1}{5}$ of the participants have lived in the community for less than 5 years and $\frac{2}{3}$ of the attendees have lived in the neighborhood for at least 10 years. If a member of the meeting is selected at random, what is the probability that the person has lived in the neighborhood for at least 5 years but less than 10 years?

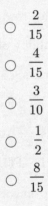

○ $\frac{2}{15}$

○ $\frac{4}{15}$

○ $\frac{3}{10}$

○ $\frac{1}{2}$

○ $\frac{8}{15}$

Here's How to Crack It

In order to solve this problem, we need to put together our probability fraction. The denominator of our fraction is going to be 375, the total number of people from which we are selecting. Next we need to figure out how many attendees satisfy the criteria of having lived in the neighborhood for more than 5 years but fewer than 10 years.

What number goes on the bottom of the probability fraction?

First, we know that $\frac{1}{5}$ of the participants have lived in the neighborhood for less than 5 years. $\frac{1}{5}$ of 375 is 75 people, so we can take them out of the running. Also, $\frac{2}{3}$ of the attendees have lived in the neighborhood for at least 10 years. $\frac{2}{3}$ of 375 (be careful not to use 300 as the total!) is 250, so we can also remove them from consideration. Thus, if 75 people have lived in the neighborhood for less than 5 years and 250 have lived for at least 10, the remaining people are the ones we want. 250 + 75 is 325, so that leaves us with 50 people who satisfy the criteria. We need to make 50 the numerator of our fraction, which gives us $\frac{50}{375}$. This reduces to $\frac{2}{15}$, and (A) is the answer.

Two Important Laws of Probability

Probability of A **and** B
= Probability of A
× Probability of B

When you want to find the probability of a series of events in a row, you multiply the probabilities of the individual events. What is the probability of getting two heads in a row if you flip a coin twice? The probability of getting a head on the first flip is $\frac{1}{2}$. The probability is also $\frac{1}{2}$ that you'll get a head on the second flip, so the combined probability of two heads is $\frac{1}{2} \times \frac{1}{2}$, which equals $\frac{1}{4}$. Another way to look at it is that there are four possible outcomes: HH, TT, HT, TH. Only one of those outcomes consists of two heads in a row. Thus, $\frac{1}{4}$ of the outcomes consist of two heads in a row. Sometimes the number of outcomes is small enough that you can list them and calculate the probability that way.

Probability of A **or** B
= Probability of A
+ Probability of B

(The full formula for the Probability of A or B includes subtracting the Probability of *both* A and B, but the GRE only uses mutually exclusive events, so both A and B can't happen, and you don't need to worry about it!)

Occasionally, instead of finding the probability of one event AND another event happening, you'll be asked to find the probability of either one event OR another event happening. In this situation, instead of multiplying the probabilities, you add them. Let's say you have a normal deck of 52 cards. If you select a card at random, what's the probability that you select a 7 or a 4? The probability of selecting a 7 is $\frac{4}{52}$, which reduces to $\frac{1}{13}$. The probability of selecting a 4 is the same; $\frac{1}{13}$. Therefore, the probability of selecting a 7 or a 4 is $\frac{1}{13} + \frac{1}{13} = \frac{2}{13}$.

Let's look at a problem:

When a pair of six-sided dice, each with faces numbered 1 to 6, is rolled once, what is the probability that the result is either a 3 and a 4 or a 5 and a prime number?

Give your answer as a fraction.

Click on each box and type in a number.
Backspace to erase.

Here's How to Crack It

Probability is fundamentally about counting. You need to be able to count all the things that can happen and count all the situations that meet the conditions of the problem. Sometimes, the easiest way to count both everything that can happen and the situations that meet the condition is to write everything out. In this case, let's use a table:

	1	2	3	4	5	6
1	✗	✗	✗	✗	✗	✗
2	✗	✗	✗	✗	✓	✗
3	✗	✗	✗	✓	✓	✗
4	✗	✗	✓	✗	✗	✗
5	✗	✓	✓	✗	✓	✗
6	✗	✗	✗	✗	✗	✗

Each cell of this table represents a result when the dice are rolled. For example, the cell at the intersection of the row shown as 1 and the column shown as 1 would represent that 1 was showing on each of the two die. This cell has been marked with an ✗ because it does not meet either condition of the problem.

The cells marked with a ✓ are the only dice rolls that meet one of the conditions of the problem. To finish, just count the ✓ marks—there are 7. (Remember that 1 is not prime. That's why combinations such as 5 and 1 are not checked.) Next, count the total possibilities—there are 36. So, the probability of rolling either a 3 and a 4 or a 5 and prime number is $\frac{7}{36}$.

One last important thing you should know about probabilities is that the probability of an event happening and the probability of an event not happening must add up to 1. For example, if the probability of snow falling on one night is $\frac{2}{3}$, then the probability of no snow falling must be $\frac{1}{3}$. If the probability that it will rain is 80%, then the probability that it won't rain must be 20%. The reason this is useful is that, on some GRE probability problems, it will be easier to find the probability that an event doesn't occur; once you have that, just subtract from 1 to find the answer.

Let's look at the following example.

Dipak has a 25% chance of winning each hand of blackjack he plays. If he has $150 and bets $50 a hand, what is the probability that he will still have money after the third hand?

○ $\frac{1}{64}$

○ $\frac{3}{16}$

○ $\frac{27}{64}$

○ $\frac{37}{64}$

○ $\frac{3}{4}$

Here's How to Crack It

If Dipak still has money after the third hand, then he must have won at least one of the hands, and possibly more than one. However, directly calculating the probability that he wins at least one hand is tricky because there are so many ways it could happen (for example, he could lose-lose-win, or W-W-L or W-L-W or L-W-L, and so on). So think about it this way: The question asks for the probability that he will win at least one hand. What if he doesn't? That would mean that he doesn't win any hands at all. If we calculate the probability that he loses every hand, we can then subtract that from 1 and find the corresponding probability that he wins at least one hand. Since Dipak has a 25% chance of winning each hand, this means that he has a 75% chance of losing it, or $\frac{3}{4}$ (the answers are in fractions, so it's best to work with fractions). To find the probability that he loses all three hands, simply multiply the probabilities of his losing each individual hand. $\frac{3}{4} \times \frac{3}{4} \times \frac{3}{4} = \frac{27}{64}$, so there is a $\frac{27}{64}$ probability that he will lose all three hands. Subtracting this from 1 gives you the answer you're looking for. $1 - \frac{27}{64} = \frac{37}{64}$. The answer is (D).

Given events A and B, the probability of
- A and B = (Probability of A) × (Probability of B)
- A or B = Probability of A + Probability of B

Given event A
- Probability of A + Probability of Not A = 1

FACTORIALS

The **factorial** of a number is equal to that number times every positive whole number smaller than that number, down to 1. For example, the factorial of 6 is equal to $6 \times 5 \times 4 \times 3 \times 2 \times 1$, which equals 720. The symbol for a factorial is ! so 4! doesn't mean we're really excited about the number 4, it means $4 \times 3 \times 2 \times 1$, which is equal to 24. (0! is equal to 1, by the way.) When factorials show up in GRE problems, always look for a shortcut like canceling or factoring. The point of a factorial problem is not to make you do a lot of multiplication. Let's try one.

Quantity A	Quantity B
$\dfrac{12!}{11!}$	$\dfrac{4!}{2!}$

○ Quantity A is greater.

○ Quantity B is greater.

○ The two quantities are equal.

○ The relationship cannot be determined from the information given.

Here's How to Crack It

Let's tackle Quantity A. We definitely don't want to multiply out the factorials since that would be pretty time-consuming: 12! and 11! are both huge numbers. Instead let's look at what they have in common. What we're really talking about here is $\dfrac{12 \times 11 \times 10 \times 9 \times 8 \times 7 \times 6 \times 5 \times 4 \times 3 \times 2 \times 1}{11 \times 10 \times 9 \times 8 \times 7 \times 6 \times 5 \times 4 \times 3 \times 2 \times 1}$. Now it's clear that both factorials share everything from 11 on down to 1. The entire bottom of the fraction will cancel and the only thing left on top will be 12, so the value of Quantity A is 12. For Quantity B, we can also write out the factorials and get $\dfrac{4 \times 3 \times 2 \times 1}{2 \times 1}$. The 2 and the 1 in the bottom cancel, and the only thing left on top will be 4×3, which is equal to 12. The two quantities are equal and the answer is (C).

PERMUTATIONS AND COMBINATIONS

Permutation problems often ask for arrangements, orders, schedules, or lists.

The basic definition of a **permutation** is an arrangement of things in a particular order. Suppose you were asked to figure out how many different ways you could arrange five statues on a shelf. All you have to do is multiply $5 \times 4 \times 3 \times 2 \times 1$, or 120. (Yes, this is another application of factorials.) You have five possible statues that could fill the first slot on the shelf, then, once the first slot is filled, there are four remaining statues that could fill the second slot, three that could fill the third slot, and so on, down to one.

Now suppose that there are five people running in a race. The winner of the race will get a gold medal, the person who comes in second will get a silver medal, and the person who comes in third will get a bronze medal. You're asked to figure out how many different orders of gold-silver-bronze winners there can be. (Notice that this is a permutation because the order definitely matters.)

First, ask yourself how many of these runners can come in first? Five. Once one of them comes in first, she's out of the picture, so how many can then come in second? Four. Once one of them comes in second, she's out of the picture, so how many of them can come in third? Three. And now you're done because all three slots have been filled. The answer is $5 \times 4 \times 3$, which is 60.

> To solve a permutation
>
> - Figure out how many slots you have.
> - Write down the number of options for each slot.
> - Multiply them.

The difference between a permutation and a combination is that in a combination, the order is irrelevant. A **combination** is just a group, and the order of elements within the group doesn't matter. For example, suppose you were asked to go to the store and bring home three different types of ice cream. Now suppose that when you got to the store, there were five flavors in the freezer—chocolate, vanilla, strawberry, butter pecan, and mocha. How many combinations of three ice cream flavors could you bring home? Notice that the order doesn't matter, because bringing home chocolate, strawberry, and vanilla is the same thing as bringing home strawberry, vanilla, and chocolate. One way to solve this is the brute force method; in other words, write out every combination.

Combination problems usually ask for groups, teams, or committees.

VCS VCB VCM VSB VSM VBM CSB CSM CBM SBM

That's 10 combinations, but there's a quicker way to do it. Start by filling in the three slots as you would with a permutation (there are three slots because you're supposed to bring home three different types of ice cream). Five flavors could be in the first slot, four could be in the second, and three could be in the third. So far, that's $5 \times 4 \times 3$. But remember, this takes into account all the different orders that three flavors can be arranged in. We don't want that, because the order doesn't matter in a combination. So we have to divide $5 \times 4 \times 3$ by the number of ways of arranging three things. In how many ways can three things be arranged? That's 3!, $3 \times 2 \times 1$, which is 6. Thus we end up with $\frac{5 \times 4 \times 3}{3 \times 2 \times 1}$. Cancel the denominators, to find that all that remains is $5 \times 2 = 10$. Bingo.

Does the order matter?

To solve a combination

- Figure out how many slots you have.
- Fill in the slots as you would a permutation.
- Divide by the factorial of the number of slots.

The denominator of the fraction will always cancel out completely, so it's best to try and cancel first before you multiply.

Always cross off wrong
answer choices on your
scratch paper.

Here's an example:

Brooke wants to hang three paintings in a row on her wall. She has six paintings to choose from. How many arrangements of paintings on the wall can she create?

- ○ 6
- ○ 30
- ○ 90
- ○ 120
- ○ 720

Here's How to Crack It

The first thing you need to do is determine whether the order matters. In this case it does, because we're arranging the paintings on the wall. Putting the Monet on the left and the Van Gogh in the middle isn't the same arrangement as putting the Van Gogh on the left and the Monet in the middle. This is a permutation question. We have three slots to fill because we're arranging three paintings. There are 6 paintings that could fill the first slot, 5 paintings that could fill the second slot, and 4 paintings that could fill the third slot. So we have 6 × 5 × 4, which equals 120. Thus, the correct answer is (D).

Here's another example:

A pizza may be ordered with any of eight possible toppings.

Quantity A	**Quantity B**
The number of different ways to order a pizza with three different toppings	The number of different ways to order a pizza with five different toppings

- ○ Quantity A is greater.
- ○ Quantity B is greater.
- ○ The two quantities are equal.
- ○ The relationship cannot be determined from the information given.

Here's How to Crack It

First, note that for both quantities we're dealing with a combination, because the order of toppings doesn't matter. A pizza with mushrooms and pepperoni is the same thing as a pizza with pepperoni and mushrooms. Let's figure out Quantity A first.

We have eight toppings and we're picking three of them. That means we have three slots to fill. There are 8 toppings that could fill the first slot, 7 that could fill the second slot, and 6 that could fill the third, so we have $8 \times 7 \times 6$. Since this is a combination, we have to divide by the factorial of the number of slots. In this case we have three slots, so we have to divide by 3!, or $3 \times 2 \times 1$. So our problem looks like this: $\frac{8 \times 7 \times 6}{3 \times 2 \times 1}$. To make the multiplication easier, let's cancel first. The 6 on top will cancel with the 3×2 on the bottom, leaving us with $\frac{8 \times 7}{1}$, which is 56. Thus, there are 56 ways to order a three-topping pizza with eight toppings to choose from. Now let's look at Quantity B.

We still have eight toppings, but this time we're picking five of them so we have five slots to fill. There are 8 toppings that could fill the first slot, 7 that could fill the second slot, 6 that could fill the third, 5 that could fill the fourth, and 4 that could fill the fifth. That's $8 \times 7 \times 6 \times 5 \times 4$, but we still have to divide by the factorial of the number of slots. We have five slots, so that means we need to divide by 5!, or $5 \times 4 \times 3 \times 2 \times 1$. Thus we have $\frac{8 \times 7 \times 6 \times 5 \times 4}{5 \times 4 \times 3 \times 2 \times 1}$. We definitely want to cancel first here, rather than doing all that multiplication. The 5 on top will cancel with the 5 on the bottom. Likewise, the 4 on top will cancel with the 4 on the bottom. The 6 on top will cancel with the 3×2 on the bottom, leaving us again with $\frac{8 \times 7}{1}$, which is 56. Therefore, there are also 56 ways to order a five-topping pizza with eight toppings to choose from. The two quantities are equal, and the answer is (C).

Let's try one more:

Nicole needs to form a committee of 3 from a group of 8 research attorneys to study possible changes to the Superior Court. If two of the attorneys are too inexperienced to serve together on the committee, how many different arrangements of committees can Nicole form?

○   20

○   30

○   50

○   56

○   336

Here's How to Crack It

This problem is a little more complicated than an ordinary combination problem, because an extra condition has been placed on the committee. Without that condition, this would be a fairly ordinary combination problem, and we'd simply calculate how many groups of three can be created with eight people to choose from.

There's more than one way to approach this problem. First, you should realize that there are two ways that we could form this committee. We could have three experienced attorneys, or we could have two experienced attorneys and one inexperienced attorney. If we find the number of ways to create each of those two possibilities, we can add them together and have our answer. It's fairly straightforward to calculate the number of ways to have three experienced attorneys on a committee: There are three slots to fill, and we have 6 options for the first slot, 5 for the second, and 4 for the third. Here the order doesn't matter, so we divide by 3! to get $\frac{6 \times 5 \times 4}{3 \times 2 \times 1}$ = 20. Thus there are 20 ways to create the committee using three experienced attorneys. What about creating a committee that has two experienced attorneys and one inexperienced attorney? We have 6 options for the first experienced attorney and 5 options for the second. Order doesn't matter so we divide by 2!. So far we have $\frac{6 \times 5}{2 \times 1}$. Next we have 2 options for the inexperienced attorney, so now we have to multiply by 2, and our calculation is $\frac{6 \times 5}{2 \times 1} \times \frac{2}{1}$ = 30. As you can see, there are 30 ways to create the committee using two experienced attorneys and one inexperienced attorney. Adding 20 and 30 gives us 50 total committees, and the answer is (C).

Here's another way that you could solve the problem. If there were no conditions placed on the committee, we could just calculate $\dfrac{8 \times 7 \times 6}{3 \times 2 \times 1}$, which would give us 56 committees. But we know some of those committees are not allowed; any committee that has the two inexperienced attorneys on it isn't allowed. How many of these types of committees are there? Let's call the inexperienced attorneys A and B. An unacceptable committee would be A B __, in which the last slot could be filled by any of the experienced attorneys. Since there are 6 experienced attorneys, there are 6 unacceptable committees. Subtracting them from 56 gives us 50 acceptable committees. Hey, the answer's still (C)!

FUNCTIONS AND THE GRE

$f(x)$ Notation

ETS often employs the use of function notation to create difficult problems. Generally speaking, the function notation is a style of math problem that causes test takers to be nervous. The function notation, $f(x)$, is unfamiliar to look at, seems difficult and involved, and evokes memories of graphs and charting lines that you may have learned in high school geometry.

The good news is that pure function problems on the GRE are much more straightforward than that and become very manageable if you utilize Plugging In strategies.

The easiest way to think about a function question is to look at an example. Take $f(x) = x + 2$, for instance. All this problem is stating is that for any value of x, the function $f(x)$ is that value plus 2. Let's say that $x = 3$; therefore, to solve this problem, take the value of x and plug it into the given equation. So if $x = 3$, the equation now reads $f(3) = 3 + 2$, or $f(3) = 5$. To solve function notation problems, all you need to do is read the instructions carefully and fill in the values for the variables where appropriate. If you used the same equation, but the value of x is 10, then the function is now $f(10) = 10 + 2$, so $f(10) = 12$.

Sometimes a function problem gives a restriction such as $x \neq 0$. If this is the case, you know that x could be equal to any value but 0, and this is generally for a good reason. If $f(x) = \dfrac{2}{x}$, then x cannot equal 0 because a number cannot be divided by 0.

Try this example of a function question on the GRE.

———————————○———————————

If $-3 \leq g \leq 2$ and $f(g) = -2g$ and g is an integer, then which of the following integers could be a value of $f(g)$?

Indicate <u>all</u> such integers.

☐ –6

☐ –5

☐ –2

☐ 0

☐ 2

☐ 4

☐ 6

Here's How to Crack It

This is a function problem with restrictions, so find all the different values that can be plugged in for g. Since g is an integer that is equal to or between –3 and 2 then there is a range for its values. Therefore, $f(g)$ (which equals $-2g$) is all the integer values between the high and low end of the range of g multiplied by 2. In other words, plug in 2 and –3 for g in the function and figure out what the range is. If $g = -3$, then $f(g)$ is $f(-3) = -2(-3) = 6$. And if $g = 2$, then $f(g)$ is $f(2) = -2(2) = -4$. So the range of $f(g)$ is $-4 \leq f(g) \leq 6$. Choices (A) and (B) are less than –4 and fall out of the range. The rest of the integers fall in the range, so they are possible values of $f(g)$. Therefore the correct answer is (C), (D), (E), (F), and (G).

Evaluating functions is all about following the directions. Just plug in the values for the variable and solve.

———————————○———————————

Functions With Uncommon Symbols: #*µ°ℽ

The GRE also tries to scare students using functions in another way: picking strange symbols and putting them in a problem. When you see a funny symbol that you have never seen before, don't stress out! It's just a function problem in disguise. Follow the directions to find the correct answer.

A problem with funny symbols may look something like the following.

If the operation λ is defined for all integers x and y as $x \lambda y = x^2 + y - 2$, then which of the following is equal to $4 \lambda -3$?

- ○ 21
- ○ 17
- ○ 15
- ○ 11
- ○ 10

Here's How to Crack It

Remember, this is a function problem, so just follow the directions. The problem wants to know the value of $4 \lambda -3$, and it states that $x \lambda y = x^2 + y - 2$. To solve this problem, plug in $x = 4$ and $y = -3$. So $4 \lambda -3 = 4^2 + (-3) - 2$. Now, solve: $4 \lambda -3 = 16 - 3 - 2 = 11$. The correct answer is (D).

You may get a different symbol when you get another problem like this, but the process is still the same. Just plug in the values given for the variables and solve the problem. If you have worked your way through this book and mastered the content, then there won't be any actual mathematical symbols on the GRE that are unfamiliar to you. If you see a symbol like that, it's a function problem!

Let's look at one more example.

For any non-negative integer x, let $x^* = x - 1$.

Quantity A	**Quantity B**
$\dfrac{15\,*}{3\,*}$	$\left(\dfrac{15}{3}\right)^*$

- ○ Quantity A is greater.
- ○ Quantity B is greater.
- ○ The two quantities are equal.
- ○ The relationship cannot be determined from the information given.

Here's How to Crack It

Just follow the directions: $15^* = 15 - 1$, or 14, and $3^* = 3 - 1$, or 2. So Quantity A is $\dfrac{14}{2}$, or 7. Don't forget PEMDAS for Quantity B. First, $\dfrac{15}{3}$ is 5. Then, $5^* = 5 - 1$, or 4. So because Quantity A is 7 and Quantity B is 4, the correct answer is (A).

You might see one group problem on the GRE.

Wrapping Up Math
You're almost done with the Math section. Tackle the Math Drills on the following pages, then give yourself a break before you dive into the Analytical Writing Section. Take a walk, eat a snack, or meet up with a pal and give yourself some downtime before you dive into Part IV.

GROUPS

Group problems, although not too common on the GRE, can be troublesome if you don't know how to set them up. When confronted by a group problem, use the group equation

$$T = G_1 + G_2 - B + N$$

In the equation, T represents the Total, G_1 is one group, G_2 is the second group, B is for the members in both groups and N is for the members in neither group. Here's an example of a typical group problem.

A biologist studying breeding groups noted that of 225 birds tagged for the study, 85 birds made nests in pine trees, 175 made nests in oak trees, and 40 birds did not build nests in either type of tree. How many birds built nests in both types of trees?

- ○ 45
- ○ 60
- ○ 75
- ○ 80
- ○ 125

Here's How to Crack It

Let's use the group equation. The total is 225, one group consists of 85 birds, the other group has 175 birds in it, and we know that 40 birds built nests in neither type of tree. Our equation would look like this:

$$225 = 85 + 175 - B + 40$$

All we have to do is solve for B. Simplifying the equation gives us $225 = 300 - B$, so B must equal 75. Choice (C) is our answer.

Et Cetera Drill

Here are some math questions to practice on. Remember to check your answers when you finish. You can find the answers in Part V.

A bowl contains 15 marbles, all of which are either red or blue. If the number of red marbles is one more than the number of blue marbles, what is the probability that a marble selected at random is blue?

○ $\dfrac{1}{15}$

○ $\dfrac{2}{15}$

○ $\dfrac{7}{15}$

○ $\dfrac{1}{2}$

○ $\dfrac{8}{15}$

If $¥(x) = 10x - 1$, what is $¥(5) - ¥(3)$?

○   15

○   18

○   19

○   20

○   46

For all positive integer values of x, $\#x = 2^{-x}$.

Quantity A	Quantity B
#8	#4

○ Quantity A is greater.

○ Quantity B is greater.

○ The two quantities are equal.

○ The relationship cannot be determined from the information given.

At a recent dog show, there were 5 finalists. One of the finalists was awarded "Best in Show" and another finalist was awarded "Honorable Mention." In how many ways could the two awards be given out?

Click on the answer box and type in a number. Backspace to erase.

Company X budgets \$90,000 total on advertising for all of its products per year. Company X budgets \$40,000 for all advertising for product A and \$30,000 for all advertising for product B. From the budgets for products A and B, \$15,000 is budgeted for advertisements that feature both products used as a system.

Quantity A	Quantity B
The total amount Company X budgets for advertising products other than products A and B.	\$20,000

○ Quantity A is greater.

○ Quantity B is greater.

○ The two quantities are equal.

○ The relationship cannot be determined from the information given.

Lee randomly selects a 2-digit prime number less than 50. What is the probability that the tens digit is greater than the units digit?

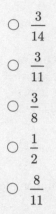

- ○ $\dfrac{3}{14}$
- ○ $\dfrac{3}{11}$
- ○ $\dfrac{3}{8}$
- ○ $\dfrac{1}{2}$
- ○ $\dfrac{8}{11}$

An elected official wants to take five members of his staff to an undisclosed secure location. What is the minimum number of staff members the elected official must employ in order to have at least 20 different groups that could be taken to the location?

- ○ 7
- ○ 8
- ○ 9
- ○ 10
- ○ 11

For all real numbers x and y, if $x \# y = x(x - y)$, then $x \# (x \# y) =$

- ○ $x^2 - xy$
- ○ $x^2 - 2xy$
- ○ $x^3 - x^2 - xy$
- ○ $x^3 - (xy)^2$
- ○ $x^2 - x^3 + x^2y$

A jar contains 12 marbles. Each is either yellow or green and there are twice as many yellow marbles as green marbles. If two marbles are to be selected from the jar at random, what is the probability that exactly one of each color is selected?

- ○ $\dfrac{8}{33}$
- ○ $\dfrac{16}{33}$
- ○ $\dfrac{1}{2}$
- ○ $\dfrac{17}{33}$
- ○ $\dfrac{25}{33}$

A set of 10 points lies in a plane such that no three points are collinear.

Quantity A	Quantity B
The number of distinct triangles that can be created from the set	The number of distinct quadrilaterals that can be created from the set

- ○ Quantity A is greater.
- ○ Quantity B is greater.
- ○ The two quantities are equal.
- ○ The relationship cannot be determined from the information given.

Comprehensive Math Drill

Let's do a drill involving all of the math topics we have covered throughout the book. Remember to check your answers when you finish. You can find the answers in Part V.

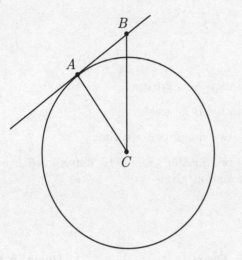

Line AB is tangent to the circle C at point A.

The radius of the circle with center C is 5 and $BC = \dfrac{10\sqrt{3}}{3}$.

Quantity A	**Quantity B**
The length of line segment AB	The length of line segment AC

○ Quantity A is greater.

○ Quantity B is greater.

○ The two quantities are equal.

○ The relationship cannot be determined from the information given.

$$x \neq 0$$

Quantity A	**Quantity B**
$\dfrac{x}{10}$	$\dfrac{\frac{x}{5}}{2}$

○ Quantity A is greater.

○ Quantity B is greater.

○ The two quantities are equal.

○ The relationship cannot be determined from the information given.

The test scores for a class have a normal distribution, a mean of 50, and a standard deviation of 4.

Quantity A	**Quantity B**
Percentage of scores at or above 58	Percentage of scores at or below 42

○ Quantity A is greater.

○ Quantity B is greater.

○ The two quantities are equal.

○ The relationship cannot be determined from the information given.

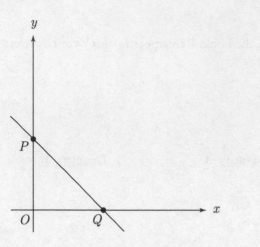

The line $y = -\dfrac{5}{6}x + 1$ is graphed on the

rectangular coordinate axes.

Quantity A	**Quantity B**
OQ	OP

○ Quantity A is greater.

○ Quantity B is greater.

○ The two quantities are equal.

○ The relationship cannot be determined from the information given.

5 of 20

At a dog show, there are 20 judges and 10 dogs in the final round.

Quantity A	**Quantity B**
The number of distinct pairs of judges	The number of possible rankings of dogs from first to third place

○ Quantity A is greater.

○ Quantity B is greater.

○ The two quantities are equal.

○ The relationship cannot be determined from the information given.

$$k > 0$$
$$l > 1$$

Quantity A	**Quantity B**
$\dfrac{1}{\dfrac{1}{k} + \dfrac{1}{l}}$	$\dfrac{kl}{\dfrac{1}{k} + \dfrac{1}{l}}$

○ Quantity A is greater.

○ Quantity B is greater.

○ The two quantities are equal.

○ The relationship cannot be determined from the information given.

7 of 20

Quantity A	**Quantity B**
The greatest odd factor of 78	The greatest prime factor of 78

○ Quantity A is greater.

○ Quantity B is greater.

○ The two quantities are equal.

○ The relationship cannot be determined from the information given.

Joe has $200. If he buys a CD player for $150, what is the greatest number of CDs he can buy with the remaining money if CDs cost $12 each?

[ ]

Click on the answer box and type in a number.
Backspace to erase.

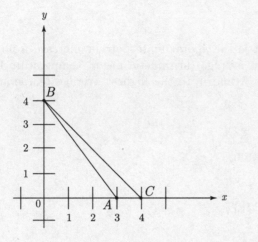

What is the area of triangle ABC in the figure above?

○ 2

○ 4

○ $4\sqrt{2}$

○ 7

○ 8

By which of the following could $10(9^6)$ be divided by to produce an integer result?

Indicate all such values.

☐ 90

☐ 100

☐ 330

☐ 540

☐ 720

Roberta drove 50 miles in 2 hours. Her rate in miles per hour is equivalent to which of the following proportions?

Indicate all such proportions.

☐ 5 to 20

☐ 100 to 4

☐ 400 to 16

☐ 20 to 500

☐ 520 to 20

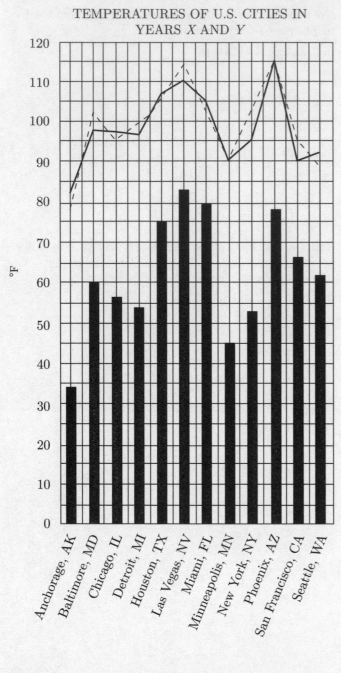

TEMPERATURES OF U.S. CITIES IN YEARS *X* AND *Y*

°F

Anchorage, AK · Baltimore, MD · Chicago, IL · Detroit, MI · Houston, TX · Las Vegas, NV · Miami, FL · Minneapolis, MN · New York, NY · Phoenix, AZ · San Francisco, CA · Seattle, WA

■ Average Temperature for Years *X* and *Y*

- - - - High for Year *Y*

——— High for Year *X*

For how many of the cities shown was the highest temperature in Year *Y* greater than or equal to the highest temperature in Year *X* ?

- ○ 4
- ○ 5
- ○ 7
- ○ 8
- ○ 12

What is the approximate percent increase from the lowest average (arithmetic mean) temperature for Years *X* and *Y* to the highest average temperature?

- ○ 60%
- ○ 82%
- ○ 140%
- ○ 188%
- ○ 213%

The average (arithmetic mean) temperature for any city in Years *X* and *Y* is the average of the high and low temperatures for those years. What is the average of the low temperatures for Baltimore for Years *X* and *Y* ?

- ○ –9° F
- ○ 11° F
- ○ 20° F
- ○ 44° F
- ○ It cannot be determined from the information given.

If $|2x - 3| + 2 > 7$, which of the following could be the value of x ?

Indicate <u>all</u> such values.

- ☐ −4
- ☐ −3
- ☐ −2
- ☐ −1
- ☐ 0
- ☐ 1
- ☐ 2
- ☐ 3

If x, y, and z are consecutive odd integers where $x < y < z$ and $x + y + z < z$, then which of the following could be the value of x ?

Indicate <u>all</u> such values.

- ☐ −3
- ☐ −1
- ☐ 0
- ☐ 1
- ☐ 3

If $4^x = 1{,}024$, then $(4^{x+1})(5^{x-1}) =$

- ○ 10^6
- ○ $(5^4)(10^5)$
- ○ $(4^4)(10^5)$
- ○ $(5^4)(10^4)$
- ○ $(4^4)(10^4)$

What is the greatest distance between two vertices of a rectangular solid with a height of 5, a length of 12, and a volume of 780 ?

- ○ 12
- ○ $12\sqrt{2}$
- ○ 13
- ○ $13\sqrt{2}$
- ○ $13\sqrt{3}$

If three boys and three girls sit in a row on a park bench, and no boy can sit on either end of the bench, how many arrangements of the children on the bench are possible?

- ○ 46,656
- ○ 38,880
- ○ 1,256
- ○ 144
- ○ 38

If 16 is the average (arithmetic mean) of p, 24, and q, what is $16(p + q)$?

- ○ 180
- ○ 192
- ○ 384
- ○ 524
- ○ 768

Summary

- Topics such as probability, permutations and combinations, factorials, and functions represent only a small percentage of the math topics tested on the GRE. Make sure you've mastered all the more important topics before attempting these.

- Probability is expressed as a fraction. The denominator of the fraction represents the total number of possible outcomes, while the numerator stands for the desired outcomes.

- If a probability question asks for the chance of event A or event B, find the probability of each event and add them together. If the question asks for the probability of event A and event B, multiply the individual probabilities.

- The key to factorial problems is to look for ways to cancel or factor out terms.

- Permutations and combinations are related concepts. A permutation tells you how many arrangements or orderings of things are possible. A combination tells you how many groupings of things are possible.

- Function problems use funny looking symbols as shorthand for the operations to perform on a certain number.

- The group equation is Total = $Group_1$ + $Group_2$ − Members of Both Groups + Members of Neither Group.

Part IV
How to Crack the Analytical Writing Section

Chapter 15
The Geography of the Analytical Writing Section

This chapter clues you in on everything you've ever wanted to know about the Analytical Writing section of the GRE. It contains important information on how the essays are used by graduate schools, the scoring system ETS graders use to evaluate your essays, and the crucial distinctions between the issue essay and the argument essay. This chapter also looks at the basic word-processing program used by ETS.

ESSAYS AND THE GRE

The Analytical Writing section of the GRE requires you to write two essays—one will be an analysis of an issue and the other will be an analysis of an argument. You will have 30 minutes for each essay.

In the past, ETS has had problems with test takers relying on preplanned essays. The essay questions have been reformulated to reduce the possibility of testers preparing their essays in advance. However, while you may not be able to plan your entire essay in advance, you can still go into your test session having a good idea of what type of essay you're going to write.

How Do Schools Use the Writing Assessment?

Even if your program doesn't care much about the essay, a poor score might still raise a red flag.

First, the essays are probably more important for international students and those for whom English is not a first language. If you are not a native English speaker, expect your essay score and the essays you wrote to receive more attention. (ETS also makes the essays available to schools, which may choose to read them or not.) Second, and not surprisingly, the essays will probably be weighted more heavily by programs for which writing is a frequent and necessary task. A master's program in applied mathematics might not care so much about your 30-minute written opinion about whether or not it's necessary for a person to read imaginative literature, but a program in creative writing probably would.

Ultimately, though, here's the most honest answer to this question: It depends. Some schools will not care at all about the Analytical Writing score, while others will say that they want only applicants who scored a 5 or higher on this section. Call the schools you're interested in and talk to people in the department. By finding out how important your target schools consider the Analytical Writing section, you'll be able to determine the appropriate amount of effort to devote to it.

More Online!
Head over to PrincetonReview.com/grad-school-advice for useful information and helpful articles about graduate school.

Regardless of your target score on this section, you should at least read through these chapters to get a better sense of what ETS is looking for. You'll have to write these essays, so no matter what, you want to do a decent job. You'll find that writing high-scoring essays is not as hard as it may seem once you've been shown how to do it.

How Will the Essays Be Scored?

What you write—the content—will be weighted more than *how* you write.

Your essays will be read by two graders, and each will assign a score from 1 to 6, based on how well you do the following:

- follow the instructions of the prompt
- consider the complexities of the issue or argument
- effectively organize and develop your ideas
- support your position with relevant examples
- control the elements of written English

The grades you receive for each essay will be totaled and averaged. For example, if you receive a 4 and a 5 on your issue essay and a 3 and a 4 on your argument essay, your Analytical Writing score will be a 4.0; 16 total points divided by 4 scores. If the graders' scores for your essays differ by more than one point, a third person will be brought in to read the essay. The graders use a holistic grading system; they're trained to look at the big picture, not to focus on minor details. Your essay is not expected to be perfect, so the graders will overlook minor errors in spelling, punctuation, and grammar. However, pervasive or egregious errors will affect your score.

Here are ETS's descriptions of the scoring levels:

Issue Essay		Argument Essay	
6	An essay that scores a 6 presents a cogent, well-articulated critique of the issue and conveys meaning skillfully.	6	An essay that scores a 6 presents a cogent, well-articulated critique of the argument and conveys meaning skillfully.
5	An essay that scores a 5 presents a generally thoughtful, well-developed analysis of the complexities of the issue and conveys meaning clearly.	5	An essay that scores a 5 presents a generally thoughtful, well-developed critique of the argument and conveys meaning clearly.
4	An essay that scores a 4 presents a competent analysis of the issue and conveys meaning adequately.	4	An essay that scores a 4 presents a competent critique of the argument and conveys meaning adequately.
3	An essay that scores a 3 demonstrates some competence in its analysis of the issue and in conveying meaning but is obviously flawed.	3	An essay that scores a 3 demonstrates some competence in its critique of the argument and in conveying meaning but is obviously flawed.
2	An essay that scores a 2 demonstrates serious weaknesses in analytical writing.	2	An essay that scores a 2 demonstrates serious weaknesses in analytical writing.
1	An essay that scores a 1 demonstrates fundamental deficiencies in analytical writing skills.	1	An essay that scores a 1 demonstrates fundamental deficiencies in both analysis and writing.

An essay written on a topic other than the one provided will receive a score of 0.

Who Are These Readers Anyway?

We'll put this in the form of a multiple-choice question:

Your essays will initially be read by

(A)   captains of industry

(B)   leading professors

(C)   college TAs working part time

If you guessed (C), you're correct. Each essay will be read by part-time employees of ETS, mostly culled from graduate school programs.

How Much Time Do They Devote to Each Essay?

ETS graders spend less than two minutes grading your essay.

The short answer is this: not much. It is unusual for a grader to spend more than two minutes grading an essay, and some essays are graded in less than a minute. The graders are reading many, many GRE essays and they aren't going to spend time admiring that clever turn of phrase you came up with. So don't sweat the small stuff—it probably won't even be noticed. Focus on the big picture—that's what the graders will be focusing on.

So How Do You Score High on the Analytical Writing Essays?

Make the graders' jobs easy. Give them exactly what they're looking for.

On the face of it, you might think it would be pretty difficult to impress these jaded readers, but it turns out that there are some very specific ways to persuade them of your superior writing skills.

What ETS Doesn't Want You to Know

In a recent analysis of a group of essays written by actual test takers, and the grades that those essays received, ETS researchers noticed that the most successful essays had one thing in common. Which of the following characteristics do you think it was?

- good organization
- proper diction
- noteworthy ideas
- good vocabulary
- sentence variety
- length

What Your Essay Needs in Order to Look Like a Successful Essay

The ETS researchers discovered that the essays that received the highest grades from ETS essay graders had one single factor in common: length.

To ace the Analytical Writing section, you need to take one simple step: Write as much as you possibly can. Each essay should include *at least* four indented paragraphs. Your Issue essay should be 400 to 750 words in length, and your Argument essay should be 350 to 600 words.

So All I Have to Do Is Type "I Hate the GRE" Over and Over Again?

Well, no. The length issue isn't that easy. The ETS researchers also noted that, not surprisingly, the high-scoring essays all made reasonably good points addressing the topic. So you have to actually write something that covers the essay topic. And in your quest for length, it's more important that you add depth than breadth. What this means is that it's better to have a few good examples that are thoroughly and deeply explored than it is to add length by tacking more and more examples and paragraphs onto your essay until it starts to feel like a superficial list of bulleted points rather than a thoughtful piece of writing.

Read the Directions Every Time

You should read the directions for each essay prompt. The instructions we provide here for each essay task are not necessarily the ones you will see on the GRE. Directions can vary in focus, so you shouldn't memorize any particular set of instructions. Visit the ETS website at **www.ets.org/gre** for a complete list of all the potential essay topics and direction variants. (Yes, you really get to see this information in advance of the test!) Practice responding to the different instructions, combined with a variety of issue and argument prompts. Be sure to mix it up; the prompt/directions pairings you see on the ETS website are not necessarily the duos you will see on the real test. Practicing with a variety of these essays will prepare you for whatever comes your way on test day.

Oh, Yes, You Can Plan Your Essays in Advance

In fact, there are some very specific ways to prepare for the essays that go beyond length and good typing skills. So how can you prepare ahead of time?

Creating a Template

When a builder builds a house, the first thing he does is construct a frame. The frame supports the entire house. After the frame is completed, he can nail the walls and windows to the frame. We're going to show you how to build the frame for the perfect GRE essay. Of course, you won't know the exact topic of the essay until you get there (just as the builder may not know what color his client is going to paint the living room), but you will have an all-purpose frame on which to construct a great essay no matter what the topic is. We call this frame the template.

Preconstruction

Just as a builder can construct the windows of a house in his workshop weeks before he arrives to install them, so can you pre-build certain elements of your essay. We call this "preconstruction."

In the next two chapters we'll show you how to prepare ahead of time to write essays on two topics that you won't see until they appear on your screen.

ISSUE VERSUS ARGUMENT ESSAY

It is worth noting at this time that the essay section gives you two very distinct writing tasks, and that a failure to appropriately address these tasks will severely reduce your score.

The Issue Essay

The Issue essay asks for your opinion; you're expected to present your viewpoint on a particular topic and support that viewpoint with various examples. The following is one example of the instructions for the Issue essay:

> You will be given a brief quotation that states or implies an issue of general interest and specific instructions on how to respond to that issue. You will have 30 minutes to plan and compose a response in which you develop a position on the issue according to the specific instructions. A response to any other issue will receive a score of zero.
>
> Make sure that you respond to the specific instructions and support your position on the issue with reasons and examples drawn from such areas as your reading, experience, observations, and/or academic studies.

Note how important it is to specifically address the assignment provided as part of the Issue prompt; not following ETS's directions will make your grader unhappy and result in a poor score on the essay.

The Argument Essay

The Argument essay requires a different type of response. Instead of presenting your own perspective, your job is to critique someone else's argument. You're supposed to address the logical flaws of the argument, not provide your personal opinion on the subject. The following is one example of the directions for the Argument essay:

> You will be given a short passage that presents an argument, or an argument to be completed, and specific instructions on how to respond to that passage. You will have 30 minutes to plan and compose a response in which you analyze the passage according to the specific instructions. A response to any other argument will receive a score of zero.
>
> Note that you are NOT being asked to present your own views on the subject. Make sure that you respond to the specific instructions and support your analysis with relevant reasons and/or examples.

In the Argument essay, the emphasis is on writing a logical analysis of the argument, not an opinion piece. It is absolutely essential that you don't confuse the two essay tasks on the GRE.

ETS graders don't expect a perfect essay; occasional spelling, punctuation, and grammar errors won't kill your score.

HOW DOES THE WORD-PROCESSING PROGRAM WORK?

ETS has created a very simple program that allows students to compose their essays on the screen. Compared to any of the commercial word-processing programs, this one is extremely limited, but it does allow the basic functions: You can move the cursor with the arrow keys, and you can delete, copy, and paste. You don't have to use any of these functions. With just the backspace key and the mouse to change your point of insertion, you will be able to use the computer like a regular word-processing program.

Take a look at the image below to see what your screen will look like during the Analytical Writing section of the test:

The question will always appear at the top left of your screen. Beside it, in a box, will be your writing area (in the writing area above, you can see a partially completed sentence). When you click inside the box with your mouse, a winking cursor will appear, indicating that you can begin typing.

As we said above, the program supports the use of many of the normal computer keys.

- The "Backspace" key removes text to the left of the cursor.
- The "Delete" key removes text to the right of the cursor.
- The "Arrow" keys move the cursor up, down, left, or right.
- The "Home" key moves the cursor to the beginning of a line.
- The "End" key moves the cursor to the end of a line.
- The "Enter" key moves the cursor to the beginning of the next line.
- "Page up" moves the cursor up one page.
- "Page down" moves the cursor down one page.

You can also use the buttons above the writing area to copy and paste words, sentences, or paragraphs. To do this, you first have to highlight the desired text by clicking on the starting point with your mouse and holding down the mouse button while you drag it to the ending point. Then click on the "Cut" button. This deletes the text you've selected from the screen, but also stores it in the computer's memory. Next, just move the cursor to wherever you would like the selected text to reappear, and click on the "Paste" button. The selected text will appear in that spot.

If you make a mistake, simply click on the "Undo" button, which will undo whatever operation you have just done. You can undo a cut, a paste, or even the last set of words you've typed in. Unfortunately, unlike many word-processing programs, ETS's program does not have a "Redo" button, so be careful what you decide to undo.

Obviously, the small box on the screen is not big enough to contain your entire essay. However, by hitting the "Page up" and "Page down" keys on your keyboard, or by using the arrows on your keyboard, you will be able to go forward and backward to reread what you have written and make corrections.

Does Spelling Count?

Officially, no. The word-processing program doesn't have a spell checker, and ETS essay readers are supposed to ignore minor errors of spelling and grammar, but the readers wouldn't be human if they weren't influenced by an essay that had lots of spelling mistakes and improper grammar—it gives the impression that you just didn't care enough to proofread.

Because pervasive spelling errors will detract from your score, pick an easier word if you're really uncertain of how to spell a word.

Summary

o   Different programs value the essay section in different ways. Check with your program to see how important the essays are.

o   Understand the criteria ETS uses for judging your essay. Organization, examples, and language use are important. Perfect grammar and spelling less so.

o   On the GRE, longer essays tend to receive better scores, so strive to write as much as you can for each essay.

o   Make sure you understand the differences in the assignments for the Issue essay and the Argument essay.

o   Issue essays ask for your opinion on a topic while Argument essays expect you to critique the logic of an argument. The ways in which you're asked to do each of these tasks will vary, so make sure you read each set of directions carefully.

o   The word processor ETS provides has only the most basic functions. You can delete, copy, and paste text, but not much more.

Chapter 16
The Issue Essay

The Issue essay of the GRE requires you to present your opinion on the provided topic. This chapter will show you the steps to take in order to write a clear, coherent essay in the limited time provided. You'll learn the key parts of a successful essay, and how to brainstorm ideas, combine them into a thesis, and then structure a cohesive essay that will get you the best possible result.

THREE BASIC STEPS

Because you don't have a lot of time to write the essays, you'll need to have a pretty good idea of how you're going to attack them as soon as you sit down at the computer on test day. Our approach to the essays involves three steps:

1. **Think.** Before you start writing, take a moment to brainstorm some thoughts about the topic.
2. **Organize.** Take the ideas you've come up with and fit them into the assignment for the prompt.
3. **Write.** Once you've completed the first two steps, the final step should be a snap.

Thirty minutes is not a lot of time to write an essay, so you have to get it right the first time out. While ETS advises you to leave enough time to proofread and edit your essay, it simply isn't feasible to expect to make any significant changes to your essay during the final minutes of the section. Furthermore, if you get halfway through your essay and realize you're stuck or you're not saying what you need to say, you'll be hard pressed to fix your essay in the time you have left.

You have to know what you want your essay to say before you can start writing.

It is essential, therefore, to make sure you spend time planning your essay before you start writing. You have to figure out what it is you want to say before you begin; otherwise, you run the risk of writing an incoherent, rambling essay. The first two steps are actually more important to a successful GRE essay than the final step; by spending a little time planning your essay, the actual writing part should be relatively painless.

> The keys to the essay: Think, Organize, Write

Essay Essentials

The basics parts of an essay include the introduction, body paragraphs, and conclusion.

As you learned in sixth-grade composition class, a basic essay has three parts: an introduction, some body paragraphs, and a conclusion. These three things are exactly what you should include in your Analysis of an Issue Essay. Each of these parts has a specific role to play.

1. The **introduction** should introduce the topic of the essay, discuss the issues surrounding it, and present the essay's thesis.
2. The **body paragraphs** should use examples to support the thesis of the essay.
3. The **conclusion** should summarize the major points of the issue, reiterate the thesis, and perhaps consider its implications.

Basically, if you try to think of each paragraph as having a specific job to do, you can pretty much preconstruct each type of paragraph and then fill in the specific details on test day.

Keys to a High-Scoring Essay

In order to write a high-scoring Issue essay, you'll want to accomplish four key tasks. A high-scoring Issue essay

- considers the complexities of the issue
- supports the position with relevant examples
- is clear and well organized
- demonstrates superior facility with the conventions of standard written English

To put it more simply, your essay should be logically organized, include good examples to support whatever position you've taken, and demonstrate that you can use the English language reasonably well in writing.

Let's continue our discussion of the Issue essay by looking at a typical prompt.

The Prompt

> "True beauty is found not in the exceptional but in the commonplace."
>
> Write an essay in which you take a position on the statement above. In developing and supporting your essay, consider instances in which the statement does and does not hold true.

The prompts are supposed to get you thinking about areas of "general interest," whatever that means. A better way of thinking about the prompt is to look at it as an agree/disagree or pro/con statement. Your task in the essay will be to look at both sides of the issue, the pro and the con side, and take a position on the statement. Let's look at how to do that.

STEP 1: THINK

"Think" is a pretty broad command, so we need to clarify this step in order to make it more useful. Specifically, we want you to think about three things.

1. **Key Terms.** What are the key words or phrases in the prompt? Do the terms need clarifying before you can properly deal with them in the essay?
2. **Opposite Side.** What would the converse of the statement be?
3. **Examples.** What are some examples that would support the statement? What are some examples that would support the opposite statement?

Let's work through these steps with our sample prompt.

Key Terms

When preparing your essay, first look more closely at the key terms in the prompt. Do they need to be clarified? Are there multiple ways of interpreting the words? In order to make your essay as focused as possible, you might need to limit the key terms to a specific definition or interpretation. If the key terms in the prompt seem pretty straightforward, you still want to note them. By repeatedly returning to these terms in your essay, you'll convey the impression that your essay is strongly organized and on topic.

For the sample prompt above, write down the key terms:

_____

_____

_____

Using key terms from the prompt throughout your essay contributes to its overall coherency.

For this prompt, the key terms are *beauty, true, exceptional*, and *commonplace*. We need to think about how we're going to use these terms in our essay. For example, what is *true beauty*? Do we want that to mean just natural beauty or can we consider man-made objects? As for the word *beauty*, do we want to limit our discussion to artistic beauty such as paintings and sculptures, or should we consider poems and literature as well? Should we discuss only natural beauty, such as stars and flowers, or should we consider personal beauty as well, such as models and GRE instructors? As you can see, we could write a lot on this topic, if we had the time. But we don't, so it's important to focus. By defining our key terms, we make the essay a lot more manageable and easier to write in a short amount of time. For this essay, let's include both natural objects and man-made artistic feats, but leave out personal beauty.

Opposite Side

In order to score well on the Issue essay, you'll have to consider both sides of the prompt. A simple "I agree, and here's why" essay won't be enough here; rather, you'll need to consider both sides of the issue and state a clear position that you can defend. Take a brief moment to look at the sample prompt again, and then write down the converse of the statement.

> "True beauty is found not in the exceptional but in the commonplace."

_____

For this prompt, the opposite side of the argument would be something along the lines of "True beauty is found not in the commonplace, but in the exceptional." Note that there is no right answer to the prompt; either side is valid. So if you find the opposite of the statement more convincing, that's fine. As long as you can support your position with some relevant examples, it doesn't matter what position you take on the prompt. This brings us to the final part of step one—brainstorming examples.

Examples

In many ways, the examples will be the most important part of your essay. Without strong, relevant examples you cannot expect to achieve a high score on the Issue essay. As the instructions state, you should support your position with examples drawn from your reading, experience, observation, and academic studies. In general, the more specific your examples are, the better your essay score. And examples from history, literature, or current events are better than personal observations or experiences. Imagine that a friend asks you to read her essay and give feedback. Which sentence would you respond more favorably to?

"Few observers would doubt the awesome beauty of the ceiling of the Sistine Chapel in Rome, a work of art produced by the great Renaissance artist Michelangelo."

"Few observers would doubt the awesome beauty of the various paintings they see in museums, works of art produced by great artists."

Both sentences essentially say the same thing and use practically the same words. But you would probably respond more favorably to the first sentence because it contains a *specific* example.

Take a moment to jot down some examples for the previous prompt. Make sure you come up with examples for both the original statement and its opposite.

_____

_____

_____

Now take a moment to look over your examples. Are they specific? Are they relevant to the topic? Do they support a position on the topic? The strength of your examples will determine the strength of your argument. It's hard to write a convincing paper with weak examples. Here are some examples that might work for our sample topic, both weaker and stronger:

Okay Example	Better Example
paintings, artwork	Leonardo da Vinci's *Mona Lisa*
buildings, churches	Notre Dame Cathedral in Paris
flowers, natural wonders	Niagara Falls

> Good examples are relevant to the topic and contain specific details.

In each case, the better example is the more specific, more detailed example. Also note that we've avoided any personal examples. While you certainly may feel that your boyfriend or girlfriend is the most beautiful person in the world, that sort of personal example won't be as effective as a more academic or global example. Use personal examples only when specifically instructed to by the prompt or as a last resort.

STEP 2: ORGANIZE

Once you've identified the key terms, considered the opposite side of the issue, and generated some examples, it's time to organize your thoughts. Basically, you'll want to do the following:

1. **Separate Your Examples.** How many of your examples support the pro side and how many support the con side? Divide your examples up and see which side has more support.
2. **Write Your Thesis Statement.** After evaluating the strength of your examples, decide what position you will take in your essay, and then write your thesis. Your thesis is the main point that you want your essay to express.

Let's continue the process on the sample prompt.

Separate Your Examples

Do this before you decide on your thesis statement. Even though you might have a strong preference for one position on the issue, you might notice that the examples you brainstormed tend to support the other side of the issue. Don't expend more time trying to think of examples to support your preconceptions; just write your essay supporting the other side! There is no right or wrong response. All that matters is being able to write a strong, coherent essay in a very limited time. Your personal views or beliefs are unimportant to the ETS graders. If we continue with the examples we used earlier, they would probably break down like this:

Pro	Con
natural wonders	*Mona Lisa*
	Notre Dame

Based on some of the examples we've come up with, it looks like we'd be better off supporting the idea that "True beauty is found not in the commonplace, but in the exceptional." While natural wonders like sunsets and flowers are pretty commonplace, we've come up with a lot more exceptional examples. And it looks like we could even argue that it is the exceptional natural wonders, such as Niagara Falls, that are truly beautiful.

Write Your Thesis Statement

Now comes the culmination of all of our work. What point do we want to make about the topic? Write it down here:

_____

Our thesis should probably be something along the lines of this: "While certain commonplace natural objects are examples of beauty, true beauty is most often found in rare, exceptional cases."

Now that we have figured out what we want to say, we can focus on proving why we believe it. But remember: Only after working through these steps are we truly ready to write!

It doesn't matter what side of the issue you take on the GRE.

Practice: Steps 1 and 2

Work through steps one and two on the following Issue essay prompts below.

PROMPT 1

> "Government funding should never be used to support art that the majority of the population finds distasteful or objectionable."
>
> Write an essay in which you take a position on the statement above. In developing and supporting your position, you should consider whether the above statement is always true or whether there are exceptions to it.

On your scratch paper, write the (1) Key Terms, (2) Opposite Side, (3) Examples, and (4) Thesis.

PROMPT 2

> "Oftentimes, the results of a particular action are not of consequence; rather, it is the way we go about the action that matters most."
>
> Write an essay in which you take a position on the statement above. In developing and supporting your position, you should consider situations in which the ways matter most as well as situations in which the results matter most.

On your scratch paper, write the (1) Key Terms, (2) Opposite Side, (3) Examples, and (4) Thesis.

Practice: Sample Responses

Obviously, your examples and thesis statements will differ from those given below, but these sample responses will give you a good indication of what to aim for in your actual essay.

Prompt 1

Key Terms: What does *support* mean? Is that just giving money to the artist, or does the government have to commission the work or promote it? What population are we using to judge—the general population, the population of artists, or some other population? What do we mean when we say art is "objectionable" or "distasteful?" What standards are we using to determine that?

Opposite Side: "Government funding should be used to support art, even if the majority of the population finds the art distasteful."

Examples: Robert Mapplethorpe controversy; National Endowment for the Arts; Supreme Court rulings on obscenity; Government censorship

Thesis: "While artists have the right to create whatever objectionable art they wish, taxpayers should not have to pay for art they find offensive or obscene."

Prompt 2

Key Terms: What do we mean by *consequence*? Does this term refer to the results of the action, or the effects the action has on the person doing the action? Similarly, when we say the way we go about something "matters most," what criteria are we using?

Opposite Side: "The way we go about a certain action is not of consequence; the results we get are what matter most."

Examples: Rosa Parks, whose actions helped further the Civil Rights movement; Gandhi, whose methods of nonviolent resistance played a part in Indian independence; Revolutionary War, whose violent methods eventually led to independence for the United States

Thesis: "While people do note the ways in which people go about certain actions, it is usually the ultimate result that matters."

STEP 3: WRITE

Now that we know how to prepare for our Issue essay, we can write it. In this section, we'll discuss various templates for essays and show you how you can pre-construct certain portions of your essay. Before we do that, though, let's revisit your goals for the essay.

Essay Essentials Review

Remember the format of your essay should be

- introduction
- body paragraphs
- conclusion

Another way to think about this structure is

- Say what you're going to say.
- Say it.
- Say what you said.

Preconstruction: The Introduction

For the Issue essay, a good introduction accomplishes the following tasks:

1. clearly establishes the topic of the paper
2. previews both sides of the issue at hand
3. presents a clear thesis

Let's look at each of these tasks in detail and discuss different ways to accomplish the goals of the introductory paragraph.

Establish the Topic

Don't just restate the prompt! Come up with a strong "hook" for the beginning of your essay.

You want to make it clear what issue the essay is going to talk about. Even though the grader will see the prompt you're writing about, he or she should be able to figure out the prompt just from reading the introduction of your essay. There are a few different ways you can quickly establish the topic, so let's return to our original prompt and preconstruct some approaches.

Here, once again, is our prompt:

> "True beauty is found not in the exceptional but in the commonplace."
>
> Write an essay in which you take a position on the statement above. In developing and supporting your essay, consider instances in which the statement does and does not hold true.

One of the worst ways of establishing the topic is to merely quote the prompt, as that shows a lack of creativity and a potential lack of understanding of the prompt itself. So let's discuss some other ways to start our essay.

Approach 1: Rhetorical Questions

This approach is a tried-and-true way of introducing your topic. Instead of simply quoting or paraphrasing the prompt, turn it into a rhetorical question. Here are a few samples:

Where does true beauty lie, in the exceptional or in the commonplace?

Do we find the exceptional more beautiful or the commonplace?

Can we find beauty only in rare, exceptional instances or does it truly lie all around us?

It is immediately clear what topic the essay will explore, from each of these examples of introductory sentences. See if you can come up with a rhetorical question for either this topic or one from the previous drill.

Approach 2: Famous Quotations

Another classic approach to beginning an essay is to use either a well-known saying or a famous quote from someone. Many of the GRE topics are fairly bland, so even if you can't think of a famous quote, there are usually some classic aphorisms you use. Here's what we mean:

"Beauty is Truth, Truth Beauty," or so said the romantic poet John Keats.

A common saying is that beauty is in the eye of the beholder.

Obviously, this type of introduction can be tough to do if something doesn't pop into your head right away. Try to come up with a quote or common saying for this topic or one from the drill.

Approach 3: Anecdote

An anecdote is a brief story. Oftentimes you can grab your reader's attention and introduce the topic with a good anecdote. Consider this example:

It is said that Cézanne, the famed French painter, was so concerned with the beauty of his paintings that he would destroy any of his works that he felt was flawed.

The Romantic poet John Keats was so struck by the beauty of Chapman's translation of Homer's work that he wrote a poem about it.

When using an anecdote you might have to write a sentence or two explaining the relevance of your story. Try out an anecdote for this topic or one of the drill topics.

Approach 4: Fact/Statistic

For some topics, it might be appropriate to start your essay by stating a fact or statistic. Factual mistakes won't cost you any points, because this is an essay, not a book report. So don't be afraid if your fact isn't 100 percent accurate. Here's an illustration:

A recent scientific study showed that the faces that people find the most beautiful are those that are the most symmetrical.

Psychologists have demonstrated that people's responses to certain phenomena are based on certain innate mechanisms in the brain.

Give this approach a shot, using this topic or one from the drill.

Approach 5: Definition

One way you may wish to start your essay is by defining one of the key terms from the prompt:

Beauty, by definition, is that which moves us or impacts us significantly.

The "exceptional" typically refers to those things that stand out, which is also a plausible definition for beauty.

The advantage to this approach is that you already spent some time thinking along these lines when you were planning your essay. Come up with a sample introductory sentence for this topic or one of the drill topics.

Preview the Issue

Once you've told the reader what the topic is, your next task is to inform the reader of the issues at hand. You want to briefly touch on both sides of the debate, explaining the pros and cons of the prompt. A good way to accomplish this is to make use of strong transition words—words like *but, despite, while,* and *although.* Here are some examples.

While some people can find beauty in the most common of places, true beauty is found only in the exceptional.

Some would argue that beauty is found everywhere, from the flowers to the stars, but others would state that true beauty is found only in rare, special instances.

Despite the assertions of many that beauty is everywhere, true beauty is found only in exceptional cases.

Although one might argue that many commonplace things are beautiful, it is the exceptional things that possess true beauty.

There can be no doubt that some of the world's most common things are beautiful. And yet, it is often the exceptional objects that possess true beauty.

Practice writing sentences that address both sides of the issue. Use the sample topic or one from the drill.

Present the Thesis

Your final task in the introduction is to present the thesis. Some writers prefer to avoid the first person, refusing to use sentences such as "I believe…" or "I feel…" However, there is no penalty for use of the first person. A more important consideration when writing your thesis is giving some indication of why you hold your particular position. You should make it clear that you've thought about and analyzed the issue. Here are some examples of thesis statements.

I believe that beauty is truly found in the exceptional, not in the commonplace, because if common things were beautiful, the very word would lose its meaning.

> A good thesis tells the reader exactly what your position is and why.

In my view, beauty is found in the exceptional, not in the commonplace, because only exceptional things really stand out as special in our minds.

It is clear that true beauty is not to be found in the commonplace but in the exceptional. On closer inspection, even so-called common objects that people consider beautiful are actually exceptional.

After weighing the evidence, it is certain that beauty is the province of the exceptional, not the commonplace. People find true beauty in things that they rarely experience, not the things they experience every day.

For each thesis, you can see that the author is also giving some justification for the viewpoint. This justification will be of course explored more thoroughly in the body paragraphs, but it's good to give a preview of how your essay will take shape. Try writing thesis statements for some of the sample prompts.

Preconstruction: Body Paragraphs

A body paragraph should do the following:

1. use a good transition/topic sentence
2. present an example
3. explain how the example supports the thesis

Body paragraphs are a little harder to preconstruct because they are the most specific part of the essay. Still, there are some handy tips for creating body paragraphs that will make for a strong essay.

Transition/Topic Sentence

One attribute of the strongest essays is that they flow well. The best way to write an essay like this is to use strong topic sentences and good transitions for each of your body paragraphs. Your topic sentence should serve as a gentle reminder of what the thesis of the essay is. Here's an example:

One example of beauty found in the exceptional is Leonardo da Vinci's Mona Lisa.

A second instance in which true beauty lies not in the commonplace but in the exceptional is Notre Dame Cathedral in Paris.

Of course, you might want to avoid using simple transitions like "the first example," and "the second example." You can make your writing stronger by leading with the example and making the transition a little more subtle, like so:

Leonardo da Vinci's Mona Lisa *is surely one of the most exceptional, and beautiful, paintings ever created.*

Consider the beauty of Notre Dame Cathedral in Paris, a building that is in no way commonplace.

Or to get even fancier, refer to the previous example in your transition sentence:

Like da Vinci's Mona Lisa, *the cathedral of Notre Dame in Paris is an exceptional, and exceptionally beautiful, object.*

The important point is that each sentence introduces the example and reminds the reader of the purpose of the example, which in this case is to support the notion of beauty as exceptional. In the next few sentences, you'll provide details about your example. It's important that you remember to link the example to your thesis.

Explain How Your Example Supports Your Thesis

On the GRE essays, don't get so caught up in providing details for your example that you forget to explain how or why your example helps your thesis. The purpose of the Issue essay is not to just list some examples; the purpose is to develop and support a position on the issue. Here's an example of a body paragraph that doesn't quite fulfill that goal:

Don't just state the example; explain why the example is relevant to your thesis.

Like da Vinci's Mona Lisa, *the cathedral of Notre Dame in Paris is an exceptional, and exceptionally beautiful, object. Notre Dame is a stunning example of gothic architecture, famous for the flying buttresses that adorn the sides of the building. The cathedral also has rows and rows of beautiful sculptures recessed into the walls, as well as a gorgeous central stained-glass window. These features make Notre Dame one of the most beautiful cathedrals in the world.*

The writer here did a good job of providing specific details about the example, which definitely strengthens this paragraph. However, the writer failed to explain why Notre Dame supports the view that true beauty is exceptional, not commonplace. Let's fix that:

Like da Vinci's Mona Lisa, *the cathedral of Notre Dame in Paris is an exceptional, and exceptionally beautiful, object. Churches and cathedrals line the streets of most major cities in Western Europe, but few possess the renown of Notre Dame. Notre Dame is a stunning example of gothic architecture, famous for the flying buttresses that adorn the sides of the building. The cathedral also has rows and rows of beautiful sculptures recessed into the walls, as well as a gorgeous central stained-glass window. These features make Notre Dame one of the most beautiful cathedrals in the world. Compared to a common church or cathedral, Notre Dame is truly awe-inspiring; Victor Hugo used the building as the backdrop for his magnificent book* The Hunchback of Notre Dame *and thousands of tourists travel untold miles to view the cathedral. That sort of beauty is not possessed by just any church on the corner.*

This is a stronger body paragraph because it is more explicit in its discussion of the thesis. The author notes that churches and cathedrals are fairly common, but then argues that Notre Dame stands out as an exceptional cathedral. The author concludes the paragraph by showing how Notre Dame is more beautiful than any typical church. Just as the topic of the essay should be clear from the introduction, the thesis should be clear from each body paragraph.

Write a body paragraph for one of the examples for this sample topic, or one of your examples from the practice. Make sure you have a good topic/transition sentence, specific details for the example, and an explanation of how or why the example is relevant to the thesis.

Preconstruction: Conclusion Paragraphs

Make sure your essay has a conclusion.

Your essay should always have a conclusion, for two reasons. First, a conclusion paragraph is evidence of good organization. It shows that you knew exactly what points you wanted to make, you made them, and now you're ending the essay. And second, an essay that lacks a conclusion seems incomplete, almost as if your writing abruptly ends before it should. This can give a negative impression of your essay. Fortunately, conclusion paragraphs are easy to write. A good conclusion:

> 1. alerts the reader that the essay is ending
> 2. summarizes the main points of the essay

Some test takers even prefer to write their introduction and conclusion first and then fill in the body paragraphs. This strategy has the advantage of making your essay seem complete even if you happen to run out of time writing the body paragraphs.

Alert the Reader

Conclusion paragraphs have their own topic/transition sentences, which generally should contain a word or phrase that signifies the end of the essay. Here are some examples:

In conclusion, it's clear that true beauty is found not in the commonplace, but in the exceptional.

Ultimately, beauty lies in the exceptional, not in the commonplace.

As the bulk of the evidence shows, the exceptional, not the commonplace, possesses true beauty.

Clearly, true beauty is found in exceptional things, not in commonplace ones.

The examples above all support the idea that we find true beauty in exceptional cases, not in commonplace ones.

Write some conclusion sentences for this topic or a sample topic from the sample prompts.

Summarize Main Points

Your conclusion should also summarize the main points of the essay, meaning that it should mention the thesis and how the examples support it. Additionally, you can briefly consider the implications of the thesis. Here are some sample conclusions:

In conclusion, it's clear that true beauty is found not in the commonplace, but in the exceptional. The Mona Lisa *and* Notre Dame Cathedral *are both exceptional examples of fairly commonplace things and it is these exceptions that are noted as truly beautiful. If anything, the commonplace serves only as a contrast to what true beauty really is.*

Ultimately, beauty lies in the exceptional, not the commonplace. While paintings and churches are fairly commonplace, only a small few of them, such as the Mona Lisa *or* Notre Dame, *truly reach the heights of beauty. It is in these exceptions that we find real beauty.*

The examples above all support the idea that we find true beauty in exceptional cases, not in commonplace ones. Common things may seem at first glance to be beautiful, but once we compare these commonplace examples to the truly exceptional ones, we see that the exceptional ones are truly beautiful.

Try your hand at constructing a conclusion paragraph, once again using this topic or one from the sample prompts.

Putting It All Together

Read through this sample essay that's based on the basic five-paragraph model. Then you'll have the chance to try writing a similar essay for a different prompt.

> "True beauty is found not in the exceptional but in the commonplace."
>
> Write an essay in which you take a position on the statement above. In developing and supporting your essay, consider instances in which the statement does and does not hold true.

Beauty, by definition, is that which moves us or impacts us significantly. Some would argue that beauty is found everywhere, from the flowers to the stars. But others would state that true beauty is found only in rare, special instances. After weighing the evidence, it is certain that beauty is the province of the exceptional, not the commonplace. People are moved most by things that they rarely experience, not the things they experience every day.

Those who would argue that true beauty is everywhere might point to the beauty of a flower, or the starlit night. These experiences are certainly common, but do they show that true beauty is commonplace? Flowers might be considered beautiful, but how often does a person stop to look at or appreciate every flower? Flowers are so common that in many cases, they are ignored or viewed as nothing special. However, on those rare occasions—exceptional occasions, one might say—when we want to commemorate an event or express emotion, we notice the beauty of flowers. Thus, it is not the commonplace flower that strikes us as beautiful, but the exceptional situations themselves that move us to appreciate the flower.

Now consider the exceptional. Leonardo da Vinci's Mona Lisa *is surely one of the most exceptional, and beautiful, paintings ever created. Few people who view the painting are not moved by the sheer beauty of it, and the* Mona Lisa *is instantly recognized as a masterpiece of art. And yet, there have been literally millions of paintings produced in human history. Is every single one of them beautiful? Does every one of those paintings have the impact that da Vinci's does? Of course not. In order to find beauty, we must separate the exceptional cases from the common ones. True beauty is such because it stands out from the masses of the average and pedestrian.*

Like da Vinci's Mona Lisa, *the cathedral of Notre Dame in Paris is an exceptional, and exceptionally beautiful, object. Churches and cathedrals line the streets of most major cities in Western Europe, but few possess the renown of Notre Dame, one of the most beautiful cathedrals in the world. Compared to a common church or cathedral, Notre Dame is truly awe-inspiring; Victor Hugo used the building as the backdrop for his magnificent book* The Hunchback of Notre Dame *and thousands of tourists travel untold miles to view the cathedral. That sort of beauty is not possessed by just any church on the corner.*

In conclusion, it's clear that true beauty is found not in the commonplace, but in the exceptional. The Mona Lisa *and Notre Dame Cathedral are both exceptional examples of fairly commonplace things and it is these exceptions that are noted as truly beautiful. If anything, the commonplace serves only as a contrast so that we can understand what true beauty really is.*

Your Turn

Try writing a similar essay for the prompt that follows this paragraph. Make sure you consider the opposing side of the argument. Devote a paragraph to looking at an example for the other side of the issue, but make sure you indicate that there is a flaw in the example or that the example is less than convincing. Set a timer for 30 minutes to practice GRE time constraints.

> "People most respect the powerful not when they exercise their power, but when they refrain from exercising it."
>
> Write an essay in which you develop and support a position on the statement above. In writing your essay, you should consider both when the statement may be true and when it may be false.

How to Score Your Essay

Now it's time to put on your essay-scoring hat and prepare to grade your own essay. If you're lucky enough to have a friend who is also preparing for the GRE, you could switch essays and grade each other's like you used to do in sixth grade. You'll need to be objective during this process. Remember, the only way to improve is to honestly assess your weaknesses and systematically eliminate them.

Set a timer for two minutes. Read the essay carefully but quickly, so that you do not exceed the two minutes on the timer.

Now ask yourself the following questions about the essay:

1. Overall, did it make sense?
2. Did you address the topic directly?
3. Did you address the topic thoroughly?
4. Did your introduction paragraph repeat the issue to establish the topic of the essay?
5. Did you consider both sides of the issue?
6. Did your examples make sense?
7. Did you flesh out your examples with details?
8. Did you explain how your examples supported your thesis?
9. Did your essay have a strong concluding paragraph?
10. Was your essay well organized, using transitions and topic sentences?
11. Did you use language that made the organization of the essay obvious?
12. Did you use correct grammar, spelling, and language, for the most part?

If you could answer "yes" to all or almost all of these questions, congratulations! Your essay would probably receive a score in the 5–6 range. If you continue to practice, and write an essay of similar quality on the real Analysis of an Issue section of the real test, you should score very well.

If you answered "yes" to fewer than 10 of the questions, you have room for improvement. Fortunately, you also know which areas you need to strengthen as you continue to practice.

If you answered "yes" to fewer than six of the questions, your essay would probably not score very well on a real GRE. An essay of this quality would not help you in the admissions process and could raise some red flags in the minds of the admissions people. You need to continue to practice, focusing on the areas of weakness that you discovered during this scoring process.

Another Sample Response

Take a look at a high scoring response to the prompt you just practiced on. Your essay might look different and that's fine. This is just one of many ways to successfully complete the Issue essay assignment.

> "The powerful are most respected not when they exercise their power, but when they refrain from exercising it."
>
> Write an essay in which you develop and support a position on the statement above. In writing your essay, you should consider both when the statement may be true and when it may be false.

What aspect of power engenders the greatest respect? Some would argue that power inspires respect only by its ability to change things or bring about results. This camp respects the powerful only when they demonstrate their power by raising a massive army or bestowing charity on the less fortunate. Others believe that the true measure of power lies not in what it is used for, but in how it is restrained. These people believe that people most respect the powerful when they choose not to use their power, such as granting clemency to a criminal on death row or allowing critics of the government to speak out. However, even in these cases of restraint, it is clear that the exercise of power is more respected because of what that restraint implies about government power and control.

Consider first the respect people hold for the exercise of power. One of the mightiest displays of power is the ability to protect and safeguard people and property and this aspect of government is what many people respect. Indeed, in Hobbes's Leviathan, *he argued that one of the reasons people sacrifice themselves for the good of the state is to preserve the power of the state to protect its members from outside attacks. And one of the stated goals of the United States massive military buildup was so that other countries would either "love us or fear us." Thus, it is clear that people have respect for displays of power. Similarly, the ability of the powerful to bestow gifts of charity on the less fortunate is also well respected. The names of philanthropists like*

Carnegie and Rockefeller are held in high esteem because they used their power to help those less fortunate than themselves.

On the other hand, the ability to show restraint can also engender respect. Recently, the governor of Illinois decided to commute the death sentences of all the prisoners on death row. Such an act of clemency brought high praise from human rights proponents around the world. Furthermore, the fact that democratic governments allow dissent when they could in many cases censor or squash unfavorable opinions also lends credence to the view that restraint of power is what people respect. For example, the arbitrary arrest and sentencing of political dissidents in Russia has brought much international criticism of the Kremlin, while countries that support freedom of speech and the press are widely respected in the world.

Ultimately, after considering both sides of the issue, it must be concluded that the exercise of power is most respected. This is because even in cases of restraint, the entity in power is still exercising its power. Granting clemency is possible only because the state holds the power of life and death. Allowing dissent is exceptional only because the government has the power to crush it. Thus, it is not the restraint of power that people most respect, it is the exercise of it.

Your essay doesn't have to be perfect. Focus on the big picture.

FINAL THOUGHTS: WHAT TO DO WITH YOUR TIME

Now that you know how to construct your essay, you have to practice writing essays in a mere 30 minutes. Here's a guideline for how to use your time.

- Find key terms, state the opposite side, brainstorm examples: 5–7 minutes
- Formulate a thesis: 2 minutes
- Write the essay: 18–20 minutes
- Proofread: 1–2 minutes

Notice that not a lot of time is allotted for proofreading. Remember that it's okay to have minor spelling and grammatical errors. Your time is better spent making sure you consider both sides of the issue completely and write an effective essay. For tons more practice, you can go to **www.ets.org/gre** for the complete list of essay topics.

Summary

- Follow the three simple steps to essay success: Think, Organize, Write.

- One of the keys to high scoring essays is good examples. Make sure your examples are relevant to the topic and as specific as possible.

- Try to use examples drawn from your readings, current events, literature, and history. Avoid personal examples.

- Spice up your writing by employing an interesting "hook" to get your readers' attention. Consider using such hooks as rhetorical questions, quotes, anecdotes, facts and statistics, and other attention-getting devices.

- A good GRE essay presents a smooth flow of ideas and examples. Make sure you use transitions to help show the progression of ideas in your essay.

- Templates can be effective ways of organizing your essay, but don't feel restricted to them. Come up with your own template or modify the existing templates as you see fit.

Chapter 17
The Argument Essay

The Argument essay of the GRE asks you to examine and critique the logic of an argument. The arguments you will see in this chapter are similar to the ones you worked with in Chapter 7, and you will need to use the same approach to breaking these arguments down. This chapter will show you how to organize and write an essay once you've found the premises, conclusion, and assumptions of a GRE argument.

You'll be able to use all the skills we've discussed for the Analysis of an Issue essays on this type of essay as well, but in a slightly different way. Instead of asking for your opinion on a topic, the Analysis of an Argument essay asks you to critique someone else's argument. Before we jump into setting up templates and other pre-construction steps, let's take a look at how Analytical Writing arguments work.

THE PARTS OF AN ARGUMENT

As you read in Chapter 7 on Critical Reasoning, an argument, for GRE purposes, is a short paragraph in which an author introduces a topic and uses reasoning or factual evidence to back up his or her opinion about that topic.

The following statement is a really simplified example of an argument:

> *My car broke down yesterday, and I need a car to get to work.*
> *Therefore, I should buy a new car.*

The car argument above is composed of the following three parts:

- the conclusion—the author's opinion and recommendation for action
- the premises—the facts the author uses to back up his or her opinion
- the assumptions—unstated conditions that must be true in order for the argument to make sense

In this argument, the author's conclusion is "I should buy a new car."

The premises the author uses to support this conclusion are that his car broke down yesterday, and that he needs a car to get to work.

The premises must support the conclusion the way table legs support a tabletop. The tabletop is the most obvious and useful part of a table—you see more of it, and you can put things on it. But without the legs to hold it up, it's just a slab of wood on the floor. The same is true for the conclusion of an argument. The conclusion is the part that gets all the attention, since it recommends some course of action, but without the premises to support the conclusion, the conclusion won't hold up.

Conclusion Words

Certain words indicate a conclusion.

- so
- therefore
- thus
- hence
- showed that

- clearly
- then
- consequently
- as a result
- concluded that

When you see these words, you can be relatively sure that you've found the conclusion of the argument.

Premise Words

Certain words indicate premises.

- because
- since
- if
- given that

- in view of
- in light of
- assume

ASSUMPTIONS

An assumption is an unstated premise that supports the author's conclusion. It's the connection between the stated premises and the conclusion. In the example of the table, the assumption is that nails or glue hold the legs and the tabletop together. Without the glue or nails, the table will fall apart. Without the assumption, the argument will fall apart.

Sometimes the assumption is described as the gap between the facts that make up the premises and the conclusion. They don't always connect, so the assumption is the gap between them.

Let's take a look back at the car argument:

> My car broke down yesterday, and I need a car to get to work.
> Therefore, I should buy a new car.

The premises are that *my car broke down yesterday* and *I need a car to get to work*. The conclusion is that *I should buy a new car*.

When you first read this argument, you may have had some questions. These questions might have been along the lines of "Why can't the author just rent a car?" or "Why can't the author just fix the car?"

As you read an argument, identifying the premises and conclusion, questions may pop into your head. Those questions are pointing out the gap that leads to the assumption. Here, the gap is between having a broken car and still needing a car to get to work on the one side, and having to buy a new car on the other side.

Therefore, the assumption must be as follows:
There is no other way to have a car.

There are all sorts of smaller assumptions here—that the car can't be fixed, that a car can't be rented, that there's no other car the author can borrow—but those are all covered in the main assumption.

The assumption fills the gap between the premises and the conclusion, and, in fact, functions as an unstated premise:
My car broke down yesterday, and I need a car to get to work. There is no other way to have a car. Therefore, I should buy a new car.

Brainstorming for the Argument Essay consists primarily of coming up with a list of assumptions.

Three Common Types of Arguments and Their Assumptions

There are three types of arguments you are likely to see. They are Sampling, Analogy, and Causal. Becoming familiar with these three types will help you identify the assumptions in the argument more quickly when the clock is ticking on the real test.

1. The Sampling Assumption

A sampling argument assumes that a small group is representative of a much larger group to which it belongs. To attack a sampling argument, show that one cannot assume that the opinions or experiences of the smaller group are necessarily representative of the larger group.

2. The Analogy Assumption

An argument by analogy assumes that A = B or that what is true for one entity will be true for another. To attack an argument by analogy, simply show that the two groups or places or individuals are nothing like each other. What is true for one does not have to be true of the other.

3. The Causal Assumption

A causal argument assumes that A causes B, or that if you remove the cause, you will remove the effect. While there may be a strong correlation between A and B, it does not always follow that it is a causal relationship or that A is the cause of B.

To attack a causal relationship, point out that there are other possible causes for B and brainstorm some possible examples.

Well, Great, But Why Do I Care?

You should care about taking apart the argument, and finding the assumptions in particular, because the key to writing a great Argument essay on the Analytical Writing section is ripping apart the argument.

Think about it. The official instructions on the test ask you to "critique" the author's argument. However, if you claim that everything the author says makes sense, you won't be able to write an essay that's more than a few sentences long. This means that in order to write a great essay, you'll need to tear the author's argument apart.

> **Danger:** The most common mistake people make in writing the Argument essay is expressing their own opinions. Don't do this! The Issue essay specifically asks you to give an opinion and then back it up. The Argument essay wants a critique of someone else's opinion, not your own.

WRITING THE ARGUMENT ESSAY

Writing the Analysis of an Argument essay requires a series of steps.

Step 1: Read the topic and identify the conclusion and the premises.

Step 2: Since they're asking you to critique (that is, weaken) the argument, concentrate on identifying its assumptions. Look for gaps in the argument, weaknesses in the logic, and new information in the conclusion that wasn't present in the premises. Brainstorm as many different assumptions as you can think of. Write these out on your scratch paper or on the computer screen.

Step 3: Select three or four of the strongest assumptions around which to build your essay.

Step 4: Choose a template that allows you to attack the assumptions in an organized way.

Step 5: Write the essay, using all the tools and techniques that you'll be learning in this chapter.

Step 6: Read over the essay and edit it.

You will have 30 minutes to plan and compose a response to the argument topic, so make sure to budget your time wisely.

KEYS TO A HIGH-SCORING ESSAY

In the Analysis of an Argument topic section, your job is to critique the argument's line of reasoning and the evidence supporting it, and to suggest ways in which the argument could be strengthened. Again, you aren't required to know any more about the subject than would any normal person—but you must be able to spot logical weaknesses. Make absolutely sure you have read and understood the previous section about taking apart the argument.

Your opinion is not the point in an Analysis of an Argument essay.

In order to write a high-scoring essay, you'll want to accomplish four key tasks. According to a booklet prepared by ETS, "An outstanding argument essay...clearly identifies and insightfully analyzes important features of the argument; develops ideas cogently, organizes them logically, and connects them smoothly with clear transitions; effectively supports the main points of the critique; and demonstrates superior control of language, including diction, syntactic variety, and the conventions of standard written English. There may be minor flaws."

To put it more simply, your essay should demonstrate all of the same things that you did for the Analysis of an Issue essay, plus one extra ingredient: a cursory knowledge of the rules of logic.

Doing the Actual Analysis of the Argument

In any Analytical Writing argument, the first thing you should do is separate the conclusion from the premises.

Let's see how this works with an actual essay topic.

Topic:

Save the fancy prose for English class! Your grader cares more that you can identify the parts of the argument than for a clever turn of phrase.

> The director of the International Health Foundation recently released this announcement:

> "A new medical test that allows the early detection of a particular disease will prevent the deaths of people all over the world who would otherwise die from the disease. The test has been extremely effective in allowing doctors to diagnose the disease six months to a year before it would have been spotted by conventional means. As soon as we can institute this test as routine procedure in hospitals around the world, the death rate from this disease will plummet."

The conclusion in this argument comes in the first line:

> *A new medical test that allows the early detection of a particular disease will prevent the deaths of people all over the world who would otherwise die from that disease.*

The premises are the evidence in support of this conclusion.

> *The test has been extremely effective in allowing doctors to diagnose the disease six months to a year before it would have been spotted by conventional means.*

The assumptions are the unspoken premises of the argument—without which the argument would fall apart. Remember that assumptions are often causal, analogical, or statistical. What are some assumptions of this argument? Let's brainstorm.

Brainstorming for Assumptions

You can often find assumptions by looking for a gap in the reasoning. "Medical tests allow early detection": According to the conclusion, this medical test leads to the early detection of the disease. There doesn't seem to be a gap here.

Early detection allows patients to survive: In turn, the early detection of the disease allows patients to survive the disease. Well, hold on a minute. Is this necessarily true?

- First, do we know that early detection will *necessarily* lead to survival? We don't even know if this disease is curable. Early detection of an incurable disease is not going to help anyone survive it.
- Second, will the test be widely available and cheap enough for general use? If the test is expensive or available only in certain parts of the world, people will continue to die from the disease.
- Third, will doctors and patients interpret the tests correctly? The test may be fine, but if doctors misinterpret the results or if patients ignore the need for treatment, then the test will not save lives.

Death rate will plummet: There's a huge gap here in that there's absolutely no explanation of how merely detecting the disease will immediately cause the death rate from it to plummet. This area is ripe for exploration.

Organizing the Analysis of an Argument Essay

We're now ready to put this into a ready-made template. In any Analysis of an Argument essay, the template structure should be pretty straightforward: You're simply going to reiterate the argument, attack the argument in three different ways (each in a separate paragraph), summarize what you've said, and mention how the argument could be strengthened. From an organizational standpoint, this is pretty easy. Try to minimize your use of the word *I*. Your opinion is not the point in an Analysis of an Argument essay.

The arguments provided for the writing assessment of the GRE typically contain more flaws than those you worked with in the multiple-choice section. The flaws are often easier to spot as well.

A Sample Template

Of course, you will want to develop your own template for the Analysis of an Argument essay, but to get you started, here's one possible structure:

The argument that (restatement of the conclusion) is not entirely logically convincing, since it ignores certain crucial assumptions.

First, the argument assumes that _____

_____ .

Second, the argument never addresses _____

_____ .

Finally, the argument omits _____

_____ .

Thus, the argument is not completely sound. The evidence in support of the conclusion is not sufficient to support the conclusion of the argument because

_____ .

Ultimately, the argument might have been strengthened by _____

_____ .

The key to succeeding on an Analysis of an Argument essay is to critique the argument clearly.

How Would the Result of Our Brainstorming Fit into the Template?

Here's how the assumptions we came up with for this argument would fit into the template:

> The argument that the new medical test will prevent deaths that would have occurred in the past is not entirely logically convincing since it ignores certain crucial assumptions.
>
> First, the argument assumes that early detection of the disease will lead to an immediate drop in the mortality rate from this disease, yet it does nothing to explain how this will happen, and so on.
>
> Second, the argument never addresses the point that the existence of this new test, even if totally effective, is not the same as the widespread use of the test, and so on.
>
> Finally, even supposing the ability of early detection to save lives and the widespread use of the test, the argument still depends on the doctors' correct interpretation of the test and the patients' willingness to undergo treatment, and so on.
>
> Thus, the argument is not completely sound. The evidence in support of the conclusion that the test will cause death rates to plummet does little to prove that conclusion, since it does not address the assumptions already raised. Ultimately, the argument might have been strengthened if the author could have shown that the disease responds to early treatment, which can be enacted immediately upon receipt of the test results, that the test will be widely available around the world, and that doctors and patients will make proper use of the test.

Customizing Your Analysis of an Argument Template

Your organizational structure may vary in some ways, but it will always include the following elements: The first paragraph should sum up the argument's conclusion. The second, third, and fourth paragraphs will attack the argument and the supporting evidence. The last paragraph should summarize what you've said and state how the argument could be strengthened. Here are some alternate ways of organizing your essay:

Variation 1

1st paragraph: Restate the argument.

2nd paragraph: Discuss the link (or lack thereof) between the conclusion and the evidence presented in support of it.

3rd paragraph: Show three holes in the reasoning of the argument.

4th paragraph: Show how each of the three holes could be plugged up by explicitly stating the missing assumptions.

5th paragraph: Summarize and conclude that because of these three holes, the argument is weak.

Variation 2

1st paragraph: Restate the argument and say it has three flaws.

2nd paragraph: Point out a flaw and show how it could be plugged up by explicitly stating the missing assumption.

3rd paragraph: Point out a second flaw and show how it could be plugged up by explicitly stating the missing assumption.

4th paragraph: Point out a third flaw and show how it could be plugged up by explicitly stating the missing assumption.

5th paragraph: Summarize and conclude that because of these three flaws, the argument is weak.

Write Your Own Template for the Argument Topic

1st paragraph:

2nd paragraph:

3rd paragraph:

4th paragraph:

5th paragraph:

You Are Ready to Write an Argument Essay

You've separated the conclusion from the premises. You've brainstormed for the gaps that weaken the argument. You've noted how the premises support (or don't support) the conclusion. Now it's time to write your essay. Start typing, indenting each of the four or five paragraphs. Use all the tools you've learned in this chapter. Remember to keep an eye on the time. Again, if you have a minute at the end, read over your essay and do any editing that's necessary.

What to Do with Your Time

Now that you know how to construct your essay, you have to practice writing essays in a mere 30 minutes. Here's a guideline for how to use your time.

- Break down the argument: 3–4 minutes
- Find 2–3 assumptions: 3–4 minutes
- Write the essay: 18–20 minutes
- Proofread: 1–2 minutes

As was the case with the Issue essay, not a lot of time is allotted for proofreading. Remember that it's okay to have minor spelling and grammatical errors. Your time is better spent making sure you consider both sides of the issue completely and write an effective essay.

Practice: Writing an Argument Essay

Practice on the following sample argument topic. If you have access to a computer, turn it on and start up a word-processing program (again, you may want to use a very rudimentary one like Notepad to simulate the ETS program you'll see on the real test). Then set a timer for 30 minutes. In that time, read the topic, brainstorm in the space provided in this book, and then type your essay into the computer.

A Sample Argument

The market for the luxury-goods industry is on the decline. Recent reports show that a higher unemployment rate, coupled with consumer fears, has decreased the amount of money the average household spends on both essential and nonessential items, but especially on nonessential items. Since luxury goods are, by nature, nonessential, this market will be the first to decrease in the present economic climate, and luxury retailers should refocus their attention to lower-priced markets.

Conclusion:

Why? (premises)

Assumptions:

Ways you can pull the argument apart:

Ways the argument could be made more compelling:

When writing your essay, make sure to use terms like *causal, analogy, sampling,* and so forth. Nothing impresses an ETS grader more than a sentence like "The argument assumes the sample is representative."

Now use the template you developed earlier in this chapter to type your essay on a computer.

How to Score Your Essay

It's time to put on your essay-scoring hat and prepare to grade your own essay. (Again, if you're lucky enough to have a friend who is also preparing for the GRE, you could switch essays.) You'll need to be objective about the process. The only way to improve is to honestly assess your weaknesses and systematically eliminate them.

Set a timer for two minutes. Read the essay carefully but quickly, so that you do not exceed the two minutes on the timer.

Now ask yourself the following questions about the essay:

1. Overall, did it make sense?
2. Did you address the argument directly?

3. Did you critique the argument thoroughly?
4. Did your introduction paragraph repeat the argument to establish the topic of the essay?
5. Did you avoid injecting your own opinion into the essay?
6. Did your essay have three strong paragraphs critiquing the arguments?
7. Did your critiques make sense?
8. Did you flesh out your points to make the weaknesses of the argument explicit?
9. Did the examples apply directly to the topic?
10. Did the essay have a strong conclusion paragraph?
11. Was the essay well organized?
12. Did you use language that made the organization of the essay obvious?
13. Did you use correct grammar, spelling, and language, for the most part?
14. Was the essay of an appropriate length (four to five paragraphs of at least three sentences each)?

If you could answer "yes" to all or almost all of those questions, congratulations! Your essay would probably receive a score in the 5–6 range. If you continue to practice, and write an essay of similar quality on the Analysis of an Argument essay on the real test, you should score very well.

If you answered "yes" to fewer than 12 of the questions, you have room for improvement. Fortunately, you also know which areas you need to strengthen as you continue to practice.

If you answered "yes" to fewer than five of the questions, your essay would probably not score very well on a real GRE. You need to continue to practice, focusing on the areas of weakness that you discovered during this scoring process.

There are more Argument topics for you to practice in the back of this book, but if you'd like to practice even more, go to **www.ets.org/gre** and view the list of real Argument topics. You cannot possibly practice writing essays on all of these real ETS topics, so don't even try. However, you should spend time reading through them to become familiar with the variety of topics that ETS may give you.

Just Keep Practicing

So now you've read everything you need to know about writing high-scoring essays on the GRE. With a little practice, writing these essays should become second nature, and you'll find yourself sitting at the word processor on test day confident and prepared. Keep it up!

Summary

o   Always start by identifying the conclusion of the argument.

o   Look for the common types of arguments: Sampling, Analogy, and Causal.

o   Brainstorm all of the assumptions that attach the premises to the conclusion.

o   Outline your essay on your scratch paper before you start writing.

o   Leave yourself two minutes to proofread your essay once you are done writing.

Part V
Answers and Explanations to Drills and Practice Sets

CHAPTER 4: TEXT COMPLETIONS

Practice: Finding the Clue (Page 47)

1. Your words: *harrowing, difficult, troubled*; Underline: *reflected in the harrowing nature…of his plays*

2. Your words: *tall, high, towering*; Underline: *second highest mountain in the world…reaching more than 28,000 feet high*

3. Your words: *negative, harmful, unhealthy*; Underline: *wind-chill warning is issued…minus 25 degrees Fahrenheit or lower*

4. Your words: *remnants, remains, artifacts* OR *devices, munitions, projectiles*; Underline: *unexploded shells… from World War II*

5. Your words: *non-interchangeable, distinct, different*; Underline: *use the terms interchangeably…mammoths were hairy with long tusks, while mastodons had low-slung bodies and fatter skulls*

6. Your words: *practical, pragmatic, apolitical*; Underline: *he crafted his policies not with an eye toward their political consequences but instead toward their practical effects*

7. Your words: *amount, volume, workload*; Underline: *he would have to read for hours and hours each day to finish it all*

8. Your words: *derived, descended, transcribed*; Underline: *word "ghoul"…from the Arabic word "Algol"*

Practice: Clues and Transition Words (Page 50)

1. Your words: *bad, poor, uneven*; Underline: *top talents…performance as a rookie almost ended his career*; Circle: *but*

2. Your words: *praise, recognition, respect*; Underline: *she brokered a diplomatic solution to a potential crisis*; Circle: *work; she*

3. Your words: *beneficial, health-promoting, healthful*; Underline: *detrimental to one's health*; Circle: *While*

4. Your words: *disconnected, apart, isolated*; Underline: *increasing technological connectivity*; Circle: *Despite*

5. Your words: *attractive, graceful, charming*; Underline: *ugliness and clumsiness*; Circle: *Although*

6. Your words: *gauge, predictor, sign*; Underline: *use holiday sales to gauge future stock prices*; Circle: *prices; thus*

7. Your words: *negativity, misgivings, doubts*; Underline: *it is somewhat ironic…negative view*; Circle: *while … rarely display such*

8.	Your words: *(devastating) effects, harms, toxicity*; Underline: *devastating effects on insects*; Circle: *insects; however…the same*

Text Completions Drill (Page 55)

1. B   sorrow

The blank is describing what *her eyes relayed* and the transition word *despite* indicates that what *her eyes relayed* must be the opposite *the smile that spread from ear to ear.* A good word for the blank is something like "sadness." Choice (A), *jubilance,* means something joyous, so eliminate it. Choice (B), *sorrow*, is a good match, so keep (B). *Lively* means energetic, so eliminate (C). *[V]ision* offers no contrast to "sadness," and *mischievousness* or naughtiness is closer to *smile* than to "sadness," so eliminate (D) and (E). The correct answer is (B).

2. D   acute

The blank is describing *black bears…claws.* The transition word *[w]hile* indicates that the *claws of black bears* are different from those of *grizzly bears* which are described as *long, flat, and somewhat blunt.* Black bears' claws are described in the sentence as *short* and *curved,* which are the opposite of *long* and *flat.* Therefore, a good word for the blank is the opposite of *somewhat blunt,* so use "sharp" and evaluate the answer choices. Choice (A) *obtuse* is a synonym for blunt, so eliminate (A). Choice (B), *abominable* may describe a bear, but the word doesn't mean "sharp" and so doesn't match the clue, eliminate (B). Choice (C), *barren,* is not a match for "sharp" so eliminate it. Choice (D), *acute,* is a good match for "sharp," so keep (D). Choice (C), *fearful* does not match "sharp," so eliminate it. The correct answer is (D).

3. C   static

The blank is describing *individual personalities.* The semicolon indicates that the clause before the semicolon should agree with the clause following it. Therefore, the duality of *stability versus change* must be matched in the second clause by the duality describing *personalities*—the word in the blank or *different.* The adjective *different* in the second clause corresponds to *change* in the first, so the word in the blank must be an adjective corresponding to *stability.* Recycle from the clue and use "stable." Choice (A) *transient,* means last for a short period of time, so eliminate (A). Choice (B), *maladjusted* is not a match for "stable" so eliminate it. Choice (C), *static,* is a good match for the "stable" so keep (C). Choice (D), *disturbed,* and (E), *discreet,* are both not poor matches for "stable," so eliminate (D) and (E). The correct answer is (C).

4. E   prodigious

The blank is describing the kind of *economic ripples* caused by *[t]he Erie Canal's completion.* The clause after the semi-colon provides further insight into the sentence: *property values and industrial output…rose exponentially.* Therefore, these ripples could thus be described as significant or "large," so use this word for the blank. Choice (A), *persistent,* is not a match for "large" so eliminate it. Choice (B), *invaluable* doesn't quite mean "large," and (C), *incredulous,* is nothing like "large" so eliminate (B) and (C). *[S]evere* might describe a significant economic effect, but that effect would be negative, not positive as implied here, so eliminate (D). Choice (E), *prodigious,* meaning impressively great or large, is a good match for "large." The correct answer is (E).

5. **B stolidity**

The blank is describing how *voters…respond to the levy of a new tax.* The clue in the sentence is the word *inured,* which means hardened to a negative situation. If *[v]oters* are *inured,* then their response *to the levy of a new tax* would not be strong. Thus the word in the blank could be "resignation." Choice (A), *amazement,* is not a match for "resignation" so eliminate (A). Choice (B), *stolidity,* or lack of emotion, is a good match so keep (B). Choice (C), *exasperation,* may describe how voters feel generally towards politicians, but is not supported by the passage so eliminate (C). Choice (D), *alarm,* and (E), *perplexity,* are both poor matches for "resignation," so eliminate both answer choices. The correct answer is (B).

6. **B commensurate**

The blank is describing *when…it is desirable to expand the yield of a harvest.* The sentence provides further insight into this by stating that *it is desirable to expand…yield,* but only if there aren't also certain *additions in time, exertion and other variable factors of production.* So, a word such as "similar" for the blank conveys the logic that expanded yield shouldn't require expanded additions in time and other factors. Choice (A), *predestined,* is not a match for "similar" so eliminate (A). Choice (B), *commensurate,* is a good match for the blank so keep (B). Choice (C), *deliberate,* is not a match for the blank, so eliminate it. Choice (D), *analogous* is close, but *commensurate* is more quantitative, so eliminate (D). While *indeterminate* or uncertain additions are certainly not desired, this choice doesn't match "similar," so eliminate (E). The correct answer is (B).

Text Completions Practice Set (Page 62)

1. **B futile**

The clue is "global interconnectedness on the rise." In such a situation, the United States might allow its own interests to be harmed if it tried to stay neutral during wartime. Thus, you need a word that means *doomed* for the blank. Something *presumptuous* is not necessarily doomed, while *pragmatic* and *admirable* take the sentence in the wrong direction. *Contemptuous,* in contrast, makes no sense in the blank's context. *Futile* is the best choice.

2. **B enamored of**

Choose carefully here. The clue is "the dancers alone made his trip worthwhile." Thus, Flaubert was impressed by them. *Enamored of* is the only choice that captures such a feeling. *Overwhelmed by* is extreme, and implies that Flaubert got into more than he could handle. *Taken aback by,* in contrast, merely suggests that our traveler was surprised by the dancers; we cannot be sure that his surprise was pleasant. Meanwhile, *beseeched by* does not indicate how Flaubert felt, whereas if he were *flustered by* the performers, he would not likely have found his encounter with them *worthwhile.*

3. **A fragile** and **E vulnerability**

Try working with the second blank first. The clue is "facade of calm that covers our anxiety." The transition *and* tells you that you are going in the same direction. Therefore, the word in the second blank should be something similar to *anxiety. Vulnerability* is the best fit. Nothing in the sentence supports a word as strong as *terror,* and *humor* goes in the wrong direction. For the first blank, if our facade is "flimsy and effortlessly ruptured," it is likely that the human race is *delicate. Fragile* is the only choice that matches.

4. **B prerogative** and **F attainable by**

Try working with the second blank first. The clue is "...when the increased popularity of dime novels, the expansion in the number of bookstores, and the introduction of the paperback made books...." Therefore, find a word for the second blank similar to *accessible*. *Attainable by* is the best choice. The first blank describes the situation before books became accessible, so buying them would have been a *privilege* limited to the well-to-do. *Prerogative* is the best choice.

5. **A an ineluctable** and **F merely denouement**

If district boundaries are designed to *protect incumbents*—that is, those already in office—then *victory* for those incumbents should be close to *assured* or *inevitable*. *Ineluctable* is synonymous with these words. *Invidious* means "causing envy" and *plangent* means "full of lamentation," neither of which is as well supported as the credited response. The second blank comes after a couple of transition words. The first is *Of course*, which might sound like the passage is continuing in the same direction, but here indicates a change of direction: The author is conceding that sometimes incumbents face challenges. The second, *Nevertheless*, also changes direction, meaning that the passage has returned to where it started, arguing that elections are essentially decided before they begin. That is what *merely denouement* means. *Seldom nugatory* means rarely inconsequential, which is the opposite of what the passage calls for; *remarkably contentious* is wrong for the same reason, as that phrase would indicate that the general election is fiercely contested.

6. **A pedantic** and **D antediluvian**

The first blank describes a group of professors. The clue is that these professors "continue to insist that video games will never be a proper object of study." The transition *While* also means that these professors are different from *the rising generation of more heterodox academics*. So, a good word for the first blank is something like *orthodox*. Of the answers, only *pedantic*, which means overly concerned with the formalisms of teaching, comes close to meaning *orthodox*. The second blank describes how the rising generation regards the talk of the first group of professors. Since the rising generation is more heterodox, they would likely regard the view of the more orthodox professors as outdated. The word *antediluvian*—literally, before the flood—means extremely old-fashioned. *Pusillanimous* means cowardly, and *jejune* means vapid and immature, so eliminate these choices.

7. **C fulfilled, F changes,** and **H perilously**

Try working with the first blank first. The clue for the first blank is "predictions generally...accurate." The transition *however* tells you that the first and second parts of the sentence are in contrast to each other. Predictions are usually right, the first part of the sentence is saying, when things go as normal. Put something like *true* in the first blank. *Fulfilled* fits nicely. The second and third blank must be filled together in order to complete the second sentence. The transition *however* shows that the second sentence changes direction. You would expect predictions to be wrong when there are *changes*, which is a choice for the second blank. *Substantial changes* would make predictions *very* wrong, so *perilously* is the best choice.

8. **B dense, F liquid,** and **G an illustration**

The clue for the first blank is the "floating" ice. So, ice is less heavy than water. Only *dense* fits. There is nothing to support that water is more *intriguing* than ice. All solids are less *aqueous* than liquids. For the second blank, the transition *than* tells you to change direction from *solid*. Another clue is *water* compared to *ice*. Only *liquid* fits. For the third blank, the clue "the floating ice in your water" is offered as an example. Only *an illustration* fits.

9. **C practicing, E articulate,** and **I unfamiliar**

For the first blank, Molly *could comprehend* Spanish before their trip, so she was *becoming familiar* with Spanish. Only *practicing* fits. *Mastering* goes too far. Now you can turn your attention to the third blank. Because she is learning Spanish, it must be a *new* language for her, and only *unfamiliar* fits for the third blank. For the second blank, the transition *although* tells you to change direction from the clue *comprehend*. She could not *state* her thoughts. Only *articulate* means "state."

10. **B demarcates, D apocryphal,** and **I senescence**

The first blank refers to what some people believe about the human lifespan representing the *outer bounds of animal longevity* in relation to that of other animals. So, look for a word that means *marker. Demarcates* is the best fit, as *belies* means contradicts, and *antedates* means comes before. The second blank refers to the stories of musket balls being found in turtle shells and how some people *tend to dismiss tales* about turtles living a long time, so a word such as *questionable* would fit. *Apocryphal* means questionable, making it the best choice. The clue for the final blank is that some turtles *show(ing) no signs of aging even as they pass the two-century mark* so look for a word that works with *negligible* to create a phrase that means "not growing old." *Senescence* means growing old and when combined with negligible, is a good fit for this clue.

CHAPTER 5: SENTENCE EQUIVALENCE

Sentence Equivalence Drill (Page 71)

1. **C modern** and **E contemporary**

The blank is describing the *observer*. The sentence gives further insight into the blank with the word *ancient* and the transition word *or* which indicates that a good word for the blank is the opposite of *ancient*. Therefore, a good word for the blank could be "modern." Choice (A), *antiquated,* is the opposite of "modern" so eliminate (A). Choice (B), *perceptive,* is a poor match for "modern," so eliminate it. Choice (C), *modern,* is a perfect match, so keep (C). Choice (D), *astute,* is not a match for "modern," so eliminate it. Choice (E), *contemporary,* is a good match, so keep it. Choice (F), *archaic,* is the opposite of "modern," so eliminate it. The correct answer is (C) and (E).

2. **D innate** and **F inborn**

The blank is describing *characteristics*. The passage gives further insight by stating that some *arise through experience* and that *[r]esearchers* are interested in the nature versus nurture debate. This duality is reflected later in the sentence when it's explained why these researchers *use identical twins…separated at birth* to *explore* this debate. Characteristics *which arise through experience* correspond to *nurture,* so the characteristics described by the blank should correspond to *nature,* so use "natural" as the word for the blank. *Intractable* is a poor match for "natural" so eliminate (A). Choice (B), *nascent,* means just coming into existence, which sounds like it could match "natural" but does not fit because something does not have to be "natural" to be called nascent. Eliminate (B). Choice (C), *erudite,* means scholarly, so eliminate it. Choice (D) is a good match for the blank, so keep it. Choice (E), *predilection,* means a preference, so eliminate it. Choice (F) is a good match for the blank, so keep it. The correct answer is (D) and (F).

3. **A** *capricious* and **D** *unconventional*

The blank is describing the *behavior* and the sentence gives further insight into the clue by stating that the Canadian Prime Minister is *eccentric*. So, a good word for the blank is "eccentric." Choice (A), *capricious,* is a good match for "eccentric," so keep (A). Choice (B), *lackluster,* means not to standard, so eliminate it. Choice (C), *poised,* is the opposite of "eccentric" so eliminate (C). Choice (D), *unconventional,* is a good match for the blank, so keep (D). Choice (E), *repulsive,* could describe behavior in some, but is not a match for "eccentric" so eliminate (E). Choice (F), *decorous,* is also the opposite of "eccentric" so eliminate (F). The correct answer is (A) and (D).

4. **B** *dynamic* and **F** *oscillating*

The blank is describing the *conditions of life.* The sentence gives further insight into the blank by listing examples of what the conditions of life could be, *such as…atmospheric pressure,…physical activity, and diet.* This clues imply that the *conditions of life* are "varying." Choice (A), *inveterate,* means have a long-standing habit, so eliminate it. Choice (B) is a good match for the blank, so keep it. Choice (C), *timorous,* means nervousness, so eliminate it. Choice (D), *cowed,* means to pressure by intimidation, so eliminate it. Choice (E), turgid, means swollen, so eliminate (E). Choice (F) is a good match for the blank, so keep it. The correct answer is (B) and (F).

5. **B commandeer** and **F appropriate**

The blank is describing what the *armed forces* did to *any working form of transportation they could find.* The sentence gives further insight into the blank by stating the *armed forces* were *without an adequate number of vehicles of their own,* after *arriving…days after Hurricane Zelda.* So, the armed forces were "taking over" any form of transportation. Choice (A), *repatriate,* means to send someone back to their home country, so eliminate (A). Choice (B), *commandeer,* is a good match, so keep it. Choice (C), *extradite,* means to hand over someone to a judicial system, so eliminate (C). Choice (D), *interdict,* means to prohibit, so eliminate (D). Choice (E), *expurgate,* means to remove something questionable, so eliminate (E). Choice (F), *appropriate,* is a good match for the blank, so keep (F). The correct answer is (B) and (F).

Sentence Equivalence Practice Set (Page 81)

1. **B affinity** and **F predilection**

The word in the blank is used to describe Jim's feelings for gumdrops. The clues "enjoyed all kinds of candy" and "his absolute favorite" indicates that the blank means *liking.* Both *affinity* and *predilection* mean *liking. Odium* and *disregard* go in the wrong direction. *Container* might sound right, but it is not related to the clue. *Nature* does not mean liking.

2. **A fiasco** and **B debacle**

The blank concerns the Wright brothers' first attempt at flying. The clue is that their "subsequent efforts similarly ended in failure." Recycle the clue, and put *failure* in the blank. *Fiasco* and *debacle* are the best matches. *Triumph* and *feat* have the opposite meaning. *Hindrance* is not close enough, and *precedent* does not mean failure.

3. **D diminishes** and **F wanes**

    The clue "due to the increased aerodynamic drag" suggests that fuel efficiency is likely to decrease as speed increases. *Diminishes* and *wanes* both mean decreases. Eliminate *equalizes* and *stabilizes* because they mean the fuel efficiency evens out. *Adapts* and *increases* do not fit the clue, and neither has a synonym among the other answer choices.

4. **B an inept** and **F a maladroit**

    Despite acts as a change-of-direction transition that, combined with "vast amount of time Francis dedicated to learning six different languages," tells you that something is wrong with Francis's communication skills. The last part of the sentence provides an additional clue: "failed to redress his inability to construct cogent prose" means that he doesn't make sense. The blank must mean *ineffective*, so *inept* and *maladroit* are the correct answers. Nothing tells us how Francis feels, so *morose* won't work. *Astute* is the opposite of what's needed. Though it's possible Francis is *florid* and *prolific*, the clues don't directly support these ideas.

5. **E temperament** and **F humor**

    The main clues are that one twin is described as *sanguine*, the other *choleric*; even if you don't know these words, the phrases "even in times of stress" and "angry outbursts" suggest that they are words used to describe *personality*. *Temperament* is a good synonym for *personality*. While it is frequently used to mean comedy, *humor* can also mean personality, especially in conjunction with words such as *sanguine* and *choleric*, which derive from the ancient belief that temperament was shaped by the levels of different fluids, or humors, in a person's body. The remaining choices don't fit: *Environment* means one's surroundings, while the other three words are concerned with the physical rather than the mental.

CHAPTER 6: READING COMPREHENSION

Reading Comprehension Drill (Page 107)

1. **A**

    The passage contains a mixture of information about the aye-aye, both from a scientific and cultural background. It gives an overview of the animal without giving a lot of detail in any one area. Choice (B) is incorrect because the passage mentions evolution only briefly, at the very end. This choice is too narrow. Choice (C) is incorrect because the style of the passage is too advanced for young students. Choice (D) is incorrect because the passage mentions religion only as it relates to the fate of the aye-aye. Choice (E) is incorrect because the information given is focused more on the aye-aye itself than on the culture of Madagascar.

2. **A**

    The author refers to the aye-aye as a "superb example of life's variety." Because this is a positive statement, look for a positive answer. Choice (D) is negative. Choice (E) means sad. Choice (B) means confused. Choice (C) is positive but is too extreme. Therefore, (A), *admiring,* is the correct answer.

3.   **"The aye-aye has been listed as an endangered species and, as a result, the government of Madagascar has designated an island off the northeastern coast of Madagascar as a protected reserve for aye-ayes and other wildlife."**

    The author draws the conclusion that the aye-aye may become extinct because the animals are killed on sight and their habitat is being cut down. If some of the animals are in a protected reserve, then not all of them will be affected by the circumstances cited by the author.

4. **A and B**

    Choices (A) and (B) can both be inferred from the passage. Choice (A) is supported by the first paragraph. The classification of the aye-aye changed, which demonstrates that such classifications are not absolute. Choice (B) is supported by the part of the passage dealing with the future of the aye-aye. It states that the aye-aye is seen as an omen of death in the traditional religion of Madagascar. *Augury* refers to the use of omens, so this statement must be true. Choice (C), however, is not supported. Although the passage states that the aye-aye is in danger, it does not directly discuss whether this is due to limited resources on the main island.

5. **A**

    In the passage, the critics argue that for a piece of literature to be great, it must be hard for the average reader to understand. Choice (A) depicts an analogous situation of avant-garde movies deemed superior to Hollywood blockbusters simply because their storylines are more complicated and presumably harder to understand.

6. **E**

    The passage states, "rather than the to-be-expected socialist harangue, Allende subtly works her political message within the fabric of the compelling narrative she weaves." In other words, a reader might have expected Allende to include strong socialist propaganda within her novel, but she did not. Choice (A) is incorrect. Although the passage talks about Allende's background, it is not clear that her novel is autobiographical in nature. Choice (B) is incorrect because although the passage states that Allende's work would have received more critical attention if the book had been thought of as great literature, it is not clear that it would have received more favorable reviews. Choice (C) is incorrect because although the passage states that Allende borrowed from García Márquez's work, it does not state that she learned magical realism from García Márquez. Choice (D) is the opposite of what the passage argues. The passage suggests that it is the very subtlety of her political message that makes Allende's work compelling.

7. **E**

    The passage states, "Yet, to remember the man solely by his associations is to miss his importance to nineteenth-century American philosophy as a whole and to the Transcendental Movement in particular," which suggests the author would agree with (A). In the second paragraph, the author refers to Alcott as a "visionary," which means ahead of his time, so the author would agree with (B). In the last sentence, the author notes that Alcott believed that "a student's intellectual growth was concomitant with his or her spiritual growth." This rules out (C). In the second paragraph, the author refers to Alcott's ideas as *polemical* at the time. *Polemical* means controversial, thereby implying that Alcott's ideas were not universally accepted, which agrees with (D). The last paragraph of the passage praises Alcott as an erudite orator, a point that is made in direct contrast with his lack of skills as a writer. Therefore, (E) is not supported.

8. **B**

    In the first paragraph of the passage, the author states that Alcott's "philosophical treatises have rightly been criticized by many as being ponderous, esoteric, and lacking focus." The term "esoteric" means understood by only a select group. Therefore, the correct answer is (B).

9. **B**

Choice (B) is correct. The author states that taxonomic classifications should be used in conjunction with other information about the animal. In (B), the team uses both observed and accepted data, which would include classification. Choice (A) is incorrect because the scientists use only taxonomic information. Choice (C) is incorrect because the zookeeper uses only observed information, ignoring the taxonomic information.

10. **B**

The author tries to convey several facts and make a point about the appropriate use of classifications. Because *didactic* means "intended to instruct," that's pretty close. Choice (A) is incorrect because nothing in the passage indicates that the author is upset. Choice (C) is incorrect because the author has a definite opinion on the matter. Choice (D) is incorrect because the author does not sound sad. Choice (E) is incorrect because the passage does not praise anything.

CHAPTER 7: CRITICAL REASONING

Practice: Identifying Conclusions (Page 117)

1. "it is unlikely that the new defense bill will pass"

2. "grass was not a significant part of the dinosaur diet"

3. "automaker *X* will have no choice but to file for bankruptcy"

4. "country *Y* will experience a decrease in obesity-related health problems"

5. "machines will soon outnumber humans as the number-one users of the Internet"

Practice: Finding the Premise (Page 121)

1. Premise: "A bipartisan group of 15 senators has announced that it does not support the legislation."

2. Premises:

    (1) "The earliest known grass fossils date from approximately 55 million years ago."

    (2) "Dinosaurs most likely disappeared from the earth around 60 million years ago."

    (3) "fossilized remains of dinosaur teeth that indicate the creatures were more suited to eating ferns and palms"

3. Premises:

    (1) "company's poor financial situation"

    (2) "the workers at automaker *X* are threatening to go on strike"

4. **Premise:** "the leading members of the nation's food industry have agreed to provide healthier alternatives, reduce sugar and fat content, and reduce advertisements for unhealthy foods"

5. **Premise:** "Recent advances in technology have led to a new wave of 'smart' appliances"

Practice: Locating Assumptions (Page 125)

1. **Conclusion:** There will be no decline in enrollment at the University.

   Why?

   Premise: The University plans to hire two highly credentialed biology professors to replace Professor Jones.

   Assumption: That the two new biology professors will be at least as attractive to prospective students as was Professor Jones.

2. **Conclusion:** "It is unjust to charge customers under the age of 25 more to rent a car than those over the age of 25."

   Why?

   Premise: "Most states allow people as young as 16 to have a driver's license and all states allow 18-year-olds the right to vote."

   Assumption: Because people under the age of 25 have the right to vote and drive there is no reason to charge them more to rent a car.

3. **Conclusion:** "Roughly 12.5 percent of planets in the universe should have life on them."

   Why?

   Premise: "In our solar system, there are eight planets and at least one of them obviously has life on it."

   Assumption: All planetary systems in the universe have the same proportion of planets with life on them as does our solar system.

4. **Conclusion:** "The leaders of State A should institute the gas tax."

   Why?

   Premise: "58 percent of voters in Township B approve of a proposed 2-cent gasoline tax."

   Assumption: The opinion of Township B is representative of the opinion of all of State A.

Critical Reasoning Practice Set (Page 139)

1. **B**

   Choice (B) indicates that, *overall*, it may not have been financially advantageous in 1989 for a company to move to a region with a lower corporate tax rate. For (A), the numbers of similar companies in regions with favorable tax policies compared with the numbers in regions with unfavorable tax policies does not explain why there was less corporate flight. The reference to numbers is out of scope. For (C), both the difficulty of the codes and the benefit to anyone other than the company are irrelevant. Though the tax codes may have been difficult to decipher, saving money would still have been good incentive to move. Choice (D) would make it even harder to explain that there was less corporate flight. Some companies would have relocated to foreign countries. For (E), individual tax rates are out of scope.

2. **C**

You need an answer that describes Tello's response to Aramayo. Aramayo concludes that the government should consolidate its leadership because the government functions most efficiently when decisions are handled by very few individuals. To make such an argument, Aramayo must assume that there are no negative consequences of consolidating the leadership. Tello responds by pointing out a negative consequence. Choice (C) says that Tello responds in such a fashion. For (A), Tello does not contradict Aramayo's reasoning, despite offering a possible negative consequence. For (B), Tello does more than uncover an assumption: Tello attacks the assumption. For (B) to be correct, Tello's response would have needed to have used words to the effect "But you assume that…." For (D), Tello does not uncover any circular reasoning. For (E), Tello does not point to any overgeneralization.

3. **B**

This is really asking for the conclusion of the argument. Choice (B) provides the conclusion. Remember that a properly drawn conclusion should pass the Why Test. Why would hiring a Chief Information Officer improve productivity? Because Chief Information Officers are like new business computer systems, which increase productivity for companies. For (A), because the actual function of a Chief Information Officer is never described in the argument, you cannot conclude anything about that function. Choice (C) contradicts the part of the passage that states "many businesses experience dramatic gains in productivity after installing a new computer system." For (D), the argument provides no basis for comparing the efficiency of a Chief Information Officer and a new computer system. For (E), the difficulty of measuring the results is outside the scope of this argument.

4. **B**

The conclusion is that the clothes washed at the Main Street Laundromat are cleaner than those washed at the Elm Street Laundromat because Main Street uses more water. The premise is that Joe's clothes are cleaner when he does them at the Main Street Laundromat and that Main Street's machines use more water per load. This is a causal argument. One way to strengthen a causal argument is to rule out an alternate cause. Choice (B) rules out different detergents as an alternate cause. Choice (A) is just a restatement of the conclusion. For (C), the Oak Street Laundromat is out of scope. For (D), how much laundry Joe does at each Laundromat is out of scope. Choice (E) would weaken the argument.

5. **A**

The argument concludes that the change from a multiple-truck delivery system to a single-truck system is the cause of the increase in the rate of complaints. The premise is that the rate of complaints increased and that there had been a change in the method of delivery. The argument is causal. Choice (A) weakens the argument by providing another cause for the increased rate: Today, the complaints are being reported to the right people. This answer choice leaves open the possibility that the actual number of complaints is unchanged from 1964, but explains why the rate of complaints has risen. For (B), whether any mail arrives late in a multiple-truck delivery system is out of scope. For (C), registered mail versus unregistered mail is out of scope. For (D), because the argument is referring to the rate of complaints, the amount of bulk mail is out of scope. For (E), the price of stamps is out of scope.

CHAPTER 8: VOCABULARY FOR THE GRE

Group 1 Exercises: Matching (Page 149)

1. C
2. J
3. E
4. G
5. A
6. L
7. K
8. B
9. N
10. H
11. M
12. I
13. D
14. F

Group 2 Exercises: Matching (Page 153)

1. B
2. M
3. F
4. J
5. N
6. A
7. D
8. E
9. L
10. C
11. H
12. I
13. G
14. K

Group 3 Exercises: Matching (Page 156)

1. D
2. G
3. K
4. I
5. M
6. A
7. C
8. N
9. H
10. F
11. E
12. B
13. J
14. L

Group 4 Exercises: Matching (Page 159)

1. I
2. L
3. N
4. C
5. K

6. B
7. J
8. A
9. G
10. E

11. M
12. D
13. H
14. F

CHAPTER 10: MATH FUNDAMENTALS

Math Fundamentals Drill (Page 206)

1. **C, D, and F**

   To solve this problem, try writing out the possibilities. The least prime number is 2. $(2 \times 2) + 3 = 7$; so (C) is correct. The next prime number is 3: $(3 \times 3) + 5 = 14$, so (D) is correct. The next prime number is 5: $(5 \times 5) + 7 = 32$, which is not an answer choice. The next prime number is 7: $(7 \times 7) + 11 = 60$, so (F) is correct. The next prime number is 11: $(11 \times 11) + 13 = 134$, which is a greater value than the answer choice possibilities. The correct answer is (C), (D), and (F).

2. **C**

   To answer this question, first write an equation with the information given. So, *number of cases ordered × $1,757 = total amount of money spent*. Now begin figuring out the answer to Quantity A and the answer to Quantity B. The number of books is equal to *number of cases × 150*, so it is possible to figure out how many cases were sold. Set up the equation and solve. *Cases × $1,757 = $10,550*, so $Cases = \dfrac{\$10,550}{\$1,757} = 6.004$ cases. Since it is not possible to order a partial case, only 6 cases can be ordered for $10,550. This results in $6 \times 150 = 900$ books. Solve for Quantity B in the same way. *Cases × $1,757 = $12,290*, so $Cases = \dfrac{\$12,290}{\$1,757} = 6.99$ cases. Since it is not possible to order a partial case, once again, only 6 cases can be ordered and Quantity B equals 6×150, or 900. The quantities are equal, and the correct answer is (C).

3. **A and E**

   To begin, find the factors of 91: 1 and 91 or 7 and 13. Remember that the product of two negative numbers is positive, so the integers could also be negative factors. The question asks for the sum of the two integers. Choice (A) is the sum of −91 and −1. Choice (E) is the sum of 7 and 13. None of the other answer choices are possible, so the correct answer is (A) and (E).

4. **D**

   List all of the distinct prime integers less than 20. The prime integers are 2, 3, 5, 7, 11, 13, 17, and 19. The problem asks for the sum, so add all of the values up to yield $2 + 3 + 5 + 7 + 11 + 13 + 17 + 19 = 77$. The ones digit is a 7, so the correct answer is (D).

5. **B, C, and D**

   A $20 scarf can be discounted as much as 50 percent, and 50 percent of 20 is $\$20 \times \dfrac{50}{100} = \$10$, so the minimum sale price of a scarf is $20 − $10 = $10. The least discount is 25 percent, and 25 percent of 20 is $\$20 \times \dfrac{25}{100} = \$5$, so the maximum sale price of a scarf is $20 − $5 = $15. Therefore, the range of possible sale prices for scarves is $10 to $15. Now, eliminate choices that fall outside of that range: Choice (A) is less than $10, and (E) is greater than $15, so eliminate both of them. The correct answer is (B), (C), and (D).

6. **300**

   There are 3 terms in the sequence and they repeat. The question asks about the product of the 81st, 82nd, 83rd, 84th, and 85th term. Use the fact that the values of the terms in the sequence repeat after every third term to determine the value of the 81st term. Divide 81 by 3 to find that there are 27 complete iterations of the sequence. The 81st term is at the end of one of these repetitions, so its value is −5. Therefore, the 82nd term is −2, the 83rd is 3, the 84th is −5, and the 85th is −2. Therefore, the product is $(−5) \times (−2) \times 3 \times (−5) \times (−2) = 300$. The correct answer is 300.

7. **C**

   Recognize the Distributive Law at work here. If the expression in Quantity A is distributed, the resulting expression is $2x + 8y$, which is the same as Quantity B. Therefore, the two quantities are equal and the correct answer is (C).

8. **A**

   Quantity A is the greatest number of consecutive nonnegative integers whose sum is less than 22, so start adding the numbers with the least value. However, Quantity A contains an important clue with the word *nonnegative*. This means that the number 0 could be a value. Start with 0 and add until the sum is the greatest it could be without exceeding 22. So $0 + 1 + 2 = 3$; $3 + 3 = 6$; $6 + 4 = 10$; $10 + 5 = 15$; and $15 + 6 = 21$. Therefore, the consecutive nonnegative integers whose sum is less than 22 are 0, 1, 2, 3, 4, 5, and 6. That is 7 values. Quantity A is greater than Quantity B, and the correct answer is (A).

9. **D**

The question asks for the greatest possible value of $x + y$. Therefore, find the greatest values of x and y. The greatest value of x is when 4 is divided by 6, which produces a remainder of 4. The greatest value of y is when 2 is divided by 3, which produces a remainder of 2. Therefore, the greatest value of $x + y$ is 6, and the correct answer is (D).

10. **E**

Follow the order of operations. Start with the parentheses first and do the division and multiplication, so $12 - \left(\frac{6}{3} - 4 \times 3\right) - 8 \times 3 = 12 - (2 - 12) - 8 \times 3$. Now finish the parentheses to find that the expression is $12 - (-10) - 8 \times 3$. Now multiply so that the expression is $12 - (-10) - 24$. Now work the rest of the problem to find that $22 - 24 = -2$, and the correct answer is (E).

CHAPTER 11: ALGEBRA (AND WHEN TO USE IT)

Algebra (And When to Use It) Drill (Page 246)

1. **19**

Plug in $100 for the cost of the item to the retailer. Therefore, the original selling price is $140, or 40 percent more than the retail price. To find the reduced price, subtract 15 percent of $140 from $140 to get $119. The difference between the reduced price and the cost of the item to the retailer is then $119 – $100 = $19. Therefore, the question is asking what percent of 100 is 19. The correct answer is 19 percent.

2. **B**

First, put the equation in standard form: $x^2 + 8x + 7 = 0$. Now factor: $(x + 7)(x + 1) = 0$. Solve: $x = -7$ or -1. Both of the possible values for x are negative, so Quantity B is always greater than Quantity A.

3. **27**

Because $9 = 3^2$; the original equation becomes $3^3 \times (3^2)^{12} = 3^x$; or, $3^3 \times 3^{24} = 3^x$; or, $3^{3+24} = 3^x$. Therefore, $x = 27$.

4. **E**

Because there are variables in the answers, Plug In. Let's make $x = 10$, $y = 7$, and $c = 3$. Then $A = 2 \times 10 - (7 - 2 \times 3)$. Solve for the numbers in the parentheses before subtracting. $A = 20 - (7 - 6)$. Therefore, $A = 19$. $B = (2 \times 10 - 7) - 2 \times 3$. Again, solve for the numbers in the parentheses before subtracting. $B = (20 - 7) - 6$. Therefore, $B = 7$. Be careful, the question is asking for $A - B = 19 - 7 = 12$. Plug $y = 7$ and $c = 3$ into the answers. Only (E) yields the target, 12. Choice (C) is a trap designed to catch test-takers who subtracted before simplifying the numbers in the parentheses.

5. **A**

While the relationship among the can prices is provided, no actual numbers are supplied, so try plugging. in some numbers for can prices. A good number to choose for the cost of the large cans is the value of the small can multiplied by the value of the medium can, or $5 × $7 = $35. This means the medium can costs $\frac{\$35}{\$5}$ = $7, and the small can costs $\frac{\$35}{\$7}$ = $5. The amount of money needed to buy 200 medium cans is 200 × $7 = $1,400. Now PITA. Start with (C). If the customer purchases 72 small cans, that will cost her 72 × $5 = $360. If she purchases 72 small cans, she also purchases 72 large cans so 72 × $35 = $2,520, which is more than the $1,400 spent on medium cans. This number is too great, so eliminate (C), (D), and (E). Choice (B) also works out to be too great, which leaves (A). 35 small cans × $5 a can = $175. 35 large cans × $35 = $1,225. $1,225 + $175 = $1,400, the same price as the medium cans. Choice (A) is correct.

6. **25**

Stack and add the first two equations. Multiply the second equation by –1.

$$6k - 5l = 27$$
$$+ \ \underline{2k - 3l = 13}$$
$$8k - 8l = 40$$

Divide by 8 to yield $k - l = 5$. Multiply by 5 to yield the final answer of $5k - 5l = 25$.

7. **B**

This problem has a relationship between variables, so Plug In. Let a = 2, so $3a$ = 6. 6 is 4 less than 10, which equals $6b$. $6b$ = 10 yields that $b = \frac{10}{6}$. $a - 2b$ yields $2 - 2\left(\frac{10}{6}\right) = -\frac{8}{6}$, or $-\frac{4}{3}$.

8. **A**

Work with one quantity at a time to compare them. Quantity A is $\frac{2^{-4}}{4^{-2}}$, which can be rewritten as $\frac{2^{-4}}{4^{-2}} = \frac{\frac{1}{2^4}}{\frac{1}{4^2}} = \frac{\frac{1}{16}}{\frac{1}{16}}$. This fraction can be manipulated by moving the fraction out of the denominator; however, that is unnecessary as the numerator and denominator are the same thing. So $\frac{\frac{1}{16}}{\frac{1}{16}} = 1$, which is the value of Quantity A. Quantity B can be simplified to $\frac{\sqrt{64}}{-2^3} = \frac{8}{-8} = -1$. Therefore, Quantity A is greater, and the answer is (A).

9. **B**

This is a simultaneous equation question. Both quantities ask for the value of $x + y$, so try to combine the equations to find that value. If you multiply $3x + 4y = 12$ by 3, the result is $9x + 12y = 36$. This can be subtracted from the other equation to find that $2x + 2y = -6$. Divide both sides of the equation by 2 to find that $x + y = -3$. Quantity A, then, is equal to -3. Quantity B is now $(-3)^{-2}$, which can be rewritten as $\frac{1}{(-3)^2} = \frac{1}{9}$. Therefore, Quantity B is greater than Quantity A, and the correct answer is (B).

10. **E**

Since there are variables in the answers, Plug In. If $a = 3$ and $b = 2$, then $x = 9$ and $y = 18$. So, $2(x + y) = 2(9 + 18) = 54$. So, 54 is the target. Now, evaluate each answer choice. Choices (A), (B), (C), and (D) all evaluate to 54 and match the target. Choice (E), however, equals 36. Since the question uses the word EXCEPT, choose the answer that doesn't match the target. Choice (E) is the correct answer.

CHAPTER 12: REAL WORLD MATH

Real World Math Drill (Page 272)

1. $\frac{1}{6}$

Plugging In your own number is a good way to tackle this. The fractions used in the problem are $\frac{1}{3}$ and $\frac{1}{2}$, and multiplying the denominators will produce a good number with which to work. Sadie started with 6 paintings and gave away one third of them: $6 \times \frac{1}{3} = 2$. She has 4 paintings left. She then sold another half of the original 6: $6 \times \frac{1}{2} = 3$. So, she has 1 painting left, or $\frac{1}{6}$ of the total.

2. **D**

When there are variables in the question stem, it's time to Plug In. For this problem, it's easier to Plug In if you simplify the equation first. Rearrange the equation to put the variables on opposite sides of the equal sign. $8x = 4y$. Then divide both sides by 4 to get that $2x = y$. Now, choose some easy numbers such as $x = 2$ and $y = 4$. In this case, Quantity B is greater, so eliminate (A) and (C). Next, try something like $x = 0$ and $y = 0$. In this case, the two quantities are equal. Eliminate (B), and the correct answer is (D).

3. **D**

The population rankings for Year X are as follows: (1) Massachusetts, (2) Connecticut, (3) Maine, (4) Rhode Island, (5) New Hampshire, (6) Vermont. The rankings for Year Y are as follows: (1) Massachusetts; (2) Connecticut; (3) Rhode Island; (4) New Hampshire; (5) Maine; (6) Vermont. Maine, Rhode Island, and New Hampshire have different rankings from Year X to Year Y.

4. **D**

In Year X, Vermont's population is 5 percent of 15 million (or 0.75 million), and Massachusetts' population is 40 percent of 15 million (or approximately 6 million). 6 million is what percent of 0.75 million? Now translate: 6 million $= \dfrac{x}{100} \times 0.75$ million: $x = 800$.

5. **D**

In Year X the population of Rhode Island was 10 percent of 15 million, or 1.5 million. In Year Y the population of Rhode Island was 15 percent of 25 million, or 3.75 million. The increase was 2.25 million, or 2,250,000.

6. **C**

Start solving this problem by assessing all the information that is given to you in the problem. A 20-gallon water jug is 20% full, so there are 4 gallons in the water jug. The question is asking how many days it will be before the jug is 85% full. 85% of 20 gallons is 17 gallons, so that is the number we are looking for. After the first three days 50% of the total water in the jug is added. There are 4 gallons in the jug, so after three days 2 more gallons are added to the jug to make a total of 6 gallons. After another three days, 50% of 6 gallons is added to the jug, so 3 gallons are added which increases the total amount of water in the jug to 9 gallons. After three more days, 50% of 9 gallons is added to the jug so 4.5 gallons, increasing the total to 13.5 gallons. After another three days the total is increased by 50% of 13.5, which is 6.75 gallons, which will increase the total to more than 17 gallons. So there were 4 increases of three days apiece, for a total of 12 days, (C).

7. **A**

This is an average question, so make an Average Pie any time the word *average* is used. Begin by figuring out how many supporters of the referendum are in each town. The question states that there is an average of 3,500 supporters in Towns B and D, so there is a total of $3,500 \times 2 = 7,000$ supporters in these towns. The question also states that Town B has 3,000 supporters, so the number of supporters in Town D is $7,000 - 3,000 = 4,000$. Additionally, the question states that there is an average of 5,000 supporters in Towns A and C, so there is a total of $5,000 \times 2 = 10,000$ supporters in these towns. It's also stated that Town A has 3,000 supporters, so the number of supporters in Town C is $10,000 - 3,000 = 7,000$. Now, compare the quantities. Quantity A is the average number of supporters for Towns C and D, and Quantity B is the average number of supporters for Towns B and C. Because both quantities use Town C, and both quantities ask for an average, those values cancel out and all that remains is to compare the number of supporters in Towns B and D. There are 3,000 supporters in Town B and 4,000 in Town D, so Quantity A is greater and the correct answer is (A). Alternatively, solve for the average given in both quantities. However, the result is the same; the correct answer is (A).

8. **E**

Plug In The Answers, starting in the middle with (C). If each A employee was given $740, each C employee was given half of that, or $370. Each B employee received one-and-a-half times the C raise, so $1.5 \times \$370 = \$555$. Now calculate the total money spent on raises. 50 A employees got $740 each, for a total of $50 \times \$740 = \$37,000$. 100 B employees got $555 each, for a total of $100 \times \$555 = \$55,500$. 150 C employees got $370 each: $150 \times \$370 = 55,500$. These add up to a total of $148,000, but the problem says that the total raise amount is $500,000. You need a much bigger answer. Rule out (A), (B), and (C). Try skipping directly to (E). If the A workers got $2,500, the C workers got $1,250, and the B workers got $1,875. $50 \times \$2,500 = \$125,000$; $100 \times \$1,875 = \$187,500$; and $150 \times \$1,250 = \$187,500$. Because these numbers add up to $500,000, (E) is correct.

9. **B**

> Median means middle. In other words, if you put all the ninth-graders in order by score, the middle student would have the median score. Thinking in terms of percentiles, the 50th percentile is the middle, so on the ninth-grade pie chart, whatever score includes the 50th percentile when you put the scores in order is the median score. According to the chart, 16 percent of the ninth-graders scored below 65, and 37 percent scored between 65 and 69 points. 16 percent + 37 percent = 53 percent. The 50th percentile, then, falls within the group that received 65–69, so 65–69 is the median score.

10. **A**

> In 1995 there were 1,350 + 950 + 625 + 500, or ≈ 3,400 students in grades 9 through 12. 3,400 is 35 percent of School District X, so $3,400 = \frac{35}{100} \cdot x$, $x \approx 9,700$, so there were 9,700 students.

11. **E**

> There were 1,200 ninth-graders in 2013. 25 percent of them, or 300, scored in the 70–79 point range. 14 percent, or 168, scored in the 80–89 point range. The difference between 300 and 168 is 132. Choice (E) is the closest.

12. **D**

> Draw a Ratio Box for each ratio. Solution X has 2 parts a and 3 parts b, for a total of 5 parts. Solution Y has 1 part a and 2 parts b, for a total of 3 parts. Solution Z has 3 parts X and 11 parts Y, for a total of 14 parts. There are 630 ounces of Solution Z, which yields a multiplier of 45, and leads to 495 ounces of Solution Y and 135 ounces of Solution X. A total of 495 ounces of Solution Y yields a multiplier of 165, which further yields 165 ounces of a from Solution Y. A total of 135 ounces of Solution X yields a multiplier of 27, which further yields 54 ounces of a from Solution X. 165 + 54 = 219 ounces of a. The correct answer is (D).

CHAPTER 13: GEOMETRY

Geometry Drill (Page 306)

1. **A, B, and C**

> You need to check if the two angles in each answer choice can be part of a right triangle. A right triangle has a 90-degree angle, and because the sum of all the angles of a triangle is 180 degrees, the sum of the other two angles must equal 180 – 90 = 90 degrees. In (A), 20 + 70 = 90 degrees, so these could be the other two angles in a right triangle. Choices (B) and (C) also add up to 90 degrees, and so they are correct as well. In (D) and (E), the two angles have a sum greater than 90 degrees, so they are incorrect.

2. **B**

> To find the perimeter of the figure, you need to add up all of its external sides. However, this is a funny-shaped figure, so begin by making the figure into two familiar shapes. Draw a horizontal line to separate the figure into a triangle and a rectangle. The side of the rectangle is now equal to the hypotenuse of the

right triangle. So, use the triangle to find the missing side. To find the hypotenuse of the right triangle recognize the common right triangle (5 : 12 : 13), or use the Pythagorean theorem ($5^2 + 12^2 = x^2$). The missing side of the rectangle is 13. Therefore, the perimeter equals $5 + 12 + 17 + 13 + 17 = 64$. Choice (A) is the perimeter without the missing side of the rectangle. If you chose (D), you included an interior side of the rectangle.

3. **A**

We know that the triangle *EFG* is equilateral because all three angles are equal. That means all of its sides equal 8. From the first equation, we know that the sides of the square also equal 8. The area of the square is $s \times s = 8 \times 8 = 64$, which is greater than Quantity B.

4. **D**

Draw it on your scratch paper, and plot the points. Both *a* and *b* must be positive, but their values could be equal or unequal. Quadrant I has (+, +) coordinates, Quadrant II has (−, +) coordinates, Quadrant III has (−, −) coordinates, and Quadrant IV has (+, −) coordinates.

5. **E**

There are variables in the answers, so Plug In. If the shorter piece is 2 yards long, then the longer piece is $3(2) + 2 = 8$ yards and *t* must be $2 + 8 = 10$. The target answer, the length of the longer piece, is 8. Plug in 10 for *t* into all of the answers. Choice (E) is the only answer choice that matches your target of 8.

6. **D**

If *CD*, the radius of the smaller circle, is 3, then the diameter of the smaller circle is 6. The diameter of the smaller circle is equal to the radius of the larger circle because the smaller circle touches the center and the edge of the larger circle. The formula for the area of a circle is πr^2, so the area of the larger circle is 36π. To find the area of the semicircle, divide by 2 to find 18π.

7. **2**

Draw it! If Karl starts *x* meters below the boat and swims straight down for 8 meters, he is now $x + 8$ meters below the boat. He swims 24 meters to his right and then swims 26 meters in a direct line back to the boat. This drawing should look like a triangle with sides $x + 8$, 24, and a hypotenuse of 26. Use the Pythagorean theorem to solve for *x*, or using special right triangles, realize that this is a 5, 12, 13 triangle multiplied by 2. $x + 8$ has to equal 10, so $x = 2$.

8. **A**

This is a Plug In problem. Make $r = 2$. The circumference of the circle will be 4π, which is approximately 12. The perimeter of the square is $2 + 2 + 2 + 2 = 8$. Quantity A is greater. Try plugging in other numbers and you will see that Quantity A will always be greater.

9. **C**

The area of the circle is 25π, so the radius of the circle is 5. This means that both *AC* and *BC* have length 5, and angles *A* and *B* are equal to each other. Because angle *C* is 60° and the total angle measure of a triangle is 180°, the sum of angle *A* and *B* must be 120°. Thus, each angle in triangle *ABC* is 60°, making this an equilateral triangle. An equilateral triangle has equal sides and equal angles, so the only possible length of the triangle legs is 5.

10. **A**

Remember the third side rule. The third side of a triangle must be less than the sum of the other two sides of a triangle, but greater than the difference. That gives us a clear range for x. It must be greater than 6 but less than 12. Quantity A, therefore, is greater than Quantity B; the answer is (A).

11. **A**

You can see that the two triangles are almost the same, except that the base length in the triangle to the right is slightly larger. Remember, you cannot trust the figure to be drawn to scale. If you look at these triangles and expand the base length, the triangle on the right starts to collapse and its height gets smaller and smaller. Thus, height f must be greater than height g. This technique works quite well in a number of GRE quant comp geometry problems!

12. **B**

In order to find the x-coordinate of a point on a line, you must first find the slope of the line. Notice that along with points A and B, the origin is also a point on the line in the figure. Using the coordinates of $(0, 0)$ and A $(2, 3)$, the slope is $\frac{(y_2 - y_1)}{(x_2 - x_1)} = \frac{3}{2}$. Because the slope of a line stays constant, you can use the value you just found to solve for the missing x-coordinate of point B. Using points A $(2, 3)$ and B $(x, 4.2)$, solve $\frac{(4.2 - 3)}{(x - 2)} = \frac{3}{2}$. Cross-multiply to find that $3(x - 2) = 1.2(2)$, so $3x - 6 = 2.4$ and $3x = 8.4$. Therefore, $x = 2.8$, and the correct answer is (B).

13. **A**

Use the 3 : 4 : 5 ratio or the Pythagorean theorem to determine that the length of AB is 4. Because the area of a triangle equals $\frac{1}{2}$ × base × height, triangle ABD has an area of $\frac{1}{2}$ × 3 × 4, or 6. Be wary of (D), which is the area of the rectangle.

14. **B**

Because the two angles have the same measure, the wedges of the circle they mark off will have the same area. The triangle is smaller than the wedge, so Quantity B is greater than Quantity A.

15. **C**

Because $LMNO$ is a parallelogram and $\angle OLM = 108°$, $\angle LON$ must be $180° - 108° = 72°$. $\angle LON$ is the same fraction of the entire circle (360 degrees) that arc AB is of the entire circumference, so $\frac{72}{360} = \frac{1}{5}$. Thus, arc AB is $\frac{1}{5}$ of the circumference. So, $\frac{1}{5} \times 15\pi = 3\pi$.

CHAPTER 14: MATH ET CETERA

Et Cetera Drill (Page 327)

1. **C**

   If there is one more red marble than blue, there must be 7 blue marbles and 8 red ones, for a total of 15. The probability of choosing a blue marble is $\dfrac{\# \text{ of blue marbles}}{\text{total} \# \text{ of marbles}}$, or $\dfrac{7}{15}$. If you selected (E), you probably computed the probability of drawing a red marble rather than the probability of drawing a blue one.

2. **D**

   Plug the values into the function. First, find ¥(5): $(5 \times 10 - 1) = 49$. Next, find ¥(3) = $(3 \times 10 - 1) = 29$. Now subtract them: ¥(5) − ¥(3) = 49 − 29 = 20.

3. **B**

   First, eliminate (D) as both quantities are numbers. Next, rewrite the function without the negative exponent. Negative exponents are used as another way to write a reciprocal—for all $x \neq 0$, $x^{-n} = \dfrac{1}{x^n}$. So, this function can be rewritten as $\# x = 2^{-x} = \dfrac{1}{2^x}$. Therefore, Quantity A is $\#8 = \dfrac{1}{2^8} = \dfrac{1}{256}$ and Quantity B is $\#4 = \dfrac{1}{2^4} = \dfrac{1}{16}$. Because $\dfrac{1}{16} > \dfrac{1}{256}$, Quantity B is greater. The correct answer is (B).

4. **20**

   Remember, in this problem order matters, so do not divide! Any of the 5 finalists could be awarded "Best in Show." There are 4 choices left for "Honorable Mention," because a different dog must be chosen. Therefore, the total number of possibilities is 5×4, or 20.

5. **A**

   Use the group equation: Group 1 + Group 2 − Both + Neither = Total. So, $40,000 + $30,000 − $15,000 + Neither = $90,000. Thus, $55,000 + Neither = $90,000. So, the company budgets $35,000 on other products. Quantity A is greater than Quantity B.

6. **B**

   List the two-digit prime numbers less than 50: 11, 13, 17, 19, 23, 29, 31, 37, 41, 43, and 47. The numbers in which the tens digit is greater than the units digit are 31, 41, and 43. Because 3 out of the 11 possibilities meet the requirement, (B) is correct.

7. **A**

Plug In the Answers, starting with (C). With 9 staff members, the elected official has $\dfrac{9 \times 8 \times 7 \times 6 \times 5}{5 \times 4 \times 3 \times 2 \times 1}$ options. This works out to 126, which is too large. Try plugging in (A). With 7 staff members, the elected official has $\dfrac{7 \times 6 \times 5 \times 4 \times 3}{5 \times 4 \times 3 \times 2 \times 1} = 21$ different groups of 5 from which to choose.

8. **E**

Plug In: Make $x = 2$ and $y = 3$. Now $x \# y = 2(2 - 3) = -2$. Watch out for traps: Choices (A) and (C) will give you -2, but because the question asks for $x \# (x \# y)$, you need to perform the operation again. $2 \# (-2) = 2[2 - (-2)] = 2(4) = 8$. Now put $x = 2$ and $y = 3$ into the answer choices to find a match for your target answer, 8. Be sure to eliminate (A), (B), (C), and (D) as soon as you realize they are negative. The only answer that matches is (E).

9. **B**

Use a Ratio Box to find that if there are twice as many yellow as green and 12 total, then there are 8 yellows and 4 greens. Two situations would fit the requirements of the problem: Pull out a yellow and then green, or pull out a green and then yellow. So, find the probability of each of these situations; then add these two probabilities together. The probability of yellow and then green is $\dfrac{8}{12} \times \dfrac{4}{11} = \dfrac{8}{33}$. The probability of green and then yellow is $\dfrac{4}{12} \times \dfrac{8}{11} = \dfrac{8}{33}$. Add these two probabilities to find $\dfrac{8}{33} + \dfrac{8}{33} = \dfrac{16}{33}$.

10. **B**

You could try to draw this all out, but it is easier to do the math. For Quantity A, if you're creating triangles, you're really choosing three points from the set of 10. This is a combination problem—order doesn't matter, because triangle ABC would be the same as triangle BCA. You could use the formula $\dfrac{10 \times 9 \times 8}{3 \times 2 \times 1} = 120$. For Quantity B, note that quadrilaterals are any four-sided figures, so you're just choosing 4 points from 10. You could use the formula for combinations: $\dfrac{10 \times 9 \times 8 \times 7}{4 \times 3 \times 2 \times 1} = 210$. The correct answer is (B).

Comprehensive Math Drill (Page 329)

1. **B**

Any line that is tangent to a circle makes a 90 degree angle with the radius of that circle at the point of tangency. The radius of the circle is 5, so the length of line segment AC is also 5. The side opposite the 90 degree angle is BC and this measures $\dfrac{10\sqrt{3}}{3}$. If you know the special right triangles, you should be able to recognize that the sides are in the ratio of a $30 : 60 : 90$ triangle. The ratio of the sides in a $30 : 60 : 90$ triangle is $x : x\sqrt{3} : 2x$, respectively. If $2x = \dfrac{10\sqrt{3}}{3}$, then $x = \dfrac{5\sqrt{3}}{3}$. Multiplying $\dfrac{5\sqrt{3}}{3}$ by $\sqrt{3}$ yields that the $x\sqrt{3}$

side of the triangle is 5. Since the $x\sqrt{3}$ side of a 30 : 60 : 90 is longer than the x side, AC is longer than

AB, and Quantity B is greater. If you didn't see the side relationship, you could always use the Pythagorean

Theorem to find the length of AB. Either way, the correct answer is (B).

2. **C**

Plug In. Let $x = 2$. Quantity A is $\dfrac{2}{10}$. Quantity B is $\dfrac{\frac{2}{5}}{2}$, which simplifies to $\dfrac{2}{5} \times \dfrac{1}{2}$, which yields $\dfrac{2}{10}$.

The quantities are equal, so eliminate (A) and (B). Plug In again. Let $x = 1$. Quantity A is $\dfrac{1}{10}$. Quantity B is

$\dfrac{\frac{1}{5}}{2}$, which also yields $\dfrac{1}{10}$. To be certain, check the other possibilities in FROZEN. The correct answer is (C).

3. **C**

Remember that the percentages for standard deviations are 34 percent, 14 percent, 2 percent in both directions from the mean. If the mean is 50, then 34 percent score between 50 and 54, 14 percent score between 54 and 58, and 2 percent score above 58. The same idea applies in the other direction: If the mean is 50, then 34 percent score between 50 and 46, 14 percent score between 46 and 42, and 2 percent score below 42. So, both quantities are equal to 2 percent.

4. **A**

The equation $y = mx + b$ describes a line where m is the slope and b is the y-intercept—the place where the

line crosses the y-axis. Hence, the y-intercept of our line, or P, is $(0, 1)$, which means the length of OP is

1. Because Q is on the x-axis, the y-coordinate must be 0, and we can use the line equation to solve for x:

$0 = -\dfrac{5}{6}x + 1$, so $-1 = -\dfrac{5}{6}x$, and $x = \dfrac{6}{5}$. That means $OQ = \dfrac{6}{5}$, and Quantity A is greater. Because this is

a quant comp, though, we can actually compare the quantities without solving them. If you recognize

from the line equation that our slope is $-\dfrac{5}{6}$, and you remember that slope is defined as $\dfrac{rise}{run}$, you might

also recognize that Quantity A, OQ, is our run, and Quantity B, OP, is our rise. Disregarding the negative

sign—distance is always an absolute value, and therefore positive—we can see that our rise is less than

our run, and Quantity A is greater.

5. **B**

For Quantity A, "pairs" tells you that you're picking two and that order does not matter so divide. You

could use the formula $\dfrac{20 \times 19}{2 \times 1} = 190$. For Quantity B, the "rankings" tells you that order matters, so do

not divide. So, you could use the formula $10 \times 9 \times 8 = 720$.

6. **D**

The denominator is the same for both expressions, so we only need to compare numerators to determine which fraction is greater. Plug in to see whether kl is greater than or less than 1. Let $k = 0.5$ and $l = 1.5$. Therefore, $kl = 0.75$. Eliminate (B) and (C). Now let $k = 10$ and $l = 10$, $kl = 100$. Eliminate (A).

7. **A**

Find all the factors of 78. $78 = 1 \times 78 = 2 \times 39 = 3 \times 26 = 6 \times 13$. The greatest odd factor is 39; the greatest prime factor is 13. Quantity A is greater than Quantity B.

8. **4**

If Joe starts with $200 and spends $150 on a CD player, he has only $200 − $150 = $50 left. Each CD is $12, so divide $50 by $12. It goes in 4 times with $2 left over. Don't round! Joe can buy only 4.

9. **A**

For triangle ABC, the base is the difference between A and C, 1. Finding the height is a little more difficult.

The height of a triangle is any perpendicular line dropped from the highest point to the level of the base. The height does not need to touch segment AC as long as it extends from B to the level of AC. For this triangle, distance from B to the origin is the height, 4. Plug in the base and height: Area $= \frac{1}{2} \times 1 \times 4 = 2$.

10. **A**

When you have a large number that needs to be divided, the best way to begin answering the question is to break that number down into its prime factors. So $10(9^6) = 2 \times 5 \times (3^2)^6$, or $2 \times 5 \times 3^{12}$. Therefore, the prime factorization of any number that $10(9^6)$ can be divided by can contain no more than one 2, one 5, and twelve 3s. Only (A), 90, meets these requirements. For example, the prime factorization of (D), 540, includes two 2s so $10(9^6)$ is not divisible by 540. Choice (A) is correct.

11. **B** and **C**

Roberta's rate is 50 miles in 2 hours. Notice that the first number in this proportion is greater than the second. Use that to eliminate (A) and (D). For (B), $\frac{100}{4} = \frac{50}{2}$, so this is the same as the original proportion. For (C), $\frac{400}{16} = \frac{50}{2}$, so this is also the same as the original proportion. Choice (E) does not produce this same proportion, so eliminate it as well.

12. **C**

There were seven cities with temperatures in Year Y higher than or equal to those in Year X: Baltimore, Detroit, Las Vegas, Minneapolis, New York, Phoenix, and San Francisco.

13. **C**

The lowest average temperature was 34° F in Anchorage, and the highest was 83° F in Las Vegas. Percent change $= \frac{\text{difference}}{\text{original}} = \frac{49}{34} \approx 144$ percent, which is closest to (C).

14. **C**

You're averaging the highs and lows for Years X and Y, so the number of things is 4. The bar shows the average of Years X and Y, which reads 60. Multiply 60 by 4 to get the total, 240. Get the average high temperatures for Years X and Y from the straight and dotted lines on the chart. They're about 103 degrees and 97 degrees. The total is $240 = 103 + 97 + $ low Year X + low Year Y. If you subtract the highs from the total, you're left with 40 degrees as the total for the lows. Because you want the average of the lows, divide this total by 2. The closest answer is 20°.

15. **A, B, and C**

First, simplify the inequality by subtracting 2 from both sides: $|2x - 3| > 5$. Now plug each answer choice into the inequality to see which value of x makes the inequality true. The correct values are those in (A), (B), and (C).

16. **A**

The question states that x is an odd integer, so eliminate (C) because 0 is not odd. Simplify $x + y + z < z$ by subtracting z from each side: $x + y < 0$. Because x is less than y, x must be negative so that when added to y, the answer will be less than zero. Therefore, eliminate (D) and (E). Now plug in the remaining answers to see which value of x will work in the inequality. Choice (A) is the only choice that works.

17. **E**

First, solve for x by multiplying 4 by itself until you get 1,024. This means that x equals 5. If you substitute 5 for x in the second equation, the equation reads, $4^6 \times 5^4$. Because the answers are expressed in terms of 4^n, 5^n, and 10^n, expand out $4^6 \times 5^4$ to get $4 \times 4 \times 4 \times 4 \times 4 \times 4 \times 5 \times 5 \times 5 \times 5$. Now try to express it using 10^n. We need to factor two of the fours and rewrite this as $4 \times 4 \times 4 \times 4 \times 2 \times 2 \times 2 \times 2 \times 5 \times 5 \times 5 \times 5$. Now, convert this back into exponents to get $4^4 \times 2^4 \times 5^4$, or $4^4 \times 10^4$.

18. **D**

First, use the volume formula to find the width: $V = l \times w \times h$. So, $780 = 12 \times w \times 5$. Thus, the width is 13. Next, draw the figure. Notice that the greatest distance is from one corner to the opposite corner, such as from the front left bottom corner diagonally to the rear right top corner. You can use the formula for diagonal of a rectangular solid, $a^2 + b^2 + c^2 = d^2$, in which a, b, and c are the dimensions of the rectangular solid and d is the diagonal, and love that you have a calculator. Thus, $(5)^2 + (12)^2 + (13)^2 = d^2$. So, $25 + 144 + 169 = d^2$, and thus $d = \sqrt{338}$ or $13\sqrt{2}$.

19. **D**

There are six spots to fill. Because no boys can sit on the ends of the bench, only the 3 girls are available to fill one spot at one end of the bench. Once one girl has been chosen to fill that spot, there are 2 girls available to fill the spot on the other end of the bench. Then, there are 4 children (boys and girls) available to fill the other four spots. Because $3 \times 4 \times 3 \times 2 \times 1 \times 2 = 144$, (D) is correct.

20. **C**

Use the Average Pie. If 16 is the average of 3 numbers, their total is 48. You know that one of the numbers is 24, so $p + q + 24 = 48$. Thus, $(p + q) = 24$. You need to find $16(p + q)$, so find $16(24)$, which equals 384.

Part VI
Practice Tests

TEST INSTRUCTIONS

It's important to become familiar with the instructions for the test now, so that you don't waste time figuring them out on test day.

General Instructions

Need More Practice?
The Princeton Review's *1,007 GRE Practice Questions* offers drills for every question type, along with detailed, comprehensive explanations.

Each exam consists of six sections—two Analytical Writing sections, two Verbal Reasoning sections, and two Quantitative Reasoning sections. The Analytical Writing sections will always be first. The Verbal and Quantitative Reasoning sections may appear in any order. You will have 30 minutes for each Analytic Writing section, 30 minutes for each Verbal, and 35 minutes for each Quantitative Reasoning section. If desired, you may take a 10-minute break after Section 4. Remember that during the actual test, there may be an additional verbal or quantitative experimental section.

Section 1	30 minutes	Analytical Writing
Section 2	30 minutes	Analytical Writing
Section 3	30/35 minutes	Verbal or Quantitative Reasoning
Section 4	30/35 minutes	Verbal or Quantitative Reasoning
Section 5	30/35 minutes	Verbal or Quantitative Reasoning
Section 6	30/35 minutes	Verbal or Quantitative Reasoning

When taking a Verbal or Quantitative Reasoning section, you are free to skip questions that you might have difficulty answering and come back to them later during the time allotted for that section. You may also change your response to any question in a section during the time allotted to work on that section. You may not go back to an earlier section of the test after time for that section runs out.

Analytical Writing Instructions

Issue Topic

You will be given a brief statement on an issue of general interest and specific instructions on how to respond to that issue. You will have 30 minutes to plan and write a response in which you develop a position on the issue. Make sure that you respond to the specific instructions and support your position on the issue with reasons and examples drawn from such areas as your reading, experience, observations, and/or academic studies.

Before you begin writing, you may want to think for a few minutes about the passage and the instructions and then outline your response. Be sure to develop your analysis fully and organize it coherently. Leave a minute or two at the end to reread what you have written and make any revisions you think are necessary.

Argument Topic

You will be given a short passage that presents an argument, or an argument to be completed, and specific instructions on how to respond to that passage. You will have 30 minutes to plan and write a response in which you analyze the passage. Note that you are NOT being asked to present your own views on the subject. Make sure that you respond to the specific instructions and support your analysis with relevant reasons and/or examples.

Before you begin writing, you may want to think for a few minutes about the passage and the instructions and then outline your response. Be sure to develop your analysis fully and organize it coherently. Leave a minute or two at the end to reread what you have written and make any revisions you think are necessary.

Verbal Reasoning Instructions

Each Verbal Reasoning section is 30 minutes long and has 20 questions. For some questions, you will be instructed to choose one or more answer choices. The instructions may or may not specify the number of answers you must choose. If the number of answers is specified, you must choose all of the correct answers in order to have your response counted as correct. If the number is not specified, choose all that correctly answer the question. No credit will be given if fewer or more than all of the correct answers are chosen.

Quantitative Reasoning Instructions

Each Quantitative Reasoning section is 35 minutes long and has 20 questions. You will be provided with a five-function calculator—one with addition, subtraction, multiplication, division, and square-root features—during Quantitative Reasoning sections.

For some questions, you will be instructed to choose one or more answer choices. The instructions may or may not specify the number of answers you must choose. If the number of answers is specified, you must choose all of the correct answers in order to have your response counted as correct. If the number is not specified, choose all that correctly answer the question. No credit will be given if fewer or more than all of the correct answers are chosen.

Some questions will require you to enter your own answer. If the question provides a single response space, enter a single number. You may enter negative signs and decimal points. If the question tells you to round your answer, do so. Otherwise, enter the entire answer. If the question provides two response spaces, you must enter your answer in the form of a fraction. You are not required to enter fractions in their most reduced form. If you are aware of more than one correct response, you should enter only one of them.

Some questions will ask you to fill blanks in the text by clicking to select from a list of choices. Sometimes all of the choices will be used, and sometimes only some of the choices will be used. The correct answer always requires you to put a different choice in every blank.

Note on Numbers and Figures

Numbers: All numbers used are real numbers.

Figures: The position of points, angles, regions, and so on can be assumed to be in the order shown, and angle measures can be assumed to be positive. Lines shown as straight can be assumed to be straight. Figures can be assumed to lie in a plane unless otherwise indicated. Any other figures are not necessarily drawn to scale, unless a note states that a figure is drawn to scale.

Chapter 18
Practice Test 1

SECTION 1: ISSUE TOPIC

Directions:

You will be given a brief quotation that states or implies an issue of general interest and specific instructions on how to respond to that issue. You will have 30 minutes to plan and compose a response in which you develop a position on the issue according to the specific instructions. A response to any other issue will receive a score of zero.

"Governments are justified in circumventing civil laws when doing so is vital to the protection of national security."

Write an essay in which you take a position on the statement above. In developing and supporting your position, you should consider ways in which the statement might or might not hold true.

SECTION 2: ARGUMENT TOPIC

Directions:

You will be given a short passage that presents an argument, or an argument to be completed, and specific instructions on how to respond to that passage. You will have 30 minutes to plan and compose a response in which you analyze the passage according to the specific instructions. A response to any other argument will receive a score of zero.

Note that you are NOT being asked to present your own views on the subject. Make sure that you respond to the specific instructions and support your analysis with relevant reasons and/or examples.

The following is from a recent email from the Diord Corp. Human Resources Manager: "Tobor Technologies found that mental health problems and mental illness were responsible for about 15 percent of employee sick days. Tobor amended its employee insurance plan so that workers receive the same coverage for mental illness as they do for physical illness. In addition, the company hired an on-site psychologist and created a system that allows workers to schedule confidential counseling appointments. After one year, the number of sick days used by employees declined by 10 percent. Diord Corp. has had an increase in employee sick days over the past two years, so we should introduce a similar insurance plan and counseling program. These measures will surely reduce employee absenteeism and cause an increase in productivity."

Write a response in which you examine the argument's unstated assumptions, making sure to explain how the argument depends on the assumptions and what the implications are if the assumptions prove unwarranted.

SECTION 3: QUANTITATIVE REASONING

For each of Questions 1 to 7, compare Quantity A and Quantity B, using additional information centered above the two quantities if such information is given. Select one of the four answer choices below each question and fill in the circle to the left of that answer choice.

(A) Quantity A is greater.

(B) Quantity B is greater.

(C) The two quantities are equal.

(D) The relationship cannot be determined from the information given.

A symbol that appears more than once in a question has the same meaning throughout the question.

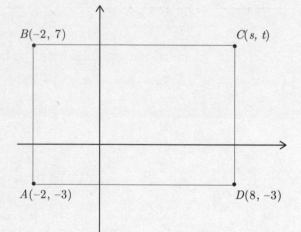

AB is parallel to CD.

BC is parallel to AD.

Quantity A	Quantity B
s	t

○ Quantity A is greater.

○ Quantity B is greater.

○ The two quantities are equal.

○ The relationship cannot be determined from the information given.

A certain punch is created by mixing two parts soda and three parts ice cream. The soda is 4 parts sugar, 5 parts citric acid, and 11 parts other ingredients. The ice cream is 3 parts sugar, 2 parts citric acid, and 15 parts other ingredients.

Quantity A	Quantity B
Parts sugar in the punch	Parts citric acid in the punch

○ Quantity A is greater.

○ Quantity B is greater.

○ The two quantities are equal.

○ The relationship cannot be determined from the information given.

The average (arithmetic mean) high temperature for x days is 70 degrees. The addition of one day with a high temperature of 75 degrees increases the average to 71 degrees.

Quantity A	Quantity B
x	5

○ Quantity A is greater.

○ Quantity B is greater.

○ The two quantities are equal.

○ The relationship cannot be determined from the information given.

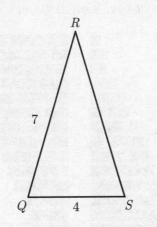

Each angle in $\triangle QRS$ has a degree measurement of either x or y and $2x + y = 180$.

Quantity A	Quantity B
Perimeter of QRS	17

○ Quantity A is greater.

○ Quantity B is greater.

○ The two quantities are equal.

○ The relationship cannot be determined from the information given.

The scores for the 500 students who took Ms. Johnson's final exam have a normal distribution. There are 80 students who scored at least 92 points out of a possible 100 total points and 10 students who scored at or below 56.

Quantity A	Quantity B
The average (arithmetic mean) score on the final exam	87

○ Quantity A is greater.

○ Quantity B is greater.

○ The two quantities are equal.

○ The relationship cannot be determined from the information given.

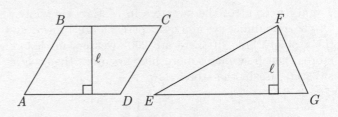

AB is parallel to CD.

AD is parallel to BC.

$$2AD = EG$$

Quantity A	Quantity B
The area of $ABCD$	The area of EFG

○ Quantity A is greater.

○ Quantity B is greater.

○ The two quantities are equal.

○ The relationship cannot be determined from the information given.

$$(3x - 4y)(3x + 4y) = 2$$

Quantity A	Quantity B
$9x^2 - 16y^2$	4

○ Quantity A is greater.

○ Quantity B is greater.

○ The two quantities are equal.

○ The relationship cannot be determined from the information given.

If $8a - 2 = 22$, then $4a - 1 =$

○ 2

○ $\dfrac{11}{4}$

○ 11

○ 12

○ 44

Twenty percent of the sweaters in a store are white. Of the remaining sweaters, 40 percent are brown, and the rest are blue. If there are 200 sweaters in the store, then how many more blue sweaters than white sweaters are in the store?

Click on the answer box and type in a number. Backspace to erase.

$$\frac{4^{13} - 4^{12}}{4^{11}} =$$

○ 0

○ 1

○ 4

○ 12

○ 16

Questions 11 through 14 refer to the following graph.

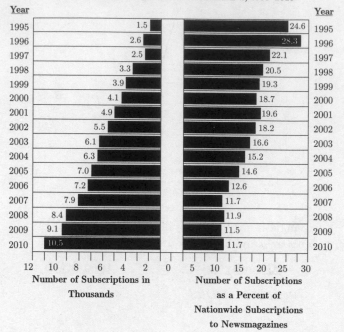

SUBSCRIPTIONS TO NEWSMAGAZINE x, 1995–2010

Year	Number of Subscriptions in Thousands	Number of Subscriptions as a Percent of Nationwide Subscriptions to Newsmagazines	Year
1995	1.5	24.6	1995
1996	2.6	28.3	1996
1997	2.5	22.1	1997
1998	3.3	20.5	1998
1999	3.9	19.3	1999
2000	4.1	18.7	2000
2001	4.9	19.6	2001
2002	5.5	18.2	2002
2003	6.1	16.6	2003
2004	6.3	15.2	2004
2005	7.0	14.6	2005
2006	7.2	12.6	2006
2007	7.9	11.7	2007
2008	8.4	11.9	2008
2009	9.1	11.5	2009
2010	10.5	11.7	2010

NATIONWIDE NEWSMAGAZINE SUBSCRIPTIONS: 1997 TO 2009

Newsmagazine	1997	2000	2003	2006	2009
x	2,500	4,100	6,100	7,200	9,100
y	1,700	3,100	4,600	5,700	7,200
z	3,600	5,800	7,600	9,400	11,400
Others	3,500	8,900	18,500	34,700	51,300

What was the total number of subscriptions for Newsmagazine x during the year in which Newsmagazine x accounted for 14.6 percent of nationwide news magazine subscriptions?

○ 1,020

○ 1,980

○ 6,300

○ 7,000

○ 7,200

In which of the following years did subscriptions to Newsmagazine z account for approximately $\dfrac{1}{6}$ of the total nationwide magazine subscriptions?

○ 2009

○ 2006

○ 2003

○ 2000

○ 1997

What was the approximate percent increase in nationwide subscriptions to newsmagazines between 1995 and 1996 ?

○   4%

○   11%

○   26%

○   51%

○   73%

In 1998, what was the approximate number of subscriptions to newsmagazines nationwide?

○   3,000

○   13,000

○   16,000

○   20,000

○   67,000

If $a = (27)(3^{-2})$ and $x = (6)(3^{-1})$, then which of the following is equivalent to $(12)(3^{-x}) \times (15)(2^{-a})$?

○ $5(-2245)(320)$

○ $\dfrac{2}{5}$

○ $\dfrac{5}{2}$

○ $5(24)(38)$

○ $5(2245)(320)$

Jill has received 8 of her 12 evaluation scores. So far, Jill's average (arithmetic mean) is 3.75 out of a possible 5. If Jill needs an average of 4.0 points to get a promotion, which list of scores qualifies Jill to receive her promotion?

Indicate all such lists.

☐   3.0, 3.5, 4.75, 4.75

☐   3.5, 4.75, 4.75, 5.0

☐   3.25, 4.5, 4.75, 5.0

☐   3.75, 4.5, 4.75, 5.0

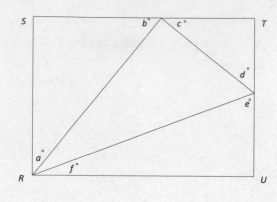

In the figure above, if $RSTU$ is a rectangle, what is the value of $a + b + c + d + e + f$?

Click on the answer box and type in a number.
Backspace to erase.

If the probability of selecting, without replacement, 2 red marbles from a bag containing only red and blue marbles is $\dfrac{3}{55}$ and there are 3 red marbles in the bag, what is the total number of marbles in the bag?

- ○ 10
- ○ 11
- ○ 55
- ○ 110
- ○ 165

All first-year students at Blue State University must take calculus, English composition, or both. If half of the 2,400 first-year students at Blue State University take calculus and half do not, and one-third of those who take calculus also take English composition, how many students take English composition?

- ○ 400
- ○ 800
- ○ 1,200
- ○ 1,600
- ○ 2,000

If $\dfrac{13!}{2^x}$ is an integer, which of the following represents all possible values of x?

- ○ $0 \leq x \leq 10$
- ○ $0 < x < 9$
- ○ $0 \leq x < 10$
- ○ $1 \leq x \leq 10$
- ○ $1 < x < 10$

NO TEST MATERIAL ON THIS PAGE

SECTION 4: VERBAL REASONING

For questions 1 through 6, select one entry for each blank from the corresponding column of choices. Fill all blanks in the way that best completes the text.

The professor is a noteworthy intellect, and as a teacher she shows more (i)_____ than her colleagues, whose teaching skills are (ii)_____ procedure.

Blank (i)	Blank (ii)
prowess	spurious
profligacy	maladroit
orthodoxies	eclectic

It would be (i)_____ for our leaders, given their responsibilities as democratically elected officials, to neglect to do everything they could to (ii)_____ an entirely (iii)_____ problem.

Blank (i)	Blank (ii)	Blank (iii)
irresponsible	forestall	benign
necessary	sustain	unimportant
frivolous	cultivate	avoidable

Despite her mentor's advice that she attempt to sound consistently _____ , the graduate student often resorted to using slang when presenting significant parts of her thesis, her habitual speech patterns overriding her years of learning.

lucid
didactic
panegyrical
erudite
rational

Although she felt Steve (i)_____ the subtlety of the delicious stew recipe with his addition of the sweet potato, she thought the pungent onion (ii)_____ the otherwise (iii)_____ taste combination.

Blank (i)	Blank (ii)	Blank (iii)
depleted	exaggerated	delicate
permeated	overwhelmed	zesty
augmented	satiated	detestable

SECTION 4: VERBAL REASONING

At first, a still-life painting can appear quite (i)_____ , its focus on such everyday objects as flowers or fruits apparently uninspired. In the hands of (ii)_____ painter, however, careful attention to slight shifts of color and texture can lead to a truly (iii)_____ and exemplary painting.

Blank (i)	Blank (ii)	Blank (iii)
vital	a gauche	unstinting
luxuriant	an adept	sublime
banal	an ascetic	prosaic

The leaders of Ukraine's "Orange Revolution" were a study in contrasts. At the center of the political storm stood Viktor Yushchenko, his once (i)_____ face transformed into a monstrous mask by dioxin poisoning; but, at his side, no one could miss the (ii)_____ Yulia Tymoshenko, soon to become the world's only prime minister to adorn the covers of fashion magazines.

Blank (i)	Blank (ii)
quiescent	prepossessing
fatuous	decorous
comely	felicitous

SECTION 4: VERBAL REASONING

For each of Questions 7 to 11, select one answer choice unless otherwise instructed.

Questions 7 through 9 are based on the following reading passage.

In analyzing the poetry of Mona Feather, we are confronted with three different yardsticks by which to measure her work. We could consider her poems as the product of a twentieth-century artist in the tradition of James Joyce, T.S. Eliot, and Wallace Stevens. However, to do so would be to ignore a facet that informs every word she writes and that stems from her identity as a woman. Yet, to characterize her solely as a woman poet is to deny her cultural heritage, for Mona Feather is also the first modern poet of stature who is also an American Indian.

Stanley Wilson has argued compellingly that the huge popularity Feather enjoys among the Indian reservation school population of the United States is creating a whole new generation of poetry enthusiasts in an age when the reading of poetry is on the wane. While this is undoubtedly true, Mr. Wilson's praise gives the impression that Feather's readership is limited to her own culture—an impression which hints that Mr. Wilson is himself measuring her by only one criterion. Radical feminist writers have long found in Feather's poetry a sense of self-pride which strikes a chord with their own more political philosophies. Her imagery, which always made use of the early Native American traditions in which the woman had an important role, was seen as the awakened sensibility of a kindred spirit.

Yet for all the "feminist" touches in her writing, it would be a disservice to consign Feather to the ranks of politicized writers, for her message is deeper than that. The despair that characterized twentieth-century modern poets is to be found in Mona Feather's work as well; she writes of the American Indians of the 1930s confined to ever-shrinking reservations and finds in that a metaphor for all of modern mankind trapped on a shrinking earth of limited resources.

The primary purpose of the passage is to

○ describe the work of Mona Feather

○ compare Feather with Joyce, Eliot, and Stevens

○ show Feather's roots in her Native American heritage

○ argue that Mona Feather's work can be looked at in several different ways

○ discuss the women's movement in America

The passage implies that the author believes Stanley Wilson's view of Feather is

○ a compelling and complete assessment of her work

○ focused too much on her status as a Native American poet

○ meant to disguise his opinion of Feather as a poet lacking in talent

○ critical of Native American children's literary judgment

○ based on all major themes and images in her poetry

The author mentions James Joyce, T.S. Eliot, and Wallace Stevens in order to

○ compare the political messages in Feather's work to those in the work of other authors

○ highlight the radical differences between male and female poets in the twentieth century

○ contrast Feather's thematic choices with those of her contemporaries

○ enumerate a list of artists whose sensibilities made them Feather's kindred spirits

○ describe a critical context in which Feather's work can be analyzed

SECTION 4: VERBAL REASONING

Questions 10 through 11 are based on the following reading passage.

Among the more interesting elements of etymology is the attempt to derive the meaning of seemingly nonsensical expressions. Take, for instance, the increasingly archaic rural phrase "to buy a pig in a poke." For centuries, the expression has been used to signify the purchase of an item without full knowledge of its condition. It relates to the common Renaissance practice of securing suckling pigs for transport to market in a poke, or drawstring bag. Unscrupulous sellers would sometimes attempt to dupe purchasers by replacing the suckling pig with a cat, considered worthless at market. An unsuspecting or naïve buyer might fail to confirm the bag's contents; a more urbane buyer, though, would be sure to check and—should the seller be dishonest—"let the cat out of the bag."

Consider each of the choices separately and select all that apply.

Which of the following phrases from the passage would help the reader infer the meaning of the word urbane as used in context?

- ☐ "increasingly archaic rural phrase"
- ☐ "without full knowledge"
- ☐ "unsuspecting or naïve buyer"

Select the sentence in which the author provides a definition for an antiquated term that may be unfamiliar to the reader.

For questions 12 through 15, select the two answer choices that, when used to complete the sentence, fit the meaning of the sentence as a whole and produce completed sentences that are alike in meaning.

Although she was such a bad-mannered child that she was sent to a boarding school, as an adult she is the very model of _____ .

- ☐ friendliness
- ☐ diffidence
- ☐ propriety
- ☐ reticence
- ☐ decorum
- ☐ brashness

Politicians sometimes appear to act in a manner that is almost _____ ; however, when all the information is released after the fact, it is apparent that they were acting according to a deliberate plan.

- ☐ pithy
- ☐ conventional
- ☐ conformist
- ☐ whimsical
- ☐ flawless
- ☐ capricious

SECTION 4: VERBAL REASONING

Forced to take an alternate road when a massive oil spill closed the highway, the two-hour detour made their already arduous trip even more _____ .

☐ irksome

☐ onerous

☐ facile

☐ glib

☐ implacable

☐ immutable

Though many of her contemporaries found her odd, Ella Wilkins is now much admired for her _____ spirit, especially her willingness to reject prevailing feminine roles and to travel to foreign lands alone.

☐ forlorn

☐ magnanimous

☐ adventurous

☐ bellicose

☐ desolate

☐ doughty

For each of Questions 16 to 20, select one answer choice unless otherwise instructed.

Microfiber synthetics have been taking the place of natural fibers in an ever-increasing number of clothes because they provide the same durability and deplete fewer natural resources. A shirt made of microfiber synthetics is, however, three times as expensive to produce as a natural-fiber shirt. It follows that the substitution of microfiber synthetic clothes for natural-fiber clothes is, at this time, not recommended from a financial standpoint.

Which of the following statements, if true, most seriously weakens the argument?

○ A microfiber synthetic shirt costs one-half the price of a natural-fiber shirt to maintain.

○ The production of microfiber synthetic clothes necessitates garment factories to renovate obsolete machinery and to hire extra workers to operate the new machines.

○ The upkeep of natural-fiber shirts is far less expensive than the upkeep of any other natural-fiber garment in current production.

○ While producers anticipate that the cost of microfiber synthetics will remain stable, they recognize that the advent of recycling programs for natural fibers should bring down the costs of natural fibers.

○ The cost of providing stain guards for microfiber synthetic shirts would probably be greater than what garment producers now spend on stain guards for natural-fiber shirts.

SECTION 4: VERBAL REASONING

Questions 17 through 18 are based on the following reading passage.

Scholars of early Buddhist art agree that Buddha images in human form emerged around the first century A.D. in the regions of Mathura, located in central India, and Gandhara, now part of Pakistan and Afghanistan. Uncertainty exists, however, about whether Mathura or Gandhara has the stronger claim to primacy. Those who believe that anthropomorphic sculptures of the Buddha first appeared in Gandhara point out that earlier Buddhist art was largely aniconic and that *bas relief* was far more common than sculpture. They argue that Greek influence in Gandhara promoted the development of the new style and form of representation of the divine. Other scholars make the case for indigenous development of such representations in Mathura, citing a centuries-long record of iconic art in pre-Buddhist traditions. They do not reject all foreign influence, but they argue that local traditions provided a strong foundation for the development of Buddhist sculpture.

Art historians bolster their arguments by highlighting distinctive features of the sculptures from each region. For example, the artists of Gandhara sculpted their Buddhas in heavy, pleated drapery, similar to that of Greek statues. Wavy lines indicating hair also reflect Greek influence. Mathura Buddhas, on the other hand, are portrayed wearing lighter robes draped in a monastic style, often with part of the shoulder and chest left bare. Elongated earlobes and strong facial features characterize Mathura images of the Buddha, whereas Gandhara images possess more angular features. Sorting out dates and directions of influence has proven difficult, but the totality of evidence suggests that the Buddha image evolved simultaneously in both regions and was shaped by the predominant cultural influences in each region.

Which of the following, if true, would those who believe that anthropomorphic images of Buddha originated in Gandhara be likely to cite as evidence for their viewpoint?

○ Pre-Buddhist subcultures in the Gandhara region created representations of their deities in human form.

○ Mathuran Buddhas' lightweight robes appear to have been modeled on the real robes of people who lived in a warm climate.

○ Gandharan artists were isolated from the larger society and not exposed to influences from outside the region.

○ Rulers from the Mathura region had political ties to Greek rulers and frequently exchanged gifts with them.

○ The hairstyles worn by Gandharan Buddhas are similar to those depicted on Greek pottery from the same period.

According to the passage, Buddhist art

○ first appeared in regions that are now part of India, Pakistan, and Afghanistan

○ experienced a period during which human representations of the Buddha were not common

○ characteristically portrayed figures with elongated earlobes and strong facial features

○ began to appear in the medium of *bas relief* as a result of Greek influence

○ was more influenced by foreign artworks than by indigenous artistic traditions

SECTION 4: VERBAL REASONING

Questions 19 through 20 are based on the following reading passage.

In 1887, Eugene Dubois began his search in Sumatra for the "missing link"—the being that would fill the evolutionary gap between ape and man. He discovered a fossilized human-like thighbone and a section of skull. He confirmed that these fossils were of significant age by examining other fossils in the same area. The thighbone's shape indicated that it belonged to a creature that walked upright. Dubois estimated the size of the creature's skull from the skull fragment and concluded that this creature's brain volume was between that of the higher primates and that of current humans. Although the concept of "missing link" has changed dramatically and a recent analysis showed Dubois's fossils to be far too recent for humans to have evolved from this "missing link," the value of his discovery and the debate it generated is unquestionable.

Consider each of the choices separately and select all that apply.

The passage supplies information to answer which of the following questions?

☐ What was the approximate age of the fossils found by Dubois?

☐ Does Dubois's find meet current definitions of the "missing link"?

☐ Do the flaws in Dubois's conclusions invalidate his work?

Select a sentence in which the author reaches a conclusion.

NO TEST MATERIAL ON THIS PAGE

SECTION 5: QUANTITATIVE REASONING

For each of Questions 1 to 7, compare Quantity A and Quantity B, using additional information centered above the two quantities if such information is given. Select one of the four answer choices below each question and fill in the circle to the left of that answer choice.

(A) Quantity A is greater.

(B) Quantity B is greater.

(C) The two quantities are equal.

(D) The relationship cannot be determined from the information given.

A symbol that appears more than once in a question has the same meaning throughout the question.

A circle with center R has a radius of 6 and is inscribed in square $ABCD$.

Quantity A	Quantity B
The area of the largest triangle that can be drawn inside square $ABCD$	The area of the circle with center R

○ Quantity A is greater.

○ Quantity B is greater.

○ The two quantities are equal.

○ The relationship cannot be determined from the information given.

$$xy \neq 0$$

$$\frac{a}{xs} = 632 \text{ and } \frac{a}{ys} = 158$$

Quantity A	Quantity B
x	y

○ Quantity A is greater.

○ Quantity B is greater.

○ The two quantities are equal.

○ The relationship cannot be determined from the information given.

Quantity A	Quantity B
The remainder when 135 is divided by 7	The remainder when 135 is divided by 19

○ Quantity A is greater.

○ Quantity B is greater.

○ The two quantities are equal.

○ The relationship cannot be determined from the information given.

a and b are integers.

$$a^2 = b^3$$

Quantity A	Quantity B
a	b

○ Quantity A is greater.

○ Quantity B is greater.

○ The two quantities are equal.

○ The relationship cannot be determined from the information given.

$$ab < 0$$

$$bc > 0$$

Quantity A	Quantity B
ac	0

○ Quantity A is greater.

○ Quantity B is greater.

○ The two quantities are equal.

○ The relationship cannot be determined from the information given.

$$|x| = 6$$
$$y = x + 4$$

Quantity A   **Quantity B**

y 10

○ Quantity A is greater.

○ Quantity B is greater.

○ The two quantities are equal.

○ The relationship cannot be determined from the information given.

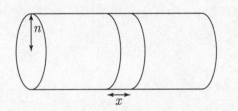

A rectangular ribbon of width x is wrapped around the circumference of a right circular cylinder of radius n, encircling the cylinder without overlap as shown in the figure above. The area of the ribbon is equal to the area of the base of the cylinder.

Quantity A   **Quantity B**

x n

○ Quantity A is greater.

○ Quantity B is greater.

○ The two quantities are equal.

○ The relationship cannot be determined from the information given.

List A: 1, 2, 7, 8, 15, 2, 3, 5, 6, 13

x is the median of the even numbers in List A.

y is the median of the prime numbers in List A.

z is the median of the least and greatest numbers in List A.

Quantity A   **Quantity B**

The median of $2x$, y, and z z

○ Quantity A is greater.

○ Quantity B is greater.

○ The two quantities are equal.

○ The relationship cannot be determined from the information given.

Oil is pumped from a well at a rate of 500 gallons per hour. How many gallons of oil are pumped from the well in 3 hours and 15 minutes?

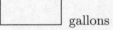 gallons

Click on the answer box and type in a number. Backspace to erase.

A certain pet store sells only dogs and cats. In March, the store sold twice as many dogs as cats. In April, the store sold twice the number of dogs that it sold in March, and three times the number of cats that it sold in March. If the total number of pets the store sold in March and April combined was 500, how many dogs did the store sell in March?

○   80

○   100

○   120

○   160

○   180

In the xy-plane, rectangle $WXYZ$ has vertices at $(-2, -1)$, $(-2, y)$, $(4, y)$, and $(4, -1)$. If the area of $WXYZ$ is 18, what is the length of its diagonal?

○ $3\sqrt{2}$

○ $3\sqrt{3}$

○ $3\sqrt{5}$

○ $3\sqrt{6}$

○ $3\sqrt{7}$

How many three-digit integers can be created using only 5 distinct digits?

○ 10

○ 15

○ 20

○ 30

○ 60

At Megalomania Industries, factory workers were paid $20 per hour in 1990 and $10 per hour in 2000. The CEO of Megalomania Industries was paid $5 million in 1990 and $50 million in 2000. The percent increase in the pay of Megalomania's CEO from 1990 to 2000 was what percent greater than the percent decrease in the hourly pay of Megalomania's factory workers over the same period?

○ 850%

○ 900%

○ 950%

○ 1,700%

○ 1,900%

Questions 14 through 16 refer to the following graph.

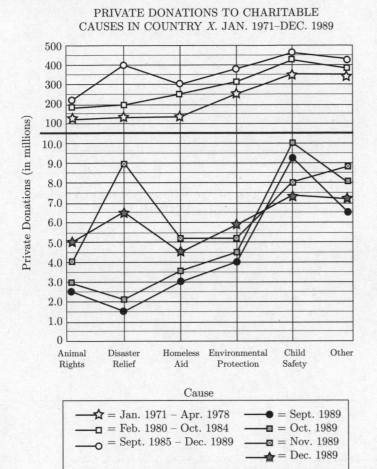

PRIVATE DONATIONS TO CHARITABLE
CAUSES IN COUNTRY *X*. JAN. 1971–DEC. 1989

Private Donations (in millions)

Cause

☆ = Jan. 1971 – Apr. 1978   ● = Sept. 1989
□ = Feb. 1980 – Oct. 1984   ■ = Oct. 1989
○ = Sept. 1985 – Dec. 1989   ⊠ = Nov. 1989
                              ★ = Dec. 1989

14 of 20

If there were 38 child safety organizations and the funds contributed to these organizations in September 1989 were evenly distributed, how much did each charity receive?

○ $12,000,000

○ $9,400,000

○ $2,500,000

○ $250,000

○ $38,000

15 of 20

From September 1985 to December 1989, what was the approximate ratio of private donations for homeless aid to private donations for animal rights?

○ 20 : 9

○ 3 : 2

○ 4 : 3

○ 5 : 4

○ 6 : 5

16 of 20

Which of the following charitable causes received the least percent increase in private donations from September 1989 to October 1989 ?

○ Animal Rights

○ Disaster Relief

○ Homeless Aid

○ Environmental Protection

○ Child Safety

In the repeating decimal 0.0653906539..., the 34th digit to the right of the decimal point is

○ 9

○ 6

○ 5

○ 3

○ 0

If $3x + 2y = 24$, and $\dfrac{7y}{2x} = 7$, then $y =$

$$\boxed{}$$
$$\boxed{}$$

Click on each box and type in a number.
Backspace to erase.

If the average (arithmetic mean) of 6, 8, 10, and x is between 6 and 12, what is the greatest possible integer value of x ?

○   8

○   11

○   23

○   28

○   44

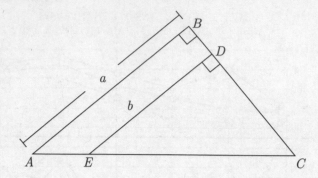

If $AB = BC$, which of the following is an expression for the area of quadrilateral $ABDE$?

○ $\dfrac{a^2}{2} - \dfrac{b^2}{2}$

○ $\dfrac{a^2}{2} + \dfrac{b^2}{2}$

○ $a^2 - b^2$

○ $\dfrac{a^2}{4} - \dfrac{ab}{2}$

○ $\dfrac{a^2}{4} + \dfrac{ab}{2}$

SECTION 6: VERBAL REASONING

For questions 1 through 6, select one entry for each blank from the corresponding column of choices. Fill all blanks in the way that best completes the text.

Many fashions that were considered daring in their time have been so widely worn and imitated that the (i)_____ style is no longer seen as (ii)_____ .

Blank (i)	Blank (ii)
proposed	outlandish
original	commonplace
revealing	copied

Western culture has so influenced Middle Eastern music that even the latter's roles of composer and performer, at one time inseparable, have now begun to _____ .

divulge
retreat
retrench
diverge
fuse

Kazan was quickly (i)_____ by many of his contemporaries for his transgression, who saw his testimony as treachery, an act of (ii)_____ which stained how they viewed him both as an artist and as a man. It was only by continually making films that he was able to (iii)_____ his perceived sins and achieve some measure of atonement.

Blank (i)	Blank (ii)	Blank (iii)
rebuked	perfidy	exacerbate
lauded	sophistry	deviate
mitigated	redemption	expiate

Although tranquilizers usually have a _____ effect, this is not always the case, especially when the abuse of these drugs results in a failure to induce the much-desired sleep.

soporific
sedulous
coruscating
debilitating
penetrating

As a rule, (i)_____ interpretations of events are rejected by modern scientists in their attempts to find secular insights into the matrix of causes and effects in our modern world. Paradoxically, this fact does not (ii)_____ the existence of individual scientists who possess views that may be (iii)_____ with a belief in supernatural causes.

Blank (i)	Blank (ii)	Blank (iii)
falsifiable	countenance	at variance
preternatural	enhance	consonant
teleological	preclude	discrepant

The Johnsons were not known for their (i)_____ ; at the very least, none of the family members was fearful of (ii)_____ , of appearing or acting differently from other people.

Blank (i)	Blank (ii)
candor	pettiness
vulgarity	eccentricity
conformity	complaisance

SECTION 6: VERBAL REASONING

For each of Questions 7 to 12, select one answer choice unless otherwise instructed.

Questions 7 through 10 are based on the following reading passage.

According to most scientists, the universe began approximately 10 to 15 billion years ago and has been expanding ever since. This theory, known as the Big Bang theory, is the fairly direct result of Hubble's law, which states that objects farther away from Earth are receding faster than those closer. This expansion implies a singular point which all matter is expanding from.

Complicating the scientific explanation is that the Big Bang cannot be thought of as an explosion from some identifiable source—rather, space and time were created in the Big Bang. Furthermore, the relationship between distance and speed is not precisely linear. So, if one were to think of galaxies as particles created in a big bang, these galaxies have both a local component of motion, as well as playing a role in the overall expansion of the universe.

A further complication is that galactic distances are so great that galactic motion, even if the galaxies are moving at incredible speeds, is difficult to observe. Scientists must therefore rely on a "standard candle," an object of known brightness within the galaxy they wish to observe. Using the inverse square law, scientists can then measure how far that galaxy is away from our own. For instance, suppose a supernova in galaxy A appears one hundred times as bright as one in galaxy B. By the inverse square law, galaxy B is ten times farther away than galaxy A, assuming, of course, that distance is the only factor affecting brightness.

7 of 20

It can be inferred from the sentence highlighted in the passage that a standard candle is useful to scientists for which of the following reasons?

○ Standard candles do not have their own locus of motion.

○ Standard candles more reliably adhere to the law of inverse squares than do other supernovas.

○ Only standard candles provide a known measure of brightness.

○ Knowledge of an object's brightness allows scientists to measure the speed at which the object is moving toward Earth.

○ Knowledge of an object's brightness allows scientists to accurately measure its distance from Earth.

Consider each of the choices separately and select all that apply.

According to the passage, if two astronomical objects of differing distances from Earth were observed, which of the following would be true of the object closer to Earth?

☐ It would not be as bright as the object farther from Earth.

☐ It would be younger than the object farther from Earth.

☐ It would be traveling away from the Earth more slowly than the farther object.

9 of 20

It can be inferred from the passage that a standard candle may not provide an accurate measure of distance if

○ the galaxy being measured is moving too quickly

○ interstellar dust makes the object measured appear dimmer than it really is

○ if the galaxy being measured has a local component of measurement

○ the particles being measured do not completely accord with a linear motion

○ the galaxies being measured move at different speeds

10 of 20

According to the passage, if two supernovas are observed and one of those supernovas is brighter than the other, scientists can conclude that

○ the brighter supernova is moving closer to our galaxy at a higher speed

○ the precise location of the supernova is measurable

○ the brighter supernova may be closer to our own galaxy

○ the brighter supernova is farther away from Earth by a distance that is roughly inversely proportional to the dim supernova

○ the distance between the supernovas and our own galaxy is inversely proportional

SECTION 6: VERBAL REASONING

Questions 11 through 12 are based on the following reading passage.

Throughout the twentieth century, it was accepted as fact that cells in our brains, called neurons, do not regenerate. Research by neurologist Elizabeth Gould overturned this core doctrine within the span of a few years. Her experiments on rats showed that even after suffering severe trauma, their brains were able to heal themselves by regenerating neurons. Gould's findings have incited a flood of new research into applications that may take advantage of neurogenesis.

One such study examines the role of reduced neurogenesis among individuals suffering from depression. It is speculated that neurogenesis may contribute to an explanation for the so called "Prozac lag." As an antidepressant, the immediate boost of serotonin caused by Prozac should have had instantaneous mood elevating effects. However, patients suffering from depression only begin to experience mood elevation weeks after beginning treatment. The study speculates that during this period, the brain may be regenerating neurons.

The author mentions the "Prozac lag" primarily in order to

○ raise a possible objection to a newly proposed theory

○ present a situation for which a new theory may serve an explanatory role

○ offer evidence that runs counter to a previously held belief

○ suggest a counterexample that undermines a newly proposed theory

○ provide supporting evidence that a newly discovered phenomenon may have unforeseen effects

In the second paragraph, select the sentence in which the author describes an unexpected observation.

SECTION 6: VERBAL REASONING

For questions 13 through 16, select the two answer choices that, when used to complete the sentence, fit the meaning of the sentence as a whole and produce completed sentences that are alike in meaning.

Plato, an important philosopher, is primarily known because he wrote down Socrates's _____ conversations. It is through Plato's record of these dialogues that Socrates's teachings have survived and continue to enlighten seekers of wisdom.

- ☐ inspiring
- ☐ edifying
- ☐ tedious
- ☐ grating
- ☐ rousing
- ☐ didactic

Even the colossal meal failed to _____ her voracious appetite.

- ☐ cadge
- ☐ exacerbate
- ☐ provoke
- ☐ satiate
- ☐ mendicate
- ☐ allay

Slicks of oil on a rain-soaked street are _____ and beautiful, but the lovely rainbows they produce on the asphalt can seem rather ugly when one reflects upon the road hazards they create and the environmental damage they entail.

- ☐ anodyne
- ☐ iridescent
- ☐ monocoque
- ☐ pavonine
- ☐ parietal
- ☐ saturnine

He had not always been so callous, but with time he became _____ to the violence around him.

- ☐ adorned
- ☐ cauterized
- ☐ sensitized
- ☐ ostracized
- ☐ inured
- ☐ attuned

SECTION 6: VERBAL REASONING

For each of Questions 17 to 20, select one answer choice unless otherwise instructed.

When the maker of Megapower, a vitamin supplement, modified its formula two years ago, Tasmania, an island off the coast of New Zealand, suffered a decrease in its export earnings. Tasmania's only export, kiwi fruit, constitutes a substantial portion of the world supply of that fruit. Researchers concluded that the old Megapower formula contained natural kiwi extract, but the new formula does not.

Which of the following, if true, gives the strongest support for the researchers' claim?

○ Some South American countries have begun to grow kiwi fruit successfully.

○ United States chemists have started development of a synthetic kiwi extract.

○ The manufacturers of Megapower chose not to renew their contract with the Tasmanian kiwi growers.

○ Imports of kiwi fruit have fallen in the country where Megapower is manufactured.

○ There was a marked drop in sales of a number of formerly profitable items that used kiwi as an ingredient.

Questions 18 through 20 are based on the following reading passage.

While art historians do not necessarily agree on the date of the birth of modern art, they do agree that mid-nineteenth century French art shows a clear and distinct break from tradition. Pressed to point to a single picture that represents the vanguard of the modern art movement, art historians will often point to Courbet's *The Painter's Studio*.

The peculiar subtitle of Courbet's work, "Real allegory summing up a seven-year period of my life" confirms that Courbet was striving to do something strikingly original with his work. The argument has been made that the painting struck a blow for the independence of the artist, and that since Courbet's work, artists have felt freed from the societal demands placed upon their work. Paintings prior to Courbet's time were most often focused on depicting events from the Bible, history, or literature. With his singular painting, Courbet promulgated the idea that an artist is capable of representing only that which he can experience through his senses of sight and touch; the true artist will then be compelled to make his representation as simply and directly as possible.

Which of the following would most effectively replace the word promulgated as it is used in the context of the passage?

○ Displayed

○ Disseminated

○ Proclaimed

○ Concealed

○ Secreted

SECTION 6: VERBAL REASONING

Select the sentence in the passage that best explains the effect of Courbet's work on other artists.

The effect that Courbet had on painting is most analogous to which situation?

- ○ An avant-garde writer who subverts novelistic conventions
- ○ A machinist who tinkers and improves his invention
- ○ A watercolor painter who paints in the same style as his peers
- ○ A scientist who comes up with a unified theory of several discordant scientific ideas
- ○ A seamstress who makes a ball gown using several different types of fabric

Chapter 19
Practice Test 1:
Answers and
Explanations

INTERPRETING YOUR RESULTS

After you check your answers on the following pages, fill out this sheet to interpret your results.

Analytical Writing

To evaluate your performance on the Analytical Writing sections, compare your response to the advice and samples in the Analytical Writing chapter.

Verbal Reasoning

Refer to the explanations to check your answers. Count the number of questions you got correct in each Verbal Reasoning section, and calculate the total number correct. Find the section of the Interpretive Guide (below) that corresponds to your total to get an idea of how your performance compares to that of other test takers.

Test 1	# Correct
Section 4	
Section 6	
Total	

Quantitative Reasoning

Refer to the explanations to check your answers. Count the number of questions you got correct in each Quantitative Reasoning section, and calculate the total number correct. Find the section of the Interpretive Guide (below) that corresponds to your total to get an idea of how your performance compares to that of other test takers.

Test 1	# Correct
Section 3	
Section 5	
Total	

Interpretive Guide

The table below provides a guide for interpreting your performance based on the number of questions you got correct in each subject.

Subject	Above Average	Average	Below Average
Verbal Reasoning	30–40	22–29	1–21
Quantitative Reasoning	33–40	24–32	1–23

Section 3

1. A

Point *C* has the same *x*–coordinate as point *D*, so $s = 8$. Point *C* also has the same *y*-coordinate as point *B*, so $t = 7$. That means that Quantity A is greater.

2. A

The punch is made with two parts soda and three parts ice cream. This means that in one mixture if you added two parts of soda, then that's $4 \times 2 = 8$ parts sugar and $5 \times 2 = 10$ parts citric acid. If you added three parts ice cream, then that's $3 \times 3 = 9$ parts sugar and $2 \times 3 = 6$ parts salt. There's $8 + 9 = 17$ total parts sugar and $10 + 6 = 16$ total parts citric acid. There's more sugar than citric acid. Choice (A) is correct.

3. B

This is a Quant Comp question with variables, so Plug In more than once. To easily compare the two quantities, recycle the number in the problems by Plugging In $x = 5$. This problem involves averages, so draw an average pie. If $x = 5$, and the average high temperature over the course of 5 days is 70 degrees, then the total temperature for the 5 days is $5 \times 70 = 350$. The problem states that one additional day has a high temperature of 75 degrees, so draw another average pie. There are now six days and the total high temperature is $350 + 75 = 425$ and the average high temperature for the six days is $\frac{425}{6} = 70\frac{5}{6}$. This is less than the 71 degree average specified in the problem. Because the two quantities cannot both equal 5, eliminate (C). If it is unclear whether the value for *x* needs to be greater or less than 5 to make the average high temperature at the end of the problem equal to 71 degrees, Plug In again. This time, try a number less than 5, such as $x = 4$. If $x = 4$, then the total temperature for 4 days with an average of 70 degrees is $4 \times 70 = 280$. The addition of one day with a high temperature of 75 degrees means that the total high temperature is $280 + 75 = 355$ over the course of 5 days. Therefore, the average is $\frac{355}{5} = 71$. Therefore, the correct value of *x* is 4 and so the value of Quantity A is 4. This is less than the value of Quantity B, so the correct answer is (B).

4. D

Because $\triangle QRS$ is isosceles, side *RS* must be equal to one of the other sides, and *x* could measure 4 or 7. Thus, the perimeter could be $4 + 4 + 7 = 15$, or the perimeter could be $4 + 7 + 7 = 18$. You can't tell if the perimeter is greater or less than 17, so the answer is (D). Remember, you cannot trust the figure to be drawn to scale!

5. **B**

Remember that a normal distribution curve has divisions of 34 percent, 14 percent, and 2 percent on each side of the mean. 80 out of 500 is 16 percent, or 14 percent + 2 percent, and 10 out of 500 is 2 percent. Draw a normal distribution curve and label it. There are three standard deviations between 92 and 56, so 92 − 56 = 36, and 36 ÷ 3 = 12. The mean is 92 − 12 = 80, which is smaller than Quantity B.

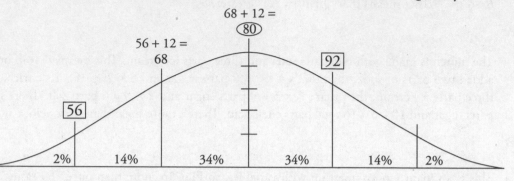

6. **C**

Plug in numbers for the sides. Let $AD = 4$, so $EG = 8$. Let $l = 3$. The area of $ABCD = 3 \times 4 = 12$, and the area of $EFG = \frac{1}{2} (3 \times 8) = 12$. The two quantities can be equal, so eliminate (A) and (B). Try changing your numbers, and you will see that the two quantities will always be equal.

7. **B**

FOIL out the equation given, and you'll get $(3x − 4y)(3x + 4y) = 9x^2 − 16y^2$, so Quantity A is 2. Quantity B is therefore bigger, and the answer is (B).

8. **C**

Solve for a by adding 2 to each side to get $8a = 24$. Divide by 8 to find $a = 3$. Plug $a = 3$ into the second equation to find $4(3) − 1 = 12 − 1 = 11$. Alternatively, you could save yourself some time by noticing that $8a − 2$ is $2(4a − 1)$. If $2(4a − 1) = 22$, divide by 2 to get $4a − 1 = 11$.

9. **56**

Twenty percent of the sweaters in the store are white, so there are $200 \times \frac{20}{100} = 40$ white sweaters. There are $200 − 40 = 160$ sweaters remaining. Of the remaining sweaters, $160 \times \frac{40}{100} = 64$ are brown. That means that $160 − 64 = 96$ are blue. There are $96 − 40 = 56$ more blue sweaters than white sweaters.

10. **D**

Because 4^{12} is a common factor of both 4^{13} and 4^{12}, you can rewrite the numerator as $4^{12}(4 − 1)$. Now look at the whole fraction: $\frac{4^{12}(4 − 1)}{4^{11}}$. You can divide 4^{12} by 4^{11}, leaving you with $4^1(4 − 1)$. Now the calculation should be much easier: $4 \times 3 = 12$, (D).

11. **D**

Refer to the right side and the left side of the "Subscription to Newsmagazine x, 1995–2010" chart. In 2005, Newsmagazine x accounted for 14.6 percent of newsmagazine subscriptions, and it had 7,000 subscriptions.

12. **B**

In 2006, Newsmagazine z accounted for 9,400 out of 57,000 newsmagazine subscriptions. Therefore, Newsmagazine z accounted for approximately 9,000 out of 57,000, or $\frac{1}{6}$, of the nationwide newsmagazine subscriptions.

13. **D**

In 1995, there were 1,500 subscriptions to Newsmagazine x, which accounted for approximately 25 percent of total nationwide subscriptions. Total nationwide subscriptions in 1995, then, were equal to about 6,000 (25 percent of total nationwide subscriptions = 1,500). Using the same process, total nationwide subscriptions in 1996 were equal to about 9,000 (30 percent of total nationwide subscriptions = 2,600). The percent increase between 1995 and 1996 is $\frac{difference}{original}$ or $\frac{9,000-6,000}{6,000} = \frac{3,000}{6,000} = \frac{1}{2}$, or 50 percent.

14. **C**

In 1998, Newsmagazine x had 3,300 subscriptions, or 20.5 percent of the total number of newsmagazine subscriptions. Set up the calculation to find the total: $3,300 = \frac{20.5}{100}x$. Solve it to find that $x = 16,000$.

15. **C**

$a = 27 \times \frac{1}{3^2} = 3$, and $x = 6 \times \frac{1}{3} = 2$. Find $(12)(3^{-x})(15)(2^{-a}) = (12)(3^{-2})(15)(2^{-3}) = \frac{(12)(15)}{(3^2)(2^3)}$. Now, reduce:

$\frac{(2 \times 2 \times 3)(3 \times 5)}{(3 \times 3)(2 \times 2 \times 2)} = \frac{5}{2}$.

16. **B and D**

Use the Average Pie to find that Jill's mean of 3.75 for 8 evaluations gives her a current total of $3.75 \times 8 = 30$ points. Use the Average Pie to find that if she needs an average of 4.0 for 12 scores, she needs $4.0 \times 12 = 48$ total points. Jill still needs $48 - 30 = 18$ points. Her four remaining scores must total 18 or greater. Only (B) and (D) have a total of at least 18.

17. **270**

To answer this question remember that each angle in a rectangle is 90 degrees and there are 180 degrees in a triangle. Look at the figure. When presented with a shape like this, look for shapes that are familiar. The rectangle has been divided into 4 separate triangles. Three of the triangles have one side of the triangle that is represented by the angle of the original rectangle. For example, a triangle is represented by the angles of a and b as well as the 90 degree angle that is represented by point S. Since there are 180 degrees in a triangle, and 90 of those degrees are found at point S, the sum of angles a and b is 90. The same principle can be applied to the triangle that is created by angles c, d, and point T, as well as the triangle created by angles e, f, and point U. Since this is true, $c + d = 90$ and $e + f = 90$. Therefore, the sum of all the angles is 270.

18. **B**

Plug In the Answers, starting with (C). If the total is 55, then the probability would be $\left(\dfrac{3}{55}\right)\left(\dfrac{2}{54}\right)$, which does not equal $\dfrac{3}{55}$. The denominator is too large, so try choice (B). If the total is 11, then the probability is $\left(\dfrac{3}{11}\right)\left(\dfrac{2}{10}\right)$, which reduces to $\dfrac{3}{55}$.

19. **D**

Use the Group formula: Total = Group$_1$ + Group$_2$ − Both + Neither. In this problem, the total is 2,400. The question also states that 1,200 students (half of the total) take calculus, so that is Group$_1$; one-third of that group (400) take both calculus and English. Because every student takes calculus or English or both, the Neither group is zero. Solve for the number of students who take English by plugging these numbers into the group formula: 2400 = 1200 + Group$_2$ − 400. The number of students who take English is 1,600, or (D).

20. **A**

To solve this expression you need to break apart the factorial of 13 to the common prime number in the denominator, in this case the number 2. 13! can be expressed as $13 \times 12 \times 11 \times 10 \times 9 \times 8 \times 7 \times 6 \times 5 \times 4 \times 3 \times 2 \times 1$. When you break apart this factorial into its prime numbers you are left with $13 \times 11 \times 7 \times 5^2 \times 3^5 \times 2^{10}$. For a fraction to result in an integer, the denominator of the fraction must share at least one prime factor with the numerator. The greatest number of 2s that can be found in the prime factorization of 13! is 10, so $x \leq 10$. Eliminate (B), (C), and (E). Now for the tricky part! Any nonzero number raised to the power 0 is 1. Since the result when any integer is divided by 1 is also an integer, 0 must be included in the range of possible x values. The answer is (A).

Section 4

1. **prowess** and **maladroit**

   The first blank has a strong clue, so begin there. The blank is describing the *professor...as a teacher* and gives further insight that *she shows more...teaching skills* then her colleagues. The transition word and indicates that there is consistency between her description as a *noteworthy intellect* and her skills as a teacher. Therefore, a good word for the first blank is "skills." Choice (A), *prowess*, is a good match for skills so keep (A). Choice (B), *profligacy*, means reckless extravagance and (C), *orthodoxies*, means beliefs. Eliminate (B) and (C). The second blank is describing the professor's *colleagues...teaching skills*. The sentence gives further insight by stating that the professor shows more skills than her colleagues. Therefore, a good word for the blank is "unskilled" or "not good." Choice (D), *spurious*, means fake which is not a match for "unskilled" so eliminate (D). Choice (E), *maladroit*, is a good match for the blank, so keep (E). Choice (F), *eclectic*, means from different sources, so eliminate (F). The correct answer is (A) and (E).

2. **irresponsible, forestall**, and **avoidable**

   The keys to the first blank are the clues "given their responsibilities as democratically elected officials" and "neglect to do everything they could." These clues indicate that the first blank should have a negative connotation; a word that means something as simple as *bad* would eliminate *thoughtful* and *intuitive*, leaving *irresponsible*. Blanks (ii) and (iii) build on the idea set up in the first half of the sentence. The second blank describes the action that would be bad, so use something that means solve. *Sustain* and *cultivate* are the opposites of what's needed for the second blank, leaving *forestall*. The last blank describes the type of problem, and entirely suggests it's a solvable problem. *Avoidable* is close, and it helps the whole sentence make sense.

3. **erudite**

   Despite is a transition word that implies a contrast between the student's actual behavior when presenting her thesis and her mentor's advice. The student resorted to using slang, language that is informal and unscholarly. Therefore, the word in the blank must mean *formal* or *scholarly*. The only word that fits that description is *erudite*, which is the best choice. The other answer choices can be used to describe speech, but none of these words contrast the mentor's advice with the student's use of slang.

4. **augmented, overwhelmed,** and **delicate**

   Start with the second blank. The clue *pungent* tells you this onion did something bad to the delicious stew. *Exaggerated* and *satiated* are positive; *overwhelmed* is the only fit. The transition *otherwise* tells you to change direction from the third blank's clue of *pungent*. Look for a word that means *subtle* or *soft*. Only *delicate* fits. For the first blank, the clue is that Steve's stinky onion hurt the delicate stew. The transition *although* tells you to change direction. So, this addition of the sweet potato was good. Only *augmented* fits.

5. **banal, an adept,** and **sublime**

   The first clue is *its focus on such everyday objects as flowers or fruits apparently uninspired,* so the first blank has to mean something such as "uninspired." *Banal,* which means predictable, matches this. For the second blank, the painter must pay *careful attention,* so the second blank must mean "careful" or "talented," which matches *an adept.* Since the painting is *exemplary,* the third blank must be *sublime.*

6. **comely** and **prepossessing**

   The first blank describes Viktor Yuschenko's face. The clue is that his face was *transformed into a monstrous mask by dioxin poisoning* and the transition word *once* tells us an appropriate word for the blank would be the opposite of monstrous; something like attractive would work nicely. *Quiescent* means calm, and *fatuous* means foolish, so those words don't work. *Comely,* which means attractive, is the only word that works. The second blank is describing Yulia Tymoshenko. Both the transition phrase *a study in contrasts* and the clue about *fashion magazines* suggest that a word that means beautiful is appropriate. Though it might not sound like it, *prepossessing* does, in fact, mean beautiful. *Felicitous* means well-expressed, and *decorous* means full of propriety, so although they are both positive words, they aren't as fitting here as the credited response is.

7. **D**

   According to the first sentence, her work can be viewed three different ways. The rest of the passage describes those ways: as the work of a modern poet, of a woman, and of a Native American. Choice (A) is too vague, and the passage doesn't so much describe her work as how it should be viewed. Choices (B) and (C) are too narrow and don't describe the overall purpose. Choice (E) doesn't match the passage.

8. **B**

   In the second paragraph the author states, "Mr. Wilson's praise gives the impression that Feather's readership is limited to her own culture—an impression which hints that Mr. Wilson is himself measuring her by only one criterion," which best fits (B). Choices (A) and (E) contradict the passage and are too broad and extreme. Choice (C) contradicts the passage, and (D) is not supported.

9. **E**

The second sentence of the passage claims, "We could consider her poems as the product of a twentieth-century artist in the tradition of James Joyce, T.S. Eliot, and Wallace Stevens." Thus, the author mentions Joyce, Eliot, and Stevens in order to describe one context—twentieth-century poetry—in which Feather's work can be analyzed. Eliminate (A) because the author doesn't compare Feather's political messages to those of these authors. Eliminate (B) because the author doesn't use these authors to discuss differences between male and female poets. Eliminate (C) because the author doesn't contrast Feather's themes with those of these authors. Although Joyce, Eliot, and Stevens were, like Feather, twentieth-century artists, the passage doesn't say that they shared sensibilities, which eliminates (D). Choice (E) is the answer.

10. **C**

Only (C) provides a clue to the meaning of *urbane* as used here: The urbane buyer is contrasted with the "unsuspecting or naïve buyer," so it must mean "not unsuspecting" or "not naïve." Choice (A) tantalizingly dangles the word "rural" before our eyes, trying to take advantage of that word's well-known association with the word urban. *Urbane*, though, means *sophisticated*. Moreover, if (A) were accepted, the strangely illogical proposition that city-dwellers knew best how to buy animals at market would have to be accepted as well. Choice (B), thankfully, presents no such difficulties of interpretation and appears in the definition of the obscure expression itself, not in the comparison between unsuspecting and urbane.

11. **It relates to the common Renaissance practice of securing suckling pigs for transport to market in a poke, or drawstring bag.**

In this sentence the author defines the term "poke" as a drawstring bag. This is the only instance in which the author gives a definition for a word that the reader may not be familiar with because the word "poke" is not a common term used to describe a drawstring bag.

12. **propriety** and **decorum**

The clue is "was such a bad-mannered child." Time acts as a change-of-direction transition ("as an adult") that indicates the blank should mean something like well-mannered. Only *propriety* and *decorum* mean well-mannered. *Diffidence, reticence,* and *brashness* are all traits that would be considered bad-mannered. *Friendliness* does not necessarily mean well-mannered.

13. **whimsical** and **capricious**

The blank describes how politicians act. The clue is "acting according to a deliberate plan." The change-of-direction transition *however* tells you that they appear not to have a plan. Words that mean unplanned or random should be in the blank. Both *whimsical* and *capricious* fit this meaning. *Conventional* and *conformist* have the opposite meaning. The other two words are unrelated to the blank.

14. **irksome** and **onerous**

The transition *even more* tells you to stay in the same direction as the clue. "Forced to take an alternate road," "two-hour detour," and "arduous trip" tell you that the journey was difficult. Put a word that means hard or tiring in the blank. Only *irksome* and *onerous* fit this meaning. *Facile* and *glib* describe something easy, and *implacable* and *immutable* describe something that doesn't change.

15. **adventurous** and **doughty**

   The transition *especially* tells you to stay in the same direction as the clue "willingness to reject prevailing feminine roles and to travel to foreign lands alone." Thus, she has a bold spirit. Only *adventurous* and *doughty* mean bold. Although she is traveling alone, there is nothing to support that she is lonely, as *forlorn* and *desolate* suggest. *Magnanimous* and *bellicose* do not fit.

16. **A**

   The argument concludes that the substitution of microfiber clothes for those made from natural fabrics is not financially sound. The premise is that microfiber clothes last as long as natural fabric clothes but are three times as expensive to produce. The argument assumes that there are no other factors that need to be considered to evaluate the cost effectiveness of switching. Choice (A) points out another factor that would affect the overall costs and so weakens the argument. Choice (B) helps to explain why the microfiber synthetic shirt is more expensive to produce than a natural fiber shirt, but it does not weaken the argument. In (C), comparing natural fiber shirts and other fiber garments is not relevant. Choice (D) strengthens the argument. Choice (E), by pointing out additional costs associated with microfibers, also strengthens the argument.

17. **E**

   The first paragraph presents the Gandhara-first view that "Greek influence in Gandhara promoted the development of the new style and form of representation of the divine." The second paragraph provides evidence Gandharan Buddhas shared certain features with Greek art. Choice (E) provides additional information about those similarities and is the best choice. Choices (A) and (C) undermine the idea that Gandharan artists were responding to outside influences. Choice (B) is irrelevant, and (D) provides evidence for outside influences in Mathura.

18. **B**

   The first sentence says that "images in human form emerged around the first century A.D.," and the middle of the first paragraph states that "earlier Buddhist art was largely aniconic." You can conclude from these statements that the earliest Buddhist art didn't usually depict the Buddha in human form. Eliminate (A); although human representations first appeared in these regions, the passage doesn't say that the first Buddhist art appeared in the same places. The passage doesn't support (C), (D), and (E).

19. **B and C**

   For (A), the passage says only that the age of these fossils was "far too recent for humans to have evolved" from them. This does not give an age for the fossils. The last sentence says that "the concept of 'missing link' has changed dramatically," which answers the question in (B). The last sentence also answers the question in (C) because it says, "the value of his discovery and the debate it generated is unquestionable."

20. **Although the concept of "missing link" has changed dramatically and a recent analysis showed Dubois's fossils to be far too recent for humans to have evolved from this "missing link," the value of his discovery and the debate it generated is unquestionable.**

   In the last sentence, the author states that the value of Dubois's fossils is "unquestionable." This statement represents the author's conclusion.

Section 5

1. **B**

   Draw the figure. You have a square with a circle inside of it that has a radius of 6. Therefore, the length of one side of the square is 12. Quantity A asks for the area of the largest triangle that can be drawn inside the square. The largest triangle cuts the square in half diagonally (subsequently creating a $45:45:90$ triangle) and has a height and base of length 12. So the area of the triangle is $\frac{1}{2}$ (12)(12) = 72. Quantity B is asking for the area of the circle with center R. So the area of the circle is $6^2\pi$, or 36π. π is approximately 3, so you know that 36 times 3 is greater than 72. Quantity B is greater.

2. **D**

   There are a lot of variables in this problem, so starting thinking about Plugging In. The variable a has to be the same for each equation. You cannot pick just any number, however, because you must satisfy the equations. When you feel stuck on a problem, start looking at the numbers; remember the math will always work out nicely. Examining the two equations you realize that $158 \times 4 = 632$, so these two numbers are related. So the easiest number to plug in for a is 632. Now you know that $xs = 1$, and $ys = 4$. Since the variable s is the same in both equations, they cancel each other out and you are left with $x = 1$ and $y = 4$. Eliminate (A) and (C). Next, try a FROZEN number such as $a = -632$. In this case, $xs = -1$ and $ys = -4$ or $x = -1$ and $y = -4$. Eliminate (B). The correct answer is (D).

3. **C**

   $135 \div 7 = 19$, remainder 2. $135 \div 19 = 7$, remainder 2. Both Quantity A and Quantity B equal 2.

4. **D**

   Plug In. Let $a = 8$ and $b = 4$. Quantity A can be greater than Quantity B, so eliminate (B) and (C). Now let $a = b = 1$. Quantity A can be equal to Quantity B, so eliminate (A).

5. **B**

   Plug in numbers for a, b, and c. If $a = -2$, $b = 3$, and $c = 4$, then $ac = -8$. Quantity B is greater; eliminate (A) and (C). If $a = 2$, $b = -3$, and $c = -4$, then ac is still negative. Quickly consider different numbers, but realize that Quantity A will always be negative.

6. **D**

   If $|x| = 6$, then $x = 6$, or $x = -6$. If $x = 6$, then $y = 6 + 4 = 10$. The quantities are equal, so you can eliminate choices (A) and (B). If $x = -6$, then $y = -6 + 4 = -2$, and Quantity B is greater. Eliminate (C), and select (D).

7. **B**

   Plug in for the radius, n, and solve for x. Let's make $n = 3$: The area of the base of the cylinder is now 9π, and the circumference of the base is 6π. The ribbon itself is a rectangle, and we now know both its area, which is the same as the area of the base, and its length, which is the same as the circumference of the base. Now we can solve for x, which is the other side of the rectangle: $6\pi x = 9\pi$, so $x = \frac{9\pi}{6\pi}$, or $\frac{3}{2}$. Our value for n is greater than our value for x, so Quantity B is greater.

8. **C**

Remember that median is the number that ends up in the middle of the list when you rewrite the list in numerical order. Find x: The even numbers are 2, 2, 6, 8. Because 2 and 6 are in the middle, find their mean: $\frac{2+6}{2}$ = 4. So, x = 4. Find y: The prime numbers are 2, 2, 3, 5, 7, 13. Remember: 1 is not prime. Because 3 and 5 are in the middle, find their mean: $\frac{3+5}{2}$ = 4. So, y = 4. Find z: The least is 1, and the greatest is 15. The median of 1 and 15 is $\frac{1+15}{2}$ = 8. So, z = 8. For Quantity A, find the median of 2(4), 4, and 8: So, the median of 4, 8, 8 is 8. Quantity B is also 8.

9. **1,625**

Set up a proportion: $\frac{1 \text{ hour}}{500 \text{ gallons}} = \frac{3.25 \text{ hours}}{x \text{ gallons}}$. Cross-multiply to find that x = 500 × 3.25 = 1,625 gallons.

10. **B**

Plug In the Answers, starting with the middle choice. If 120 dogs were sold in March, then 60 cats were sold that month. In April, 240 dogs were sold, along with 180 cats. The total number of dogs and cats sold during those two months is 600, which is too large, so eliminate (C), (D), and (E). Try (B). If there were 100 dogs sold in March, then 50 cats were sold; in April, 200 dogs were sold along with 150 cats. The correct answer is (B) because 100 + 50 + 200 + 150 = 500.

11. **C**

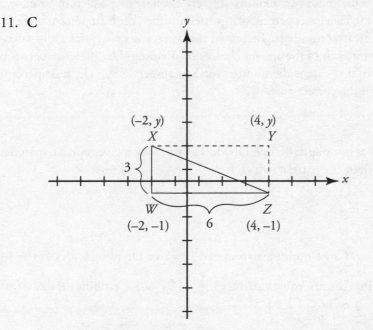

Notice that the length of WZ is 4 – (–2) = 6. If area is 18 = 6 × w, then w is equal to 3. Now you have a right triangle with legs of 3 and 6. Use the Pythagorean theorem: $3^2 + 6^2 = c^2$, or 9 + 36 = c^2. So, $c = \sqrt{45} = \sqrt{9 \times 5} = 3\sqrt{5}$.

12. **E**

Order matters in this problem, so remember you do not divide; you multiply! For the first integer, you have 5 options. For the second, you have 4. For the third, you have 3; 5 × 4 × 3 is 60, which is (E).

13. **D**

The percent increase in the CEO's pay was $\frac{\$50 - \$5}{5} \times 100\% = 900$ percent. The percent decrease in the factory workers' pay was $\frac{\$20 - \$10}{20} \times 100\% = 50$ percent. To find what percent greater 900 percent is than 50 percent, do the following: $\frac{900\% - 50\%}{50\%} \times 100\% = 1,700$ percent, or (D).

14. **D**

Divide the $9.4 million in private donations received by child safety organizations in September 1989 by the 38 organizations operating at the time. The amount is approximately $250,000.

15. **C**

From the line graph, you see that homeless aid groups took in about $300 million in private donations, and animal rights groups about $225 million. The ratio of $300 million to $225 million is 4 to 3.

16. **E**

Identify the markers for September 1989 and October 1989 on the chart. The question is asking about the least percent increase between these two data points. So, begin by evaluating the data points. All of the differences between the data points for these two months are very similar; they all seem to have a difference of approximately 0.5. Because 0.5 is a lesser percent of a greater number, the least percent increase corresponds to the data point with the greatest numbers. Therefore, the correct answer is (E), child safety. Alternatively, find the percent increase for each of the answer choices by dividing the difference between the two points by the original, which in this case is the number for September 1989. The least percent increase is still (E), child safety, which is the correct answer.

17. **D**

This is a pattern problem. The pattern has five digits: 06539. Divide 34 by 5, which gives you a remainder of 4. So the 34th digit will be the fourth in the pattern, which is 3.

18. $\frac{48}{7}$

First, solve for x using the equation $\frac{7y}{2x} = 7$. Cross-multiply to find that $7y = 14x$. Dividing both sides by 14 yields $\frac{1}{2}y = x$. Substitute this expression into the first equation to get $3(\frac{1}{2}y) + 2y = 24$. Combine the like terms to get $\frac{7}{2}y = 24$; multiply both sides by $\frac{2}{7}$ to find $y = \frac{48}{7}$.

19. **C**

Plug In the Answers, which are the possible values of x. Start with (C). Find the average of 6, 8, 10, and 23, which is 11.75, which is in the correct range. Eliminate (A) and (B) because the question asks for the greatest possible value of x. Next, try (D). The average of 6, 8, 10, and 28 is 13, which lies outside of the range. The correct answer is (C).

20. **A**

Plug In! To find the area of quadrilateral *ABDE*, find the area of right $\triangle ABC$ and subtract the area of right $\triangle EDC$. Make $a = 4$ and $b = 2$. Because $AB = BC$, we know that this triangle has a height and base that are both equal to 4. The area of *ABC* is $4 \times 4 \times \dfrac{1}{2} = 8$. The area of *EDC* is $2 \times 2 \times \dfrac{1}{2} = 2$. The area of *ABDE* is $8 - 2 = 6$. Plug in for a and b and find that (A) is the only one that works. Alternatively, to find the area of quadrilateral *ABDE*, find the area of right $\triangle ABC$ and subtract the area of right $\triangle EDC$. Both the base and the height of $\triangle ABC$ are a, so the area equals $\dfrac{1}{2} \times a \times a$, or $\dfrac{a^2}{2}$. Both the base and the height of $\triangle EDC$ are b, so the area equals $\dfrac{1}{2} \times b \times b$, or $\dfrac{b^2}{2}$. Therefore, the area of quadrilateral *ABDE* is $\dfrac{a^2}{2} - \dfrac{b^2}{2}$.

Section 6

1. **original** and **outlandish**

   Try working with the second blank first. The clues are that the fashions were "considered daring" and then "imitated." Starting with the second blank, the sentence suggests that the fashions have changed from what they once were—in other words, daring. *Outlandish* is a good synonym for daring and it makes sense that, in the first blank, the fashions were *original* and then lost their impact because of excess imitation.

2. **diverge**

   Take note of the time transition *at one time inseparable...now,* which indicates that the combined roles in Middle Eastern music are now not inseparable. You need a word that means divide or separate. *Divulge* starts with the proper root, but its meaning is way off. Meanwhile, neither *retreat* nor *retrench* means divide, while *fuse* is the opposite of what you want. *Diverge* is the correct answer.

3. **rebuked, perfidy,** and **expiate**

   Start with the second blank, which must mean something close to an act of "treachery." *Perfidy* means this. Since his contemporaries believed Kazan had committed treachery, they would have "harshly criticized" him, so the first blank means rebuked. For the last blank, he was able to achieve *atonement,* which is what *expiate* means.

4. **soporific**

   The sentence requires you to figure out the effect that "tranquilizers usually have," and this is provided by the clue in the later part of the sentence, when we read that the "abuse of these drugs results in a failure to induce the much-desired sleep." You can infer that the usual effect of tranquilizers is to produce sleep. *Soporific,* which means sleep-inducing, is the correct answer choice. While *sedulous* might remind you of "sedative," it actually means hard-working.

5. **preternatural, preclude,** and **consonant**

The clue for the first blank is "are rejected by modern science in its attempts to find secular insights." Otherworldly interpretations contrast the secular, and the best choice for the first blank is *preternatural*. There would be a paradox only if scientists could hold non-secular beliefs. Therefore, a good word for the second blank is *prevent*, and a good phrase for the last blank would be *in agreement*. *Preclude* is synonymous with *prevent*, and *consonant* is synonymous with *in agreement*, making these the correct answers.

6. **conformity** and **eccentricity**

Try working with the second blank first. The clue is "none of the family members were fearful…of appearing or acting differently from other people." Therefore, find a word for the second blank that means uniqueness. *Eccentricity* fits the bill. Considering the clue, "The Johnson's were not known for their," the two blanks must be opposites. Eliminate *candor* and *vulgarity* based on the clue and the word choice for the second blank, and choose *conformity*.

7. **E**

In the last paragraph, the author discusses the difficulties inherent in measuring intergalactic distances. He notes that scientists use a standard candle in combination with the inverse square law to measure those distances.

8. **C**

The passage states in the third paragraph that brighter objects are closer than dim objects, so eliminate (A). The passage never specifies what scientists know about the age of astronomical objects, so eliminate (B). The first paragraph says that, according to Hubble's law, "objects farther away from Earth are receding faster than those closer." This means that the farther object will travel faster, so (C) is correct.

9. **B**

According to the last line in the paragraph, "By the inverse square law, galaxy B is ten times farther away than galaxy A, assuming, of course, that distance is the only factor affecting brightness." Therefore, if interstellar dust affects the brightness of an object, the brightness of the object is affected, and the distance scientists measure may be inaccurate.

10. **C**

According to the passage, "By the inverse square law, galaxy B is ten times farther away than galaxy A, assuming, of course, that distance is the only factor affecting brightness." Therefore, assuming that all other factors affecting brightness can be known, we can conclude that the brighter of the supernovas will be closer to Earth.

11. **B**

"Prozac lag" is a phenomenon for which there is currently no explanation, but neurogenesis may offer a solution. Choice (A) contradicts this. The passage offers "Prozac lag" as supporting evidence of a new theory, not disproving an old one, as (C) suggests, or disproving a new one, as (D) states. Choice (E) goes too far by discussing "unforeseen effects." Choice (B) is the best option.

12. **However, patients suffering from depression only begin to experience mood elevation weeks after beginning treatment.**

   The second paragraph has five sentences, so this question has five answer choices. For an "unexpected observation," a good place to start would be to check the transition words. The fourth sentence starts with the word "however." While the effects should occur immediately, these don't occur until weeks after starting treatment. The answer is the fourth sentence.

13. **edifying** and **didactic**

   The blank describes Socrates's conversations. The clue is "Socrates's teachings have survived and continue to enlighten seekers of wisdom," so the blank must mean instructional. *Edifying* and *didactic* are the closest in meaning. *Tedious, grating, inspiring,* and *rousing* could all be used to describe Socrates's conversations, but they do not match the clue.

14. **satiate** and **allay**

   You would expect "the colossal meal" to fill someone up, but the sentence says that "failed to…her voracious appetite." Thus, she was not full, and the meal failed to satisfy. *Satiate* and *allay* are the best match. *Cadge* and *mendicate* mean the meal begged her hunger. *Exacerbate* and *provoke* go in the wrong direction.

15. **iridescent** and **pavonine**

   The clue for this sentence is "the lovely rainbows they produce," which suggests that the blank should be filled by a word meaning colorful. Both *iridescent* and *pavonine* mean exactly that. Even if you don't agree that the blank necessarily refers to rainbows of color, the missing word does have to agree with *beautiful* due to the transition word *and*, and none of the other four options does: *Anodyne* means eliminating physical pain, *monocoque* means constructed in one piece, *parietal* mean college-related, and *saturnine* means gloomy.

16. **cauterized** and **inured**

   The clue for this sentence is *callous,* so the blank must mean "used to," or "didn't notice." Choices (B), *cauterized,* and (E), *inured,* mean this. Choice (F) is incorrect because he didn't notice the violence more, but rather noticed it less.

17. **D**

   The conclusion of the argument is that the old formula for Megapower contained natural kiwi extract, while the new formula does not. The evidence is that Tasmania suffered a decrease in its kiwi exports. The assumption is that Megapower is not getting kiwi fruit from Tasmania. Choice (D) strengthens the argument by pointing out that kiwi imports have fallen in the country that produces Megapower, which would reinforce that assumption that the manufacturer is not getting kiwis from Tasmania. Choice (A) would weaken the argument by providing a potential alternate source for kiwi fruit. Choice (C) weakens the argument by providing evidence that the manufacturer of Megapower could be getting kiwi fruit from another source. Choices (B) and (E) are not relevant to the conclusion.

18. **C**

   While the word *promulgated* can take on the meanings given in (A), (B), or (C), within the context of the sentence it is clear that Courbet is taking a stand on what he believes art should be. Therefore, (C) is closest to the correct meaning.

19. **The argument has been made that the painting struck a blow for the independence of the artist, and that since Courbet's work, artists have felt freed from the societal demands placed upon their work.**

While the rest of the passage enumerates Courbet's ideas on painting, only this sentence points to the effect that Courbet's work may have had on other artists when it states that "since Courbet's work artists have felt freed from the societal demands placed on their work."

20. **A**

According to the passage, Courbet broke with convention by "striving to do something strikingly original." Only (A) provides that sense of defying a convention to do something original.

Chapter 20
Practice Test 2

SECTION 1: ISSUE TOPIC

Directions:

You will be given a brief quotation that states or implies an issue of general interest and specific instructions on how to respond to that issue. You will have 30 minutes to plan and compose a response in which you develop a position on the issue according to the specific instructions. A response to any other issue will receive a score of zero.

"Studying foodways—what foods people eat and how they produce, acquire, prepare, and consume them—is the best way to gain deep understanding of a culture."

Write an essay in which you take a position on the statement above. In developing and supporting your position, you should consider ways in which the statement might or might not hold true.

SECTION 2: ARGUMENT TOPIC

Directions:

You will be given a short passage that presents an argument, or an argument to be completed, and specific instructions on how to respond to that passage. You will have 30 minutes to plan and compose a response in which you analyze the passage according to the specific instructions. A response to any other argument will receive a score of zero.

Note that you are NOT being asked to present your own views on the subject. Make sure that you respond to the specific instructions and support your analysis with relevant reasons and/or examples.

Fossil evidence indicates that the blompus—an extremely large, carnivorous land mammal—inhabited the continent of Pentagoria for tens of thousands of years until its sudden decline and ultimate extinction about twelve thousand years ago. Scientists have determined that the extinction coincided with a period of significant climate change and with the arrival of the first humans. Some scholars theorize that the climate change so altered the distribution of plants and animals in the environment that the food chain upon which the blompus depended was irretrievably disrupted. Others contend that predation by humans is the more plausible explanation for the rapid population decline.

Write a response in which you discuss specific evidence that could be used to decide between the proposed explanations above.

SECTION 3: VERBAL REASONING

For questions 1 through 6, select one entry for each blank from the corresponding column of choices. Fill all blanks in the way that best completes the text.

The (i)_____ with which a statement is conveyed is frequently more important to the listener in determining the intended meaning than the actual words (ii)_____ . For example, a compliment, when delivered sarcastically, will be perceived by the receiver as fairly insulting.

Blank (i)	Blank (ii)
inflection	implied
pitch	repudiated
accuracy	utilized

Though a film studio produces works that are (i)_____ and artistic, its priorities often dictate that creativity be (ii)_____ to a secondary position since the creative process can (iii)_____ the organization and hierarchy necessary to running a large company.

Blank (i)	Blank (ii)	Blank (iii)
expressive	compared	respond to
tedious	uplifted	conflict with
tiresome	relegated	coexist with

Science and religion each have core tenets that are considered _____ ; however, because some scientific tenets are in conflict with some religious ones, these tenets cannot all be correct.

historic
axiomatic
disputable
ubiquitous
empirical

Although most preventative medical ointments commonly in use would have (i)_____ an infection, the particular one Helen applied to her sores actually, much to her dismay, (ii)_____ her (iii)_____ .

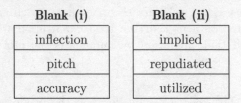

Blank (i)	Blank (ii)	Blank (iii)
surrendered to	contributed to	medicine
exacerbated	detracted from	salve
staved off	disbursed with	affliction

A single (i)_____ remark can easily ruin the career of a politician, so most are trained to avoid such offhand remarks and instead stick to prepared talking points. This training can result in a lack of (ii)_____ , however, and elicit merely (iii)_____ , lukewarm responses from crowds.

Blank (i)	Blank (ii)	Blank (iii)
elated	spontaneity	ardent
glib	equanimity	tepid
pedantic	rigidity	morose

Oscar Wilde's *The Importance of Being Earnest* satirizes the _____ nature of upper crust British society; its characters take trivial concerns seriously while thoughtlessly dismissing important ones.

maladaptive
insincere
unusual
insignificant
shallow

SECTION 3: VERBAL REASONING

For each of Questions 7 to 12, select one answer choice unless otherwise instructed.

Questions 7 through 10 are based on the following reading passage.

In 1798, economist Thomas Robert Malthus stated in his "Essay on the Principle of Population" that "population increases in a geometric ratio, while the means of subsistence increases in an arithmetic ratio." However, Malthus's dire prediction of a precipitous decline in the world's population has not come to pass. The miscalculations in what has come to be known as the Malthus Doctrine are partly due to Malthus's inability to foresee the innovations that allowed vast increases in worldwide wheat production.

In the late nineteenth century, the invention of the tractor staved off a Malthusian disaster. While the first tractors were not particularly powerful, the replacement of animals by machinery meant that land that had been devoted to hay and oats could now be reclaimed for growth of crops for human consumption. Nevertheless, the Malthusian limit might still have been reached if crop yield had not been increased.

A natural way to increase crop yield is to supply the soil with additional nitrogen. In 1909, chemist Fritz Haber succeeded in combining nitrogen and hydrogen to make ammonia, the white powder version of which, when added to the soil, improves wheat production. Haber nitrogen, however, was not widely used until later in the twentieth century, largely due to farmers' resistance to spreading an unnatural substance on their crops. Haber's invention had a further drawback: If applied in incorrect quantities, the wheat crop would grow taller and thicker, eventually toppling over and rotting.

Interestingly, in the late twentieth century the discovery of genetic engineering, which provides a means of increasing rice and maize production, met with equal resistance, this time from the environmental movement. Even without direct genetic engineering, it is likely that science will discover new methods to improve agricultural production.

According to the passage, which of the following is true about Haber nitrogen?

- ○ Haber nitrogen is more effective at increasing the yield of wheat crops than that of maize or oat crops.

- ○ Undesired effects can result from the application of surplus quantities of Haber nitrogen.

- ○ Haber nitrogen was the first non-naturally occurring substance to be applied to crops as fertilizer.

- ○ Haber nitrogen may not be effective if applied at an improper time in wheat's growth cycle.

- ○ Farmers were quick to adopt Haber nitrogen because it made their crops grow taller and thicker.

The passage implies all of the following EXCEPT

- ○ world food production has kept pace with world population growth

- ○ technological innovation is one factor that allowed for an increase in crop production

- ○ farmers are not the only group that has opposed artificial efforts to increase crop yield.

- ○ the Malthusian limit might well have been reached if new methods to increase crop production had not been found

- ○ a Malthusian disaster would have been ensured if it were not for the invention of genetic engineering

SECTION 3: VERBAL REASONING

Which of the following, if true, would best represent Malthus' contention in the first paragraph?

○ By 2040 the world's population increases marginally, and food production keeps pace with demand.

○ By 2040 the world's population decreases marginally, and food production outstrips demand.

○ By 2040 the world's population remains unchanged, and food production declines slightly.

○ By 2040 the world's population has significantly increased, and food production has increased slightly.

○ By 2040 the world's population has significantly decreased, and food production has decreased slightly.

Which of the following most nearly means the word *precipitous*, as used in context?

○ anticipated

○ deliberate

○ gradual

○ risky

○ sharp

Questions 11 through 12 are based on the following reading passage.

The dearth of natural resources on the Australian continent is a problem with which government officials there have long struggled. As long distance travel has become less of an obstacle, the tourism industry has become ever more important to the national economy. Tourism represents more than 10 percent of national export earnings annually, and in less developed regions such as the Western Territory, the percentage is much higher.

Unfortunately, this otherwise rosy prospect has one significant cloud on the horizon. In recent years, there has been a move towards returning some of the land to the Aboriginal people. As Western society and culture have flourished on Australian soil, tribal people have been forced ever farther inland in an attempt to maintain their traditional ways of living, a desire that the government has striven to respect.

One of the central beliefs of the Aboriginal religion is that certain natural formations have spiritual significance and must be treated accordingly. Strict guidelines determine who may visit these sites and at what times. Unfortunately, many of these sites are the very natural wonders tourists flock to see. If non-Aboriginal people are forbidden to visit these natural wonders, many may choose not to vacation in a region that sorely needs the income generated by tourism.

The Australian government has dealt with this dilemma thus far by trying to support both sides. The Aboriginal council is still trying to put an end to such use of certain sites, however, and it remains to be seen whether respect for tradition or economic desires will ultimately triumph.

In the context of the passage, which of the following most closely matches the meaning of the phrase "otherwise rosy prospect has one significant cloud on the horizon"?

○ A colorful sunset is marred by a dark storm cloud.

○ A generally promising future has a potential problem.

○ The view is beautiful but partially blocked.

○ The future of the Aboriginal people is doubtful.

○ Although the situation looks good, in reality it is hopeless.

Consider each of the choices separately and select all that apply.

According to the passage, which of the following is a cause of the current dispute between the Aborigines and the Australian government?

☐ economic hardships in certain regions of the country

☐ increasing dominance by European norms and lifestyles

☐ limited natural resources in most of Australia

SECTION 3: VERBAL REASONING

For questions 13 through 16, select the two answer choices that, when used to complete the sentence, fit the meaning of the sentence as a whole and produce completed sentences that are alike in meaning.

George was a mercurial character; one moment he was optimistic about his prospects, and the next he was _____ .

- [ ] immoral
- [ ] hopeful
- [ ] witty
- [ ] morose
- [ ] dour
- [ ] buoyant

Growing up in a wealthy suburb, she felt quite the _____ as she began her first job as a llama caretaker on a rural farm.

- [ ] tyro
- [ ] concierge
- [ ] agronomist
- [ ] cultivator
- [ ] neophyte
- [ ] curator

William Shakespeare's *Macbeth* was based upon a highly _____ version of events that the playwright wrought from Raphael Holinshed's *Chronicles of England, Scotland, and Ireland*; King Duncan's death at the hand of Macbeth comprises the play's only historical truth.

- [ ] anachronistic
- [ ] effusive
- [ ] embellished
- [ ] prosaic
- [ ] serpentine
- [ ] colored

While comic book artists such as Neal Adams demonstrated a more thorough mastery of human anatomy than did the generation that preceded them, some readers wondered whether the superheroes they drew were really supposed to be so _____ that every detail of their musculatures would be visible through their clothing.

- [ ] thewy
- [ ] sinewy
- [ ] superfluous
- [ ] pneumatic
- [ ] flocculent
- [ ] atrophied

SECTION 3: VERBAL REASONING

For each of Questions 17 to 20, select one answer choice unless otherwise instructed.

Questions 17 through 18 are based on the following reading passage.

One of the most curious structures in cellular biology is the telomere, a length of repeated bases located at the end of every chromosome that, unlike the rest of the DNA strand, carries no useful genetic information. While the telomere seems on the surface to be nothing more than a useless afterthought of DNA, a closer look proves that it is not only important, but also crucial to the functioning of any organism. Indeed, without this mundane structure, every cell division would be a step into senescence, and the onset of old age would begin at birth.

Scientists have found that during cell division not every base of the DNA strand can be replicated, and many, especially those near the end, are lost. If, instead of telomeres, our chromosomes stored valuable genetic information at the end of the DNA strand, then cell division would cause our cells to lose the ability to code for certain information. In fact, many ailments associated with normal old age begin only after the telomere buffer has been exhausted through years of cell division.

Consider each of the choices separately and select all that apply.

Which of the following can reasonably be inferred based on the passage?

☐ An individual who aged faster than the average person may have had a shorter telomere buffer than the average person.

☐ Scientists once believed that telomeres served no useful purpose.

☐ If DNA degradation were absent, then telomeres would be less important to human health.

The passage suggests that if telomere buffers did not exist

○ problems associated with aging would begin earlier in life

○ people would age so rapidly that almost no one would live past childhood

○ cellular senescence would probably be prevented by DNA bases

○ chromosomes would lose the ability to store genetic codes

○ DNA strands would contain only useful genetic information

SECTION 3: VERBAL REASONING

Questions 19 through 20 are based on the following reading passage.

Music education in America emerged in the early eighteenth century out of a desire to ensure that church goers could sing the weekly hymns in tune. In 1721, John Tufts, a minister, penned the first textbook for musical education entitled *An Introduction to the Singing of Psalm Tunes.* Tufts's pedagogical technique relied primarily on rote learning, omitting the reading of music until a student's singing abilities had improved.

In the same year that Tufts's publication emerged, Reverend Thomas Walter published *The Ground and Rules of Music Explained,* which, while also focusing on preparing students to sing religious music, took a note-based approach by teaching students the rudiments of note reading from the onset. The "note versus rote" controversy in music education continued well into the mid-nineteenth century. With no curriculum to guide them, singing school teachers focused on either the rote or note method with little consistency.

The author discusses Walter's pedagogical technique in order to

- ○ suggest that rote learning is superior to note learning

- ○ present a contrast with Tufts's educational technique

- ○ argue that rote learning improves a student's singing ability

- ○ show the origin of Tufts's educational techniques

- ○ show that rote learning was inconsistently practiced

Select the sentence in the passage that best describes the endurance of the tension between pedagogical techniques.

SECTION 4: QUANTITATIVE REASONING

For each of Questions 1 to 8, compare Quantity A and Quantity B, using additional information centered above the two quantities if such information is given. Select one of the four answer choices below each question and fill in the circle to the left of that answer choice.

(A) Quantity A is greater.

(B) Quantity B is greater.

(C) The two quantities are equal.

(D) The relationship cannot be determined from the information given.

A symbol that appears more than once in a question has the same meaning throughout the question.

Quantity A	Quantity B
$\dfrac{98^7}{7^{63}}$	$\dfrac{2^7}{7^{49}}$

○ Quantity A is greater.

○ Quantity B is greater.

○ The two quantities are equal.

○ The relationship cannot be determined from the information given.

5 is r percent of 25.

s is 25 percent of 60.

Quantity A	Quantity B
r	s

○ Quantity A is greater.

○ Quantity B is greater.

○ The two quantities are equal.

○ The relationship cannot be determined from the information given.

g and h are positive integers such that the value of g is twice the value of h.

Quantity A	Quantity B
The ratio of g to 1	The ratio of 1 to h

○ Quantity A is greater.

○ Quantity B is greater.

○ The two quantities are equal.

○ The relationship cannot be determined from the information given.

Quantity A	Quantity B
The average (arithmetic mean) of 67, 78, x, and 101	The average (arithmetic mean) of 66, 79, x, and 102

○ Quantity A is greater.

○ Quantity B is greater.

○ The two quantities are equal.

○ The relationship cannot be determined from the information given.

In a certain country the total weight of recycled newspapers increases annually by 0.79 million tons.

Quantity A	Quantity B
The percent increase in the weight of recycled newspapers in 1989 over 1988	The percent increase in the weight of recycled newspapers in 1990 over 1989

○ Quantity A is greater.

○ Quantity B is greater.

○ The two quantities are equal.

○ The relationship cannot be determined from the information given.

SECTION 4: QUANTITATIVE REASONING

Quantity A	**Quantity B**
The total weight of m peanuts with a weight of $n + 3$ mg each	The total weight of n almonds with a weight of $m + 3$ mg each

○ Quantity A is greater.

○ Quantity B is greater.

○ The two quantities are equal.

○ The relationship cannot be determined from the information given.

Quantity A	**Quantity B**
$5^{27}(575)$	$5^{28}(115)$

○ Quantity A is greater.

○ Quantity B is greater.

○ The two quantities are equal.

○ The relationship cannot be determined from the information given.

Alejandro has a six-sided die with faces numbered 1 through 6. He rolls the die twice.

Quantity A	**Quantity B**
The probability that he rolls two even numbers	The probability that neither number rolled is a multiple of 3

○ Quantity A is greater.

○ Quantity B is greater.

○ The two quantities are equal.

○ The relationship cannot be determined from the information given.

If $4(r - s) = -2$, then what is r, in terms of s ?

○ $\dfrac{-s}{2}$

○ $s - \dfrac{1}{2}$

○ $s - \dfrac{3}{2}$

○ $s + 2$

○ $2s$

At Tenderloin Pharmaceuticals, 25 percent of the employees take the subway to work. Among those who ride the subway, 42 percent transfer from one subway line to another during their commutes, and the rest do not transfer. What percent of all employees transfer lines?

 percent

Click on the answer box and type in a number. Backspace to erase.

$$\frac{\left(a + \dfrac{b}{c}\right)}{\left(\dfrac{d}{e}\right)}$$

If the value of the expression above is to be halved by doubling exactly one of a, b, c, d, or e, which should be doubled?

○ a

○ b

○ c

○ d

○ e

SECTION 4: QUANTITATIVE REASONING

$$\left(\sqrt{5}-\sqrt{3}\right)^2 =$$

- ○ $2-2\sqrt{15}$
- ○ $2-\sqrt{15}$
- ○ $8-2\sqrt{15}$
- ○ 2
- ○ $8-2\sqrt{5}$

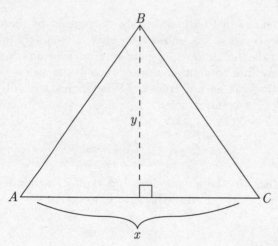

$\triangle ABC$ has an area of 108 cm². If both x and y are integers, which of the following could be the value of x ?

Indicate all such values.

- ☐ 4
- ☐ 5
- ☐ 6
- ☐ 8
- ☐ 9

Questions 14 through 16 refer to the following graphs.

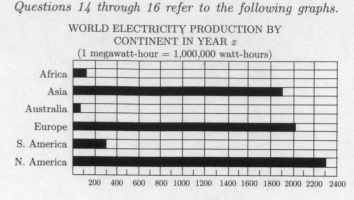

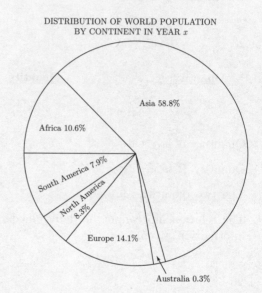

In Year x, on which other continent did electricity production most closely equal electricity production in Europe?

- ○ Africa
- ○ Asia
- ○ Australia
- ○ South America
- ○ North America

In Year x, for which continent was the ratio of electricity production to percent of population the greatest?

○ Africa

○ Asia

○ South America

○ Europe

○ North America

In Year x, if South America had a population of approximately 368 million, what was the approximate population, in millions, of Africa?

○ 494

○ 470

○ 274

○ 150

○ 39

The average (arithmetic mean) weight of 5 crates is 250 pounds. The 2 lightest crates weigh between 200 and 205 pounds each, inclusive, and the 2 heaviest crates weigh between 300 and 310 pounds each, inclusive. If the weight of the fifth crate is x pounds, then x is expressed by which of the following?

○ $220 \leq x \leq 250$

○ $230 \leq x \leq 260$

○ $240 \leq x \leq 270$

○ $250 \leq x \leq 270$

○ $260 \leq x \leq 280$

In a certain sequence, s_1, $s_2 \ldots s_x$ if $s_1 = 2$, $s_2 = 2$, $s_3 = 2$, and for $x \geq 4$, $s_x = 2s_{x-1} + s_{x-2}$, what is the value of s_6?

○ 30

○ 34

○ 37

○ 38

○ 40

Y is a point on line segment XZ such that $XY = \dfrac{1}{2} XZ$. If the length of YZ is $4a + 6$, and the length of XZ is 68, then $a =$

Click on the answer box and type in a number.
Backspace to erase.

Talk show host Ralph Burke has exactly one guest on his show each day, and Burke's show airs every Monday through Friday. Burke always schedules politicians on Mondays and Wednesdays, actors on Tuesdays and athletes on Thursdays, but can have a guest of any one of these three kinds on Friday. No guest appears more than once per week on Burke's show. If Burke has five politicians, three actors and six athletes he could invite, and if no politician is also an actor or an athlete and no actor is also an athlete, how many different schedules of guests from Monday to Friday could Burke create?

○ 30

○ 1,200

○ 3,600

○ 4,500

○ 6,300

SECTION 5: VERBAL REASONING

For questions 1 through 6, select one entry for each blank from the corresponding column of choices. Fill all blanks in the way that best completes the text.

Despite what _____ philosophies of child-rearing suggest, there is no imperative that the day-to-day action of raising a child be simple, unambiguous, and unchanging—no requirement, in other words, ensures that life follows philosophy.

inexact
aggressive
random
shameless
systematic

All the greatest chess players in the world know that it is folly to be (i) _____ when facing a formidable opponent, as stubbornness will almost surely lead to mistakes that force a player to (ii) _____ to the prevailing strategy of his or her opponent.

Blank (i)	Blank (ii)
finicky	capitulate
obdurate	dissent
vituperative	repudiate

The novel emphasizes the innate (i) _____ of all humans, showing how each and every character within the narrative is, ultimately, (ii) _____ . This motif becomes tiresome due to its (iii) _____ , however, as character after character is bribed, either explicitly or implicitly, into giving up his or her supposedly cherished beliefs.

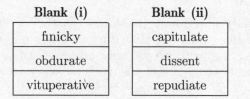

Blank (i)	Blank (ii)	Blank (iii)
zealousness	adroit	redundancy
corruptibility	cunning	triviality
optimism	venal	subtlety

Although pirating software, such as borrowing a friend's copy of an installation CD or downloading software from unapproved sources is (i) _____ , many people continue to do so (ii) _____ , almost as if they were unaware that such acts amount to theft.

Blank (i)	Blank (ii)
uncommon	savagely
illegal	sensibly
difficult	unabashedly

Having squandered his life's savings on unprofitable business ventures, the _____ entrepreneur was forced to live in squalor.

former
unlikely
insolvent
perturbed
eccentric

Teachers of composition urge their students to (i) _____ in their writing and instead use clear, simple language. Why use a (ii) _____ vocabulary when (iii) _____ phrasing conveys one's meaning so much more effectively?

Blank (i)	Blank (ii)	Blank (iii)
exscind obloquy	recreant	an arcane
eschew obfuscation	redolent	a limpid
evince ossification	recondite	a droll

SECTION 5: VERBAL REASONING

For each of Questions 7 to 11, select one answer choice unless otherwise instructed.

Questions 7 through 8 are based on the following reading passage.

Neurobiologists have never questioned that axon malfunction plays a role in neurological disorders, but the nature of the relationship has been a matter of speculation. George Bartzokis's neurological research at UCLA suggests that many previously poorly understood disorders such as Alzheimer's disease may be explained by examining the role of the chemical compound myelin.

Myelin is produced by oligodendrocyte cells as a protective sheathing for axons within the nervous system. As humans mature and their neurochemistries grow more complex, oligodendrocyte cells produce increasing amounts of myelin to protect the byzantine circuitry inside our nervous systems. An apt comparison may be to the plastic insulation around copper wires. Bereft of myelin, certain areas of the brain may be left vulnerable to short circuiting, resulting in such disorders as ADHD, schizophrenia, and autism.

Consider each of the choices separately and select all that apply.

It can be inferred from the passage that the author would be most likely to agree with which of the following statements regarding the role of myelin?

- ☐ The levels of myelin in the brain can contribute to the neurological health of individuals.

- ☐ Increasing the levels of myelin in the brain can reverse the effects of neurological damage.

- ☐ The levels of myelin in the brain are not fixed throughout the lifetime of an individual.

In the context in which it appears, byzantine most nearly means

- ○ devious
- ○ intricate
- ○ mature
- ○ beautiful
- ○ electronic

The cost of operating many small college administrative offices is significantly reduced when the college replaces its heavily compensated administrative assistants with part-time work-study students whose earnings are partially subsidized by the government. Therefore, large universities should follow suit, as they will see greater financial benefits than do small colleges.

In the above argument it is assumed that

- ○ replacing administrative assistants with work-study students is more cost-effective for small colleges than for large universities

- ○ large universities usually depend upon small colleges for development of money-saving strategies

- ○ the financial gains realized by large universities would not be as great were they to use non-work-study students in place of the administrative assistants

- ○ work-study students at large universities could feasibly fulfill a similar or greater proportion of administrative assistant jobs than what they could at small colleges

- ○ the smaller the college or university, the easier it is for that college or university to control costs

SECTION 5: VERBAL REASONING

Questions 10 through 11 are based on the following reading passage.

The nineteenth century marked a revolutionary change in the way wealth was perceived in England. As landed wealth gave way to monied wealth, investments became increasingly speculative.

A popular investment vehicle was the three-percent consol which took its name from the fact that it paid three pounds on a hundred pound investment. The drawback to the consol was that once issued, there was no easy way for the government to buy back the debt. To address the problem, the British government instituted a sinking fund, using tax revenue to buy back the bonds in the open market. The fact that the consol had no fixed maturity date ensured that any change in interest rate was fully reflected in the capital value of the bond. The often wild fluctuation of interest rates ensured the consol's popularity with speculative traders.

Which of the following best describes the relationship of the first paragraph of the passage to the passage as a whole?

○ It provides a generalization which is later supported in the passage.

○ It provides an antithesis to the author's main argument.

○ It briefly compares two different investment strategies.

○ It explains an investment vehicle that is later examined in greater detail.

○ It provides a historical framework by which the nature of the nineteenth-century investor can more easily be understood.

In the second paragraph, select the sentence that describes a solution to a problem.

For questions 12 through 15, select the two answer choices that, when used to complete the sentence, fit the meaning of the sentence as a whole and produce completed sentences that are alike in meaning.

Owing to a combination of its proximity and _____ atmosphere, Mars is the only planet in our solar system whose surface details can be discerned from Earth.

☐ viscous

☐ ossified

☐ rarefied

☐ estimable

☐ copious

☐ meager

Using the hardships of the Joad family as a model, John Steinbeck's *The Grapes of Wrath* effectively demonstrated how one clan's struggles epitomized the _____ experienced by an entire country.

☐ reticence

☐ adversity

☐ repudiation

☐ quiescence

☐ verisimilitude

☐ tribulation

SECTION 5: VERBAL REASONING

The Mayan pyramid of Kukulkan is more than just _____ edifice; this imposing structure was built to create a chirping echo whenever people clap their hands on the staircase. This echo sounds just like the chirp of the Quetzal, a bird which is sacred in the Mayan culture.

- ☐ a venerable
- ☐ a humble
- ☐ a beguiling
- ☐ an august
- ☐ a specious
- ☐ a prosaic

Some wealthy city-dwellers become enchanted with the prospect of trading their hectic schedules for a bucolic life in the countryside, and they buy property with a pleasant view of farmland—only to find the stench of the livestock so _____ that they move back to the city.

- ☐ bovine
- ☐ pastoral
- ☐ noisome
- ☐ atavistic
- ☐ olfactory
- ☐ mephitic

For each of Questions 16 to 20, select one answer choice unless otherwise instructed.
Questions 16 through 18 are based on the following reading passage.

Often the most influential developments initially appear to be of minor significance. Consider the development of the basic stirrup for example. Without stirrups horse and rider are, in terms of force, separate entities; lances can be used from horseback, but only by throwing or stabbing, and mounted warriors gain only height and mobility. In medieval times, a lance couched under the rider's arm, unifying the force of rider and weapon, would throw its wielder backwards off the horse at impact. Stirrups unify lance, rider, and horse into a force capable of unprecedented violence. This development left unusually clear archaeological markers: With lethality assured, lances evolved barbs meant to slow progress after impact, lest the weight of body pull rider from horse. The change presaged the dominance of mounted combat, and increasingly expensive equipment destroyed the venerable ideal of freeman warriors. New technology demanded military aristocracy, and chivalric culture bore its marks for a millennium.

The primary purpose of the passage is to

- ○ discuss the influence of a recent archeological discovery
- ○ explore the societal significance of a technological innovation
- ○ assess the state of research in a given field
- ○ lament the destruction of certain social ideals
- ○ explicate the physics of combat artillery

SECTION 5: VERBAL REASONING

It can be inferred from the passage that the author believes which of the following about innovations in military technology?

○ Their study merits additional research.

○ They had more lasting influence than did those of the ancient world.

○ Most of them had equally far-reaching repercussions.

○ Prior to their application, the military value of horses was considered insignificant.

○ Many of them are archaeologically ambiguous.

Select the sentence in the passage in which the author cites the physical effects of a technological innovation being discussed as an example of a previous generalization.

Questions 19 through 20 are based on the following reading passage.

Few mathematical constructs seem as conceptually simple as that of randomness. According to the traditional definition, a number is random if it is chosen purely as the result of a probabilistic mechanism such as the roll of a fair die. In their groundbreaking work regarding complexity and the limitations of formal systems, mathematicians Gregory Chaitin and A.N. Kolmogorov force us to consider this last claim more closely.

Consider two possible outcomes of throwing a fair die three times: first, 1, 6, and 2; second 3, 3, and 3. Now let us construct two three-member sets based on the results. Though the first set—{1,6,2}—intuitively seems more random than the second—{3,3,3}, they are each as likely to occur, and thus according to the accepted definition, must be considered equally random. This unwelcome result prompts Chaitin and Kolmogorov to suggest the need for a new standard of randomness, one that relies on the internal coherence of the set as opposed to its origin.

Which of the following best describes the organization of the passage as whole?

○ A concept is introduced; a traditional definition is put forward; a thought experiment is described; a new definition is proposed; the traditional definition is amended as a result.

○ A concept is introduced; a traditional definition is supported by authorities; a thought experiment is described; the implications of the experiment are discussed.

○ A concept is introduced; a traditional definition is considered and rejected; a thought experiment is described; a new definition is proposed.

○ A concept is introduced; a traditional definition is called into question; a thought experiment is described; the implications of the experiment are discussed.

○ A concept is introduced; authorities are called in to reevaluate a definition; a thought experiment is described; the implications of the experiment are considered and rejected.

Consider each of the choices separately and select all that apply.

Which of the following is an inference made in the passage above?

☐ The results of the same probabilistic mechanism will each be as likely as the other to occur.

☐ According to the traditional definition of randomness, two numbers should be considered equally random if they result from the same probabilistic mechanism.

☐ Different probabilistic mechanisms are likely to result in similar outcomes.

NO TEST MATERIAL ON THIS PAGE

SECTION 6: QUANTITATIVE REASONING

For each of Questions 1 to 7, compare Quantity A and Quantity B, using additional information centered above the two quantities if such information is given. Select one of the four answer choices below each question and fill in the circle to the left of that answer choice.

(A) Quantity A is greater.
(B) Quantity B is greater.
(C) The two quantities are equal.
(D) The relationship cannot be determined from the information given.

A symbol that appears more than once in a question has the same meaning throughout the question.

$$\frac{x}{6} + 2 = \frac{6}{2}$$

$$\frac{y}{3} + 2 = \frac{9}{3}$$

Quantity A	Quantity B
$\dfrac{(x-1)}{y}$	$\dfrac{(y-1)}{x}$

○ Quantity A is greater.

○ Quantity B is greater.

○ The two quantities are equal.

○ The relationship cannot be determined from the information given.

Quantity A	Quantity B
The distance that Bob drives in 3 hours at an average speed of 44 miles per hour	The distance that Inez drives in 2 hours and 30 minutes at an average speed of 50 miles per hour

○ Quantity A is greater.

○ Quantity B is greater.

○ The two quantities are equal.

○ The relationship cannot be determined from the information given.

The height of a rectangular solid is increased by p percent, its depth is decreased by p percent and its width is unchanged.

Quantity A	Quantity B
The volume of the new rectangular solid if $p = 20$	The volume of the new rectangular solid if $p = 40$

○ Quantity A is greater.

○ Quantity B is greater.

○ The two quantities are equal.

○ The relationship cannot be determined from the information given.

In $\triangle ABC$, $AB = AC$

Quantity A	Quantity B
The sum of the degree measures of angle B and angle C	90

○ Quantity A is greater.

○ Quantity B is greater.

○ The two quantities are equal.

○ The relationship cannot be determined from the information given.

12.5 percent of k is 80.
k is y percent of 80.

Quantity A	Quantity B
y	650

○ Quantity A is greater.

○ Quantity B is greater.

○ The two quantities are equal.

○ The relationship cannot be determined from the information given.

SECTION 6: QUANTITATIVE REASONING

Set $P = \{a, b, c, d, e, f, g\}$

Set $Q = \{a, b, c, d, e, f\}$

a, b, c, d, e, f, and g are distinct integers

Quantity A	**Quantity B**
Range of Set P	Range of Set Q

○ Quantity A is greater.

○ Quantity B is greater.

○ The two quantities are equal.

○ The relationship cannot be determined from the information given.

Sequence F is defined as $F_n = F_{(n-1)} + 3$ and $F_1 = 10$.

Quantity A	**Quantity B**
The sum of F_4 through F_{10}	The sum of F_6 through F_{11}

○ Quantity A is greater.

○ Quantity B is greater.

○ The two quantities are equal.

○ The relationship cannot be determined from the information given.

A number, n, is multiplied by 6 and the product is increased by 24. Finally, the entire quantity is divided by 3. Which of the following is an expression for these operations, in terms of n ?

○ $\dfrac{n}{3} + 8$

○ $\dfrac{n + 24}{2}$

○ $2n + 8$

○ $3n + 24$

○ $16n$

The average (arithmetic mean) of a and b is 10, and the average of c and d is 7. If the average of a, b, and c is 8, what is the value of d ?

Click on the answer box and type in a number. Backspace to erase.

In the xy-plane, square $ABCD$ has vertices at A (3, 7), B (3, 12), C (8, x), D (8, y). What is the area of $ABCD$?

○ 16

○ 20

○ 25

○ 30

○ 36

Houses Sold in July		
Week	Peter	Dylan
Week 1	4	9
Week 2	6	3
Week 3	10	10
Week 4	4	2

The table above shows the number of houses sold per week for the month of July by two real estate agents, Peter and Dylan. What is the difference between the median number of houses sold per week by Dylan and the median number of houses sold per week by Peter?

○ 0

○ 1

○ 2

○ 5

○ 6

SECTION 6: QUANTITATIVE REASONING

At Flo's Pancake House, pancakes can be ordered with any of six possible toppings. If no toppings are repeated, how many different ways are there to order pancakes with three toppings?

- ○ 20
- ○ 40
- ○ 54
- ○ 120
- ○ 720

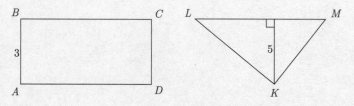

The area of triangle *KLM* is equal to the area of rectangle *ABCD*. If the perimeter of *ABCD* is 16, what is the length of *LM* ?

- ○ $\dfrac{3}{2}$
- ○ 3
- ○ $\dfrac{16}{5}$
- ○ 5
- ○ 6

Questions 14 through 16 refer to the following graph.

TELEVISION RATINGS* IN THE UNITED STATES
1980–1987

*Ratings equal the percent of television households in the United States that viewed the program.

For how many of the years shown did the ratings for Program *y* increase over the ratings for Program *y* in the previous year?

- ○ Two
- ○ Three
- ○ Four
- ○ Five
- ○ Six

In 1995, there were 95 million television households in the United States. In 1983, if the number of television households was 80 percent of the number of television households in 1995, then approximately how many television households, in millions, viewed Program y in 1983 ?

○ 80

○ 76

○ 15

○ 12

○ 10

If there were 20 million television households in the United States in 1983, then the number of viewers of Program x is how much greater than the number of viewers of Program y in 1983 ?

Click on the answer box and type in a number.
Backspace to erase.

Each of the 576 houses in Tenantville is owned by one of the following landlords: Matt, Gavin, Angela, or Susan. Matt and Angela together own twice as many houses as Gavin and Susan own. If Gavin owns 100 more houses than Susan owns, and Matt owns 100 more houses than Angela owns, how many houses does Susan own?

○　46

○　142

○　146

○　192

○　242

One-fourth of the cars that an automobile manufacturer produces are sports cars, and the rest are sedans. If one-fifth of the cars that the manufacturer produces are red and one-third of the sports cars are red, then what fraction of the sedans is red?

Click on each box and type in a number.
Backspace to erase.

A candy jar has 4 lime, 10 cherry, 8 orange, and x grape candies. If Tom selects a candy from the jar at random and the probability that he selects an orange candy is greater than 20 percent, which of the following could be the value of x ?

Indicate all such values.

☐ 10

☐ 14

☐ 18

☐ 22

☐ 24

☐ 28

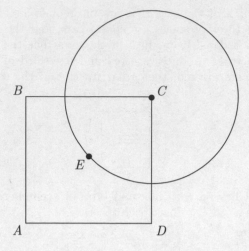

Square $ABCD$ and a circle with center C intersect as shown. If point E is the center of $ABCD$ and if the radius of circle C is k, then what is the area of $ABCD$, in terms of k ?

○ $\dfrac{k^2}{2\pi}$

○ $\dfrac{\pi k^2}{2}$

○ πk^2

○ k^2

○ $2k^2$

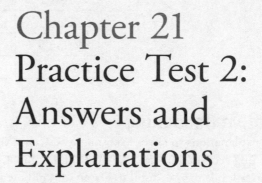

Chapter 21
Practice Test 2:
Answers and
Explanations

INTERPRETING YOUR RESULTS

After you check your answers on the following pages, fill out this sheet to interpret your results.

Analytical Writing

To evaluate your performance on the Analytical Writing sections, compare your response to the advice and samples in the Analytical Writing chapter.

Verbal Reasoning

Refer to the explanations to check your answers. Count the number of questions you got correct in each Verbal Reasoning section, and calculate the total number correct. Find the section of the Interpretive Guide (below) that corresponds to your total to get an idea of how your performance compares to that of other test takers.

Test 2	# Correct
Section 3	
Section 5	
Total	

Quantitative Reasoning

Refer to the explanations to check your answers. Count the number of questions you got correct in each Quantitative Reasoning section, and calculate the total number correct. Find the section of the Interpretive Guide (below) that corresponds to your total to get an idea of how your performance compares to that of other test takers.

Test 2	# Correct
Section 4	
Section 6	
Total	

Interpretive Guide

The table below provides a guide for interpreting your performance based on the number of questions you got correct in each subject.

Subject	Above Average	Average	Below Average
Verbal Reasoning	30–40	22–29	1–21
Quantitative Reasoning	33–40	24–32	1–23

Section 3

1. **inflection** and **utilized**

   For the first blank, the transition "more important" tells you to change direction from "actual words." Also, *sarcastically* is an example of tone. Look for a choice that means tone. *Inflection* fits tone. *Pitch* is nonverbal, but it does not match the example of sarcastically. *Accuracy* does not fit. For the second blank, look for a word that means *conveyed* or *spoken*. *Utilized* is the best match. *Implied* and *repudiated* don't fit.

2. **expressive, relegated,** and **conflict with**

   Try working with the first blank first. The clue is *artistic*, and the transition *and* indicates the first blank should be a word that is the same as artistic. *Expressive* is the best choice; neither *tedious* nor *tiresome* works. *Though* changes the direction of the sentence—though the studio likes the creative/artistic aspect, something negative must be happening to creativity—it's brought down to a secondary position. Eliminate *uplifted* and *compared* for blank (ii) because they are not negative, and choose *relegated*. Turning to the third blank, "organization and hierarchy" are in opposition to *creativity*, so *conflict with* makes the most sense.

3. **axiomatic**

   You are given the clue that the beliefs "are in conflict" and "cannot all be correct." Therefore, whatever goes into the blank must be synonymous with *correct* or something we can infer correctness from. The correct answer is *axiomatic*, which means self-evident or universally true. *Disputable* is the opposite of what the sentence requires, and *ubiquitous* and *historic* are not synonymous with self-evident. Although *empirical*, meaning derived from observation, might fit science, it is not a good fit for religion.

4. **staved off, contributed to,** and **affliction**

   The clue "Although most preventative medical ointments commonly in use" tells you that most ointments would prevent an infection, but the one Helen used did not. Recycle the clue, and put a word that means prevent in the first blank; *staved off* is the best match. Work with the second and third blanks together. The ointment did not prevent an infection, and the clue "much to her dismay" tells you that something bad happened. The only pair that makes sense together is *contributed to* and *affliction* because they tell you that the ointment made her problem worse.

5. **glib, spontaneity,** and **tepid**

   For the first blank, the clue is *offhand remarks*, so the blank means something like "offhand." *Glib*, which means "superficial or showing a lack of concern," is the closest match for this. Sticking to *prepared talking points* can result in a lack of "excitement" or "naturalness," which *spontaneity* matches. For the last blank, you know the crowd's responses are *lukewarm*, so the answer for that blank is *tepid*.

6. **shallow**

   The clue is the entire clause that follows the semicolon: "its characters take trivial concerns seriously while thoughtlessly dismissing important ones." Look for a word that means superficial or petty to go in the blank. The only one that fits is *shallow*.

7. **B**

The third paragraph states that if incorrect quantities of Haber nitrogen were applied, "the wheat crop would grow taller and thicker, eventually toppling over and rotting." Losing a crop would be an undesirable effect, making (B) the correct answer. Eliminate (A) because the passage doesn't compare the effects of Haber nitrogen on different kinds of crops. The passage doesn't provide any information to support (C) and (D). Choice (E) contradicts the passage, which says the farmers were wary of the substance.

8. **E**

According to the first paragraph, there has been no sharp decline in the world's population and, therefore, we can surmise that food production has been sufficient to allow for the existing population growth, as in (A). In the second paragraph, the author mentions the invention of the tractor as one of the factors that allowed more crops to be grown for human consumption. This reflects the technological innovation in (B). In the last paragraph, the author notes that the environmental movement has opposed efforts at genetic engineering. Thus, (C) is implied as well. The author notes that increases in crop production through the invention of the tractor and ammonia prevented Malthus's predictions from being realized, and this rules out (D). The extent of the impact of genetic engineering is not clear. We don't know that a Malthusian disaster would have been a *certainty* without genetic engineering. Therefore, the correct answer is (E) because it is not implied.

9. **D**

The first paragraph states that Malthus believed that "population increases in a geometric ratio, while the means of subsistence increases in an arithmetic ratio." More simply put, Malthus argued that population growth happens at a significantly faster rate than food production. Only (D) demonstrates this.

10. **E**

The first paragraph presents Malthus's prediction about what would happen if population growth were to outstrip food production. If there were too many people and not enough food, you would expect a significant or rapid population decline. Look for a word to replace *precipitous* that is similar to *significant* or *rapid*. *Sharp*, (E), is the best word.

11. **B**

The "rosy prospect" refers to the previous paragraph's discussion of the booming tourism industry in Australia, which implies a positive future, and the "cloud on the horizon" refers to the conflict between the rights of the Aborigines and the need for the money from tourism, a potential problem. Choice (A) incorrectly interprets the quote as referring to a literal *horizon and prospect*. Choice (C) is also too literal, taking *prospect* to mean view. Choice (D) is incorrect because, although this may be true based on later information in the passage, it is not an accurate interpretation of this phrase. Choice (E) is too strong because the future is described as generally good, not hopeless.

12. **A, B, and C**

All three statements are given as sources of the conflict. Choice (A), economic hardships, is mentioned in the third paragraph. Due to financial difficulties, many regions are unwilling to give up the income derived from tourists visiting Aboriginal lands. Choice (B) is discussed in the second paragraph. The expansion of Western culture is the reason that the Aborigines have moved inland and abandoned other sacred sites. Choice (C) is mentioned in the first sentence. Tourism is described as particularly important due to the "dearth of natural resources."

13. **morose** and **dour**

   The first part of the clue is "mercurial character," which means George's moods change frequently. The second part of the clue is "one moment he was optimistic about his prospects," and the transition is *the next he was.* Thus, the blank should be the opposite of optimistic; look for words that mean pessimistic. *Morose* and *dour* are both similar to pessimistic. *Hopeful* and *buoyant* have the opposite meaning, and *witty* and *immoral* are not related.

14. **tyro** and **neophyte**

   The clue is that she "began her first job." Also, the contrast of "wealthy suburb" and "llama caretaker on a rural farm" suggests that she'd feel out of place or lacking in experience at her first job. Look for words that mean beginner. *Tyro* and *neophyte* are the only words that mean beginner. *Agronomist* and *cultivator* are traps for people who focused too heavily on the farm. *Concierge* and *curator* are traps for people who focused too heavily on *caretaker.*

15. **embellished** and **colored**

   The clue "King Duncan's death at the hand of Macbeth comprises the play's only historical truth" tells you that the version of events related in Macbeth was not very accurate. Does *anachronistic* mean inaccurate? No; cross it out. What about *effusive*? No. In contrast, *embellished* works well, but *prosaic* and *serpentine* do not. Finally, *colored*—which, like embellished, means *misrepresented* or *distorted*—fits the blank nicely.

16. **thewy** and **sinewy**

   The word that goes into the blank describes superheroes, of whom the clue phrase states that "every detail of their musculatures would be visible through their clothing." Clearly, something like *muscular* is called for, and both *thewy* and *sinewy* fit the bill. The other four words don't fit: *Superfluous* means unnecessary, *pneumatic* means full of air, *flocculent* means covered in wool, and *atrophied* means shriveled due to disuse.

17. **A and C**

   Choice (A) is correct because the passage states that "...without this mundane structure, every cell division would be a step into senescence, and the onset of old age would begin at birth." Choice (B) is not correct because we have no information about what scientists used to think about telomeres. Choice (C) is correct because we are told that one function of telomeres is to mitigate the loss of DNA bases. If no bases are lost, then this role is not important any more.

18. **A**

   The first paragraph says that without telomere buffers "every cell division would be a step into senescence, and the onset of old age would begin at birth," and the last sentence of the passage states that "many ailments associated with normal old age begin only after the telomere buffer has been exhausted through years of cell division." If the protection offered by the buffers didn't exist, you could expect problems related to aging to start sooner, as (A) suggests. Choice (B) goes too far; though the passage speaks on the onset of old age at birth, we can't be sure that almost no one would live past childhood. The passage provides no support for (C), (D), or (E).

19. **B**

The passage as a whole provides a short history of two types of early musical education, the rote method and the note method. Nowhere in the passage does the author come out in favor of either method, thereby ruling out (A) and (C). Given that Reverend Walter taught music by the note method he developed, (D) doesn't make sense. While it is true that rote learning was inconsistently practiced, as (E) states, this does not answer the question.

20. **The "note versus rote" controversy in music education continued well into the mid-nineteenth century.**

The use of the word "controversy" in the final paragraph is the only indication the author gives that the decision between "note" or "rote" as a musical learning technique was in any way contentious.

Section 4

1. **C**

The Quantities have numbers with great exponents and none of the exponent rules can be applied, so look for a way to factor. In Quantity A, factor 98^7 into its prime factors. The prime factors of 98 are $2 \times 7 \times 7$, so 98^7 can be rewritten as $(2 \times 7^2)^7$. Use the Power-Multiply rule to combine the exponents and simplify to $2^7 \times 7^{14}$. Quantity A can be rewritten as $\dfrac{2^7 \times 7^{14}}{7^{63}}$. Use the Divide-Subtract rule to combine the exponents with base 7 to find that $\dfrac{2^7 \times 7^{14}}{7^{63}} = \dfrac{2^7}{7^{49}}$. Therefore, the quantities are equal. The correct answer is (C).

2. **A**

Translate and solve each expression. The expression "5 is r percent of 25" becomes $5 = \dfrac{r}{100} \times 25$. So, $r = 20$. The expression "s is 25 percent of 60" becomes $s = \dfrac{25}{100} \times 60$. So, $s = 15$, and Quantity A is greater.

3. **A**

Plug In for this question. Let $h = 3$, which makes $g = 6$. Quantity A equals $\dfrac{6}{1} = 6$ and Quantity B equals $\dfrac{1}{3}$. Quantity A can be greater than Quantity B, so eliminate answer choices (B) and (C). Because g and h are positive integers, Quantity A will always be greater than 1 and Quantity B will always be less than or equal to 1. Quantity A will always be greater than Quantity B.

4. **B**

The average is the sum divided by the number of elements. Because three elements make up both averages, you can simply compare the sum of each set. $67 + 78 + 101 + x = 246 + x$, and $66 + 79 + 102 + x = 247 + x$. Thus, Quantity B is greater.

5. **A**

Plug In! Say there were 10 million tons in 1988. The percent increase was $\dfrac{0.79}{10}$. Then in 1989 there were 10.79 tons, so the percent increase from 1989 to 1990 was $\dfrac{0.79}{10.79}$. Quantity A must be greater.

6. **D**

Plug In. Make $m = 2$ and $n = 3$. For Quantity A, the weight of 2 peanuts at $3 + 3$ mg each is $2 \times 6 = 12$ mg. For Quantity B, the weight of 3 almonds at $2 + 3$ mg each is $3 \times 5 = 15$ mg. Eliminate (A) and (C). Plug In again to see if you can get a different result. Keep $m = 2$, and change n to 2. For Quantity A, the weight of two peanuts at $2 + 3$ mg each is $2 \times 5 = 10$ mg. For Quantity B, the weight of two almonds at $2 + 3$ mg each is $2 \times 5 = 10$ mg. Eliminate (B), and choose (D).

7. **C**

Remember, when you have large exponents, try to break them down into their prime factors. You can rewrite Quantity A as $5^{27}(5)(115)$, or $5^{28}(115)$. The quantities are equal.

8. **B**

For Quantity A, there are three ways to get an even number (these are 2, 4, 6). So, the probability of "rolling an even" and then "rolling an even" is $\frac{3}{6} \times \frac{3}{6} = \frac{1}{4}$. For multiple independent events, multiply the probabilities. For Quantity B, there are four ways to not get a multiple of 3 (these are 1, 2, 4, 5). The probability of "not rolling a multiple of 3" then "not rolling a multiple of 3" is $\frac{4}{6} \times \frac{4}{6} = \frac{4}{9}$. Quantity B is greater than Quantity A.

9. **B**

There are variables in the answer choices, so Plug In. If $r = 2$, then $4((2) - s) = -2$. Divide both sides by 4 to find $2 - s = -0.5$. So, $s = 2.5$. The target answer is r, which is 2. Go to the answer choices and plug in 2.5 for s. Choice (B) is the only answer choice that matches your target of 2.

10. **10.5**

Plug In! Let's say there are 100 employees. 25 percent of the employees take the subway to work, so $\frac{25}{100} \times 100 = 25$. Of the 25 employees who ride the subway, 42 percent of them transfer during the commute, so $\frac{42}{100} \times 25 = 10.5$. Therefore, 10.5 out of 100 employees transfer lines. This is 10.5 percent.

11. **D**

Plug In. If $a = 3$, $b = 6$, $c = 3$, $d = 5$, and $e = 10$, the value of the equation is $\dfrac{10\left(3 + \dfrac{6}{3}\right)}{5} = 10$. Half of 10 is your target of 5. Try doubling each variable to find the one that yields 5. The only one that works is doubling d to 10 so that the equation is $\dfrac{(10)\left(3 + \dfrac{6}{3}\right)}{10} = 5$.

12. **C**

For this question, you can FOIL: $\left(\sqrt{5}\right)^{2} - \left(\sqrt{3}\right)\left(\sqrt{5}\right) - \left(\sqrt{5}\right)\left(\sqrt{3}\right) + \left(\sqrt{3}\right)^{2}$. This simplifies to $5 - 2\sqrt{15} + 3$, or $8 - 2\sqrt{15}$.

13. **A, C, D, and E**

    Plug the information given into the formula for the area of a triangle to learn more about the relationship between x and y: $A = \dfrac{bh}{2} = \dfrac{xy}{2} = 108$. The product of x and y is 216, so x needs to be a factor of 216. The only number in the answer choices that is not a factor of 216 is 5. The remaining choices are possible values of x.

14. **B**

    Europe's electricity production (2,000 megawatt-hours) most closely matches that of Asia (1,900 megawatt-hours).

15. **E**

    The ratio for North America is 2300 to 0.083 or, $\dfrac{2300}{0.083} = 27{,}710$. This is the greatest ratio of any of the continents.

16. **A**

    Africa's population is 10.6 percent on the pie chart; South America's is 7.9 percent. Right away, you can eliminate all of the answer choices that are smaller than 368. Now you are left with (A) and (B). Because the question gives you South America's population (368 million), you can use a proportion to find the population of Africa. The proportion would look like this: $\dfrac{0.079}{368} = \dfrac{0.106}{x}$, where x is equal to the population of Africa. Cross-multiplying gives you $0.079x = 0.106 \times 368$, so $x = 493.7$.

17. **A**

    If the average of 5 crates is 250, then their total $= 5 \times 250 = 1{,}250$. To find the high end of the range for the fifth crate, make the other crates as light as possible: Make the two lightest crates 200 each, for a total of 400, and the two heaviest crates 300 each, for a total of 600; together, those four crates weigh 1,000 pounds, leaving 250 pounds for x. Because only (A) sets 250 pounds as the high end, you can eliminate (B), (C), (D), and (E).

18. **B**

    Substitute 6 for x in the equation, $s_x = 2s_{x-1} + s_{x-2}$ and work carefully from there. $s_6 = 2s_{6-1} + s_{6-2}$, which simplifies to $s_6 = 2s_5 + s_4$. However you don't know s_5 or s_4. Use the equation to find these missing terms. $s_4 = 2s_3 + s_2$ and the problem tells you s_2 and s_3 are equal to 2. $s_4 = (2 \times 2) + 2$, which is 6. Now you need to find s_5. Using the equation, you get $s_5 = (2 \times 6) + 2$, which is 14. Now that you know s_5 and s_4, go back to your original equation, $s_6 = 2s_5 + s_4$, and $s_6 = (2 \times 14) + 6$, which is 34.

19. **7**

    Always draw a figure when one is not provided. In this case, line segment XZ has a length of 68. Point Y is the midpoint of the segment, because $2XY = XZ$. To find the lengths of these segments, divide 68 by 2. Segment $YZ = 34$. Because $YZ = 4a + 6$, you know that $34 = 4a + 6$, so $a = 7$.

20. **C**

Make a spot for each day and fill in the number of guests who could occupy that spot. Burke has 5 choices for Monday, 3 choices for Tuesday, 4 choices for Wednesday (because one politician was chosen on Monday), 6 choices for Thursday, and 10 choices for Friday (because 4 of the 14 potential guests have already been chosen). Multiply these to arrive at 3,600 different schedules.

Section 5

1. **systematic**

   The clue is "simple, unambiguous, and unchanging." The transition phrase is *in other words*. The transition maintains the direction of the clue. Therefore, find a word that means regimented. *Systematic* is the best match.

2. **obdurate** and **capitulate**

   Try working with the second blank first. The second blank is talking about what a player will be forced to do if he's stubborn. The clue is that the "mistakes" the player makes will lead to the "prevailing strategy of his or her opponent." Because of these clues, we know that a word that means "to give in" would be a good match. *Capitulate* is the only word that works, as *dissent* means to disagree and *repudiate* means to reject. Now look at the first blank. The first blank is referring to something all great chess players know. The clue tells us that they know *stubbornness will almost surely lead to mistakes that force a player to capitulate to the prevailing strategy of his or her opponent*. As you can see, we needed to solve for the second blank first, as we would not have known what *stubbornness* would lead to without doing so. Recycle the word *stubbornness* as your word for the blank. *Obdurate* is the only word that works for the first blank. *Finicky* means to be overly particular, and *vituperative* means to be combative.

3. **corruptibility, venal**, and **redundancy**

   The first two blanks are related, but there isn't a strong clue for either one in the first part, so let's start with the third blank. Since the motif is *tiresome,* the third blank must mean something close to "repetitive." *Redundancy* matches this. At the end of the paragraph, each character is *bribed...into giving up...beliefs*. So the first two blanks must mean "bribable." *Corruptibility* in the first blank and *venal* in the second both match this.

4. **illegal** and **unabashedly**

   For the first blank, the clues "pirating software" and "downloading software from unapproved sources" describe unauthorized activities, so *illegal* is the best fit. *Uncommon* and *difficult* are incorrect because the sentence says that "many people continue to do so." If people are doing something despite its illegality and "almost as if they were unaware that such acts amount to theft," you could describe them as acting *brashly. Unabashedly* is the best fit.

5. **insolvent**

   The phrase "squandered his life's savings on unprofitable business ventures" tells you that the entrepreneur had no money left. The blank needs a word that means broke. *Former* and *unlikely* are tempting choices, but they don't match broke. Eliminate them. *Eccentric* also doesn't match, while *perturbed* only describes the entrepreneur's possible feelings. *Insolvent* agrees with the clue, so keep it.

6. **eschew obfuscation, recondite,** and **a limpid**

The key clue is that the teachers urge students to "use clear, simple language." The transition *instead* indicates that the phrase that goes into the blank will present an alternative to using clear, simple language, while the *and* indicates that the phrase will nevertheless agree with the clue. Something like "avoid difficult language" would be best: Difficult language is the alternative to clear, simple language, but the two phrases still agree because the difficult language is something to avoid. Thus, *eschew obfuscation* is best: *Eschew* means avoid, while *obfuscation* means the act of hiding the meaning of something. *Exscind obloquy* means to cut out critical language, while *evince ossification* means to show excessive rigidity, neither of which is appropriate here. The second blank needs a word that means difficult or obscure because teachers call into question the use of difficult vocabulary; *recondite* means obscure and hard to understand. *Recreant* means cowardly; *redolent* means fragrant. The final blank requires a word like *clear* because that is the type of language that "conveys one's meaning so much more effectively." *Limpid* means easily understood, so it is correct.

7. **A and C**

Choice (A) is supported because the passage says that myelin protects the brain's circuitry. Choice (C) is supported by the fact that "as humans mature" increasing levels of myelin need to be produced. While the passage suggests that a lack of myelin leaves the brain vulnerable, that doesn't mean that increasing the levels of myelin will reverse damage.

8. **B**

In the passage, *byzantine* refers to the "circuitry inside our nervous systems." Previously, the circuitry is described as growing more complex, so you need to find a word with a similar meaning. Choice (A) is an alternate meaning for byzantine, but it is not supported by the passage. Choices (C), (D), and (E) do not have meanings similar to complex.

9. **D**

The argument concludes that large universities should utilize work-study students rather than administrative assistants. The premise is that a similar strategy realizes a cost savings at small colleges. This is an argument by analogy. Hence, the argument assumes that there are similar conditions at small colleges and at large universities. Choice (D) says that students at universities are just as qualified to take over the administrative roles as they are in small colleges. In other words, the administrative jobs at universities are not appreciably different than those at colleges. For (A), whether the practice would be of greater benefit to the small colleges is out of scope. For (B), whether large universities usually depend on small colleges for ideas is out of scope. For (C), the issue of non-work-study students is out of scope. For (E), whether anyone has an easier ride than anyone else is out of scope.

10. **A**

The first paragraph acts as an introduction to the rest of the passage. The author notes that in the nineteenth century "investments became increasingly speculative." In the last paragraph, the author explains that due to fluctuating interest rates, the consol was popular with speculative investors. There is no support in the passage for (B), (C), or (D). Although the first paragraph provides a historical framework, as suggested in (E), it does not provide a way "by which the nature of the nineteenth-century investor" could be understood.

11. **To address the problem, the British government instituted a sinking fund, using tax revenue to buy back the bonds in the open market.**

    The second paragraph has five sentences, so this question has five answer choices. The third sentence begins, "To address the problem...." This is a clear indication that the sentence describes a solution to a problem. The correct answer is the third sentence.

12. **rarefied** and **meager**

    What sort of atmosphere would make Mars the only planet "whose surface details can be discerned from Earth?" You need a word that means transparent or thin for the blank. *Viscous* takes you in the wrong direction, so toss it. The next choice, *ossified*, makes no sense; toss that one too. In contrast, *rarefied* works well, so hang onto it. Meanwhile, a *copious* atmosphere would definitely not be easy to see through, so cross out that choice. *Meager* fits nicely and agrees with *rarefied*, making those two the correct answers.

13. **adversity** and **tribulation**

    The clue is "Using the hardships of the Joad family as a model." Recycle *hardships* and use POE. Does *reticence* mean *hardships?* No; cross it out. *Adversity* works, so leave it. Do the same for the remaining choices. Only *tribulation* agrees with *hardships,* so that's the other correct answer.

14. **a venerable** and **an august**

    The blank is a description of the pyramid. The clue is "imposing structure" because this is the only other description of the pyramid. *Venerable* and *august* are the only words that match *imposing*.

15. **noisome** and **mephitic**

    The word that fills the blank must describe "the stench of the livestock," which is so malodorous that it drives the newcomers back to the city; it must mean something like, well, "stinky." Both *noisome* and *mephitic* are appropriate choices. The other words don't work; if you were tempted by *olfactory*, realize that it simply means "related to the sense of smell" and does not actually describe a particular scent.

16. **B**

    Choice (B) correctly sums up the purpose of the passage: It explores the significance—the creation of a military aristocracy and chivalric culture—of a technological innovation—the stirrup. Choice (A) is incorrect because nothing in the passage suggests that this discussion has a basis in recent discovery. Choice (C) is too broad for the limited subject matter discussed. Choice (D) is too extreme. Choice (E) is incorrect because the physics, while important in connecting the stirrup to its social effects, isn't really the point of the passage—and, in any event, the physics relates to cavalry, not artillery.

17. **E**

    Choice (E) is supported by the passage because the sixth sentence suggests that the development of the barbed lance serves as an "unusually clear" marker. Choice (A) is incorrect because no additional subjects for research are brought up in the passage. Choices (B) and (C) require comparisons beyond the scope of the information in the passage: No other technology, ancient or medieval, was discussed. Choice (D), finally, is an extreme overstatement: Although the stirrup increased the military value of the horse, nowhere is it suggested that it had previously been considered militarily insignificant.

18. **Stirrups unify lance, rider, and horse into a force capable of unprecedented violence.**

In this sentence, the author says that stirrups improve the ability of a lance and rider. This is an improvement on the issues discussed earlier when the author states that a "lance couched under the rider's arm, unifying the force of rider and weapon, would throw its wielder backwards off the horse at impact."

19. **D**

Choice (D) describes the organization of the passage. Choice (A) can be eliminated because the traditional definition is never amended. Choice (B) can be eliminated because the authorities do not support the traditional theory. Choice (C) can be eliminated because no new definition is proposed. Choice (E) can be eliminated because the "implications of the experiment" are not rejected.

20. **A and B**

The author's dismissal of the traditional definition of randomness rests upon the premises that the results of the same probabilistic mechanism will all have the same likelihood of occurring, and, as such, should be considered equally probable. The passage never mentions how the results of different probabilistic mechanisms relate to each other, so eliminate (C).

Section 6

1. **A**

   Solve for x in the top equation, $\frac{x}{6} + 2 = \frac{6}{2}$, by reducing the right side: $\frac{x}{6} + 2 = 3$. Subtract 2 from both sides, and multiply both sides by 6 to find that $x = 6$. Solve for y in the second equation, $\frac{y}{3} + 2 = \frac{9}{3}$, by reducing the right side: $\frac{y}{3} + 2 = 3$. Subtract 2 from both sides, and multiply both sides by 3 to find that $y = 3$. If $x = 6$ and $y = 3$, Quantity A becomes $\frac{5}{3}$, and Quantity B becomes $\frac{2}{6} = \frac{1}{3}$.

2. **A**

   Use the equation *distance = rate × time*. Bob's time is 3 hours, and his rate is 44 miles per hour, so his distance is 3 × 44 = 132 miles. Inez's time is 2.5 hours, and her rate is 50 miles per hour, so her distance is 2.5 × 50 = 125 miles.

3. **A**

   Plug In! Let's say that the height is 10, the depth is 20, and the width is 20. If the height is increased by 20%, the new height is 12. If the depth is decreased by 20%, the new depth is 16 and the width remains 20. The new volume is 12 × 16 × 20 = 3,840. If you use those same numbers but make the changes by 40%, the new volume is 14 × 12 × 20 = 3,360. Quantity A is greater. However, make sure you switch the numbers to check all possibilities. Make the height 20, the depth 10 and the width 20. The volume of the new 3D figure if p is 20 is 24 × 8 × 20 = 3,840. The volume of the new 3D figure if p is 40 is 28 × 6 × 20 = 3,360. The quantities are the same regardless of what numbers you plug in. The answer is (A).

4. **D**

Draw the figure. Triangle ABC has two adjacent sides, AB and AC, that are equal in length. The angles that are opposite these sides, angles B and C, are also equal. One common triangle that has two equal sides is the $45 : 45 : 90$ triangle. If angles B and C were both 45 degrees, then their sum would be 90 and the answer would be (C). However, we know nothing about the third side of the triangle so it is possible that this is equal as well, which creates an equilateral triangle with angles of 60. The sum of the angles in Quantity A is now 120. You cannot determine which is greater, so the answer is (D).

5. **A**

Translate: $\dfrac{12.5}{100}k = 80$, so $\dfrac{1}{8}k = 80$, and $k = 640$. Use this information in the other equation:

$k = 640 = \dfrac{y}{100} \times 80,$ and solve for y: $y = \dfrac{10}{8} \times 640 = 800$. Quantity A is greater than Quantity B.

6. **D**

Plug in values for each set. If $P = \{1, 2, 3, 4, 5, 6, 7\}$ and $Q = \{1, 2, 3, 4, 5, 6\}$, the range of Q is smaller. Eliminate (B) and (C). If you change P to $\{1, 2, 3, 4, 5, 7, 6\}$, and Q to $\{1, 2, 3, 4, 5, 7\}$, the range of Q is equal to that of P. Eliminate (A), and select (D).

7. **A**

One way to attack this problem is to list F_1 to F_{11}: 10, 13, 16, 19, 22, 25, 28, 31, 34, 37, 40. Notice that F_6 through F_{10} are included in both quantities, so focus on what's different. Quantity A is $F_4 + F_5$ and Quantity B is F_{11}. Quantity A is $19 + 22 = 41$, and Quantity B is 40. Alternatively, you know that F_4 has had 3 changes from F_1. So, $F_4 = F_1 + 3(3) = 10 + 9 = 19$. F_5 has had 4 changes from F_1, so $F_5 = F_1 + 3(4) = 10 + 12 = 22$. F_{11} has had 10 changes from F_1, so $F_{11} = F_1 + 3(10) = 10 + 30 = 40$.

8. **C**

Plug in a number for n. Let $n = 5$. Because $5 \times 6 = 30$, the product is 30. Add 24 to get 54. Divide by 3 to get 18 as your target. If you plug in 5 for n in each answer choice, only (C) matches the target: $2n + 8 = 2(5) + 8 = 18$.

9. **10**

If the average of a and b is 10, then $a + b = 20$. Likewise, if the average of c and d is 7, then $c + d = 14$. If the average of a, b, and c is 8, then $a + b + c = 24$. Because $a + b = 20$, $c = 4$. If $c = 4$, then $d = 10$.

10. **C**

To find the area of a square, you need the length of a side. To find a side, find the distance between two vertices. If A is at $(3, 7)$ and B is at $(3, 12)$, then the length of a side is equivalent to the difference in the y-coordinates: $12 - 7 = 5$. So, side AB has a length of 5. Square this to find the area: $5^2 = 25$. The fact that there are variables for the y-value of points C and D is irrelevant to solving this problem.

11. **B**

Get Dylan's median by putting his weekly sales into increasing order and finding the middle value. Dylan's set is $\{2, 3, 9, 10\}$, and his median is the average of 3 and 9, or 6. Next, do the same thing for Peter's sales numbers. Peter's set is $\{4, 4, 6, 10\}$, so his median is the average of 4 and 6, which is 5. The difference between the medians is $6 - 5 = 1$.

12. **A**

Order doesn't matter, so remember you must divide by the factorial of the number of decisions made. For the first topping, you have 6 options. For the second topping, you have 5 options. For the third topping, you have 4 options. $\dfrac{6 \times 5 \times 4}{3 \times 2 \times 1} = 20$, (A).

13. **E**

Because you know the perimeter of the rectangle, you can figure out that both BC and $AD = 5$. Thus, the area of the rectangle is $3 \times 5 = 15$. The area of the triangle is therefore also 15. Because the area of a triangle $= \dfrac{1}{2} bh$, you can put in the values you know to find $15 = \dfrac{1}{2}(b \times 5)$ and solve for the base, which is 6. LM is the base of the triangle, so $LM = 6$.

14. **C**

From 1981 through 1984, the ratings for Program y were higher than they were in the previous year.

15. **E**

There were 95 million times 80 percent, or 76 million, television households in 1983. Thirteen percent of them viewed Program y. 76 million times 13 percent (0.13) is 9.88 million, or approximately 10.

16. **500,000**

The number of television households that were viewers of Program x is 3.1 million. The number of television house-holds that were viewers of Program y is 2.6 million. The difference between the numbers is $3.1 - 2.6 = 0.5$ million, or 500,000.

17. **A**

Plug In the Answers, starting with (C). If Susan owns 146, Gavin owns 246, and together they own 392. Matt and Angela together would own 784, and the total number of houses would be 1,176. Choice (C) is too large, so also cross off (D) and (E). Try a smaller number. For (A), if Susan owns 46, Gavin owns 146, and together they own 192. Matt and Angela together would own 384, and the total number of houses would be 576.

18. $\dfrac{7}{45}$

Plugging In is a great way to tackle this question. Multiply the denominators of $\dfrac{1}{4}$, $\dfrac{1}{5}$, and $\dfrac{1}{3}$ together to get 60, which will be an easy number with which to work. Make the total number of cars 60. $60 \times \dfrac{1}{4} = 15$ sports cars, and $60 - 15 = 45$ sedans. The number of red cars is $60 \times \dfrac{1}{5} = 12$. The number of red sports cars is $15 \times \dfrac{1}{3} = 5$, which means that there are $12 - 5 = 7$ red sedans. The fraction of the sedans that are red is $\dfrac{7}{45}$.

19. **A and B**

Plug In the Answers. Start with one of the middle values, such as choice (C). If there are 18 grape candies, then there are 40 total candies in the jar. The probability of selecting an orange candy is $\frac{8}{40}$, or 20 percent. The question states that the probability of selecting an orange candy is greater than 20 percent, so (C) cannot work. Values larger than 18 also do not work because when the denominator becomes larger than 40, the probability becomes less than 20 percent. The only choices that could work are (A) and (B).

20. **E**

Plug in for k, and let $k = 3$. CE is a radius and also half of the square's diagonal. If k is 3, then CE is 3, and the diagonal is 6. The diagonal of a square is also the hypotenuse of a 45 : 45 : 90 triangle. To get the hypotenuse from a side, you multiply by $\sqrt{2}$; so, to get a side from the hypotenuse, divide by $\sqrt{2}$. The sides of the square are each $\frac{6}{\sqrt{2}}$. To find the area, square the side to find $\left(\frac{6}{\sqrt{2}}\right)^2 = \frac{6^2}{\sqrt{2}^2} = \frac{36}{2} = 18$. Plug $k = 3$ into the answers to find one that yields your target of 18. Choice (E) yields the target of 18.

Appendix: Accommodated Testing

If you plan to request accommodations, you need a copy of the Testing Accommodations Request Form, which is part of the Bulletin Supplement for Test Takers with Disabilities or Health-Related Needs. The Bulletin Supplement is at **https://www.ets.org/s/disabilities/pdf/bulletin_supplement_test_takers_with_disabilities_health_needs.pdf**, or you can request it by phone at 866-387-8602 (toll-free for test takers in the United States, American Samoa, Guam, Puerto Rico, U.S. Virgin Islands and Canada) or 609-771-7780. You can also write to:

ETS Disability Services
P.O. Box 6054
Princeton, NJ
08541-6054

Available accommodations include the following:

- extended testing time (There are no untimed tests.)

- additional rest breaks

- test reader

- scribe

- sign language interpreter for spoken directions only

- screen magnification

- large print

- trackball

- audio recording

- braille

This is not an exhaustive list. ETS will consider any accommodation requested for a disability or medical condition.

Processing a request for accommodations takes time, so you should submit your request as early as possible (at least six weeks before you intend to take the test). The request must include the following:

- a completed Computer-Based Test (CBT) Authorization Voucher Request form and the proper test fee

- a completed Testing Accommodations Request Form

- a Certification of Eligibility: Accommodations History (COE), which verifies your use of accommodations at your college, university, or place of employment. In some cases, the COE is sufficient to document a disability and can be used in place of sending full documentation to ETS. If you are eligible to use the COE in this way, the documentation on file with the college, university, or employer must meet all ETS documentation criteria. Please see the Bulletin Supplement for details.

- documentation (unless you are using the COE as described above)

    o If you have a psychiatric disability, physical disability or health-related need, traumatic brain injury, or autism spectrum disorder, you must submit documentation.

    o Documentation must also be submitted if your disability has been diagnosed within the last twelve months, regardless of the accommodations you are requesting.

The documentation you submit must meet the following criteria:

- Clearly state the diagnosed disability

- Describe the functional limitations resulting from the disability

- Be current: within the last five years for a learning disability or autism spectrum disorder, last six months for a psychiatric or physical disability or a health-related need, or last three years for other disabilities. Documentation of physical or sensory disabilities of a permanent or unchanging nature may be older if it provides all of the pertinent information.

- Include complete educational, developmental, and medical history relevant to the disability

- Include a list of all test instruments used in the evaluation report and all subtest, composite, and/or index scores used to document the stated disability

- Describe the specific accommodations requested

- State why the disability qualifies you for the requested accommodations

- Be typed or printed on official letterhead and be signed and dated by an evaluator qualified to make the diagnosis. The report should include information about the evaluator's license or certification and area of specialization.

If you have a learning disability, ADHD, a physical disability, a psychiatric disability, a hearing loss or visual impairment, a traumatic brain injury, or an autism spectrum disorder, refer to the ETS website at **www.ets.org/ disability** for specific documentation.

ETS will send you an approval letter confirming the accommodations that have been approved for you.

- **National Paper-Based Testing (PBT)**
When you receive your approval letter, you are registered. The approval letter will identify the testing location and test administrator. If the testing center cannot accommodate your request on the scheduled testing date, you will be contacted by the test administrator to arrange an alternate test date.

- **Computer-Administered Testing (CBT)**
The approval letter will include instructions that you must follow to schedule your test. **Do not schedule a CBT test until you receive your approval letter.** When scheduling your test, be prepared to provide the authorization/voucher number and the information contained in the letter.

- **Alternate-Format Testing**
A representative from ETS Disability Services will contact you to confirm the accommodations approved for you and to schedule your test.

International Offices Listing

China (Beijing)
1501 Building A,
Disanji Creative Zone,
No.66 West Section of North 4th Ring Road Beijing
Tel: +86-10-62684481/2/3
Email: tprkor01@chol.com
Website: www.tprbeijing.com

China (Shanghai)
1010 Kaixuan Road
Building B, 5/F
Changning District, Shanghai, China 200052
Sara Beattie, Owner: Email: tprenquiry.sha@sarabeattie.com
Tel: +86-21-5108-2798
Fax: +86-21-6386-1039
Website: www.princetonreviewshanghai.com

Hong Kong
5th Floor, Yardley Commercial Building
1–6 Connaught Road West, Sheung Wan, Hong Kong
(MTR Exit C)
Sara Beattie, Owner: Email: tprenquiry.sha@sarabeattie.com
Tel: +852-2507-9380
Fax: +852-2827-4630
Website: www.princetonreviewhk.com

India (Mumbai)
Score Plus Academy
Office No.15, Fifth Floor
Manek Mahal 90
Veer Nariman Road
Next to Hotel Ambassador
Churchgate, Mumbai 400020
Maharashtra, India
Ritu Kalwani: Email: director@score-plus.com
Tel: + 91 22 22846801 / 39 / 41
Website: www.scoreplusindia.com

India (New Delhi)
South Extension
K–16, Upper Ground Floor
South Extension Part–1,
New Delhi-110049
Aradhana Mahna: aradhana@manyagroup.com
Monisha Banerjee: monisha@manyagroup.com
Ruchi Tomar: ruchi.tomar@manyagroup.com
Rishi Josan: Rishi.josan@manyagroup.com
Vishal Goswamy: vishal.goswamy@manyagroup.com
Tel: +91-11-64501603/ 4, +91-11-65028379
Website: www.manyagroup.com

Lebanon
463 Bliss Street
AlFarra Building–2nd floor
Ras Beirut
Beirut, Lebanon
Hassan Coudsi: Email: hassan.coudsi@review.com
Tel: +961-1-367-688
Website: www.princetonreviewlebanon.com

Korea
945-25 Young Shin Building
25 Daechi-Dong, Kangnam-gu
Seoul, Korea 135-280
Yong-Hoon Lee: Email: TPRKor01@chollian.net
In-Woo Kim: Email: iwkim@tpr.co.kr
Tel: + 82-2-554-7762
Fax: +82-2-453-9466
Website: www.tpr.co.kr

Kuwait
ScorePlus Learning Center
Salmiyah Block 3, Street 2 Building 14
Post Box: 559, Zip 1306, Safat, Kuwait
Email: infokuwait@score-plus.com
Tel: +965-25-75-48-02 / 8
Fax: +965-25-75-46-02
Website: www.scorepluseducation.com

Malaysia
Sara Beattie MDC Sdn Bhd
Suites 18E & 18F
18th Floor
Gurney Tower, Persiaran Gurney
Penang, Malaysia
Email: tprkl.my@sarabeattie.com
Sara Beattie, Owner: Email: tprenquiry.sha@sarabeattie.com
Tel: +604-2104 333
Fax: +604-2104 330
Website: www.princetonreviewKL.com

Mexico
TPR México
Guanajuato No. 242 Piso 1 Interior 1
Col. Roma Norte
México D.F., C.P.06700
registro@princetonreviewmexico.com
Tel: +52-55-5255-4495
+52-55-5255-4440
+52-55-5255-4442
Website: www.princetonreviewmexico.com

Qatar
Score Plus
Villa No. 49, Al Waab Street
Opp Al Waab Petrol Station
Post Box: 39068, Doha, Qatar
Email: infoqatar@score-plus.com
Tel: +974 44 36 8580, +974 526 5032
Fax: +974 44 13 1995
Website: www.scorepluseducation.com

Taiwan
The Princeton Review Taiwan
2F, 169 Zhong Xiao East Road, Section 4
Taipei, Taiwan 10690
Lisa Bartle (Owner): lbartle@princetonreview.com.tw
Tel: +886-2-2751-1293
Fax: +886-2-2776-3201
Website: www.PrincetonReview.com.tw

Thailand
The Princeton Review Thailand
Sathorn Nakorn Tower, 28th floor
100 North Sathorn Road
Bangkok, Thailand 10500
Thavida Bijayendrayodhin (Chairman)
Email: thavida@princetonreviewthailand.com
Mitsara Bijayendrayodhin (Managing Director)
Email: mitsara@princetonreviewthailand.com
Tel: +662-636-6770
Fax: +662-636-6776
Website: www.princetonreviewthailand.com

Turkey
Yeni Sülün Sokak No. 28
Levent, Istanbul, 34330, Turkey
Nuri Ozgur: nuri@tprturkey.com
Rona Ozgur: rona@tprturkey.com
Iren Ozgur: iren@tprturkey.com
Tel: +90-212-324-4747
Fax: +90-212-324-3347
Website: www.tprturkey.com

UAE
Emirates Score Plus
Office No: 506, Fifth Floor
Sultan Business Center
Near Lamcy Plaza, 21 Oud Metha Road
Post Box: 44098, Dubai
United Arab Emirates
Hukumat Kalwani: skoreplus@gmail.com
Ritu Kalwani: director@score-plus.com
Email: info@score-plus.com
Tel: +971-4-334-0004
Fax: +971-4-334-0222
Website: www.scorepluseducation.com

Our International Partners

The Princeton Review also runs courses with a variety of partners in Africa, Asia, Europe, and South America.

Georgia
LEAF American-Georgian Education Center
www.leaf.ge

Mongolia
English Academy of Mongolia
www.nyescm.org

Nigeria
The Know Place
www.knowplace.com.ng

Panama
Academia Interamericana de Panama
http://aip.edu.pa/

Switzerland
Institut Le Rosey
http://www.rosey.ch/

All other inquiries, please email us at
internationalsupport@review.com

The Princeton Review®

BONUS MATERIALS

GRE INSIDER

Admissions and Program Advice

While *Cracking the GRE* will prepare you for your exam, the *GRE Insider* will help you navigate what comes next. The bonus materials included here contain invaluable information about degree options, application considerations, and assorted fields of study. We wish you the best of luck on your studies and preparation for graduate school.

Table of Contents

Part 1

Beyond The GRE: Graduate School and More

So Much More Online
To learn more about graduate school admissions, check out your Premium Portal for articles, advice, and lots more.

Graduate schools continue to draw more applicants, more enrollees, and more graduates in almost every field, with a few exceptions. The most important thing for a prospective graduate student to know is that there really is no simple, cookie-cutter way to describe graduate school. While many elements from program to program are similar, like taking classes, writing papers, conducting lab or field work, studying advanced theory and sitting for exams, the category is so broad that until now, we have not found a graduate school guide that does it justice. The goal of this *GRE Insider* is to pull back the covers on specific graduate program areas, examine the data and trends in each area (as well as associated careers), and highlight opportunities or things to think about before making this critical life choice.

One of the best ways we've found to describe graduate school is as a critical stage of career development. In fact for many careers discussed in this guide, an advanced degree is a requirement in order to get a job in that field. While some might joke that getting an advanced degree is a great way to put off getting a "real job", the reality is that graduate school programs are designed by professionals and researchers in each field to prepare students for the day-to-day demands and challenges of that specific profession.

For example, there are many master's programs considered to be "professional" because they are designed not to prepare graduates for further study necessarily, but to step right into a recognized profession. These jobs typically require some kind of certification or licensure that is regulated by state law, as is commonly the case for counselors, engineers, librarians, social workers, teachers, and therapists. In such cases, master's programs are often geared toward and will include elements that specifically prepare students for state-regulated exams.

Other master's programs are also considered professional, not because they launch students into careers in regulated professions, but because they prepare students for jobs that require a high level of proficiency in a field that has a fairly well-defined range of accepted practices. Examples of these fields include business management, government, information management, journalism, and museum curation. There are still other master's programs designed to prepare students for either further study in the same field or for careers in which their general skills (though perhaps not their full range of content knowledge) are applicable. Examples of these programs can be found in the liberal arts disciplines, such as humanities and social sciences.

Doctoral programs prepare individuals to become experts in a particular field but also prepare graduates for specific career paths. Most PhD programs, for example, are designed explicitly to prepare students for careers as professors in higher education institutions or as researchers in the private, public, or nonprofit sectors. Other doctoral programs, such as those granting a Doctor of Psychology and Doctor of Education, are designed to produce practitioners in selected professions, such as counseling or education. Given that the typical length of a doctoral program is in the range of five to eight years (depending on the discipline), it's even more important for prospective doctoral students to understand what kind of career they're preparing for than it is for prospective master's students.

Whatever your reasons for reading this guide, we hope it gives you a better sense of which path to take for success in your future career. Good luck!

Tune In Online
Your Premium Portal contains a bunch of helpful videos that cover content review for the GRE, plus vocab strategies, how to guidelines, and much more!

Part 2

Introduction to Graduate School

The decision to apply to graduate school is one that requires careful thought about your career goals, awareness of the different paths to reach your goals, and an understanding of the job market and prospects. In other words, will your degree help you reach your goals, and ultimately pay off?

For many careers in the graduate arts and sciences disciplines, obtaining a master's degree or a PhD is required to be considered for certain jobs. An advanced degree can also provide an edge in increasingly competitive industries or for the best jobs in fast-growing industries.

SELECTING A PROGRAM

Expert Advice
Visit PrincetonReview.com/ GRE for tried-and-true GRE and graduate school advice and information.

Programs come in many shapes and sizes. Rather than blitzing every program with an application, it is best to do your research, focus your attention and apply to carefully chosen schools. In some fields, it may be important to consider the prestige of the institution or even the professor with whom you want to conduct your research. Other fields that require state-based licensure might cause you to consider the location of your program for the best possible preparation.

It might be helpful to divide potential graduate schools into categories based on your chances of admission, just as you did when applying to undergrad. Select two schools you're fairly certain will accept you, two with whom you have a fighting chance and one school that you'll get into if lightning strikes. This is your target list; add more schools only if you have the time and money to do so.

Be sure to include making personal connections as part of your research process. While you can gather a lot of good information about programs online, make every effort to pick up the phone or go visit a school on your list. If you are going to spend three to six years in your program, it's important to make connections beforehand with the professors, ask questions and find out how your work (and goals) will be supported. Likewise, talk to graduate students in the program for a better picture of the atmosphere. It may be the only way to find out about the things you can't learn about online.

DEGREE OPTIONS

Do you need a master's or a PhD? Generally speaking, if you want to conduct research and development or teach in a postsecondary setting, a PhD is required.

PhD Degree

PhD programs are designed to give you extensive expertise in a specialized field, training you to pursue a life in academia as a professor or researcher (although not all candidates follow this path). Typically you spend five to six years earning your degree with the first three years focused on required coursework, writing a dissertation proposal, and developing relationships with your professors. In years four through six, you take fewer (or no) courses and focus on writing your dissertation, which is supposed to constitute a new and meaningful contribution to knowledge in your field.

Some fields offer alternative terminal degrees to the PhD. For example, engineering offers a Doctor of Engineering Science (EngScD) while a Doctor of Psychology (PsyD) is a practitioner-based degree with less focus on research.

Master's Degree

Just like in college, first-year master's students take courses to fulfill degree requirements. However, the workload is heavier, the course topics are more specific, and much more is expected of you than in college.

At the beginning of the master's program, you'll choose (or be assigned) a faculty member who will serve as your advisor. This person will help you develop an academic focus and potential topics for your thesis or final project.

As a second year master's student, you decide on your research focus and—in one semester or two—complete your master's thesis or final project. If you show promise, you may be encouraged to continue toward a PhD.

Fields seeing more job applicants than job opportunities can experience growth in those opting for a PhD instead of a master's degree. Be sure to consider whether the programs you choose offer master's only or also have PhD options. Remember that within some programs, you can enroll for a master's degree and later choose to pursue a PhD if you are so inclined; conversely, you can enroll in a PhD program and leave after earning your master's if the academic lifestyle fails to entice you further.

LETTERS OF RECOMMENDATION

GRE for Business School?
More and more Business Schools are accepting GRE scores for admissions consideration. Check out *The Best 294 Business Schools* from The Princeton Review to learn more.

The value that an objective third-party can provide gives the application reviewing committee great insight into your value as a candidate for their program beyond the test scores, GPA, and your own personal statement. Most programs require three letters of recommendation, so consider that when selecting a recommender, much weight will be given to recommendations from academics in your field. However, practice-oriented programs, particularly ones that value fieldwork as part of your application, would likely value recommendations from the professionals you worked with during your internship, job, or fieldwork. If in doubt about recommendations, consider what kinds of input your audience, in this case the admissions committee, would most like to help them make their decision, and don't be afraid to ask them either.

ESSAYS

Putting yourself in the shoes of the admissions committee is a good rule of thumb for essays while research is the best way of preparing to actually write. Of course it's important to talk about the research you would like to pursue in a graduate program, but make sure you are able to demonstrate a solid understanding of what the school has to offer. Research their program strengths as well as their professors' research and publications; the more your areas of interest align with the program's strengths, the easier it will be to write your essay. Also, be as detail-oriented as possible.

WORK SAMPLES AND INTERVIEWS

Remember that the application and admission process is all about giving the admissions committee the most complete picture of you and your work as possible in a relatively short amount of time. Work samples and interviews are a great way to highlight your strengths as well as make yourself stand out from other applicants.

Reading through the application requirements early will help you pull together any necessary requirements, such as a portfolio or audio or video samples of your work (for areas like performing arts). Some programs will require or recommend an interview, so don't be afraid to practice! Talking about your goals for graduate school with others, and being able to think on your feet, will give you an edge once you sit down for an interview.

Part 3

Graduate School Programs By Type

ART, DESIGN, AND ARCHITECTURE

Creativity and artistic expression come to mind as the most important skills for careers in art and architecture. This is especially true in the studio arts or dramatic and theater arts. So why obtain a graduate degree at all—can't I just paint, act, or play music?

Well, yes, but…just as a graduate degree in any other field provides relevant training and detailed knowledge required for a job in the field, an advanced degree in the arts gives students an opportunity to develop, refine, and practice their art with direct access to the resources, materials, and support they need to grow.

And for art historians, preservationists, conservators, as well as art and film critics, a balanced background of studying and creating the work provides a full preparation. Many of these programs focus on history, foreign languages, and cultural studies.

For the various fields within architecture, there is a unique "marrying" of creative design and construction with the cultural and social dynamic of the areas in which architects work, whether it is a streetscape, a renovation of a historic building, or designing a new home. Programs require that applicants have a year of college-level math, such as calculus or physics.

Degrees Offered

All areas of art and architecture have experienced growth in advanced degrees conferred, most notably in architecture and related fields. For many fields in this area, the terminal degree is a master's degree, particularly for those offering the Master of Fine Arts (MFA).

In order to be a licensed architect, one must possess a BArch (a five-year undergraduate program) or MArch. While a MArch takes about three years to complete, those entering the program with a BArch can often complete the program much faster. A Master's in Interior Architecture (MIA) or Landscape Architecture (MLA) generally take two to three years to complete, depending on undergraduate experience, and culminate in a thesis as well as oral and written exams.

While students in graduate programs for studio and performing arts receive the terminal degree in their field (MFA), many choose graduate school because it provides a unique and focused opportunity in which to develop themselves as artists. Grad school provides the necessary preparation, resources, and exposure to dramatically influence one's success as an artist, writer, performer, or musician. Most programs last two to three years and culminate in, among other things, a presentation of work produced.

Quick Snapshot: Art and Architecture

SAMPLE DEGREE PROGRAM	NO. OF SCHOOLS OFFERING PROGRAM	DEGREE OPTIONS	APPLICATION CONSIDERATIONS
Architecture	Master's: 112 Doctorate: 23	MArch	Architecture degree or relevant coursework; portfolio of undergraduate work
Art History, Criticism & Conservation	Master's: 114 Doctorate: 55	MA, MS Conservation PhD	Study of at least one foreign language; classes in studio art or art history helpful
Drama & Dramatics/ Theater Arts	Master's: 143 Doctorate: 32	MA PhD	Portfolio of dramatic work
Industrial Design	Master's: 19 Doctorate: 1	MA, MFA (terminal degree)	Undergraduate degree or equivalent coursework in industrial design
Interior Architecture	Master's: 13 Doctorate: 0	MIA	Bachelor's degree in a related field such as architecture, fine arts, or art history
Landscape Architecture	Master's: 58 Doctorate: 2	MLA PhD	Courses in calculus and physics; work experience preferable
Playwriting and Screenwriting	Master's: 26 Doctorate: 0	MFA	One full-length dramatic writing sample
Studio Arts	Master's: 319 Doctorate: 5	MFA (terminal degree)	Portfolio demonstrating applicant has been actively practicing his/her art for some time

You can find more detailed information to guide you on the right path from these trade organization websites.

TRADE ORGANIZATIONS YOU SHOULD KNOW	
American Film Institute afi.com	The American Film Institute is dedicated to advancing and preserving the art of the moving image.
American Institute of Architects aia.org	News, conferences, education, government affairs and everything else an architect should know.
American Society of Landscape Architects asla.org	The ASLA provides information on seminars, jobs, and history of the profession.
National Association of Dramatic and Speech Arts, Inc. nadsainc.com	A professional organization for all dramatics professionals, including performers, educators, administrators, and students.
National Trust for Historic Preservation preservationnation.org	A not-for-profit organization dedicated to saving historic buildings, neighborhoods, and landscapes that form communities.
Writers Guild of America, West wga.org	Offers tools for writers of all genres and professions.

Typical Admissions Requirements

Despite the wide range of degrees in art and architecture, all of them generally require a portfolio as part of the application. Many of the degree programs in art and architecture are directly linked to creative work, meaning that a portfolio is the best way for the admissions committee to review the demonstrated ability of the applicants.

Here are some examples:

- Acting: live auditions or performance tapes

- Architecture/Interior Architecture: portfolio of work, typically created during undergraduate study

- Graphic Design: portfolio of work

- Landscape Architecture: portfolio of work that can include designs, drawings, and photography

- Playwriting/Screenwriting: at least one full-length dramatic writing sample

- Studio Arts: samples, photographs of work

For architecture programs, it is often required to have a bachelor's degree in the same or related field while many also require one year of undergraduate physics and mathematics, such as calculus.

General graduate school requirements:

- Bachelor's degree from an accredited college or university

- Official transcript(s) from all colleges or universities attended

- GRE General Test scores (different programs require different minimum scores)

- TOEFL score (if necessary)

- Academic letters of recommendation

- Letter of intent or statement of purpose

- Application forms

- Application fee

Some degree programs will also require:

- Interview or audition

- Supplemental essays or writing sample

- Proficiency in a foreign language (art history or architectural history)

- Portfolio of work, including audio, video, pictures and samples of work

BIOLOGY AND LIFE SCIENCES

Biology is a natural science that invloves the study of life and living organisms. There are many subdivisions of biology, categorized by the scale and method with which they approach the subject: biochemistry, molecular, cellular, physiology (organs, tissues, organ systems), and ecology. Within these subdivisions, one typically focuses on either basic or applied research.

Much of the grant-funded basic research serves as a starting point for applied research, which finds practical applications of biological knowledge in areas as diverse as new drugs, treatments, and medical diagnostic tests, increased crop yields, and new biofuels.

A career path for those who are interested in studying biology and life sciences is pharmacology. Pharmacologists are often thought of in tandem with toxicologists, as both research the effects of chemicals on cells. However, toxicologists examine the effects of poisons on cells while pharmacologists remain focused on drug-related chemical interactions.

Advanced degrees are required for many jobs in this area. A PhD is required for researchers seeking funding and post-secondary teachers while a master's degree can also be useful in the sales, marketing and publication aspects of biological sciences.

Degrees Offered in Biology and Life Sciences

An MS in biology and life sciences generally takes two to three years to complete. Masters programs culminate in a written examination, as well as a thesis with oral defense. A PhD is generally required for those expecting to conduct independent research, especially in academia, or for high-level administrative positions. You can expect to spend five to six years of full-time study and research in a PhD program.

Some programs, like neuroscience and toxicology, are inherently interdisciplinary and combine disciplines with other graduate departments. Those that offer masters degrees in neuroscience are often steps toward PhDs or combined MD/PhDs. Likewise, a masters degree in toxicology is rarely seen as terminal—most students spend another four plus years earning their PhD.

Quick Snapshot: Biology and Life Sciences

SAMPLE DEGREE PROGRAM	NO. OF SCHOOLS OFFERING PROGRAM	APPLICATION CONSIDERATIONS
Biochemistry	Master's: 144 Doctorate: 147	GRE Subject in Biochemistry, Cell and Molecular Biology
Biology, Biomedical Sciences	Master's: 478 Doctorate: 233	Coursework in biology, GRE Subject Test in Biology
Ecology	Master's: 50 Doctorate: 46	Coursework in sciences, especially upper level biology or environmental science
Molecular Biology	Master's: 83 Doctorate: 110	Some schools require a minimum GPA and undergraduate coursework in organic chemistry, physics, and calculus
Neuroscience*	Master's: 735 Doctorate: 103	If not a neuroscience major, then coursework in natural sciences
Toxicology	Master's: 40 Doctorate: 43	Undergraduate major or significant course work in biology, chemistry, or biochemistry
Zoology/Animal Behavior	Master's: 26 Doctorate: 25	Emphasis placed on research interest and work experience; some require GRE Subject Test in Biology

* Neuroscience is interdisciplinary, and programs and coursework may be found in psychology, molecular biology, biochemistry, and others.

You can find more detailed information to guide you on the right path from these trade organization websites.

TRADE ORGANIZATIONS YOU SHOULD KNOW	
American Board of Clinical Pharmacology abcp.net	Recently created organization that administers an optional accreditation for clinical pharmacologists.
American Institute of Biological Sciences aibs.org	A membership organization advancing research, education, and public policy issues for the biological sciences. Publishes a peer review journal.
Society for Neuroscience sfn.org	World's largest organization of scientists and physicians devoted to understanding the brain and nervous system. Includes an extensive Higher Education and Training section.
Association of Zoos and Aquariums aza.org	Links to job opportunities, conferences, and professional training opportunities.
Society for Human Ecology societyforhumanecology.org	The society is an "international interdisciplinary society" whose mission is to promote "the use of an ecological perspective in research and application."
Society of Toxicology toxicology.org	Plenty of information about schools, degrees, grants and fellowships, links to career information, and other resources.

Typical Admissions Requirements

While many programs in biology and biological sciences might not require a specific major for admission, if they require a GRE Subject Test in either Biology or Biochemistry, Cell and Molecular Biology, then an undergraduate major or significant coursework is typically the best preparation.

General graduate school requirements:

- Bachelor's degree from an accredited college or university
- Official transcript(s) from all colleges or universities attended
- GRE General Test scores (different programs require different minimum scores)
- TOEFL score (if necessary)
- Academic letters of recommendation
- Letter of intent or statement of purpose
- Application forms
- Application fee
- Interview

Some degree programs will also require:

- GRE Subject Test: Biology
- GRE Subject Test: Biochemistry, Cell and Molecular Biology
- Curriculum vitae
- Research statement (as part of letter of intent)

COMMUNICATIONS, JOURNALISM, AND MEDIA STUDIES

Radio, TV, Internet, smartphones and tablets…the evolution of media consumption has driven dramatic changes and opportunities in the field of communications, journalism, and media studies.

Companies such as Google, Facebook, YouTube, Tumblr, Vine, and Twitter, along with easy-to-use technology and publishing tools (digital cameras, free blogging sites) give anyone with access to a computer or smartphone the opportunity to reach an audience with their message. Twenty-four-hour news channels (and their companion websites or social media outlets) mean that news and information are pumped out at an unprecedented speed and volume.

Just as important in this evolution are the communications professionals who either create, or react to, the news on behalf of their employers. These days, it goes beyond for-profit companies and government organizations to include nonprofits, school districts, and yes, celebrities and personalities.

So what distinguishes an amateur from a professional? An advanced degree in communications, journalism or media studies provides a graduate student with the skills she needs to be an effective and educated resource, honing any raw skills and nurturing a passion for the field. With rapidly changing technologies and new social media outlets, students can learn the latest trends and technologies to understand how they can work together for the biggest impact. A graduate degree can also give professionals in this area of study the solid background and experience to strike out on their own with more credibility.

Degrees Offered

The few PhDs pursued in this field are for post-secondary teaching and research, though there has been a a small surge in PhDs with 31-percent growth between 2008–2009 and 2013–2014. The majority of the 32,000 enrollees in this discipline pursue a master's degree.

Though programs vary by institution, if you want to report the news (writing, broadcasting, or publishing), you'd probably want to look at journalism programs. If you want to study forms of communication, methods, culture, or media, then you probably want to look into communications programs. Again, research both disciplines (sometimes housed in the same department) to determine the best path for your career.

The Master of Arts tends to be more common than the Master of Science in journalism, and the differences between programs vary from institution to institution. Remember, a broad knowledge of history and current events strengthens the quality of your work in the field while perseverance and experience tend to play a big role in making a good journalist great. Try to find programs that teach more than just core skills and feature a depth of writing experiences and frequent fieldwork. Some programs also provide the opportunity to focus in a particular subject area such as health care, science, business, etc. Master's programs in communications also offer a range of foci including advertising and marketing, politics, law, public policy, and the global and cultural aspects of communication in society or within an organization.

Depending on your career goals and your industry of preference, combined or interdisciplinary degrees can be found at many institutions, depending on where they house their communications, journalism and media studies programs.

MA Journalism (2–3 years)

MS Journalism (1–2 years)

MA Communications or Mass Communications (2–5 years)

BA / MA Journalism (5 years, starting junior year of college)

PhD Communications or Journalism (5–7 years, including dissertation)

Quick Snapshot: Communications, Journalism, Media Studies

SAMPLE DEGREE PROGRAM	NO. OF SCHOOLS OFFERING PROGRAM	DEGREE OPTIONS	APPLICATION CONSIDERATIONS
Communications and Media Studies	Master's: 101 Doctorate: 24	MA PhD	PhD candidates need experience; others do not but background courses a bonus
Journalism	Master's: 77 Doctorate: 6	MA, MS PhD	Background courses and sample work helpful; required for PhD candidates
Mass Communications/ Media Studies	Master's: 58 Doctorate: 0	MA, PhD	
Radio and Television	Master's: 23 Doctorate: 0	MA PhD	

You can find more detailed information to guide you on the right path from these trade organization websites.

TRADE ORGANIZATIONS YOU SHOULD KNOW	
The Associated Press ap.org	The AP is the momma bear of all journalistic agencies.
The Poynter Institute poynter.org	From its "Mission & History" statement: "The Poynter Institute...is the world's leading instructor, innovator, convener and resource for anyone who aspires to engage and inform citizens in 21st Century democracies."
American Society of Magazine Editors magazine.org/asme	The American Society of Magazine Editors is the professional organization for print and online magazine editors. Its website lists jobs, hosts discussion boards, and offers courses for junior editors, among other things.
National Communication Association natcom.org	The National Communication Association advances communication as the discipline that studies all forms, modes, media and consequences of communication through humanistic, social scientific and aesthetic inquiry. Find resources, publications, and careers on their website.
National Press Photographers Association nppa.org	Promotes photojournalism with competitions, workshops and seminars, and job listings.

Typical Admissions Requirements

Experience in journalism, whether in the classroom or on the streets, is a plus but not required. Writing samples from undergraduate study, undergraduate GPA, recommendations, essays and, in some cases, GRE scores are required. While undergraduate prerequisites vary, most programs require a bachelor's degree in a related field.

General graduate school requirements:

- Bachelor's degree from an accredited college or university

- Official transcript(s) from all colleges or universities attended

- GRE General Test scores* (different programs require different minimum scores)

- TOEFL score (if necessary)

- Letters of recommendation

- Letter of intent or statement of purpose

- Academic or professional writing samples

- Application forms

- Application fee

*Not required for all programs

COMPUTERS AND TECHNOLOGY

The field of computers and information technology includes three main disciplines: computer science, information systems, and information technology. The fields do overlap in terms of certain training and curriculum. A bachelor's degree is sufficient for many careers in these fields, but for those looking to advance within their organizations, manage teams, or teach, a graduate degree boosts your potential. In addition to Master of Science degrees, one might consider an MBA with a focus in technology.

Graduate programs focus on both theoretical frameworks, along with applied research and lab work. Because this is a rapidly changing field, a strong theory-based knowledge coupled with a practical orientation keeps students not only current, but in some cases on the cutting edge of advancing new technologies.

Computer scientists contribute to new technologies, including interactive multimedia and virtual reality systems. Time is divided between class and lab work to ensure that students are equipped with the necessary skills in software development, systems development, and new computer systems creation.

Information technology covers the entire spectrum of computer-based content, and those who undertake study in this field will learn about it all. Courses cover computer hardware and software; how to view and send information by computer plus how to adapt, control, and improve the experiences had by computer users. In addition, graduate students will learn how to create and modify the very systems that transmit the information—and how to best distribute that information to the target audience. Study will also include web-based computer applications, the fundamentals of e-commerce, the importance of web security, ethical issues and finally, how information technology affects business and society.

Those interested in more of a management-based career might want to consider a graduate program in management information systems (MIS). Studies in MIS will include management strategies and theories, how management can best use information systems and applications and security. You'll also learn how skillful use of information systems can lead to business solutions, help with decision-making and ways to improve the corporation.

Degrees Offered in Computers and Technology

Advanced degrees in computer science include either the Master of Arts or Master of Science, and of course, the PhD. Graduate students study broad, theoretical frameworks and then exercise that knowledge through lab work. Many who choose to pursue a doctorate select a concentration. Be sure to look for programs that produce and contribute to the latest research in computer science given that it is a rapidly changing field. Degree programs related to computer science include:

- Information Science

- Information Technology

- Management Information Systems (MIS)

- Systems Engineering

- Web/Multimedia Management

Graduate work in information technology covers everything from hardware and software to managing and transmitting the information as well as the end-user experience. Your hands-on graduate work culminates in a MS in information technology or information technology and management. Students wishing to teach or pursue more research can advance with a PhD program in either information technology or another computer-related field. For those interested in a more management-based IT career, consider an MS in management information systems (MIS), which prepares graduate students for management careers in technology. Alternatively, one could pursue an MBA with a focus or concentration in information systems.

Quick Snapshot: Computers and Technology

SAMPLE DEGREE PROGRAM	NO. OF SCHOOLS OFFERING PROGRAM	DEGREE OPTIONS	APPLICATION CONSIDERATIONS
Computer Science	Master's: 432 Doctorate: 274	MA, MS PhD	Higher math and computer programming courses
Information Science	Master's: 128 Doctorate: 26	MS PhD	Computer sciences background
Information Technology	Master's: 95 Doctorate: 11	MS IT, MS ITM PhD	Proficiency in computer science, basic computer programming, and higher mathematics
Computer Information Systems	Master's: 122 Doctorate: 5	MS, CIS PhD	Accounting, statistics, calculus, and computer programming; some require work experience

You can find more detailed information to guide you on the right path from these trade organization websites.

TRADE ORGANIZATIONS YOU SHOULD KNOW	
Association of Information Technology Professionals aitp.org	Education, peer support, and information for IT professionals in government, industry and academia.
HDI thinkhdi.com	The largest association for IT service and support professionals produces numerous publications, hosts several symposiums and conferences each year, and certifies hundreds of help desk and service desk professionals each month.
Society for Information Management simnet.org	Provides information and a community of shared experience among professionals.
TechAmerica TechAmerica.org	Public sector and public policy department of CompTIA, the IT industry trade association.

EDUCATION AND TEACHING

Many enter the teaching profession in order to make that connection with children or young adults where the proverbial light bulb goes on and the student "gets it." While the monetary rewards in teaching may not be substantial, the personal satisfaction in helping students develop intellectually and socially is a driving force behind the decision to teach.

Thanks to projected population growth, enrollment increases are expected across all grade-levels and so the outlook for teaching professionals is good. However, increased demands have been placed on teachers and administrators alike, meaning that it takes a special talent to be a successful classroom teacher or an effective administrator. Increased accountability, emphasis on standardized testing, more ESL students and growing classroom sizes are just a few of the challenges new teachers face every day. While the number of advanced degrees has decreased overall, and Master's degrees have decreased by 6 percent, the number of doctorates has increased by 21 percent. Demand for teachers continues to be highest for those who will work in rural or urban areas, or those who specialize in bilingual education, math and science, or special education.

Degrees Offered in Education and Teaching

There are literally thousands of programs in education, many of which require a teaching credential. Those who do not have a valid teaching credential or even an undergraduate background in education should look for programs that allow students to pursue licensure during their course of study.

For special ed (MS, MEd), and elementary and secondary school teaching (MS, MA, MEd), MS and MA programs usually require students to write a culminating thesis based on classroom research, whereas MEd programs usually do not. MS programs may also require more class work in methodology and research than MA or MEd programs. Most of these programs can be completed in one to two years with flexible part-time, evening, or summer options for current teachers.

Master's programs in educational administration usually span about one or two years and require successful performance in advanced level coursework, as well as participation in a practicum, research project, or internship. Some schools also require students to complete a master's thesis. After completing a master's degree in educational administration, students may choose to continue their studies in an Educational Specialist (EdS) program, designed for students who want to engage in advanced fieldwork, internship experience, or research in a specific area of education. Doctoral programs in educational administration usually focus on research or public policy as it relates to school leadership.

Post-secondary teachers require a PhD or the terminal degree in the field in which they want to teach (for example, an MFA to teach arts and music at the post-secondary level). See also the Humanities and Cultures section for more information on many post-secondary fields.

More Reading
To learn more about teacher certification, check out our book *Cracking the Praxis, 2nd Edition*.

Quick Snapshot: Education and Teaching

SAMPLE DEGREE PROGRAM	NO. OF SCHOOLS OFFERING PROGRAM	DEGREE OPTIONS	APPLICATION CONSIDERATIONS
Art Teacher Education	Master's: 140 Doctorate: 9	MA PhD	Prior coursework or other formal training in fine or studio arts
Bilingual and Multilingual Education	Master's: 50 Doctorate: 3	MA, MS, MEd, MBE, PhD	Proven proficiency in a second language
Early Childhood Education and Teaching	Master's: 213 Doctorate: 13	MA, MAT, MS PhD	Teaching experience and certification
Education Leadership and Administration	Master's: 581 Doctorate: 308	MA, EdS PhD	Teaching or administrative credential, plus two years professional experience
Elementary Education and Teaching	Master's: 464 Doctorate: 15	MS, MA, MEd PhD	Valid state teaching credential and teaching experience
Secondary Education and Teaching	Master's: 345 Doctorate: 9	MS, MA, Med PhD	Major in education or in the subject matter one plans to teach
Special Education	Master's: 564 Doctorate: 65	MS, MEd PhD	Major or some coursework in education or special education

You can find more detailed information to guide you on the right path from these trade organization websites.

TRADE ORGANIZATIONS YOU SHOULD KNOW	
AASA: The School Superintendents Association aasa.org	AASA is a national association of school system leaders. Their website contains a job board, industry related articles, membership information, and links to state associations.
National Association for Bilingual Education (NABE) nabe.org	A professional association for bilingual educators. The site has information about the field and a great page of links to related sites.
National Association of State Boards of Education nasbe.org	The National Association of State Boards of Education will help you find information about state-specific school districts including links about certification requirements, teaching standards, and a section on early childhood education.
National Science Teachers Association nsta.org	The National Science Teachers Association is a national organization of science teachers. Check their web site for information on conferences, news, publications, and other education resources.
United States Department of Education ed.gov	Information about Every Student Succeeds and other federal programs on education.

Typical Admissions Requirements

Students applying to education and teaching programs typically have several years of teaching or administration experience along with a valid teaching credential. However, some master's level programs will include a certification component for students interested in entering the education field without prior experience or certification.

General graduate school requirements:

- Bachelor's degree from an accredited college or university
- Official transcript(s) from all colleges or universities attended
- GRE General Test scores (different programs require different minimum scores)
- TOEFL score (if necessary)
- Academic letters of recommendation
- Letter of intent or statement of purpose
- Application forms
- Application fee

Some degree programs will also require:

- Interview
- Miller Analogies Test (MAT)
- Portfolio (Arts Education)

ENGINEERING

Engineering is a long-respected field leading to many challenging and exciting careers that draw upon creativity, innovative thinking, and a strong foundation in math and science. Engineers are the link between scientific discovery and the commercial application and production of those innovations in society.

There are over 1.4 million engineers employed in the United States, with 4 percent growth expected through 2024. All advanced degrees conferred grew 5 percent through 2013–2014, and PhDs saw an impressive 30 percent growth. With ancient roots dating back to the building of the pyramids, modern engineering trends show a dramatic increase in biomedical engineering as well as higher demand for infrastructure projects to preserve aging buildings, bridges, and transportation systems. Electrical engineering programs are the largest, with nearly a third of all engineering student enrollment.

Degrees Offered

Engineering offers a wide range of degree programs, each of which contains many concentrations for specialization. For example, a civil engineer could specialize in construction, hydrosystems, structural, or transportation engineering.

Most master's programs are one to two years in length. While not all programs require a relevant bachelor's degree, they do require a strong background in math, science, and engineering undergraduate courses. For those interested in research or academia, further study is required for a Doctorate in Engineering. An alternative to the PhD is a Doctor of Engineering Science (EngScD).

Quick Snapshot: Engineering

SAMPLE DEGREE PROGRAM	NO. OF SCHOOLS OFFERING PROGRAM	% OF ENGINEERING ENROLLMENT*	% OF ENGINEERING EMPLOYMENT **	SPECIAL APPLICATION NOTES
Aerospace	Master's: 61 Doctorate: 44	3%	5%	BS aerospace engineering or significant math and engineering coursework
Biomedical	Master's: 131 Doctorate: 109	6%	2%	
Chemical	Master's: 142 Doctorate: 113	6%	2%	
Civil	Master's: 190 Doctorate: 125	13%	19%	Very competitive admission. Strong scores in engineering, math & science undergraduate courses.
Electrical, Electronics	Master's: 239 Doctorate: 150	32%	22%	BS electrical engineering or related field, minimum 3.0 GPA
Materials	Master's: 80 Doctorate: 72	5%	2%	BS in related field or significant coursework in math and science
Mechanical	Master's: 219 Doctorate: 140	16%	19%	BS in engineering or related subject; minimum GPA; math & science pre-requisites

*National Science Foundation/National Center for Science and Engineering Studies

**Bureau of Labor and Statistics, Occupational Outlook Handbook, 2014–15.

You can find more detailed information to guide you on the right path from these trade organization websites.

TRADE ORGANIZATIONS YOU SHOULD KNOW	
National Society of Professional Engineers nspe.org	The National Society of Professional Engineers has the scoop on all the latest technologies and licensing regulations.
American Engineering Association aea.org	The American Engineering Association provides a support system for all engineers. Included on the site are links to information for computer and electrical engineers.
American Society of Civil Engineers asce.org	The American Society of Civil Engineers is the best clearing house for the field. This is the place to look for news, jobs, and licensing information.
Institute of Electrical and Electronics Engineers ieee.org	IEEE is the most complete site dealing specifically with electrical engineering. It also contains job information, interesting articles on the field, and even a virtual museum.
ASME asme.org	An excellent resource for both experienced workers and newcomers to the field. They have a very thorough Career & Education section.
NASA (National Aeronautics and Space Administration) nasa.gov	The site includes recent news about NASA and its accomplishments.

Typical Admissions Requirements

Most graduate engineering programs look for substantial coursework in math and science at the undergraduate level, and some require specific classes or majors within the field. Be sure to carefully review admissions requirements well in advance so you can meet all requirements before you apply. Depending on the program, schools might require a minimum GPA.

General graduate school requirements:

- Bachelor's degree from an accredited college or university
- Official transcript(s) from all colleges or universities attended
- GRE General Test scores (different programs require different minimum scores)
- TOEFL score (if necessary)
- Letters of recommendation
- Application forms
- Application fee

Some degree programs will also require:

- Interview
- Letter of intent or statement of purpose
- Supplementary essays

ENVIRONMENTAL SCIENCE, NATURAL RESOURCE MANAGEMENT, CONSERVATION, AND SUSTAINABILITY

As green issues grow in importance, popularity, and sometimes controversy, the professional fields that employ environmental scientists, conservationists, and natural resource managers are expanding.

In fact, the National Center for Education Statistics did not even track graduate enrollment in natural resources and conservation in the mid 1990s, but reported 22,000 graduate enrollees as of 2011–2012. Job growth in this sector is projected at 11 percent through 2024.

Whether driven by the science behind these issues or the laws and policies (informed by the science and social issues) that impact the environment, people enter this field to make a difference and help keep our planet in good shape for the next generation. Many schools create interdisciplinary programs to encompass the various subjects that impact this field; one might take courses across departments of biology, law, anthropology, sociology, and business or economics. In addition, graduates students can specialize in their particular area of interest, whether more focused on wildlife, water, forestry, land-use, etc.

In general, environmental science takes a more scientific, research-based approach to the problems while environmental studies encompasses the social, historical, political, and legal aspects of the field, with a foundation in scientific data. Be sure to research a specific school's program description and curriculum, as environmental studies is open to interpretation by a school's faculty and departments. If your interest area is specific to forestry, flora and fauna (wildlands), fisheries and aquatic life, or mammals (wildlife), there are master's and PhD programs for these subject areas. Also, think about your geography, as your fieldwork can be greatly enhanced by the location of your graduate program.

Degrees Offered

While there are opportunities for those with bachelor's degrees to work in this field, master's degrees provide opportunities for advancement and management positions including leading research teams or controlling the direction of projects. Master's degree programs also give students an opportunity to conduct in-depth research employing scientific methods and fieldwork, and exploring the broad spectrum of environmental issues, like the laws and policies that impact this discipline. Of course, a PhD is required for some teaching, research, or senior positions at policy institutes and government agencies.

When choosing your degree program, consider whether you want a broad approach to natural sciences with a specific focus area or would prefer a scientific approach within your area of focus. Degree options include:

- MA or MS in Environmental Studies/Science

- PhD in Environmental Studies/Science

- Master of Forestry, MS or PhD Forestry

- MS or PhD Natural Resources Management and Policy

- MS or PhD Wildlife or Wildlands Science and Management

Quick Snapshot: Environmental Sciences

SAMPLE DEGREE PROGRAM	NO. OF SCHOOLS OFFERING PROGRAM	DEGREE OPTIONS	PROGRAM CONSIDERATIONS
Environmental Science	Master's: 107 Doctorate: 39	MA, MS PhD	Some schools offer thesis and non-thesis options. Also consider broader study versus an area of focus, like water, animals, land, etc.
Environmental Studies	Master's: 70 Doctorate: 13	MA, MS PhD	This discipline provides a broader approach to the issues, covering the environment including social, political, historical, scientific, etc.
Forestry	Master's: 46 Doctorate: 32	MFR, MS PhD	Master of Science and PhD degrees are more research-oriented than the Master of Forestry degree.
Natural Resources Management and Policy	Master's: 34 Doctorate: 12	MS, JD/MS PhD	Check for interdisciplinary programs or joint degree programs in law or business to tailor your focus.
Wildlife and Wildlands Science	Master's: 26 Doctorate: 16	MS PhD	Applicants should have undergraduate coursework/major in biology or related sciences.

You can find more detailed information to guide you on the right path from these trade organizations websites.

TRADE ORGANIZATIONS YOU SHOULD KNOW	
Joint Forestry Team jointforestryteam.org	Different organizations join resources to make recommendations that result in coordinated interagency delivery of forestry and conservation assistance for working forests, farms, and ranches: USDA-National Resources Conservation Service (NRCS), the National Association of State Foresters (NASF), the National Association of Conservation Districts (NACD), and the USDA Forest Service (USFS).
National Audubon Society audubon.org	For more than a century, the Audubon Society has been committed to conserving and restoring natural ecosystems, particularly for birds and wildlife.
Natural Resources Conservation Service nrcs.usda.gov	Established by Congress in 1935 as the Soil Conservation Service, this agency's name was changed in 1994 to reflect its broadening scope.
League of Conservation Voters lcv.org	A national non-profit that works to keep environmental issues as national priorities, often through grass-roots campaigning, awareness, and education.

Typical Admissions Requirements

Depending on your area of focus, programs may look for a variety of coursework, including anthropology, biology, sociology and more. Undergraduate GPA, recommendations, essays, and GRE scores are required. While undergraduate prerequisites vary, some programs look for an undergraduate degree in a field such as the natural sciences, social sciences, or engineering. For students pursuing subject matter related to policy or economics, schools will look for relevant majors/coursework in those areas.

General graduate school requirements:

- Bachelor's degree from an accredited college or university
- Official transcript(s) from all colleges or universities attended
- GRE General Test scores (different programs require different minimum scores)
- TOEFL score (if necessary)
- Letters of recommendation
- Letter of intent or statement of purpose
- Application forms
- Application fee

Some degree programs schools also require:

Specific coursework in a related field. Some schools give conditional acceptance until students earn credits for a specific area that is lacking.

HEALTH CARE AND PUBLIC HEALTH

The field of health care is experiencing explosive growth due to the growing elderly population and technological advances in the treatment and diagnosis of illness, disease, injury, and other physical and mental impairments. With a fantastic job outlook, all graduate degrees conferred grew 40 percent in five years (from 2008–2009 to 2013–2014). Many careers in this field require advanced education and/or specialization, and the number of advanced degrees conferred mirrors the growth pattern in this industry, with a 55-percent increase in master's degrees and 23-percent increase in PhD's conferred (from 2008–09 to 2013–14).

Degrees Offered in Health Care and Public Health

Graduate degrees in health care or public health are required for many careers in this field. For audiologists, speech pathologists, occupational or physical therapists, and many other health careers, a master's degree or professional degree prepares you for work with patients whether in hospitals, clinics, ambulatory care centers, or physicians' offices. Some nurses and public health graduates interested in administration or management pursue joint degrees, such as a joint MBA program.

Growth in the health care industry is evidenced by the dramatic growth seen in advanced degrees conferred. Particularly notable is the rise in the number of doctorates or professional degrees, which grew to over 64,000 in 2013.

Some master's degree programs are coupled with undergraduate programs while others allow you to enter without a specific bachelor's degree as long as you meet prerequisites. Some examples include Master of Science in Nursing, Master in Public Health or Master of Science in Public Health, Master of Science in Physical Therapy, etc. Another possible career path in health care is the Doctor of Medicine (MD) or the Doctor of Osteopathic Medicine (DO). Admission to these programs is very competitive and it's worth noting that admission requires a strong background in sciences and math as well as solid MCAT scores.

Further Reading
Are you thinking about taking the MCAT? Prepare with some of our fantastic MCAT review products: Our series of MCAT Review books by subject (collect all 6!)

Quick Snapshot: Health Care & Public Health

SAMPLE DEGREE PROGRAM	NO. OF SCHOOLS OFFERING PROGRAM	DEGREE OPTIONS	APPLICATION CONSIDERATIONS (*required or recommended)
Audiology	Master's: 103 Doctorate: 113	MA, MS PhD	Credits in biology, physical science, mathematics, behavioral or social sciences, and speech and language development
Family Nurse Practitioner Studies	Master's: 162 Doctorate: 319	MS PhD	Solid background in physics and mathematics
Health Care Admin., Hospital Management	Master's: 342 Doctorate: 37	MHA, MPH, MBA PhD	Some work experience; background in statistics, accounting, or economics
Nursing Administration	Master's: 148 Doctorate: 14	MS PhD	Background in chemistry, physics, calculus; Specific pre-reqs based on area of focus
Occupational Therapy	Master's: 150 Doctorate: 32	MS PhD	BS OT or relevant coursework, i.e., anatomy, physiology, or psychology
Physical Therapy	Master's: 45 Doctorate: 222	MPT, DPT, MS PhD, Ed D	BS PT or relevant coursework
Public Health	Master's: 225 Doctorate: 61	MPH, DPH Joint Degrees (MD, MPH, RN)	College-level math or biostatistics and the sciences*

You can find more detailed information to guide you on the right path from these trade organization websites.

TRADE ORGANIZATIONS YOU SHOULD KNOW	
American Association of Nurse Practitioners aanp.org	The American Association of Nurse Practitioners is an advocacy and policy oriented organization of nurse practitioners.
American College of Epidemiology acepidemiology.org	The American College of Epidemiology is a professional organization dedicated to continued education for epidemiologists and their efforts to promote the public health.
American Physical Therapy Association apta.org	The American Physical Therapy Association has scholarship listings, seminar information, and related resources.
American Public Health Association (APHA) apha.org	The APHA is an organization dedicated to promoting research on issues in public health and influencing public health policies for over 125 years.
Nursing Center nursingcenter.com	The Nursing Center is a resource for professional nurses. Its website offers articles, job listings, CE activities, and message boards.

Typical Admissions Requirements

Requirements vary depending on the program you wish to pursue—be sure to read about specific prerequisites for the schools on your list. Most professions in this field need majors or coursework in the sciences and statistics while business and economics are common admissions requirements for managerial positions.

Trends in Health Care and Public Health

Technological advances in healthcare mean more options for treating illnesses and diseases. Coupled with an increased emphasis on preventative care, this will drive demand for more nurses, already the largest healthcare occupation at over 2.75 million.

Hospitals are one of the largest employers of healthcare workers; despite this, hospitals will see a slower rate of new jobs because clinics and other outpatient care sites are growing in use.

Fourteen of the top twenty fastest growing occupations (across all occupations) are healthcare related, meaning that the industry as a whole should see 18-percent growth in jobs through 2024.

The aging baby boom population will increase demand in specialties like occupational therapy, physical therapy, audiology, and speech pathology.

HUMANITIES AND CULTURES

Socrates taught the adage "Know thyself." Our need to find meaning and connect with one another runs deep in our humanity. The various degree areas of focus in the humanities and cultures provide a context that allows us to better understand "who we are" through the study of literature, culture, gender or ethnic identity, philosophy, religion, and even the very languages we speak. The analytical thinking and writing skills required for many of these disciplines translate well to many jobs in our modern economy.

Post-secondary teaching and writing opportunities show solid competition for jobs, but job outlook remains fair depending on the area pursued. Growth in advanced degrees has remained steady at 9 percent over a five-year period (from 2007–08 to 2012–13), however there was a 2 percent dip in between 2013 and 2014.

SAMPLE DEGREE PROGRAM	NO. OF SCHOOLS OFFERING PROGRAM	DEGREE OPTIONS	APPLICATION CONSIDERATIONS (*required or recommended)
Creative Writing	Master's: 183 Doctorate: 3	MA, MFA PhD	High grades in previous creative writing courses*; manuscript in area of focus
English Language and Literature	Master's: 413 Doctorate: 143	MA PhD	GRE Subject Test in Literature in English*; foreign language
Liberal Arts & Sciences, Humanities	Master's: 288 Doctorate: 17	MA, MS PhD	Background coursework or undergraduate major
Linguistics	Master's: 93 Doctorate: 57	MA, MS PhD	Writing sample, curriculum vitae
Philosophy, Philosophy & Religion	Master's: 158 Doctorate: 109	MA, MTA/MTS MDiv/Mphil, PhD	Relevant coursework or major recommended

Degrees Offered in Humanities and Cultures

Most master's degree programs in humanities and cultures take one to two years to complete, with a culminating thesis and exams. This is true for creative writing, but students also have the option to pursue a Master of Fine Arts, which usually takes two to four years and typically requires a manuscript of publishable quality to complete the program.

Those who choose to go on to pursue a PhD can expect to spend five to seven years fulfilling course requirements, writing a thesis and ultimately, defending it orally. Many PhD programs also have written exam requirements. For degrees in comparative literature and even other areas of literature, there are also foreign language requirements.

A master's level (MA or MS) degree in linguistics covers core areas of language structure, field methods, and research. Programs may be class-based or thesis-based; most take about two years. A PhD in linguistics may take an additional three to four years. Most doctoral programs encompass master's level material but focus on theoretical topics in language structure, language acquisition, and processing.

You can find more detailed information to guide you on the right path from these trade organization websites.

TRADE ORGANIZATIONS YOU SHOULD KNOW	
American Academy of Religion aarweb.org	The world's largest organization of academics researching and teaching religion-related topics.
American Comparative Literature Association acla.org	Provides links to journals, prizes, conferences, and also to affiliated associations and research sources.
Linguistic Society of America linguisticsociety.org	This is the largest linguistic society in the world; an interest in the field is the only requirement for membership. In addition to a regularly published journal, *Language*, the LSA hosts annual meetings and summer institutes
The Modern Language Association of America mla.org	Information on periodicals, conferences, readings, jobs, and style guides. It also provides a quarterly newsletter and links to accredited universities.
The Voice of the Shuttle vos.ucsb.edu	An online compendium of sites for academic research. It contains searchable areas from multiple disciplines in the humanities.

Typical Admissions Requirements

Admissions requirements vary across the broad spectrum of programs within humanities and cultures, but most programs require excellent writing skills, so essays, statement of purpose, and/or academic writing samples will often be required as part of the admissions process. For American or English literature as well as comparative literature, be ready to take the GRE Subject Test in Literature in English in addition to the GRE.

General graduate school requirements:

- Bachelor's degree from an accredited college or university
- Official transcript(s) from all colleges or universities attended
- GRE General Test scores (different programs require different minimum scores)
- TOEFL score (if necessary)
- Academic letters of recommendation
- Letter of intent or statement of purpose, essays
- Application forms
- Application fee

Some degree programs will also require:

- Curriculum vitae
- GRE Subject Test: Literature in English
- Academic writing samples

MATHEMATICS AND STATISTICS

Mathematics is a unique field that requires more than just a mastery of existing techniques and theories; it actually gives mathematicians the opportunity to discern the need for and test the creation of new theories.

The advanced study of mathematics and statistics develops problem solving and critical thinking skills that are sought after and applied in many different career paths. An advanced degree in mathematics or statistics is required for university-level teaching and advanced research.

When looking for graduate programs, know that academic institutions vary the way they structure their programs and departments. Some statistics departments are housed within the mathematics department while others are separate. Some schools break out applied mathematics to differentiate it from "pure" mathematics. While not all professionals agree on the exact distinctions, applied math generally refers to the mathematical methods used in specific areas such as business, science and engineering, or industries like insurance, healthcare, and finance. Applied math often results in the development of new mathematical models, which are in turn studied in pure mathematics, which covers more theory and generalities.

As a pure mathematician, career opportunities are more competitive unless the degree is coupled with an area of industry focus. Some careers that benefit from advanced math and stats knowledge are physics, actuarial science, biostatistics, engineering, operations research, computer science, marketing, business and industrial management, economics, finance, chemistry, geology, life sciences, behavioral sciences, and many other fields.

Quick Snapshot: Mathematics and Statistics

SAMPLE DEGREE PROGRAM	NO. OF SCHOOLS OFFERING PROGRAM	DEGREE OPTIONS	APPLICATION CONSIDERATIONS
Applied Mathematics	Master's: 99 Doctorate: 56	MA, MS PhD	Recommend background in linear algebra, real analysis, probability or statistics, theoretical computer science.
Computational Mathematics	Master's: 13 Doctorate: 12	MS PhD	Often combined with applied mathematics, heavy focus on developing computer models.
Mathematics	Master's: 326 Doctorate: 158	MA, MS PhD	Math background, incl. Abstract Algebra and Advanced Calculus. Some have minimum GPA requirements.
Statistics	Master's: 131 Doctorate: 65	MS PhD	Pre-requisites include Calculus, Linear Algebra, Statistics, and knowledge of a programming language.

Degrees Offered in Mathematics and Statistics

Master's degrees can be pursued on their own, but are also pursued by doctoral candidates in other related fields such as computer science, engineering fields, physics, business, finance, etc. Schools often have thesis and non-thesis options, which in some cases means the MA option is non-thesis and the MS option is thesis track, but this is not always the case. Other schools track the MA option for secondary school or community college-level teaching, but again, programs vary. Read the department descriptions about each option to see how it best fits to your intended career path. Degree options include:

- MS or MA Mathematics (12–24 months)

- MS or MA Applied Mathematics (12–24 months)

- MS or MA Statistics (12–24 months)

- PhD Mathematics (4–6 years)

- PhD Statistics (4–6 years)

The PhD track is best suited for teaching and research at the university level, or for quantitative research and development in industry or government.

TRADE ORGANIZATIONS YOU SHOULD KNOW	
American Mathematical Society (AMS) ams.org	A rich resource for news and events, publications, jobs, and research (as you might expect, AMS has lots of data and statistics on education and careers in mathematics).
American Statistical Association amstat.org	The world's largest community of statisticians provides resources, news and events, career information, and even scholarships and grants for statisticians worldwide.
Data.gov	A website run by the federal government; its goal is to make executive branch data sets accessible and available to the public. Among other things, it encourages app development, and community interaction by area, such as energy or health.
Society for Industrial and Applied Mathematics siam.org	SIAM's mission is to build cooperation between mathematics and the worlds of science and technology through publications, research, and community.

Typical Admissions Requirements

- Minimum GPA

- Major in math, statistics, or related area with a background in calculus (multivariate, probability) and linear algebra

Some programs require the GRE Subject Test in Mathematics.

Some graduate programs in mathematics (typically pure math PhD track) have a foreign language requirement, particularly in French, Russian, or German. Many programs require knowledge of a programming language.

General Graduate School Requirements

- Bachelor's degree from an accredited college or university

- Official transcript(s) from all colleges or universities attended

- GRE General Test scores* (different programs require different minimum scores)

- TOEFL score (if necessary)

- Letters of recommendation

- Letter of intent or statement of purpose

- Writing samples

- Application forms

- Application fee

*Not required for all programs

PHYSICAL AND EARTH SCIENCES

A highly analytical and research-intensive area, the physical and earth sciences attempt to understand the universe and everything in it: the earth's atmosphere, the earth itself and its oceans, right on down to subatomic particles.

To observe, measure, interpret and develop theories, the understanding and use of mathematics is a critical component to these sciences. Knowledge gained in research is used to design new technologies. Many of these scientists opt to apply their skills in engineering.

For most jobs in physical and earth sciences, an advanced degree is required. Enrollment, as well as the number of degrees conferred, has shown consistent growth to fill these jobs. Projected job growth is forecasted to average 8 percent in all areas (2014–2024 projection), but closer examination shows more competition in areas like chemistry (the largest field in the group), and very good job opportunities in hydrology and geosciences. Funds from the federal government are helping to boost job growth in the physical sciences as well. In 2007, Congress passed the America COMPETES Act (reauthorized by Congress in 2010), which funds government agencies employing physical scientists to boost the nation's standing in technology and innovation.

Quick Snapshot: Physical & Earth Sciences

SAMPLE DEGREE PROGRAM	NO. OF SCHOOLS OFFERING PROGRAM	DEGREE OPTIONS	APPLICATION CONSIDERATIONS (*required or recommended)
Astronomy	Master's: 30 Doctorate: 28	MS PhD	Astronomy major or strong background in physics*
Chemistry	Master's: 320 Doctorate: 209	MS PhD	Chemistry major* GRE Subject Test in Chemistry
Geological and Earth Sciences	Master's: 210 Doctorate: 123	MS PhD	Background in chemistry, physics, calculus; specific pre-reqs based on area of focus
Physics	Master's: 257 Doctorate: 187	MS PhD	Physics major,* GRE Subject Test in Physics

Typical Admissions Requirements

Without an undergraduate degree in the same field, which many programs will require, a strong background in the physical sciences and mathematics is preferred, and is the best preparation for graduate school. In addition to the GRE, schools may require the GRE subject test in Chemistry or Physics.

Given the research-oriented nature of a graduate degree in physical sciences, be sure to do your homework about the areas of research among the faculty, so you can tailor your letter of intent or statement of purpose to the research or specialty you want to pursue in graduate school.

American Chemical Society acs.org	Publishes numerous scientific journals and databases, convenes major research conferences, and provides educational, science policy, and career programs in chemistry. Also grants more than $22 million in funds for basic research.
American Institute of Hydrology aihydrology.org	Establishes the standards for the certification of hydrologists; encompasses both student and professional chapters.
American Institute of Physics aip.org	Umbrella society for physicists and astronomers, students, and teachers of those subjects. Publishes journals, and website lists valuable resources and job postings.
American Meteorological Society ametsoc.org	Provides certification, as well as a wealth of information about the field including job postings and grants.
American Physical Society aps.org	Second largest organization of physicists which hosts meetings, publishes journals, and provides career information through its website.

General graduate school requirements:

- Bachelor's degree from an accredited college or university
- Official transcript(s) from all colleges or universities attended
- GRE General Test scores (different programs require different minimum scores)
- TOEFL score (if necessary)
- Academic letters of recommendation
- Letter of intent or statement of purpose
- Application forms
- Application fee

Some degree programs will also require:

- GRE Subject Test: Chemistry
- GRE Subject Test: Physics
- Interview or campus visit
- Relevant work experience

PSYCHOLOGY

Psychology is a science that attempts to better understand mental processes and predict human behavior through careful observation, study and research. It is a popular field with many areas of focus, from industrial and organizational (that applies the principles of psychology in the workplace) to clinical or counseling psychology, where one can focus on children, families, or senior citizens, to name a few.

In general, those interested in psychology follow either a research/teaching track or a counseling track. Psychologists work in schools, hospitals and assisted living centers, and teach or conduct research in schools, colleges, and universities.

About 34 percent of all psychologists are self-employed. In a field that has limited job prospects for those with a bachelor's degree, competition for admission to graduate programs is high. Those with a doctoral degree will find the best job prospects in the field, particularly with a focus in a subfield such as health. For those seeking a master's degree, job prospects are best in industrial-organizational psychology. Though the job outlook for psychology is good, the number of advanced degrees conferred is growing at 15 percent (2008–09 to 2013–14).

Be sure to consider all the possible paths to reach your goals, such as Doctor of Medicine in Psychiatry, a Master's in Social Work for counseling, or pursuing an advanced degree in education with certification in counseling.

Degrees Offered in Psychology

Students in clinical psychology who wish for a practitioner-based degree with less focus on research can pursue the PsyD (Doctor of Psychology), while students with more research-focused or teaching interests can pursue a PhD in many of the fields of psychology. Both degrees take around five years to complete and are highly competitive. Some students choose to pursue their clinical psychology interests by earning a Master's in Social Work (MSW). Social workers are licensed after completing their MSW program from a Council on Social Work Education (CSWE) accredited program (usually about two years long) and passing their state's Association of Social Work Boards exam. Students should think carefully about their interests and career goals before selecting a program.

Students can also earn a terminal MS degree in their respective field of psychology (clinical, school, etc.), usually within two to three years; however as with most professions, the higher you go, the more careers open up to you. Graduate work in counseling psychology usually culminates in either a PhD or an EdD, both of which take around five years to complete. The PhD is more research-intensive than the EdD, and both are slightly less academically rigorous than the PhD or PsyD in clinical psychology.

For school psychology the minimum required degree tends to be a master's from a state-approved, two-year school psychology program with at least one year of internship experience. Many states require a more research-heavy Educational Specialist (EdS) degree, and a good number of school psychologists also hold doctorate degrees.

Quick Snapshot: Psychology

SAMPLE DEGREE PROGRAM	NO. OF SCHOOLS OFFERING PROGRAM	% OF EMPLOYMENT	SPECIAL APPLICATION NOTES
Clinical Psychology	Master's: 162 Doctorate: 161	91%	Coursework in natural or social sciences; GRE Subject Test: Psychology
Counseling Psychology	Master's: 252 Doctorate: 76	See Clinical	Coursework in natural or social sciences a bonus.
Developmental and Child Psychology	Master's: 20 Doctorate: 15	8%	Coursework in psychology often required
Educational Psychology	Master's: 91 Doctorate: 68	See Developmental	College coursework in statistics, education & developmental psychology
Experimental Psychology	Master's: 29 Doctorate: 23	See Developmental	
Industrial and Organizational Psychology	Master's: 61 Doctorate: 30	1%	Psychology major or coursework required
School Psychology	Master's: 150 Doctorate: 66	See Clinical	Psychology and education background a bonus, but not required
Social Psychology	Master's: 10 Doctorate: 15	See Developmental	

You can find more detailed information to guide you on the right path from these trade organization websites.

TRADE ORGANIZATIONS YOU SHOULD KNOW	
American Psychological Association apa.org	The American Psychological Association offers information on all areas within the field.
Association for Psychological Science psychologicalscience.org	The Association for Psychological Science publishes news, research, and journals and promotes scientific research within the field of psychology.
American Counseling Association counseling.org	The American Counseling Association offers information on all areas within the field, including information on state certification.
National Association of School Psychologists (NASP) nasponline.org	Official website of the NASP, dedicated to sharing resources, studies, and strategies in order to help the public and policymakers recognize the effects of students' mental health on their development, as well as the importance of school psychological services.
Association of State and Provincial Psychology Boards asppb.org	Contains information about state licensing requirements.

General graduate school requirements:

- Bachelor's degree from an accredited college or university

- Official transcript(s) from all colleges or universities attended

- GRE General Test scores (different programs require different minimum scores)

- TOEFL score (if necessary)

- Academic letters of recommendation

- Letter of intent or statement of purpose
- Application forms
- Application fee

Some degree programs will also require:

- GRE Subject Test: Psychology
- Interview

PUBLIC AFFAIRS AND POLICY

Public affairs is an umbrella that unites public policy and public administration, drawing upon the fields of political science and economics, to promote and advance policies and solutions that seek to address the public good. For those who like to keep their opinions to themselves, note that public administration is considered a non-partisan environment focused on method and historical context. Public policy discussions, on the other hand, are inherently partisan, as those involved seek to advance their agenda and view of the world as the "rule of the day."

Job outlook is good, but the number of advanced degrees is growing faster than projected job growth. Historically, advanced degrees led to government jobs, but many graduates now work in think tanks, as lobbyists, in academia, for unions or labor relations groups, and in other non-profit and community organizations. Given the economic crises faced by many state and local governments (which employ about 8.3 million people), be sure to keep options open when seeking employment, especially considering the growing popularity of the field. The number of advanced degrees conferred has grown by 31 percent in just five years (2008–09 to 2013–14).

Quick Snapshot: Public Affairs & Policy

SAMPLE DEGREE PROGRAM	NO. OF SCHOOLS OFFERING PROGRAM	DEGREE OPTIONS	SPECIAL APPLICATION NOTES
Public Administration	Master's: 368 Doctorate: 49	MPA PhD (rare)	Previous work experience sometimes required.
Public Policy/ Analysis	Master's: 80 Doctorate: 40	MPA PhD (rare)	Coursework in in economics, statistics, or college-level math helpful.

TRADE ORGANIZATIONS YOU SHOULD KNOW	
American Society for Public Administration aspanet.org	The American Society for Public Administration has a wealth of information on everything from the latest policy-making decisions and resource centers to job listings.
Association for Public Policy Analysis and Management appam.org	The Association for Public Policy Analysis and Management has information on conferences, internships, educational programs, jobs, joint degrees, and awards.
National Academy of Public Administration napawash.org	The National Academy for Public Administration is committed to monitoring and improving governance systems of all kinds.
Network of Schools of Public Policy, Affairs, and Administration naspaa.org	Accredits schools of public affairs, including those with dual accreditation. For example, business schools like Willamette University are accredited by both AACSB and NASPAA.

Typical Admissions Requirements

There are no major requirements necessary to apply for advanced degrees in public policy or administration. Many students have at least one year of work experience prior to starting their program. For public policy, helpful background coursework includes economics, statistics, or college-level math.

General graduate school requirements:

- Bachelor's degree from an accredited college or university
- Official transcript(s) from all colleges or universities attended
- GRE General Test scores (different programs require different minimum scores)
- TOEFL score (if necessary)
- Letters of recommendation

- Letter of intent or statement of purpose

- Application forms

- Application fee

Some degree programs will also require:

- Work experience

SOCIAL SCIENCES

Social sciences encompass the academic study of fields that fall outside of the natural sciences and focus on society, including the study of groups, organizations, institutions, social and economic systems, cultures, and governments. These disciplines adopt scientific method, with both quantitative and qualitative analysis geared to social understanding and improvement.

As globalization creates more complex economies, immigration and social media bring more cultures together, and political systems shift to reflect changes in society, the importance of the social sciences is perhaps greater than ever before.

While the employment outlook for social sciences is competitive in places like history and economics, many social sciences are experiencing much faster than average growth. This is somewhat reflected in the number of candidates receiving an advanced degree, which has grown by 12 percent (2008–09 to 2013–14).

Quick Snapshot: Social Sciences

SAMPLE DEGREE PROGRAM	NO. OF SCHOOLS OFFERING PROGRAM	DEGREE OPTIONS	SPECIAL APPLICATION NOTES
Anthropology	Master's: 161 Doctorate: 99	MA PhD	Proficiency in at least one foreign language
Economics	Master's: 189 Doctorate: 116	MA, MS PhD	Elementary economics & statistics background
Geography	Master's: 132 Doctorate: 62	MA, MS PhD	Some programs require minimum GPA or GRE
International Relations & Affairs	Master's: 82 Doctorate: 14	MA, MIA, Joint Degrees (Law, Journalism)	Proficiency in foreign language
Political Science and Government	Master's: 223 Doctorate: 122	MA PhD	Political science or government background preferred, but not required
Sociology	Master's: 228 Doctorate: 115	MSoc, MS PhD	Social science majors or some background in sociology or statistics
Social Sciences, General	Master's: 81 Doctorate: 16	MSSc PhD	Varies

TRADE ORGANIZATIONS YOU SHOULD KNOW

American Anthropological Association aaanet.org	The American Anthropological Association has offered anthropology professionals support, information, and services since 1902.
American Planning Association planning.org	The American Planning Association has advice on planning in urban and rural areas as well as fellowship and conference information.
American Political Science Association apsanet.org	More than 15,000 members in more than 80 countries share knowledge, professional advice and advancement, and a supportive environment conducive to the professional study of politics.
American Sociological Association asanet.org	Information for sociologists, students, and the general public including job opportunities, research grants, and newly-published reports from members.
International Economic Development Council iedconline.org	Offers information and services for those interested in economic development.
International Studies Association isanet.org	The International Studies Association promotes international affairs research and education.

Typical Admissions Requirements

While many advanced degree programs do not require specific majors or coursework, many programs recommend background in the area. In addition, programs like anthropology, international economics, and international relations require foreign language proficiency. For fields involving math and research, some coursework in statistics will be helpful background to your advanced studies as well. When making your application to-do list or calendar, be sure to note any special application requirements in advance, especially things like work experience or foreign language requirements, though some programs may allow you to study a language while working toward your degree.

General graduate school requirements:

- Bachelor's degree from an accredited college or university

- Official transcript(s) from all colleges or universities attended

- GRE General Test scores (different programs require different minimum scores)

- TOEFL score (if necessary)

- Academic letters of recommendation

- Letter of intent or statement of purpose

- Application forms

- Application fee

Some degree programs will also require:

- Interview

- Relevant work experience

- Supplemental essays or writing sample

- Proficiency in a foreign language

SOCIAL WORK

Social workers collaborate with other human services professionals to look for solutions to the complex problems of modern society. While some social workers opt for counseling or clinical practices, others work in public policy and administration, research, or teaching. Because social workers face society's most challenging problems, working in this vital field takes a lot of effort, a lot of patience, and most of all, lots of passion.

Master's degree programs in social work vary widely in scope and specialty. Some programs focus on methodology and public policy, while others are more clinically focused, preparing professionals for a direct practice in psychotherapy. Still others provide students with the background they need for a career in public and non-profit social service agencies, or for social planning and social change. When you are choosing a program, it is important to consider where you can get training that is in line with your larger career goals. Upon entering some programs, students are required to choose a specialty, such as mental health, employee assistance, aging, health care, corrections, and child welfare.

The job outlook for social workers is good, growing faster than the national average, particularly for those interested in aging populations, rural settings, or working with substance abuse programs. The number of advanced degrees conferred has grown 31 percent in just a few short years between 2008–09 and 2013–14. According to the Council on Social Work Education, women dominate this field, making up about 86 percent of master's degree enrollment, while historically underrepresented groups comprise about 37 percent of full-time enrollment and 40 percent of part-time enrollment.

Quick Snapshot: Social Work

DEGREE PROGRAM	NO. OF SCHOOLS OFFERING PROGRAM	DEGREE OPTIONS	APPLICATION CONSIDERATIONS
Clinical Social Work	Master's: 8 Doctorate: 2	CSW PhD	A BSW is not required, but social studies related field is preferred; minimum GPA or GRE score; field work (volunteer or paid)
Social Work/Social Work, Other	Master's: 229 Doctorate: 70	MSW, DSW PhD	BSW applicants may be able to enroll with advanced standing status
Substance Abuse/Addiction Counseling	Master's: 19 Doctorate: 0	MA or MS in Substance Abuse MSW, focus in Substance Abuse	Coursework in psychology or social work helpful; experience in clinical setting (volunteer or paid)

TRADE ORGANIZATIONS YOU SHOULD KNOW	
American Board of Examiners in Clinical Social Work abecsw.org	Features job postings, newsletters, and resources for students of social work.
American Counseling Association counseling.org	The American Counseling Association offers information on all areas within the field, including information on state certification.
Association of Social Work Boards aswb.org	A professional association that regulates social work, and develops and maintains the licensing exam.
National Association of Social Workers socialworkers.org	The largest member organization of professional social workers, offering networking, advocacy, books and journals.

Typical Admissions Requirements

While a BSW is not required for admission to social work programs, some programs allow enrollees with a BSW to receive advanced standing, thereby shortening the amount of fieldwork and coursework you are required to complete.

Many students entering graduate programs in social work have majored in social work, psychology, or public policy. Otherwise, coursework in social and biological sciences will be useful. Some basic knowledge of statistics and research methodologies will also be beneficial to graduate students in social work.

General graduate school requirements:

- Bachelor's degree from an accredited college or university

- Official transcript(s) from all colleges or universities attended

- GRE General Test scores (different programs require different minimum scores)*

- TOEFL score (if necessary)

- Letters of recommendation

- Letter of intent or statement of purpose

- Application forms

- Application fee

*Some social work programs accept the Miller Analogy Test in lieu of GRE Scores.

Some degree programs will also require:

- Interview

- Work experience (paid or volunteer)

NOTES